DMT & My Occult Mind II

INVESTIGATION OF OCCULT REALTIES USING THE SPIRIT MOLECULE

Book Two

DICK KHAN

There is no religion higher than Truth.

The Truth is no words.

Table of Contents

Upon our planet there are thousands of different types of creatures, from tiny one-celled forms on up. Studying these creatures, we observe many finely gradated steps of structure, from the simple to the complex, and many finely gradated steps of intelligence. Why should we assume that these steps reach their highest point at man? Wouldn't it be more logical to assume the sequence continues *beyond* man, in a hierarchy of form and intelligence, and consciousness that may not be visible to man but nonetheless real?

GINA CERMINARA, *Insights for the Age of Aquarius*

INTRODUCTION

In law and philosophy lies the concept of 'burden of proof'. This is an obligating burden placed upon one making a claim to furnish sufficient proofs in support of that claim. In law, the term actually divides between two kinds of burden. There is the 'burden of production', which is centred upon the production of evidence in support of a claim; and there is the 'burden of persuasion', which is centred upon the production of persuasive evidence in support of a claim. For the avoidance of doubt, I am not a lawyer. I am certainly not a lawmaker and I am very far removed from dispensing justice on behalf of the judiciary of a sovereign state. I would not wish to rule myself out as a philosopher; although I must admit my philosophical seat of office would not extend very much beyond the bounds of an armchair.

When looking to the law we find various phrases for both criminal and civil matters centred upon a 'standard of proof'. Here were find phrases such as: 'reasonable suspicion'; 'reasonable to believe'; 'some credible evidence'; 'substantial evidence'; and 'clear and convincing evidence'. We find that 'on the balance of probabilities', something either is true, or it is not true. In the very same vein, we find on the 'preponderance of the evidence', something either is true, or is not true. If a matter is 'beyond a reasonable doubt', it is not an absolute certainty, but it is a proof sufficiently convincing to rely upon, based upon the facts of the matter in question. The strictest standard of proof is 'beyond the shadow of a doubt', because the requirement is one wherein there is a complete absence of doubt. It is widely considered as an impossible standard to meet. Canada has a standard of proof that is used to determine whether or not a criminal defence may be used; it is known as 'air of reality'.

In the preceding DMT & My Occult Mind, I committed to publishing the findings from my own research programme, investigating what was behind the profound and oftentimes bizarre experiences rapidly following inhalation of DMT in the vaporous state. I also committed to sharing some personal memories which seemed pertinent to an inquiry of this nature. The central theme running throughout DMT & My Occult Mind is my occult-influenced mindset. That is, the mentality I have fostered through reading and considering the content of literature that would generally be considered as esoteric or occult. Esoteric may be considered a more agreeable term than occult. The latter term comes loaded and burdened with a reputation for all kinds of irreputable motives and maleficent

1

practices. But as in the previous publication, my interpretation and use of the word is generally taken as to mean hidden, or knowledge of the hidden. In that sense, I am using occult in its lite guise.

To reiterate my personal motive for such a work: from my early childhood I harboured innate certainty there was something of profound importance the adults in my life were not speaking about. There was talk of God, but it was mostly in vague or uninspiring terms; or designed to induce obeyance through fear. Classic OBE's and other inexplicable occurrences supported my absolute certainty that there was something of very great importance not spoken about by those around me. In adulthood I found that unspoken something in Helena Petrovna Blavatsky's occult masterpiece – *The Secret Doctrine*. Considering philosophically occult matters imbued me with a mindset that has proven particularly helpful for pursuing investigative research with what Rick Strassman so aptly labelled, the *Spirit Molecule*. An occult interpretation permeated the previous edition of DMT & My Occult Mind and it will continue to be an occult interpretation inculcating this edition. After all, as Blavatsky herself stated in *The Key to Theosophy:* "Truth is of two kinds - one manifest and self-evident; the other demanding incessantly new demonstrations and proofs."

Profound questions arise when asserting the reality of spiritual agency accessible through administration of a potent mind-manifesting substance. Through analyses of my own experiences using DMT I became absolutely certain that one of a class of powerful discarnate intelligences was interacting with me; or rather, was imposing upon me in a manner that almost defies explanation. By 'powerful discarnate intelligences', I mean powerful minds, devoid of a physical body – at least as far as we empirically understand the term 'physical'. I have referred to those entities generally and interchangeably as 'spirit beings', 'ethereal beings', and 'occult beings.' At this stage in my own investigative pursuit I believe data collection is far more important than nomenclature. However, I foresee clamour for kudos and arguments for intellectual supremacy among the learned and the lettered as they vie to scientifically rebaptise those entities of hidden nature.

Having set out to record and analyse my own experiences from smoking DMT, I initially wondered whether it was my mind working solely under its own steam that was creating the truly bizarre and incredibly hypervivid visual experiences. But as I progressed, it became increasingly evident that something else was absolutely central to the experience. Indeed, that same 'something else' was actually dictating the experiences. You can call that 'something else' 'entity contact' or even 'alien life'. But all told, it amounts to mind-on-mind interaction between a human and one of a class of powerful discarnate entities from hidden nature.

Amazing questions arise from such an argument. For example, if discarnate entities really do exist relative to our terrestrial globe, then wouldn't they exist progressively and hierarchically relative to this solar system, the wider cosmos, and the infinite universe? Can a spiritual realm project evolutionary motives and ideals into the temporal world? Are powerful yet subtle external influences playing upon the collective human consciousness and subconsciousness? Perhaps such influences have long-term and far reaching consequence and significance for human evolution and culture?

In this second edition, I have included the remaining experiments from my unauthorised DMT research programme. But I have elected to include only those reports that I considered worthwhile based on the actual DMT experience, my interpretation of the mechanics of the experience, my enjoyment in writing a particular report, or simply feeling there was a story worth sharing. There seemed little merit including those experiments in which the outcome was lacklustre, mundane or mediocre. Remaining resolute and steadfast to reporting with complete honesty, and employing no literary licence to embellish or enrich any report in any given particular, continues to be an unwavering principled precept.

My approach has remained one of maintaining eyes open and a preference for daylight conditions. I know what occurs when one smokes DMT in a darkened setting. And I completely understand that eyes open or closed matters not a jot in the typical breakthrough experience. But I am more interested in what is behind the actual hallucinations rather than the content of those amazingly hypervivid otherworldly visions and vistas. And that's not to disparage the hallucinatory content. On the contrary, a whole new genre of art has been borne from immersive interactions with DMT entities. One only needs to see the works of Alex Grey and Samuel Ferrand to appreciate this. One major difference from the previous documented experiences was taking my research outside into the small and relatively private rear garden. This proved incredibly enlightening in respect of my investigative inquiries. Indeed, it was by taking my research outdoors that I was able to come to a much better understanding of the occult mechanics involved in the bizarre interactive experiences.

I am loath to pontificate about how times are changing because times are always changing. Life doesn't evolve through stasis. One can suspect or even set out to show there are periods within our history where change appears to hurtle along at breakneck speed; the old order of things seems increasingly outdated by the year, the month, the week, and even by the day. How western society will respond to the occult arguments that arise through psychedelic research with DMT is one that is many magnitudes of order more profound than I can presently imagine. That life-changing experiences can result from interaction with powerful non-human intelligence through the administration of DMT – at this particular stage in western civilisation – is culturally game-changing to an unforeseeable extent.

We should not forget how that seed of cultural change came to be planted in the first place. I am not about to seek favour by fawning over Dr Rick Strassman. Indeed, I strongly suspect he would disavow of unauthorised research with DMT. And I am equally convinced my overt references to matters occult would rankle his academic high office. However, Strassman deserves applause for having the ambition and tenacity to jump through several very high administrative hoops in order to satisfy the American regulatory authorities that his research with this very potent psychedelic drug had genuine scientific validity. It was arguably through Strassman's hunch of the pineal gland being the biological locus for providing mystical states, coupled with his ground-breaking research programme administering DMT at the University of New Mexico between 1990 – 1995, along with his personal revaluation in coming to accept what his own research volunteers insisted they were experiencing during DMT inebriation, that has surely seeded the birth of an exciting new science of esoteric enquiry into the nature of mind – incarnate and discarnate – human and non-human.

Part One recounts the story behind what occurred after publishing DMT & My Occult Mind. As a self-published author with no prior social media presence whatsoever, the initial strategy developed in an effort to market the book proved laborious yet enlightening in respect of the burgeoning psychedelic zeitgeist. Part Two documents the main findings from my unauthorised research programme. It details the occult mechanics that arise following inhalation of dimethyltryptamine; endeavours to give rational explanation to what is essentially a very exceptional human experience; advances the argument that powerful spiritual agents of hidden nature are central to the DMT experience; and includes a selection of DMT trip reports and analyses that arguably give an air of reality to such assertions. Part Three builds on those arguments by taking a more in depth look at certain key experiences and further details the occult mechanics that typically played out in the documented experiences. New age, gnostical and ufological considerations are introduced as well as a controversial theory of mind in an effort to understand some of the bizarre experiences and observations perceived under DMT inebriation. The legendary Terence McKenna is cited with reference to the magnitude of impact that DMT must surely have upon western culture; which leads us onto the nomenclature for DMT. Something so powerful, with so much latent potential to change one's ontological viewpoint really does deserves an appropriate title.

PART 1

Experimenters are the shock troops of science.

MAX PLANCK

Only in the irrational and unknown direction can we come to wisdom again.

JACK PARSONS

I have learned to believe that communion between the denizens of this planet and her spirit spheres, should constitute the highest, purest, most normal and healthful exercise of our soul's religious faculties.

UNKNOWN

There is a little story to be told here. A story about the first edition of DMT & My Occult Mind. In the weeks and the months leading up to publication I occasionally found myself wondering whether or not the Police would forcibly break down my front door. Was some intelligence agency of the deep state cognisant of my psychedelic research? Perhaps they knew I was intending to publish a book about my personal experiences smoking DMT. And if so, would my family and I find ourselves rudely awakened at dawn with great hullaballoo as the Police execute a search warrant on the basis of concerns about my use of the Spirit Molecule? Given that I had no social media presence whatsoever, those fears proved completely misguided.

Upon publishing DMT & My Occult Mind, my mood was unexpectedly muted. There was no sense of achievement or triumphalism. A small bottle of cheap champagne purchased weeks earlier especially for that very occasion remained unopened and untroubled. The publishing of a book that I had putten my heart and soul into resulted in a most unexpected solemn frame of mind. After untold hours of work, spanning months and months and months, the feeling was one of great expectation. But great expectation at what exactly? It was such a peculiar and unexpected mindset. In one sense, I felt I'd just dropped the literary equivalent of an incendiary device. And yet in another sense, I felt no one really gave a damn about DMT and so-called occult entities and so-called occult realties. Some twenty muted minutes after uploading my book for retail sale, it dawned on me that I would need to actively market the book. Yet in realising as much, I simply did not consider there would be any semblance of a psychedelic community on Facebook, Twitter, or Instagram.

I was thoroughly convinced my arguments in support of powerful spiritual entities as beings of unseen nature would find great favour among the learned and the lettered. All I had to do was simply reach out to them and politely pitch my message. I was convinced my approach was revolutionary; revolutionary in the sense that I had dared to embark upon my very own unsanctioned research programme, using a very powerful and highly illegal psychedelic drug, and was now postulating the existence of powerful spiritual entities as a factual reality of occult nature. The DMT experience is exactly as Terrence Mckenna said it was: DMT really is very big headline news! I duly set out my stall by creating a very simple marketing strategy. I would identify those bodies, those agencies, and those individuals whom I suspected would take an avid interest in my work, and I would contact them. I began by attempting to contact some very well-known and some lesser known authors, whose work I greatly admired. Some were easy to contact. Others were impossible to find. Those that I least expected to reply were prompt, polite and congratulatory in their response. Others less so, or not at all. I joined Academia.edu and attempted to connect with those academics who shared or specialised in the following research interests: DMT; Psychedelics; Occultism; Western Esotericism; Theosophy; Near Death Experiences; Spirituality; Entheogens; UFOlogy; Philosophy of Religion; Paranormal; Psychical Research; Metaphysics; and, Altered States of Consciousness.

I then turned my attention to the SETI (Search for Extra-Terrestrial Intelligence) Institute. I was as naïve as I was absolutely convinced that they would welcome my research with open arms. As an organisation searching for extra-terrestrial intelligence, on a mission to explore and understand life in the universe, I felt we at least shared common values. But alas, my sixty-eight emails to named individuals fell upon deaf ears. It was with the exact same naive enthusiasm that I felt absolutely certain some of the big brains at NASA would delight in taking a look at my book. But those big brains just did not respond.

Nevertheless, over the following several months, I expended a great deal of my time, effort and energy in reaching out to a diverse audience by means of email; online message; postcard or registration with relevant online forums. I tabulated all my efforts; amassing a whopping 218-page Word document, comprising some 1,649 rows containing a multitude of names, websites, email address, postal addresses and occasional bits of relevant informative miscellany. I sent well over 1,000 emails; wrote 88 messages; posted 42 postcards; registered with 26 online forums and posted four books to those asking for a copy on the promise of a review. It would have been tiresome and arduous work, were it not for an indefatigable energy prompting me to press ahead far beyond the yawns and sighs of tiredness and fatigue. Hour after hour, week after week, month after month; whilst continuing to maintain a high standard of practice in my paid employment; and a high standard of parenting with two highly energetic and increasingly spirited young boys. I trawled and trawled and trawled for names and contact details and began casting my marketing net far and wide.

In terms of academic institutions, I was absolutely convinced those in exalted office would take very great interest in my research and my arguments. How could they not? It did not matter to me whether their position was: Reader; Lecturer; Postdoctoral Fellow; Fellow by Special Election; Research Associate; Associate Professor; Assistant Professor; Adjunct Professor; Distinguished Research Professor; Adjunct Distinguished Professor; Professor by Special Appointment; Honorary Professor; Honorary Visiting Professor; Professor Emeritus; Professor Emeritus and Distinguished Adjunct; or just a plain and simple, Professor.

I sought to identify those branches of academic research and learning that I considered were best suited to a work asserting the reality of powerful spiritual entities as a fact of hidden nature. As a consequence, I found myself directing communications to those schools, departments and faculties specialising in the study of: Consciousness; Ecology, Spirituality and Religion; Philosophy; Religion and Philosophy; Philosophical Theology; Theoretical Philosophy; Physics; Divinity; Theology; Mind and Action; Anthropology; Neurology; Transformative Inquiry; Philosophy of Physics; Ancient Philosophy; Mental Philosophy; Philosophy of Mind; Psychology; Metaphysics; Moral and Social Theology; Experimental Therapeutics; and Visual Cognition.

Occasionally, a stated specialism, study area, or research interest of the learned individual would capture my attention sufficiently for me to make a note. For example: 'the role of truth in metaphysics' and 'the moral responsibility of psychopaths', really caught my eye. These made me realise how very far removed I was from the world of high academia and how very far removed high academia was from my own little world of back garden research using dimethyltryptamine in a psychonautic context. The following hodgepodge is a bastardisation rendering of some of the more eye-catching and noteworthy academic specialisms, study areas, and research interests that caught my eye:

plasma blobs hint at new form of life; uncoiling the spiral: maths and hallucinations; a group of particles that has properties of hypothetical dark matter; explorations of the role of electricity at planetary and stellar scales; how we come to be justified in our beliefs and how this relates to our ability (or otherwise) to justify ourselves to those who don't think like us; the scope and limits of scientific method; ontology (especially Nothing); the existence and nature of God; death and metaphilosophy; researching metaphysics (including time travel); what is fundamental to subject and object: consciousness, thought, reason, space, time, possibility; belief and its connection to truth; some of the oldest and worst arguments that the history of Western Philosophy has known: the arguments from illusion and hallucination; how novelty impacts and shapes human experience; the epistemology of uncertain beliefs; interdisciplinary research on auditory verbal hallucinations; social, religious and philosophical changes which are conducive to esotericism; phenomenological philosophy; the topics of sleep, unconsciousness, death, and human finitude; whether your beliefs are supported by your evidence at that time; experimental philosophy; questions concerning evil, virtue, vice, and forgiveness; the neurobiological basis of offending behaviour, and some psychiatric conditions.

In addition to red brick and common or garden academic highness, I also conducted an extensive search of online UFO Groups. That search was made on the basis of my personal conviction that the UFO phenomena is the manifestation of a spiritual phenomenon. My thinking in that regard being heavily influenced by the literary output and arguments put forth by great luminaries such as Jacques Vallee and John Keel. I was quite certain the world of ufology would welcome the world of DMT. Thus, I messaged, e-mailed and sent postcards to numerous UFO study groups; societies; research groups; research networks; investigations committees; organisations, and organizations.

With the very same limitless and undented enthusiasm I reached out to a multitude of lodges and grand lodges of the Masonic and Freemasonic fraternity. Those people of all people would surely take an avid interest in someone ardently arguing for the reality of spiritual agency, evident through inhaled administration of a very powerful mind-manifesting substance extracted from Mother Nature. I knew Dr Strassman's game-changing work with DMT had been partly grant-funded by the Scottish Rite Foundation (a branch of the Freemasons) through their Schizophrenia Research program. I figured the Freemasons would receive my research with open heart.

Tirelessly without cessation or complaint I maintained my marketing focus. Pushing my literary effort; digging through the goldmine of globalised internet connectivity and connectedness; unearthing dozens and dozens of dotcoms and dotorgs whose relevancy somehow related to the anomalous; mysterious; Fortean; noetic; esoteric; parapsychological; philosophical; exploratory; psychedelic; entheogenic; psychical; metaphysical; epistemological; psychological; spiritual; or occult. Email after email after email. Message after message after message. It's noteworthy that I took genuine intertest in the mission statement or expressed mindset of whichever dotcom or dotorg website I was contacting. This seemed preferable to simply beating a drum and shouting: "DMT facilitates powerful spiritual interaction! Please buy my book!" The sincerity of taking an interest in those whom I was messaging proved somewhat illuminating.

Somewhat illuminating in the sense that it provided me with good insight into the emerging psychedelic zeitgeist; a zeitgeist arguably evinced in the following pseudoscientific hodgepodge comprising a mash-up of scraps and snippets taken from a handful of websites whose online content chimed with my occult mind: to investigate on a wide range of anomalous phenomena; the whole realm of the strange, unknown and unexplained; delving into subjects of the paranormal; investigating phenomena that is beyond the scope of normal scientific understanding; it is wisdom that sets a man free; enhancing scientific knowledge; support people having unusual and anomalous personal experiences; extraordinary states of consciousness; spiritual or parapsychological phenomenon; close encounters with non-human entities; advancing the exploration of human consciousness; the experience of expanded states of awareness; a path to creating a life of personal freedom; devoted to facilitating and promoting scholarly research outside the confines of traditional academic research; genuine scepticism is a virtue in science; self-proclaimed guardians of science are committed to conventional taboos against psychic phenomena; fundamentalists who attack any challenge to their beliefs; promote the study and integration of psychical and spiritual experience; the science of how people change; such experiences seem to challenge contemporary conceptions of human nature and the physical world; the transfer of information and the influence of physical systems independently of time and space via mechanisms we cannot currently explain; the primary objective is to achieve a scientific understanding of these experiences; explore the meaning and impact of psychic experiences; assess the possibility of practical applications; promoting scholarship and scientific inquiry into currently unexplained aspects of human experience; disseminating responsible information to the wider public; integrating this information with knowledge from other disciplines; people engaged in creating a new worldview for the 21st century; dedicated to advancing science for the benefit of humanity; promoting public understanding of scientific research; envisions a world in which public policy is made using the best evidence; religious beliefs are no longer seen as an excuse for bigotry or a cause to receive special treatment from government; dedicated to the advancement of philosophy; promoting public understanding; answering the most profound questions relating to the mysteries of ourselves; the universe and our relationship with it; the perennial wisdom underlying the world's religions, sciences, and philosophies; dedicated to responsible stewardship and evolution of consciousness; what would take place if other practices like meditation, yoga, painting, or dancing were made illegal; articulate a new educational paradigm; examine claims of psychic and paranormal phenomena; advance and secure the academic study of esotericism; balance the public conversation about psychedelics, spread accurate information; give a new face to psychedelia; become ambassadors for the psychedelic experience; study of paranormal experiences; an interdisciplinary dialogue on issues of the paranormal; move beyond the sceptic vs. advocate impasse; new avenues for enquiry and understanding; exploratory perspective on a wide range of experiences; beliefs and phenomena often called paranormal, supernatural or anomalous; in-depth exploration of topics that are unusual in nature; and therefore considered by most to be paranormal; exploring exceptional human experience.

Sat at my aged wooden writing desk entailed hours and hours of work. Over weeks and weeks and weeks. Day following day after day; fingers tapping away furiously on my little laptop computer; a multitude of messages sent; a mass of forum usernames and passwords generated; numerous online registrations begetting numerous account activation links; posting postcard after postcard after postcard. No complaints! No days off! No quibbles! Just pressing the message: DMT really is very big news! Very big news indeed! Replies were thin and meagre. Yet each one always served to completely revitalise and redouble my energies, as I forged ahead with unwavering commitment and complete positivity in undertaking my own little DMT promotional mission.

Throughout my online research, I had occasionally noted links to facebook accounts held by established authors; publishers; celebrities; academics; pundits; comedians; media outlets; futurists; theosophists; UFO researchers; and consciousness groups. This eventually prompted me to consider the option of securing myself a social media presence. But I genuinely did not suspect there would be any semblance of a DMT community on Facebook, Twitter, or Instagram. How could there be? Psychedelics are Class A substances. Schedule I drugs. On par with crack, smack and coke. They may induce freedom of thought and freedom of expression, but legislatively speaking, they tend to invoke the very antithesis of freedom with merciless authoritarian might.

There was one particular moment in my marketing, where having emailed and messaged and reached out to so many individuals and institutions, that I began to feel fatigue at the repetitiveness of the work. It was from that moment that I decided I should sign up for an account with Facebook. Having done that, a whole new world suddenly opened up before my eyes. I discovered a great number of accounts dedicated to psychedelics. The ability to so easily make connections and even forge friendships and bonds with like-minded individuals was a wholly unexpected revelation. I was able to secure book a swap with popular panpsychist philosopher Peter Sjöstedt-H (Noumenautics); popular freemasonic scholar P.D. Newman (Alchemically Stoned); and the mythological reimagining-cum-rediscoveries promoted by R. N. Vooght (The Spirit in the Sky).

Shortly thereafter, I joined Twitter. And eventually, despite harbouring deep misgivings and absolute certainty that Instagram would be a wholly inappropriate and unwelcoming platform for psychedelically inspired individuals, I signed up for an account. And duly discovered a very welcoming and burgeoning community of psychedelically-active and psychedelically-minded individuals. Exposing DMT & My Occult Mind to social media was a boon; an opportunity to make friends; an insight into just how rarefied the world of psychedelics actually is from the mainstream; and an opportunity to feed into, and feed from, the emerging mind-manifesting zeitgeist.

However, socialising with so many like-minded individuals and reading so many amazing DMT trip reports had an unexpected effect on me as I came to realise just how brazenly bold some psychonauts were in their commitment to the molecule. That is to say, the more I read about the experience's others were having with DMT, the less satisfied I became with my own exploits; other people's trips sounded way more intense or more deeply immersive or cosmically rewarding than my own. It's fair to say I gulped at what I had produced as a follow-up publication to DMT & My Occult Mind. I began to take the view that adhering to a principle of including each and every trip report – no matter what the outcome – effectively marred the work. Thus, I duly decided something of a revision was required.

I absolutely contend that with the right mindset, there is something to be learned from each and every DMT experiment. But that's not to say each and every DMT experiment that I undertook was bizarre, insane or awesome; and that's not to say each and every DMT experiment resulted in an overpoweringly mesmeric and immersive encounter with a powerful spiritual entity; and that's not to say my DMT crystals never lost their potent zing through repeated exposure to their inherent environmental sensitivities; and that's not to say my lighter never ran out of fuel midway through vaping; and that's not to say I didn't go for one whole month unaccountably producing wholly impotent crystals no matter what changes I made in my extraction process; and that's certainly not to say there wasn't a great deal of immensely interesting observational material to be had when using light and threshold doses of DMT with eyes open in outdoor daylight conditions.

But the feeling that what I had produced as my second book was not quite up to the mark took seed and a feeling of disenchantment slowly grew within me. This became an unwelcome malaise, and although I knew there was a solution to be had, it was just a question of whether I had the wherewithal to make the right decision, rather than publish what I had already produced and be damned. Upon making my decision to revise the project, so as to include the very best experiments from both my second and my third year of research, I suddenly found my spirits lifted enormously. My literary energies became buoyant to such an extent I felt as though some non-human agency shared in or even impelled me to heightened positivity, on account of my decision. I had made the right choice! And that is the story to be told of this particular book. It underwent a revision so as to include the best remaining experiences from my research programme; and to remove or dismiss those experiences that I personally felt would add very little to this second edition of DMT & My Occult Mind. By the best experiences, I mean those experiences that were the most thrilling, playful, insightful, frightening, dramatic, mysterious, engaging, or just downright phenomenal. Or simply, those experiences from which I derived a great personal pleasure simply from documenting. For beside my reverence for what I have experienced through inhaling the Spirit Molecule, I have found a pleasure and passion in exercising my literary creativity.

DICK KHAN

PART 2

My observation of the Universe convinces me that there are beings of Intelligence and power of a far higher quality than anything we can conceive of as human; that they are not necessarily based on the cerebral and nervous structures that we know; and that the one and only chance for mankind to advance as a whole is for individuals to make contact with such Beings.

ALEISTER CROWLEY, *Magick Without Tears*

It may seem somewhat back to front to state the findings from my research programme before having documented those remaining experiences that led me to the following conclusions. My reasoning here is simple; for as much as I feel I have answered the original question that motivated my research – even if only to my own satisfaction – I suspect I have not even scratched the surface of the DMT mystery. It comes as no real surprise to find myself having a multitude of questions unanswered and an insufficiency of candidates posing as answers. The original intention behind my research programme was simply to understand what was behind the bizarre otherworldly experiences that manifested with such rapidity after smoking the phenomenally potent mind-manifesting dimethyltryptamine crystals.

DMT is a very powerful amplifier of human consciousness. That is to say, one's consciousness, one's mind-stuff, appears to undergo a very rapid expansion or projection from a latent baseline state. Typically, that sudden projection – of what can esoterically be described as psycho-spiritual substance – rapidly expands bubble-like from the region of one's head; whereupon it becomes evident as an uncommonly dense and ultra-crystal-clear transparent medium before slowly collapsing back on itself; infolding to its latent baseline state. In so doing, one can gain some appreciation of the density, fluidity and apparent elasticity exhibited in that incredibly rapid outward expansion, followed by slow contraction. But that same psycho-spiritual medium can also project from the researcher as a rapidly spiralling torrent of bountiful proportion; exhibiting incredible beauty in its visually arresting complex geometric interior. It is the uncommon high density characterising that psycho-spiritual substance that likely accounts for the unambiguous visibility to the one projecting that psycho-spiritual medium.

Highly amplified human consciousness serves as a signal that is of great interest to conscious, intelligent and otherwise unperceived lifeforms; discarnate spiritual entities that are presently outside the cataloguing of life as we know it by traditional science. We can choose to call these: spiritual beings; conscious energies; intelligent discarnate entities; non-human intelligences; hyperspatial entities; fourth dimensional beings; higher entities; ultraterrestrial agents; demons; aliens; angels; ascended masters; occult masters; djinn; or whatever esoteric label or novel nomenclature we feel is apt to describe those denizens of hidden nature.

Upon significantly projecting one's psycho-spiritual substance with DMT, what typically follows is the emergence of one such entity into one's immediate setting with terrific or near instantaneous rapidity. I have occasionally managed to observe the onset of that emergence as a localised turbulence, rapidly manifesting from an ambiguously defined point source, which rapidly expands to fill the volume of the room – or expands to an unknown volume in an outdoor setting. Such observation make it appear that the entity actually emerges out of thin air; whereupon it undergoes expansion with terrific immediacy.

The psycho-spiritual volume of the manifesting entity exhibits extreme density and a capacity to powerfully impose itself in a manner that mesmerises the user. By mesmerise, I mean the will of the entity is used to magically overcome the will of the researcher, thereby overwhelming and transfixing the percipient's cognition. The esoteric mechanism appears to be the entity forcibly and temporarily melding its mind (psycho-spiritual substance) into the expanded mind (psycho-spiritual substance) of the researcher; thereby making one's psyche and one's physiology accessible to the entity, to varying degrees. The entity is thereby able to induce varying degrees of mesmerisation upon the researcher, commonly enabling the imposition of very highly defined hallucinatory visions and other bizarre miscellany upon the researcher's amplified mind and perceptions. One is effectively immersed within, and temporarily overwhelmed by, the mind of a very powerful entity of hidden nature.

It is the uncommon density of that psycho-spiritual substance that arguably creates the appearance of a reality appearing far more real than ordinary everyday reality appears. In a somewhat lucid dreamlike rendering, surfaces appear improbably smooth and true; wholly without blemish, dimple or imperfection. Colours appear highly saturated or rendered with radiant brilliance and captivating lustre; lines and edges display an incredible and almost improbable sharpness, in a manner that seems to typify and characterise the dimethyltryptamine inebriation.

The entities engaging in these interdimensional interactions are able to manipulate a portion of their mind in a manner that creates a truly bizarre quasi-physical-like substance. This substance has the capacity to operate invasively and with mobility. It has the ability to exhibit extremes of strength and subtleness. Additionally, these powerful entities have the capacity to manipulate the human psyche, inducing extremes of emotion such as joyous uncontrollable laughter, fervent ecstasy, and even confusion and mental insensibility. They can impel one to feel immense burden; impose profoundly terrifying fear; and frequently leave the user speechless through extreme amazement and astonishment. They exhibit a capacity to quickly and sequentially squeeze a range of extreme emotions from the human psyche in a manner that seems to define the terrain and qualities of humanness. In such encounters one feels not unlike a puppet, undergoing expert manipulation by a very powerful and very skillful puppet master.

The potency of DMT – even without any interaction from a powerful entity of hidden nature – is such that it can induce extremely blissful states, wherein one feels completely aloof from humanity. One feels so completely and utterly serene that the only vague concern one holds, as one slowly comes down from that beatifically heavenly state, is whether or not the creator of the universe was cognisant of the event. For such is the magnitude of the experience, it feels like a momentous event of such universal import and significance as to demand cosmic attention.

Specific to outdoor research was the frequent observation of what some would classify as black orb UFO's; and earth lights – balls of light of varying size manoeuvering seemingly playfully and even manifesting at close proximity. I have found it remarkable that such sightings induce huge transformation in mood; quickly moving me to childlike exuberance. Inky black orbs, or skyborne irregular shaped masses, exhibiting red, orange, creamy or even reflective surfaces and evident in consensus reality surely give credence to the interdimensional hypotheses of UFOlogy. Possibly in this terrestrially visible guise, these forms are the very same powerful entities who have temporarily contracted their psycho-spiritual volume into a superdense form.

There is no amount of words, no choice of words and no sequence of words that can convey the truly phenomenal power these beings can impose as they undergo rapid increase in frequency and intensity over mere seconds, in one's immediate setting. It is simply unimaginable. Indoors or outdoors, one's immediate setting suddenly becomes occupied with energy that is perceptibly and singularly impossibly solid, and yet paradoxically all pervasive. The extent to which that power imposes seems to have a proportionate relationship to the degree of mesmerisation imposed upon the researcher. Mesmerisation is generally understood to be the overcoming of one's will be a will of greater force. The DMT researcher is induced into an otherwise abnormal state wherein the powerful spiritual entity has liberty to exercise influence upon one's perceptions, one's psyche, and even one's physiology.

It is on the basis of that incredible capacity to impose unimaginable power within one's immediate setting that one can perceive oneself to be raised off the ground by some small distance; and thereby experience illusory states of motion. The powerful spiritual entity is able to manipulate a portion of its mass in a quasi-physical manner beneath one's recumbent physical body, in such a manner as to convincingly create the illusion of motion. One may experience a gliding sensation or feel transported on something that feels exactly like a conveyor belt. Depending upon the experience, one usually only becomes aware of that incredible circumstance as the experience draws to a close; whereupon one marvels at the softness, slowness, subtleness, and near imperceptibility of a very slow and very short descent.

My experiences with DMT have suggested a very gradual progression or initiatory aspect is at play, such that later experiences became more challenging and yet more revealing as to what is actually behind those oftentimes bizarre and apparently otherworldly hallucinatory environs. Many of my later experiences would have seen me off had they been among my first. In the latter half of my research programme –after heading outdoors – I was able to observe the powerful spiritual entity directly above me, before it had interacted with me and without it engulfing me and imposing highly defined otherworldly hallucinatory visions upon my perceptions. Those sights were truly marvelous; principally because it was so overwhelmingly evident that I was witnessing a truly rare sight – a being of hidden nature, in the guise of a large multi-faceted form; exhibiting phenomenally complex symmetrical geometry; dense beyond anything terrestrially tangible and yet completely transparent. The involuntarily reaction to dry heave and retch in sickness upon witnessing such a sight was surely indicative of the impact from facing such a stark occult reality in otherwise consensus reality. However, that is not to assume such sights in the terrestrial environment represent the true form of the entity as it would ordinarily appear within its own realm. But out of all my research thus far, those sights remain by far the most rewarding.

As should be expected, the uncommon high density of psycho-spiritual substance displays a capacity to transmit sound pressure waves far more readily than the air alone. This would account for apparent improvement in perceived acoustic characteristics of sounds as well as perceived increases in loudness of sounds. In certain settings, it also permits direct visual observation of compression and rarefaction phases in low frequency sounds emitted from speaker cones as they superimpose upon the psycho-spiritual medium, which is itself superimposed upon the air. Conversely, I have experienced wholly improbable environmental silences during indoor and outdoor DMT trips – a complete shutting out of all ambient sounds. I suggest this capacity derives from the ability of those powerful spiritual entities to manipulate their volume of mind in such a manner as to temporarily form an impressive acoustic barrier; one exhibiting the relevant properties of density, rigidity and imperforation.

The extent to which dimethyltryptamine-amplified psycho-spiritual substance expansively projects from the researcher, seems to have a proportional relationship to the intensity and frequency of energetic reaction taking place at what feels like the pineal site of the brain. Obviously, dose and factors relating to skillfulness in vaporising the substance; pneumonic contact time and the number of inhalations is relevant. Indoors, with a sufficient dose inhaled, one's amplified psycho-spiritual substance appears as a visually very obvious volume of energy filling the volume of the room. This rapidly becomes visually very turbulent and is also perceptible at once both within and without the researcher. Here, one could argue the Beer-Lambert law is applicable. This law states that when radiant energy impinges upon a surface it is either transmitted, reflected, or absorbed. One can suppose the characteristic uncommon high density of psycho-spiritual substance readily transmits through the solidity of flooring, walls, ceiling, doors and glazing. But that's not to suppose some of that energy is not absorbed within the building fabric; or even reflected from those surfaces. It took me a great many indoor experiments to work that out because it was usually within mere seconds, if not apparently instantaneously, that an entity had emerged in my immediate setting and imposed itself upon me powerfully.

When outdoors, I have witnessed my psycho-spiritual substance spiralling out of me as an incredible torrent; evident as an expanding mass of dense mind-stuff filled with complex geometry and bountifully filling the sky high above me. That such a thing can occur while one's rational senses remain totally intact is no less astonishing than the sight itself. Upon seeing so much of my mind-stuff bountifully filling the sky, my reaction was to feel great vulnerability and even maternal concern that so much of my essential-self was outside the confines of my physical body.

On several occasions I have been the unwise fool that underestimates the potency of freebase DMT crystals. The unstoppable intensity of ultra-high frequency energy emanating from one's pineal site is sure sign the experience will be memorable. Lying in the garden as highly energised psycho-spiritual substance rapidly and unstoppably spirals out from me in a swirling geometric torrent; my rational capacities completely forsake me. I barely know what I am, let alone who I am, or where I am. My mouth feels hinged open at an impossible angle of 180 degrees. My tongue involuntarily sweeps around and around the inside of my mouth, as though suffering from severe athetosis. My lips feel greatly enlarged and rubberised. My entire mouth feels improbably well lubricated. The refreshing feeling of my tongue involuntarily sweeping around my heavily salivated mouth is an oral pleasure beyond compare. There is such a great volume of my own dense mind-stuff outside my body that something has arrived to offer assistance. A spacious spiritual entity is now caring for me in a mothering capacity. An improbably dense portion of its great mass of mind has fluidly melded into my head; visibly evident as a broad and pendulous cylindrical mass. I am able to feel the incredible density of that mass inside and outside my skull. As the entity slowly pulls away from me, it creates an almost painful suction-like pull on my brain. This results in long-forgotten and deeply buried memories to stir within me. I am suddenly aware that I have experienced this pull on my brain before. I am absolutely certain of it. As a young bairn, all alone, in bed at night.

How many impossibly highly defined visions must one experience before beginning to feel discontent through familiarity with the DMT experience? How many times can one genuinely be made to feel absolutely convinced that one has died and departed the land of the living? Did I genuinely suspect I had reached the limits of the DMT experience? Or was I subtly been led toward a significant change in the experiences? One notable experiment in my bedroom, without any visionary content, cemented my suspicion that these experiences really were interactions with one of a class of powerful spiritual entities – beings of hidden nature. In the otherwise consensus reality of the bedroom, I watched in awe as the manifested entity filling the volume of the sunlit room failed to misdirect my attention, as had occurred many times before during previous experiences. Immediately prior to its departure, I earnestly and eagerly voiced aloud: "I am not missing this!" An incredibly beautiful transparent entity then silently and serenely peeled itself away from the bedroom walls and slowly exited the room. Now I knew beyond a shadow of doubt that I was dealing with spiritual beings; or rather, they were dealing with me. And yet despite that knowledge, it made my commitment to pursuing further experiments no easier. If anything, it made it doubly difficult, because now not only did I need to trust in the capacity of my own courage, but I also needed to invest my trust in the intention of those that were interacting with me.

On the floor, in the small landing area at the top of the staircase, I sat up and emptied a pipe in three proficient pulls before reclining. With tremendous rapidity, a powerful spiritual entity manifested and filled the entirety of the setting with intense high frequency energy. In just an instant, all around me appeared ultra-highly defined. Everything in sight appeared far more real than its ordinary everyday appearance. White paintwork looked impossibly white, and lustrous. Every colour was greatly intensified. Every surface appeared true and pristine; without defect, dimple, blemish or any imperfection whatsoever. Highly defined hallucinatory scenery and highly defined humanlike entities appeared all around me. The actions of the humanlike entities evidently related to the intense high frequency energy that was both audible and perceptible within me and without me. That very high frequency energy was so overwhelmingly central to the unfolding experience. The frequency continued to rise, higher and higher and higher. The humanlike entities positioned themselves all around me. One appeared poised and ready to pounce into me. The frequency and intensity of the energy was immense and increasing. I gulped. But more from dryness of mouth than from fear or fright. But that one single gulp immediately caused the phenomenal energy to reset itself to a lesser intensity and a lower frequency. By non-verbal means the humanlike entities beseeched me to remain still and remain silent. I duly obliged. The frequency of that energy then quickly reached an excruciatingly impossible pitch. I remained motionless. The frequency rose ever higher and higher. It quickly reached a truly impossible sonic level and continued to rise, higher and higher and higher, until it reached a truly sanity defying level. And then my situation changed remarkably.

Now, something was active inside my body. And not only was something active inside my body, but it was able to manipulate me from within. Somehow, it was either able to physically manipulate my internal physiology, or it was able to radically alter my perception of my anatomical physiology, to such extent that it truly belied my existence as a living creature composed of blood and bone. I was now as good as a marionette in the hands of a very powerful occult puppet master. There was no pain, but my body felt eerily and impossibly strange; as though it was synthetic, composite, fluidless, flexible and constructible. There was hollowness in the midst of all my limbs; the joints of which felt like they could so very easily be uncoupled and re-coupled by this incredibly powerful entity. I felt completely devoid of all liquid content. And yet my consciousness was completely clear and lucid. Then suddenly, a strange movement inside my throat made it feel as though my voice box had suddenly been repositioned outside of me. I remonstrated rather loudly: "Hey! You can't do that!"

But now my voice sounded to be emanating somewhere outside me. It also sounded incredibly clear and clipped, and far louder than usual. The shock of hearing my voice speaking from without was mind blowing. I cried aloud: "Whoa! Whoa! That's impossible! That's impossible! You can't do that! How can you do that? How can you do that?" But clearly, it wasn't impossible. I felt compelled to speak again and again and again, simply in order to marvel at hearing the unusual acoustic qualities characterising my voice. At the same time, the interior of my upper body felt like it was undergoing the most impossible physical manipulations. I could only cry out: "Hey! You can't do that! That's impossible! How can you do that?" The situation was just so utterly impossible. And yet there I was, in my rational senses, being skillfully manipulated by an intelligence that was surely conscious of what it was doing to me. It surely knew the extent of my immeasurable astonishment. Midway through this bizarre interaction, a very small and very remote region of my mind had sufficient capacity to consider that this experience was a reward; a reward for pursuing the DMT experience in an honest investigative manner.

I was profoundly affected by this experience. As it concluded, I burst into tears of shock and disbelief. Having dried my eyes, I then headed downstairs. My wife had heard me shouting. I lay down on the sofa without saying a word. But as I reflected, my emotions erupted and I again burst into tears. My wife, showing great concern, asked if I was alright. And of course, I was. I just needed to have an energetic emotional reaction in order to counterbalance the extreme astonishment from having been subjected to an invasive experience. This invasive capacity opened up a whole new chapter in my research. Henceforth, the powerful entities performed invasively; usually orally, thoracically or abdominally. But also, cranially and even ocularly.

On one occasion, an indoor experiment was aborted prematurely through the onset of fear. This premature cessation resulted in very long and very slender quasi-physical tentacular portions of the powerful entity, slowly and palpably withdrawing from my interior physiology. The value of insight gained from terminating that particular interaction was well worth the feeling of ruefulness at failing to fully commit to the experience. The invasive experiences went so far as to purposefully stymie my capacity to breathe; by steadily reducing the effective internal diameter of my windpipe, until gasping for breath, and on the verge of outright panic, I would suddenly find myself all alone and free to breathe without restriction. The rejoice and rejuvenation at realising one is alive when death seemed inevitable was surely the purpose of that dark trickery.

Another invasive machination of the entities involved sealing up my lips from within by using that strange quasi-physical-like substance. On numerous occasions I had suspected my lips were being tightly sealed-up, rendering my mouth unopenable. But my mesmeric state had always precluded the capacity or the courage to test the integrity of that seal. Implicit trust seems paramount in these encounters. When I did eventually find sufficient capacity of mind to test the integrity of that seal, by trying to open my mouth, it came as no surprise that I was completely unable to overcome its strength. And yet had I panicked, I have no doubt the quasi-physical orally-imposed seal, and the powerful spiritual entity imposing it upon me, would've vanished in an instant.

I chose to inhale a moderate dose indoors one day, despite fervent appeals from my inner voice beseeching me not to proceed. The outcome of that one single experience was a regrettable temporary change in my mental health; one that I document only as far as I dare in this book. The result of that experience, after a period of abstinence from DMT, was to take my experiments outdoors. At that stage in my research, the usual hallucinatory visions had all but ceased. Heading outdoors was greatly advantageous to my research in that it enabled me to observe some of the phenomenally configured entities of hidden nature responsible for imposing the oftentimes bizarre encounters I had experienced indoors.

Outdoors, from the confines of a small suburban back garden in broad daylight, in otherwise consensus reality, I was witness to phenomenally configured entities of an otherwise occult existence, ranging from large to vast – relative to my physical size. Some displayed complex symmetrical geometry, giving them an appearance akin to an outlandishly oversized, multi-faceted and superdense transparent diamond. Such sights can only ever serve to inform the percipient, beyond any shadow of doubt, that humanity is not the pinnacle of evolution and neither are we alone. For me at least, those sights represented a humbling triumph in my investigative research.

But that's not the whole story. Because now, the experiences imposed by those powerful occult beings changed yet again. Just what does one experience of oneself when one is completely overwhelmed in a fight or flight situation; a situation wherein one is powerless to fight, and from which one cannot flee? The intensity of the interdimensional encounters I was subjected to increased remarkably. I experienced roughhousing; disturbing mind games; forcefully invasive encounters; and levels of drama, excitement and entertainment that no movie could ever possibly hope to equal. I was emotionally moved to violently tearing open my buttoned-up shirt. But only because I was incapable of tearing open my chest, and offering up my heart to the very large and very powerful entity above me as it more than capably tested the qualities of my soul.

There is very much more that could be said and very much that should be said about these entities and the experiences they impose. Science cannot ignore this field of research if it wishes to remain true to its roots. One thing that really excites me about these arguments in support of occult entities, occult realms and occult nature, is in considering how such arguments will be incorporated into western culture; how such arguments will reshape that culture; how science will adapt to such arguments; and what nomenclature science will employ in order to prevent it unwittingly or unwillingly getting into bed with theosophy and theology. It has been argued that science is based on materialism, and materialism excludes the idea of spirit. This idea of spirit within humanity and without humanity is one that will need to be pushed if it is to challenge the orthodoxy of traditional materialist science.

Report: #1

Location: Bedroom (~10:15hrs)

Dose: 30mg

Heave-Ho

The room was awash in beautiful bright sunlight. I knew the substance would attract a powerful spiritual being from the occult realms. After inhaling the dose, the room suddenly filled with a moderately powerful energy. This quickly underwent three stepped changes increasing in both intensity and frequency. The concluding visual effect was the bedroom appeared to be jarring back and forth rather violently and the air throughout the bedroom made it appear that I was underwater. The energy was not particularly prodigious but it was significant. Emotionally, I could not fail to sense the presence of a masculine entity. Intensively, I likened the discarnate presence to a very big and very strong albeit small-minded giant. For reasons unknown to me, his sole purpose in life was to heave the ground. I could easily sense the entity appealing to me. He was wanting me to share in his urgency for the task he was undertaking and quickly became frustrated with me for failing to share his concern. He went back to whatever it was he was doing. But in doing so, the left side of my body was slowly being raised up from the bedroom floor. I was terrifically surprised at this and remained in a slightly tilted position until the seething energy slowly subsided and withdrew. I felt extremely frustrated that something so bizarre and unexpected had presented itself. But I was resolute I would report honestly on that which I experienced. I urged myself to remain super sharp and as perceptive as possible, in order to learn as much as I possibly could. My hand ventured down my pants on a little mission to scratch away an itch running through my scrotum. But suspecting I was not quite as alone as I thought I was, I slowly and self-consciously withdrew my hand.

Report: #2

Location: Bedroom (~14:30hrs)

Dose: 31mg

Getting it in the Neck

I scrutinised the empty air before drawing down the dose of DMT, knowing it would rapidly expand my mind and thereby attract something from an unseen kingdom; something conscious, intelligent and alive. As my head sank back into the pillows, I implored myself to be sharp and observant. That was the exact moment the room rapidly filled with an energy of mind different to my own. Momentarily the room appeared awash with transparent seething energy, giving a characteristic underwater appearance. Within mere seconds the energy ramped up hugely. The bedroom was now subject to a tremendous ultra-high frequency energy. It was prodigious and I knew from experience that such a level of energy was easily sufficient to give the attending occult entity easy access to my physiology. I swallowed and could feel its psycho-spiritual presence moving and coating the walls of my throat. That same energy was also slowly sweeping across the room towards me. Upon swallowing I could feel the motion of the thin substance as it sealed up the opening of my mouth from the inside. I could also feel an interior presence around the general region of my throat. That presence was felt to be as solid as concrete. My head was being held firmly in position from within. I dared not test the strength of the entity and so I remained stock still, breathing through my nose and swallowing only very occasionally for comfort. Each time I swallowed it felt like something physically very stiff and very strong was present around the interior front of my throat. The presence of the entity inside my head gave me a distinct sensual appreciation of my cranial physiology. It was clear that any attempt to move my head would either be resisted or simply unfruitful. An illusion of forward motion was created. Very slowly, it appeared as though I was moving ever closer to the oak trees visible through the bedroom window. But each incremental move seemed barely perceptible. After a few minutes, the trees duly appeared to be very much closer to me than my actual view from the bedroom would ordinarily permit. In addition, the trees seemed somehow different. They appeared far less detailed, as though they had somehow been made much tidier. Even more oddly, it seemed my vision of the trees was completely unhindered by the presence of the lace curtain. There was a notable dimness of daylight within the bedroom, which I knew was caused by the transparent but uncommonly dense body of the entity. The rigid and stiff physical presence within my neck persisted. I waited patiently for a couple of minutes before even daring to open my mouth. Upon doing so I satisfied an urge to move my tongue vigorously around my mouth. The apparent rigidity within my neck immediately dissipated. The experience had concluded. I felt like blurting out tears and laughter in equal measure, but refrained.

Report: #3

Location: Bedroom (~11:00hrs)

Dose: 25mg

11:11:11:11

I looked into the empty while begging the question: How empty is the air, really? A tremendous quantity of vapour was produced from all three inhalations. A mere second after my head sank into the pillows the room filled with a familiar energy – giving a transparent but turbulent appearance throughout the room. Within mere seconds that energy went through several stepped changes. But there was something different about those changes today that I cannot quite put my finger on. The intensity and the frequency increased. But in those tumultuous few seconds I felt there had been something uniquely different. The room was now seething with energy. I immediately sensed the presence within that seething energy. Indeed, the presence was that seething atmosphere. I felt I was under scrutiny and could feel a slight pressure on each side of my head that I instinctively understood related to that. It seemed that a protrusive mass of energy had reached down into my head and was engaged in reading my mind. It was a very frightening situation, principally because I had the overriding sense this particular high-minded entity was not really in the business of troubling itself with humans on a one-to-one basis. It was here with me now simply in order to understand the source of amplified psychic signal. My inner voice spluttered to convey my situation – undertaking practical occult research and writing about that research. My internal narration made me feel like a jabbering fool. The atmosphere within the room was still seething. The entity seemed fascinated with me. But it was the same fascination that a streetwise tomcat would hold for a naive little house mouse. I swallowed and felt a thin psycho-spiritual film coating the roof of my mouth. Suddenly, far off in the distance and totally unrelated to my undertaking, a booming noise of considerable power sounded. I suspected a major incident had just occurred. Several more booms of equal loudness sounded out in succession. It was obvious the booms were distant but significantly loud at source. I imagined some devastating major catastrophe was now unfolding. My focus was no longer on the energetic being sharing the bedroom with me. With great concern I jumped up and went over to the window. Everything was just as it should be. I raced downstairs. My wife was in the lounge. I asked if she had heard any booming noises. She said she thought she had heard someone banging down the lid down on a wheelie bin. The potent substance was still very active within me. Our plain beige carpet exhibited extensive patterning and my head was still ringing with amplified psychic energy well above baseline level. I sat down on the sofa and thought about the energetic entity I had rudely abandoned in the bedroom. I looked up to the ceiling and wondered whether the entity might make its way through there in order to find me. I waited impatiently for a few seconds and then headed back upstairs and lay upon the bedroom floor in the same position. My occult guest had vacated. I wondered about the booming sounds. Had a chemical factory just blown up? Had a petrol tanker exploded? Was a terrorist incident unfolding? I stood up and went downstairs. I met my wife in the kitchen and chanced to glance up at the wall clock. It was 11:11hrs. I then realised the date was the 11th day of the 11th month. I now realised the booms I had heard were cannon fire from the WW1 Remembrance Day in central London.

Report: #4

Location: Bedroom (~13:15hrs)

30mg

Extra-Cerebral Residential

When I was a small boy it was religious that every Sunday morning, we would drive over to see my grandparents in Dewsbury, West Yorkshire. It was a long and boring motorway drive. To pass the time we would play eye-spy, or we'd count red cars, or blue cars, or green cars, or whatever colour of car we chose to count. Eventually I would tire of that game and my own thoughts would keep me relatively entertained. I'd wonder about the people in the cars on the motorway. Where did they come from? Where did they live? What were they like? Where were they going? Eventually we would exit the motorway and drive for a few miles through a town called Ossett before arriving at our destination. We would drive by thousands and thousands of houses. And again, my mind would wonder about the individuals living inside those houses. What did each of them do within their own little house?

The bedroom was enjoying a brief spell of sunlight. Nerves aplenty were swimming inside me. After a minute I sat upright and got on with it. Three careful pulls produced a terrific amount of vapour. After exhaling the final intake, I lay back and urged myself to remain sharp in my observations. The room suddenly filled with a moderate and mildly turbulent transparent energy. As soon as it manifested it increased in intensity. I could hear and feel the same increase in the midst of my head. The frequency of the energy also visibly increased. After just a few short seconds the whole room appeared to be jarring back and forth significantly. I realised however that too many seconds had passed for the entity to secure any significant interaction with me. The psychic energy audibly ringing inside my head suddenly reduced, yet remained well above baseline level. The jarring effect throughout the bedroom reduced and then ceased. The bright sunlight waned and the room fell dull. A nearby crow cawed three times. Up to my right, I now observed the very slow manifestation of an entity. I watched it carefully while wondering how much potency my crystals had lost. Suddenly, something began slowly squeezing itself into the left side of my head. I could feel its dense psycho-spiritual-physicality as it squeezed itself inside my head. It felt like an oversized quasi-physical grub. I could feel it slowly moving around. It was exerting an unusual degree of pressure as it moved around inside my brain. The pressure from its presence was becoming startling. I began to consider it could be something unwelcome; a minor occult entity of uncertain character or unsavoury disposition; a morbid maleficent entity looking to squat inside my head and lay lots of ill-motived machinations. Immediately upon thinking those thoughts I sat bolt upright in mild panic and wondered what I should do. I thought it best not to worry and just lay back down. But upon laying back down, I felt the very same pressure. The very same oversized psycho-spiritual grub and its overtly pronounced movements caused the very same fears to flood my mind once again. I began to imagine a host of despicable occult beings all around me; closing in on my mind for a feeding frenzy upon my psychic energies. I thought I could see them – evident as short-lived sparkly twinkles in the air above me. I began to question: What if that oversized psycho-spiritual grub never leaves my head? That was enough! I leaped to my feet and walked over to the bedroom window. I looked outside and then turned on my heels and cried aloud: "I'm frightening the bloody life out of myself here!" The beige carpet was awash with tryptamine patterning. I shook my head vigorously and let out a guttural bray, as though to assure myself that I was still myself. I headed downstairs to the kitchen while whispering appeals of anxious self-concern to myself. I told my wife I was gonna to take a shower. Following which, I strode naked into the bedroom feeling thoroughly refreshed. But I had one question at the forefront of my mind: Was there anything extra-cerebral resident in my head? Is it possible that something occult can actually accommodate itself inside my head, and influence my thoughts and my feelings? And if that is so, are there beings that can bring about positive and benevolent influence? And are there beings that can bring about malevolent and negative influence? Or, perhaps such entities simply amplify the thoughts and the feelings of the individual; in much the same way that feeding into a negative stream of consciousness can quickly make a great mountain out of a molehill; in much the same way that a clear-cut positive stream of consciousness breeds clear-cut positive thoughts and actions. Can the influence of extra-dimensional beings bring about that which most right-thinking people would consider to be good, and that which most right-thinking people would consider to be bad? How would I know my mind had, or indeed had not succumbed to a psychic intruder? What if I wake up in the morning but am not quite myself? What if I awaken with nefarious inclinations? Ill-begotten notions that simply will not go away? This is no joke! What if I suddenly snap out from an overbearing trance-like state and find my family bloodily slain? That's not jocular! Demonic possession, or the very possibility of such a thing is no laughing matter when real life horror manifests in the flesh. But surely the notion of demonic entities, and the possession of human subjects thereof by such lifeforms, is downright ludicrous.

[Wikipedia: Michael Taylor (Ossett)]

http://en.wikipedia.org/wiki/Michael_Taylor_(Ossett)

This 1974 murder case centred upon alleged demonic possession. Taylor was a married man. He and his wife attended a Christian Fellowship Group. The lay leader of the group was Marie Robinson. Taylor's wife stated aloud at one group meeting that relations between her husband and Marie Robinson were of a carnal nature. Michael Taylor, who admitted feeling evil within himself, verbally attacked Robinson and she screamed back at him. At the next meeting however, Taylor received absolution – he was forgiven. Despite that, his actions became increasingly erratic, to the extent that a local vicar and other ministers experienced in deliverance prepared to cast out the demons they assumed to be residing within him. An exorcism was arranged and duly carried out at St Thames church in Barnsley.

> According to Bill Ellis, an authority on folklore and the occult in contemporary culture, the exorcists believed that they had: "In an all-night ceremony ... invoked and cast out at least forty demons, including those of incest, bestiality, blasphemy, and lewdness." At the end, exhausted, they allowed Taylor to go home, although they felt that at least three demons –insanity, murder, and violence – were still left in him."

> The exorcism rite, which lasted until 6 a.m., exhausted the priests, who allowed the man to return home. Nevertheless, they cautioned that although they had cast out forty spirits from Michael Taylor, a few remained, including the demon of murder. While at home Michael Taylor brutally murdered his wife, Christine, and strangled their poodle. He was found by a policeman, naked in the street, covered with blood. At his trial in March, Taylor was acquitted on the grounds of insanity.

> [From Wikipedia, the free encyclopedia]

That's a truly tragic and gruesome tale of real-life horror. And one in which there was no evidence and there could be no evidence for the actual existence of any of those supposed demonic beings. Taylor admitted feeling evil within himself. But could anyone really had known with any certainty whether Taylor was inherently evil and insane; or whether those tendencies developed within him from his relations with the people in his life; or whether something conscious and unseen had either introduced that malignancy into him or amplified that which was already there? The idea that unseen beings can influence us to such an extent as that is an incredibly thought-provoking and terribly discomforting notion. But what if it is possible that unseen things – discarnate beings made of mind-stuff – really can influence our thoughts and our actions? Terrible things do happen. Someone snaps; loses their temper; flies into a fit of anger or rage; acts violently. In the aftermath, we hear: "I don't know what came over me," "Something came over me," "I wasn't myself," "I wasn't in my right mind," "The red mist descended upon me," "I didn't do it," "I heard voices inside my head." It's unnerving and very frightening to consider some of our thoughts and promptings may not be of our own making. Is that why we: "Perish the thought?" And just suppose that such things really do occur. Where does the blame lie? Can a man upon killing his wife, or a wife upon killing her man, excuse themselves with: "Something came over me!" Clearly it would be ludicrous to pin the blame upon an unseen being of occult nature and blindly accept such explanation. But that doesn't necessarily mean it wasn't so. So, I need to be certain. Have I gotten something discarnate and extraneous into my head; something that is going to lay ill-begotten ideas deep within my psyche; terrible viral mind seeds that will take root and slowly grow into full blown malevolent madness? Will my mind crack and crizzle as I wreak unspeakable horror on those around me? Clearly, one needs to have absolute certainty upon the interpretations one arrives at when dealing with mind manifesting realities. I knew I was okay. But only because I felt okay. There was no doubt that something psycho-spiritual and shaped very much like an oversized grub had been rummaging around inside my brain. But I was absolutely certain it had been a quasi-physical protrusion from a powerful DMT entity. An unseen portion of that being had entered into my head, either in an investigatory capacity or an action purposefully designed to put the heebie-jeebies upon me.

Report: #5

Location: Bedroom (~11:45hrs)

Dose: 27mg

The Energy Question

My nerves and fears were terrifying me. I insisted upon lying down. But only to sit straight back up and begin. Three pulls emptied pipe. As I lay back, I implored myself to remain sharp and astute. Transparent energy rapidly emanated from me and filled the bedroom. It appeared uniformly turbulent. With equal immediacy the intensity of that energy increased. No sooner had I made that observation when the intensity and the frequency increased phenomenally in magnitude. In particular, the frequency became so incredibly high as to make the entire field of energy feel homogenous and solid; a mass of paradoxically solid yet invisible energy, to which physical things could offer no resistance. I could feel it upon my bones; especially the bones of my fingers. I could feel as it drove into my head without the slightest hindrance. And then suddenly, everything in the bedroom appeared as though I were seeing through a filter. Everything in the room appeared very much cleaner, much more colourful, and altogether brighter and tidier, with a notable radiant appearance. I swallowed. Straightaway it became obvious a portion of the occult entity was inside me. A very physical presence was easily perceptible inside my head. There was no pain and no apparent reason for me to be worried. But the strange cranial presence was absolutely rigid; making it feel as though my head were being held very firmly in position. This scenario continued for perhaps two to three minutes. I was breathing nasally, rhythmically and heavily. Suddenly, there was a very rapid and palpably very obvious movement of energy away from me. I suspected the occult entity was transferring itself to another location within the bedroom. That sudden lurching movement indicated the beginning of the end of our interaction. I remained motionless while strange interior movements indicated psycho-spiritual portions of the entity were slowly withdrawing from my physiology. I could feel it exiting through a small localised area to the rear left side of my neck; feeling something like a liquid under high pressure surging through a small-bore pipe. Above me the entity slowly condensed into superdense visible state – appearing as an amorphous mass of transparent spherical cells. As the being exited along the inside lengthy of my torso, I had the distinct impression that I was somehow being physically maneuvered. The emotional atmosphere within the bedroom was one of utter seriousness. It seemed there was an implicit understanding between us; an understanding that I was fully aware of exactly what was occurring, and would therefore remain completely calm and patient, until those long psycho-spiritual tentacular lengths had worked their way out of my physiology. My emotions in the aftermath of the experience were quite matter of fact. It felt to me like this interaction had been cut short.

Report: #6

Location: Bedroom (~13:45hrs)

Dose: 29mg

Divinely Decorative

My fears and nerves were in advanced state. I walked over to the bedroom window and looked outside. The awareness of being alone in this research washed over me. There was no support and no assistance. There is only me that can make progress with my investigations. My heart was beating fast. I took a couple of deep breaths and demanded courage from within. I lay down and after some silently spoken words of urgency I sat back up and began the first of three very slow and very careful inhalations. I lay back while imploring myself to be sharply perceptive as the room filled with my own psycho-spiritual energy. Its intensity rapidly increased. Within all of two seconds, another source of psycho-spiritual energy arrived. And that energy was off the scale. It was prodigious and ominous. It filled the room and imposed such an incredibly willful display of its own spiritual power that I became genuinely scared the plasterboard walls were going to be forced asunder under the almighty otherworldly pressure. Within mere seconds the bedroom took on a divine transformation. It was the same bedroom. But it now looked heavenly. Everything white was now whiter than white, radiant and dazzling – visually stunning! Nothing within my sight had any blemish or any imperfection whatsoever. Everything material appeared to have been spiritualised. Every item and every finish appeared as though it had been given a magnificent divine rendering of a quality that was simply impossible to produce within the earthly realm. And yet there it was – throughout the entire bedroom – and I was in the midst of it. Even the very air within the bedroom seemed illuminated and radiant. A portion of the occult entity was inside me. I swallowed and the action gave away its unmistakable presence. It had secured a very firm purchase throughout my cranium, in much the same way one's fingers tightly grip a ten-pin bowling ball prior to launch. I swallowed once again and could feel the psycho-spiritual substance moving along the roof of my mouth. It seemed the entity was securing itself more firmly but was also allowing me the comfort to swallow freely. The trees outside the bedroom window were rendered in a fashion that suggested they too had been spiritually redecorated. My breathing was rhythmical and fast with adrenaline coursing through my veins. It then appeared I was subject to a very slow and progressive forward motion, even though I knew I was completely stationary. But coupled with that illusion of motion, my view of the trees outside the bedroom window suggested I was slowly moving closer and closer toward them, such that their proximity eventually appeared extraordinarily and impossibly close to me. This highly bizarre visual effect and illusion of motion then slowly reversed itself. I was now apparently undergoing a progressive retrograde motion. The trees seemed to slowly resume their normal proximity and appearance. I could still feel the presence of the entity within me. I knew what the finale would be – an imperceptible exit of the entity from within me and from the bedroom. I knew it would take place so slowly and so subtly that I would not detect even one single little change from the divine appearance of the bedroom back to its ordinary mundane appearance. I began thinking out loud; feeling quite certain the occult entity could understand me. I praised its skill and asked whether I too would evolve to be so configured in the far distant future. I stated that I wished it to be so. And then, having become bold, I called out aloud: "Yes! I know you can hear me! One day, I want to be just like you!"

Report: #7

Location: Bedroom (~10:45hrs)

Dose: 25mg

Psychically Psyched

I forced myself into a progressive mentality. With courageous bravado I oversaw three very good inhalations before lying back and urging myself to be perceptive and astute. The room suddenly filled with energy that appeared to visibly race away from me at a very rapid rate. It immediately filled the bedroom and resulted in a very turbulent dense atmosphere. Straightaway, that energy increased noticeably in its intensity. The whole room appeared to be jarring back and forth violently. Something arrived. Something unmistakable arrived. Very quickly the room filled with a very different kind of energy to what I am used to. There was no ultra-high frequency characterising this energy. The room was now filled with a terribly foreboding density of mind; its energy was palpable to my entire being. The atmosphere was visually and palpably very turbulent. I could feel the density of the discarnate mind and could actually see it filling the room. The apparent physicality and emotional heaviness of its presence was truly frightening – terrifying and ominous. From within the midst of that widespread turbulent atmosphere, I observed a sizeable spiralling protrusion of mind-stuff quickly and purposefully corkscrewing its way down towards me. I knew it was coming down for a closer analysis of me. And I knew this was not good. This entity was an occult heavyweight. I had attracted something immense. Something oversized had deigned to investigate the spike of psychic output from my DMT-amplified mind. And much to its displeasure, it had found a human – a mere surface dweller. The descending protrusion reached me. It reached my solar plexus. It pushed down gently onto my solar plexus like an invisible oversized finger of tremendous proportion, whereupon it maintained a firm physical pressure upon that region of my anatomy. I straightaway realised something terribly worrying. I realised the pressure imposing upon the centre of my chest, and the formidable palpable mentality behind that imposing pressure, filling the entire bedroom like a controlled storm, could snuff me out on a whim. I attempted to communicate with the terrifying presence. I silently conveyed that I am writing a book. But the sheer heaviness of its mental presence immediately told me this being was not in the least bit interested in anything about me whatsoever. I ceased my communication. There I was, trapped beneath an occult being; an entity made of mind-stuff characterised by such awful powerful weightiness that all it had to do was impose upon me gently and my soul would surely be terminally squeezed from my body. Frightened just does not adequately convey the fearfulness I was feeling. I was smaller than small. I was at the complete and utter mercy of something far more powerful than me on every conceivable and relevant level. Silently, I began to make appeals; appeals that I am just a human; appeals that I am a parent; genuine appeals that I wished to remain alive. But this being was simply not interested in anything I had to say. Its sheer power conveyed a deep and troubling capacity for danger without remorse, and that worried me in the extreme. I knew this experience must eventually come to an end. But I was worried I may not see that end; or I may not see that end with the same soundness of mind that I began this experiment with. Worryingly, there was no indication this experience was coming to an end. I sensed it was truly within the gift of this being to reconfigure my psyche in ways that would be disastrous to me. I was very scared. I was scared for my mind and for my future and for my life. I thought about jumping up. And I did jump up. I jumped up to remove myself from the terrifying being whose presence was quite literally weighing very heavily upon me. As I jumped up, the first thing I noticed really surprised me. That is, I did not notice anything unusual. There was no strange energy. The entity had vanished. Had my jumping up broken the psychic waveband we were interacting on? There was no sense of a heavy menacing presence anywhere at all. I was so shocked at how very different things had been just a second ago. I descended the stairs in great haste and outlined to my wife just how frightening this experience had been. It was petrifying – damnable and wretched! It was a truly god-awful experience! For some time afterwards, I felt greatly aggrieved at this incursion. I felt shocked at the power of the entity, and totally amazed at the clarity with which I had visually observed it and palpably felt it.

This was undoubtedly one of the most significant experiences of my research programme. There were no visions and no bizarre hallucinations. There was no psycho-spiritual substance operating invasively within my physiology. It was simply the unmistakable suffocating weight of superdense mind-stuff that made this experiment really standout. This was a truly fearsome and powerful being; one that felt far in excess of the measure of my own mind. But what kind of occult being was it? How does one even go about cataloguing such beings? Could it really have squeezed the life out of me, with as much ease as I could squeeze the juice from an overripe grape under the trifling pressure of my index finger? Had that occult entity ever belonged to the human kingdom in aeons past? I imagined it would've been of prodigious size and almighty strength. And similarly, its mind would have been singular, ambitious, and uncontrollably determined – knowing full well that evolutionary advancement means progressive acquisition of power at all costs. Freed from the bonds of terrestrial flesh, it now evolves on a different plane; an unseen plane; exercising its powerful mind while fully conscious of its own evolution; fully conscious of that which it has been and that which it is progressively becoming. And just as it was minding its own business, out went my tiny little psychic signal – a short-lived spike of psychic noise; audible in an otherwise relatively peaceable yet unseen non-physical realm. Today, I was psychically out-psyched. It was a classic fight or flight situation. But without the remotest sense that I could fight. What would've happened had I stayed there; I just don't know? Maybe this being was merely testing my courage and my resolve. And on this occasion, I was found wanting? I didn't feel foolhardy enough to remain any longer beneath of its fearsome presence – which could've resulted in a terrible psychic comeuppance for me. Was it about to snaffle my mind and leave me as an empty shell, with nothing but subconscious capabilities – nothing more than an internal echo of who I once was? Whatever that being was, I know I will have to progress with my research. And knowing that such beings as that exist out there is truly worrying. Do I run away at every troublesome encounter in order to keep my mind ensouled within my body?

Report: #8

Location: Bedroom (~14:30hrs)

Dose: 20mg

Mother's Day

I sat up and inhaled. The substance tasted far from fresh. It had a certain dry and powdery taste upon my tongue. The onset of the substance took a second or two longer than expected. Intense energy rapidly pervaded the entire bedroom. The whole room appeared to be jarring back and forth at a mediocre rate. I wasn't expecting much from this experience. And I should not have been scared. But there was something terribly ominous about the energy. Its diminution seemed to make me fearful of the outcome. Suddenly, without any warning whatsoever, the room flooded with an energy that made me regret ever messing about with this substance. Instinctively, I felt this unseen entity had been watching me. It had been reading my mind. It completely understood how poorly prepared I was for this encounter; an encounter with an occult entity exhibiting such tremendous forcefulness that its power made the aged plasterboard walls creak and groan under its immense imposing pressure. In the instant it arrived it rapidly imposed its prodigious might throughout the entire bedroom. The bedroom became incredibly radiant. The air throughout appeared dense and radiant. Ultra-high frequency energy imposed immensely upon the aged plasterboard walls and they began creak and groan – audibly flexing under the terrific force imposing upon them. I felt like a child that had been caught out. Caught out with a dose of DMT that had tasted far from fresh. I began to worry that this experience would take me so far out of my comfort zone that I'd soon be calling for the love and comfort of my dear old mum. Here was an entity of immense capacity. It was upon me and over me and throughout as though it had been watching me all along – just waiting for me to empty my pipe. I felt like I had wandered into the wrong neighbourhood. I was terrified. I thought my number was up. I made began making silent appeals about the welfare of my children; and several other appeals, which did include fond remembrance of my dear old mum. Unexpectedly and rather rapidly, the energy within the room either completely vanished or attuned itself to such an accurate frequency with ordinary terrestrial reality that its visual presence throughout the bedroom was completely undetectable. I swallowed. A portion of the entity was inside me for sure. Its distinct psycho-spiritual presence was all around in the interior of my mouth. And emotionally, there was no doubting its presence whatsoever. I realised it was busy beneath me. It was doing something at the mid-point and centre of my back. I have no idea what it was doing there. It was slowly working its way around the outside of me in a very purposeful yet unseen manner. Upon swallowing I could feel the thin psycho-spiritual substance moving around the inside my mouth. After completing whatever it had been doing with my back, I sensed the entity had gone. But there was an overwhelming feeling there would be a second part to this experience. A continuation of sorts, sometime in the future. I mouthed aloud: "This will come back to me!" The experience took around seven minutes to complete. I remained lain for a further seven or eight minutes. During that time, I exhibited a strange emotion; it was neither joyful nor despairing; neither happy or sad. It was none of those emotions. There was complete neutrality to my emotions. And although that did not trouble me, I wanted to better understand what was at the root of that strange state of mind. I introspectively scrutinised myself. I consciously amplified and magnified just how I was feeling until at last I got my answer. I was learning. Tears and laughter would merely cloud my mind. The strange neutral emotion was a clear-cut progressive desire to learn from this research.

Report: #9

Location: Bedroom (~13:45hrs)

Dose: 25mg

Indescribable Multicoloured Miscellany

The only available excuse to avoid furthering my research was to listen to my fears. They were certainly whispering unto me. Like a pre-programmed unthinking automaton, I sat at my desk and prepared the pipe. From the bedroom floor I sat up and made three pulls. Whilst inhaling, I realised there was not a jot of nervousness nor mote of fear about me. I was absolutely 100% committed to my research undertaking. A mildly turbulent and crystal-clear fluid-like medium quickly filled the bedroom. There had been just a hint that it had rapidly projected forth from me. The strange fluid-like medium became increasingly turbulent and intense and very soon the entire bedroom appeared to be jarring back and forth. Just then, with tremendous rapidity, a highly energetic occult being arrived and imposed its own prodigious power throughout the room. I cannot ever see myself becoming comfortable with the intensity and incredible ultra-high frequency of such energy. It is a stunning and devastating display of otherworldly power. I could feel it thrilling right through me; penetrating the very core of my body. I instinctively understood this display of power was the occult entity's means of securing its bizarre and temporary psychic interaction with me. Not so much a case of attuning itself with my own psychic signal, but more a case of it imposing upon me so powerfully that it could totally dictate the course of the interaction. As that conscious energy imposed itself throughout the bedroom and drove powerfully into me, it created a visual effect that made the entire room appear hauntingly divine and eerie. The room appeared as though veiled beneath radiant white and grey gossamer drapery. In taking on that haunting appearance, everything therein appeared incredibly rigid and brittle, improbably stiff and delicate. Even the daylight within the bedroom appeared static, stiff and starched. But this appearance was fleeting – maybe no longer than two or three seconds. Because then, from within the volume of its own spiritual body, the occult entity produced a vast vista of scenery that was truly stunning to behold. It was simply beyond words. The depth of the bright white scenery appeared to stretch out far into the distance. The foreground was filled with untold magical and indescribable multicoloured miscellany; highly active yet impossible content. Everything was wrought in a depth of colour and a quality of definition that seemed far more real than real life appears. It was as good as being in another world. It also appeared that I was actually moving through that magical environment, in a slow and swirling fashion. It was simply stunning. And the truth is, I could have lain there for hours and hours and hours, marvelling at that dreamlike otherworld. But in truth, I was nowhere else other than within my bedroom, laid upon my bedroom floor. I was in the midst of the mind of a very powerful and apparently very imaginative occult being; one imposing a visionary world upon my perceptions from within its own non-corporeal psycho-spiritual body. For some reason my mood was strangely neutral. Despite the thoroughly astonishing appearance of this magical and evidently non-terrestrial kingdom, I did not seem in any way emotionally astonished. As that vision slowly subsided, I noted the room appeared to be out of kilter, as though the entire bedroom and all contents therein had been slightly twisted, from top to bottom. The air filling the bedroom also displayed a very distinct dark beige hue. I suspected that was visual evidence of the occult entity slowly diminishing its strange temporary liaison with me. As I was observing that withdrawal take place, something very strange presented itself. I should have been quite shocked at the occurrence. But I immediately accepted both the possibility and the reality of the situation. My head was rested on a couple of pillows. Significant movement from the pillow behind my head ensued. It was as though a hand was moving beneath the pillow, repeatedly pushing upwards. There was no mistaking the occurrence. The action was clearly meant to be significant and noticed. There was simply no way one could fail to observe such an overt action. It continued on and on and on, to such extent I eventually considered: If you're going to do that, you may as well be right up in my face! It then abated. And that coincided with the room returning to its ordinary semblance.

Report: #10

Location: Bedroom (~11:00hrs)

Dose: 27mg

Home Alone

I was home alone. The weather perfectly matched my preference for DMT research – brilliant bright sunshine. I sat up and inhaled three good pulls before lying back and listening for the increase in my psychic sound. But surprisingly, there was no audible increase at all. After just a couple of seconds the room appeared as though it were jarring back and forth, moderately. The visible jarring effect increased – not hugely, but noticeably. There was something distinctly foreboding and terribly scary about the energy imposing this jarring effect. But it was in no way obvious whether that energy had actually emanated from within me or without me. An awfully frightening emotion filled the bedroom. It really was incredibly frightening and was focussed solely upon me. Its strength was so certain and so obvious, and so terribly ominous, that I gave real thought to racing out from the bedroom. I was feeling genuinely very scared at the menacing emotion filling the room. There was a sudden movement beneath my back, as though something very small had moved very quickly and taken advantage of the small space between my lower back and the bedroom floor. With the menacing atmosphere filling the bedroom, this completely shredded my nerves. I then felt the faintest hint of movement beneath the pillows cushioning my head. That worried me terribly. Not because such a thing had never occurred before. But because the mood within the bedroom was on par with a spine-chilling horror-cum-thriller, steadily building up to a scene that was absolutely certain to make me scream for my life. I tried ignoring the movement beneath the pillows. I implored myself to be brave. But the movement beneath the pillows became evident once again. I was so taken aback that I sat bolt upright. I knew I would find nothing beneath the pillows, but I looked anyway. My imagination overtook my bravery. I began to imagine my neck being gripped from behind by an unseen force. I was now giving serious thought to jumping up and vacating the room. Where was that moody and sullen energy coming from? I had not expected such a dark experience in such fine, bright weather. I was home alone – a grown ass man in bright daylight, yet feeling genuinely as scared as a little boy all alone in bed at midnight, with something outside scratching at the window pane. Suddenly, and without any warning whatsoever, there was a single loud snapping sound. It was a short-lived godawful noise that immediately ruined what was left of my nerves. My stomach imploded in one single rippling spasm. I quickly computed that I'd heard the inner flap on the letterbox closing with a snap after the postman had pushed our mail through the letterbox. I was truly pleased to stand up and resume my day with ordinary everyday business.

Report: #11

Location: Bedroom (~14:00hrs)

Dose: 27mg

Misadventuring

I really thought this research would become easier with time. But it's contrariwise. I lay still for a short while, visually inspecting the bedroom. Even after all this time, it still does not seem at all possible that such a thing as I say occurs, actually and factually does occur. Is it really the case that inhaling the potent tryptamine vapour attracts an occult entity into my immediate setting? Looking around the bedroom in all its ordinary glory, it seemed so improbable. My third pull on the pipe drew in a truly lung-filling volume of vapour. Upon exhaling I besought hawkish perceptiveness from all my senses. The bedroom immediately filled with a strange fluid-like psycho-spiritual medium. Upon filling the room, it quickly increased in intensity, until the whole room appeared to be jarring back and forth violently. Within mere seconds that energy increased exponentially, in both intensity and frequency. I could feel the incredible power thrilling through my entire being. My vision appeared to be tuning into a different view of the same reality. Momentarily the room became foggy, and yet far more colourful. The power this entity was imposing was immense. So immense that I genuinely feared the building fabric of the bedroom was about to be rent asunder. And then, all that prodigious power suddenly subsided. It now appeared that there was nothing unusual within the bedroom. Even though I sensed the strength of a presence all around me. I swallowed to lubricate my throat. A distinct psycho-spiritual presence was palpably evident above the roof of my mouth. Not coating the roof of my mouth, but actually above the roof of my mouth – inside my cranium. It had a significant and solidly defined presence. I could even feel the straight-edged detail of its presence. It felt exactly like a four faced pyramid with a flattened top, approximately 2cm in height. I was puzzled as to how this entity could impose such a strong and apparently rigid physicality inside my brain, whilst there was not even the slightest visual hint of its presence anywhere else within the bedroom. I was certain it was invisibly filling the entire room. I could sense it. I marvelled at the ordinary appearance of the bedroom, whilst the rigid physical presence of the four-faced flattened-topped pyramid was so tactilely obvious inside my brain. I then sensed movement inside my abdomen. The entity was active inside there, moving around freely. It slowly began to work its way up inside me, evidenced by a really obvious physical feeling as it moved towards my torso. Suddenly, there was an urgent sense of a huge commotion unfolding somewhere outside. Concurrently, there was an immediate wholesale shift in the non-human emotion filling the bedroom; as though whatever was occurring outside demanded the entity's immediate attention. Now, I really could feel the physicality of the entity inside my abdomen. It quickly began racing up inside my body. It was moving through me as though desperately seeking an exit. But I sensed there was a problem. I began to wonder whether it was possible this entity had made a gross miscalculation. Was it possible this particular portion of the entity could actually become trapped inside me? And if so, what would happen to me? I implicitly trust that these entities know exactly what they are doing. But what if one of them gets it completely wrong? The nondescript commotion from somewhere outside – whatever it was – continued unabated. A bird was tweeting noisily, nonstop. I sensed there was indeed a very serious problem with this interaction. The portion of entity trapped inside me really had left things far too late. The movements quickly became frantic and erratic. It was pushing up around the region of my throat. Repeatedly trying to push and force itself out of me without any success. I was extremely concerned and began seriously considering the possibility this could bring about my demise. Death through misadventure with DMT! The entity redoubled its efforts to escape. But in so doing, it effectively reduced the diameter of my windpipe, resulting in a rapidly increasing restriction on my capacity to breath. I could actually feel the tubular physicality of my windpipe being squeezed closed. Panic time was fast approaching and I mentally prepared to yell for my wife to dial the emergency services. My windpipe was literally being squeezed from within. But the occult entity inside me was also panicking, as it too realised the desperateness of its plight. I was now in a fretful panic and genuinely fearing for my life. I sat bolt upright. And just as soon as I did, there was no sense of the entity's presence anywhere, within me or without me. I jumped up and raced downstairs and headed outside. I made great long strides to the foot of the garden, whilst vigorously moving my tongue around and around my mouth to be absolutely certain there nothing trapped inside of me. I headed back indoors where I stood trancelike looking out of the kitchen window. The memory of the bird tweeting nosily non-stop and the nondescript commotion occurring outside resurfaced in my mind. The tweeting had sounded as though it had been playing on a loop. It was at that moment I realised I'd been expertly tricked by a master manipulator. I'd been had. The sound of the bird tweeting, and the unknown commotion outside, were both fabrications – auditory and possibly emotional hallucinations imposed upon me. Upon realising the truth of that, I was filled with applause and appreciation for the deftness that the occult entity had displayed in misleading me so convincingly.

Report: #12

Location: Bedroom (~10:15hrs)

Dose: 27mg

Sex Publication Issues

A tug o' war was taking place. An internal skirmish between my desire for sex with my wife before she left for work and my desire to progress with my DMT research. My spirit was indeed willing to pursue research with the potent mind-manifesting crystals. But my flesh was far more than willing to partake in the pleasure of sex. But why even make the matter of sex vs. smoking DMT an issue? Why not simply have my cake and eat it? Have sex, and then smoke DMT. It's just a hunch, but something tells me that satisfying sexual desire before proceeding with the research experiment would likely have a significant bearing on the outcome of the experiment. Sex before DMT feels like I am cheating my research mentality by not paying enough respect to the energies required to fully commit to the DMT experiment. And to smoke DMT simply in order to get it out of the way, and then pursue sex, seems somehow discordant with the nature of the research. I spoke to my wife about this yesterday in a jocular manner, just after we'd had sex. She laughed, and then imposed a two-week hiatus on any further sex between us. From the bedroom floor a tide of urgency surged through me. I sat up and made three vaporous pulls from the fresh crystals. The vapour was pale and cool; smooth and relatively tasteless. The room immediately filled with a semi-transparent fluid-like substance. Straightaway, this strange medium began jarring back and forth. I implored myself to be observant but had hardly completed that self-imploration when it became all too evident an occult entity had just arrived. It imposed its tremendous power throughout the bedroom and down upon me. Its arrival had taken mere seconds. The entity secured a quasi-physical presence inside my head. A very rigid quasi-physical presence was anchored in the pineal region of my head. I could easily feel its presence and there was a definite shape to it. The room was now otherwise absolutely ordinary in its appearance, but there was an overwhelming emotional energy powerfully imposing down upon me. It readily translated into unspoken words: "Who are you?" And had that question actually been spoken, it would've been spoken loudly and sternly, in a demanding and indignant manner. I did my best to say nothing and think nothing. Just see what happens, I told myself. I became acutely aware of the entity's strange quasi-physical presence deep inside my head. It really had anchored itself within there. This overwhelmingly underlined the relative powers between us. Me – a human spirit housed in a physically mortal body. The occult entity – a powerful spirit divested of any obvious physical body and exhibiting sufficient capacity to anchor a quasi-physical portion of itself rigidly in the midst of my head. I suspected that should such an entity ever wish to impose upon me nefariously, I may well find myself forcibly and terminally evicted from my bodily shell. I doubted it would do such a thing. But I certainly did no doubt it had that capacity and that power. My inner voice began stammering appeals along the lines of: I am family man, with children to raise; and stammering a host of other life-bargaining pleas. The entity remained for a short while longer before I sensed its sudden departure. Yet the strange physicality remained present inside my head. I opened my mouth widely and moved my tongue around. The physical feeling of its rigid presence inside my brain immediately dissolved.

Report: #13

Location: Bedroom (~09:45hrs)

Dose: 31mg

Critical Cranial

I was home alone; committing to furthering my research by capably keeping nerves and fears at a safe distance. I sat up and emptied the pipe. As my head was halfway down to reaching the pillows, the room was already filling with that strange, transparent, superdense, fluidic, psycho-spiritual medium. It rapidly became intensely turbulent. Almost immediately, there were two or three very rapid and completely unmissable increases in the intensity and frequency of that energy. Immediately after which, a phenomenal level of energy imposed itself throughout the entire bedroom. The incredible spiritual energy had a paradoxically wholesale palpable solidity and yet it pervaded my head without hindrance. The visual effect as that took place was stunning. The bedroom appeared to take on a quality of reality that made it appear far more real than its ordinary everyday appearance. Colours, lines, contours and finishes appeared cleaner, straighter, sharper, and very much smoother. There were no imperfections whatsoever. The bedroom had momentarily taken on a spiritualised rendering. But there was also a significant amount of red-coloured miscellany incorporated throughout. And yet there are no red coloured items anywhere within the bedroom; save for one solitary canister of a proprietary brand pain-relieving heat spray standing proud upon the pine dresser. That incredible visual effect was short-lived – lasting mere seconds. The room suddenly appeared normal again. Except it was anything but normal. Because it was filled with an unseen (and thereby truly occult) entity. That same entity had secured an incredibly strong and very rigid presence throughout my entire cranial environment – starting immediately above the roof of my mouth. I swallowed and it felt as though the volume of my mouth had reduced. I swallowed twice more and this confirmed the presence and the strength of the entity in that critical region of my physiology. Some kind of activity began taking place to the right of my torso. I focussed on what was occurring. It was difficult to be absolutely certain, but it felt as though the right side of my body was being very gently and ever so subtly raised up. It was occurring so very slowly that it barely registered as perceptible. But something really was taking place in that region of my body. It then felt like a portion of the unseen entity was entering into my physiology from that same region. It soon became very apparent that a portion of the entity was moving around inside my chest cavity. I had no doubt this entity knew what it was doing, and the likelihood of harm was remote. But my subconscious mind, sensing the presence of an occult intruder, was far less willing to peaceably accept the reality of the situation. As a consequence, my breathing became faster and faster. The entity then formed a significant quasi-physical presence in the midst of my chest, just above my sternum. That strange quasi-physical presence suddenly bunched itself up into a large knotted mass, which felt as though it had bulged outwards from my chest and significantly distended the skin. I could feel it. It felt so awfully real. My breathing was now cycling at a rapid rate. There was a hint of thought-transference from the entity; assuring me that I was okay and assuring me that I would be okay. But I felt very far from okay. I felt as though something inside my chest had bulged outwards whilst remaining under my skin. It felt as though a very prominent knotted mound had formed. After just a short while I guessed or sensed the occult entity had vacated. However, I could still distinctly feel the very same physical presence throughout my head. And I could still feel that strange knotted mass bulging out of from my chest. I dared to move slightly and those bizarre tactile presences suddenly dissolved.

Report: #14

Location: Bedroom (~14:15hrs)

Dose: 17mg

Telegraphing Lightning

The house was empty. I was full of fear and holding a pipe loaded with a 17mg dose. Just outside the front of the house a couple of telephone engineers were busy fixing a telephone line that had suffered damage by a lightning strike a few days ago. Occasionally they would holler at each other. The disturbance put my commitment to experimenting in the balance. After a period of silence, I lay upon the floor. There was a strange interior feeling; something quite like a fluttering effect just beneath the surface of my sternum. I guessed it was a strange physiological response as my body knew what was about to take place. On a whim I sat up and emptied the pipe. As I reclined, I realised I was still dealing with my nerves. After just a few seconds the sound in the midst of my head increased in intensity; not hugely, but noticeably. I realised the crystals lacked full potency. There was a very gradual build-up of energy throughout the bedroom. After just a few seconds it appeared the entire room was vibrating back and forth significantly. An acute realisation of just how scary this initial phase really is imposed upon my mind. The room suddenly ceased its apparent jarring. An invisible and reasonably intense energy slowly rose upwards from beneath my feet and continued until it had reached about three-quarters of the way up my shins. I had not expected that and found it quite unsettling. It felt as though I was wearing very thickly insulated and incredibly tight-fitting snow boots. Whilst marvelling at that strange effect, I observed the incoming manifestation of a huge and transparent psycho-spiritual being. It was a truly amazing sight. I watched as it slowly made its way over to me. It was coming in through the front facing wall of the bedroom. I knew it had reached me when I perceived a wave like form passing through my brain. I watched in awe as the psycho-spiritual form continued streaming towards me and realised how spectacularly valuable these experiments are in giving clear visual evidence of lifeforms that seem to have eluded modern science.

To recall the events of the storm. My wife and I had been observing its approach from our bedroom window. Privately, I wondered how safe we were, given the close proximity of three huge oak trees to the front of the house. The storm was a spectacular visual display with accompanying claps and rumbles of thunder. Somewhat recklessly perhaps, I imagined being hit by a lightning strike, before I turned to leave the room. Suddenly, there was an almighty flash and a sharp deafening bang that caused me to jump with fright and cover my face. When I opened my eyes the landing area was fizzing with sparks. Feeling startled, my first thought was to wonder why fireworks were being used inside the house. I then looked up to see a redundant telephone terminal on the doorframe. Its casing had blown off and several severely blackened wires jutted out proudly and horizontally from the force of the current that had just thrilled through them. The event was so sudden and so incredibly scary. I was in awe at the exhibition of natural power I had just witnessed.

Report: #15

Location: Bedroom (~10:15hrs)

Dose: 16mg

Pushed & Shoved

Upon emptying the pipe, the bedroom appeared to be jarring back and forth quite violently. Within that bizarre energetic environment, I was able to observe the emergence of a turbulent transparent atmosphere, filling the upper portion of the bedroom. That turbulent transparent atmosphere was conducting an unspoken conversation with a third party. I looked up to the wall clock. Upon doing so the wall clock immediately filled the role of that third party. The turbulent transparent atmosphere was now saying to the wall clock, something along the lines of: "You said you were going to do this to him and you said you were going to do that to him." There was a palpably uneasy feeling emanating from within the turbulent and transparent energetic environment. I urged myself not to flee. I then felt a quasi-physical portion from that turbulent billowing cloud buffeting into the left side of my head. It felt as though it were unsuccessfully trying to gain access to my head. It was very unnerving, and in the midst of such a turbulent and palpably frightening environment, I couldn't stop myself from forming the notion that my interior psychic energy was going to serve as feeding fodder for hungry occult entities of uncertain character and unsavoury disposition. I raised my head from the pillows and shook it vigorously before resting it back down. I imagined the action was sufficient to stop whatever was trying to access my head from actually accessing my head.

Report: #16

Location: Bedroom (~11:15hrs)

Dose: 18mg

My Lips Are Sealed

I forced myself to make progress with my research. Paradoxically, I had to use my willpower to force myself against my own will to lie down on the floor and make myself ready. The second pull was voluminous and emptied the pipe. As I reclined, I told myself not expect too much from this experiment. The moment that my head sank into the pillows was the exact moment the room began jarring back and forth. I marvelled at the observation. I had not noticed any strange energy emanating from me. And yet the room appeared to be jarring back and forth quite violently. The energy suddenly subsided. Immediately I became aware of a slight though unmistakable pressure increase throughout my brain; and to a lesser extent throughout my upper torso. I knew this was evidence of the presence of a portion of spiritual entity within my physiology. I suspected the entity was invisibly filling the bedroom, though I saw absolutely nothing to confirm its presence. I wondered if anything really was inside me. I swallowed. Something was definitely inside me. I could feel its distinct presence, thinly coating the interior of my throat. I maintained nasal breathing steadily and rhythmically. I could feel as the entity slowly and deliberately worked its way up through my torso and into my throat. The strange psycho-spiritual substance slowly began to coat the walls of my mouth. As I swallowed, I could feel the substance purposefully moving around the walls and roof of my mouth. I swallowed again and felt its progression toward the opening of my mouth. I knew what was about to occur. My mouth was going to be sealed up shut from the inside. Once again, I swallowed. This time with considerable difficulty, as my lips really were sealed up shut from within. I tried to open my lips but they would not part. I implicitly trusted the entity that was imposing this experience upon me. There was no panic, no increase in my rate of breathing and no noticeable increase in my heartbeat. I tried to open my lips once again, but they were truly sealed-up tight from the inside. I marvelled at the experience. The bedroom appeared perfectly ordinary. And yet here I was, experiencing something occult skillfully sealing up my mouth from within. I wondered at what stage in my own evolution would I be capable of accomplishing such a feat. My mouth remained sealed up. I wondered whether I would be able to sense the departure of the entity. In that same instant I guessed the entity had gone, though I did not perceive its departure. I tried to open my lips and they opened. I opened my mouth widely and fully, as though emitting a non-existent yawn. I shook my head slowly for a very long time in utter astonishment. Tears and laughter both felt appropriate and yet inappropriate, in equal measure. Neither of those emotions manifested.

Report: #17

Location: Bedroom (~11:45hrs)

Dose: 20mg

The Human Condition

One single inhalation emptied the pipe. As my head sank down into the pillows, I hardly had time to gather my thoughts when the room filled with an unmistakable and familiar energy. The was a slight increase in intensity and an incredibly palpable emotional presence above me. It was unmistakable. The emotional energy emanating from the entity felt palpably solid. I suspected it was looking right at me and right into me – analysing me. There was a profound sense that something completely out of my control could happen without any warning at any given moment. The energetic emotional atmosphere continued like that for a short while before suddenly subsiding. In the absence of that energetic psycho-spiritual medium the appearance of the bedroom returned to normal.

Report: #18

Location: Bedroom (~09:15hrs)

Dose: 25mg

Energy Supplier

I was home alone. After inhaling the dose, the room immediately filled with psycho-spiritual energy. Immediately that energy went through rapid phased increases in both intensity and frequency. The audible high-pitched sound in the midst of my head changed concurrently and proportionally with those increases. Within seconds it was apparent the attending entity had secured a strange quasi-physical anchoring inside my head; especially around the back of my mouth. The room now appeared completely ordinary, except for a faint hint of another transparent medium superimposing upon the air. If there was a visible difference however, it was very subtle. I swallowed and was able to feel the stiff physicality of the being around my oral physiology. It had a very clearly defined interior hold upon me. I swallowed again. The strange substance coating the back of my throat caused an incredible oral dryness. The apparent physicality imposed within me was of sufficient strength to prevent me moving my head to the left or the right. My eyes were flitting and roving around the room. I wondered what was going to happen. I began second guessing possibilities. There was now an incredibly weighty and physical internal stiffness all around my lower jaw and my throat region. I wondered whether I would be able to sense the departure of this entity. But no sooner had that thought arisen when I sensed a huge emotional lurch over to my left. But it was of such a magnitude that 'to my left' was unthinkingly interpreted as, 'far away in the east'. There was an intense and urgent sense that something of incredible importance was taking place far away in an easterly direction. Even the trees outside gave the emotional impression of sharing in that sudden shift. As I looked upon the trees, they seemed to be directing genuine concern toward whatever was occurring far away in the east. I guessed that sudden occurrence marked the exit of the entity. I opened my mouth and moved my head and the residual physical presence suddenly dissolved. The strong emotional concern directed to the east remained. Suddenly, there was an unexpected knock at the door. I jumped up and raced downstairs whereupon I flung open the front door and bade the caller a very good morning. The caller proceeded to offer me the best energy supplier in London. I politely declined and explained I was already fully signed up with the very best energy supplier known to mankind. I wished him well and closed the door.

Report: #19

Location: Bedroom (~09:15hrs)

Dose: 21mg

Ventriloquism Mentalism

This experiment was made from upon the bed rather than on the floor. I sat up and made two long and slow inhalations. A mostly transparent energy soon pervaded the bedroom. I suspected the strange energy had emanated from within me. I also perceived a very subtle pressure imposing upon the outside of my body. There was a jarring effect on objects within my vision. The wall clock appeared to rapidly and repeatedly dart back and forth, left and right of centre. I became aware of a very strange effect upon my mind which I can only recount in general outline. It seemed my inner voice had divided itself. A portion of my inner-voice had somehow divided and moved from its usual centre stage and was busy making valid observations about that very effect. The location of that strangely autonomous portion of inner voice seemed to be positioned an arms-length distance over to my left. I then became aware the very same effect was mirrored over on my right side. My inner voice had seemingly divided; removed itself from centre and was now exhibiting a degree of autonomy from two different positions. Between them, they were both making separate observations about the observable effects of the experience, and were responding to each other about their own respective observations. In addition, whilst that strange conversation between two separate portions of my own inner voice was underway, I found that whenever I looked up at the light shade, it either exuded a strong desire to be a part of the ongoing conversation, or it held a mild degree of concern over my mental wellbeing. The more I focused on the externally sited and divided discourse of my own inner voice, the more I realised how thoroughly bizarre this experience was. I analysed just how I felt at that very moment and realised my mind felt incredibly open; there was an acute level of openness to suggestibility and vulnerability. My voices continued until I decided I'd had quite enough of hearing my own inner voice divided and exteriorised. I vocalised some half humorous appeals to cease this ongoing nonsense, and it ceased.

The initial phase that follows after inhaling the potent vapour has such a truly mysterious character to it. I can suspect the psycho-spiritual energy that appears to suddenly manifest actually emanates from me. I can even suspect its sudden increase in intensity results from some of that energy reflecting off the hard surfaces within the room. Could the notion that DMT causes the human mind to suddenly expand outwards account for the apparent duality and non-locality of my inner voice? Could the division between the left and right hemispheric configuration of the brain somehow account for what occurred today?

Report: #20

Location: Bedroom (~10:00hrs)

Dose: 27mg

Brain Massage

On a spur of impulse rather than premeditated courage I sat up and began inhaling. Immediately upon doing so, a reassuring courageousness surged through me. I was inhaling potent spirit-invoking vapour. And was in the best possible frame of mind. The usual transparent energetic medium rapidly manifested. But as my head sank down into the pillows the intensity of that energy increased remarkably. It was imposing powerfully down upon me; perceptible as a horizontal plane of high frequency energy buffeting into me. It was all taking place so incredibly fast. Then it suddenly abated and the main part of the experience began. The bedroom and all contents therein appeared more or less as they usually do, except the air was now wrought in exceptional crystal-clear clarity. Everything within the room was rendered in degree of realness that was markedly above its ordinary everyday appearance. It was obvious the spiritual entity – in whose midst I was within – was also inside me. Not only could I detect its unmistakable presence throughout my mouth as I swallowed, but my lips were totally sealed up from the inside. I continued with deep and steady nasal breathing. I was absolutely calm; principally because I could intuit the charter of the entity. This was the type of entity that operates as an absolute master when imposing itself upon the DMT inebriated human. I felt safe, assured and comfortable – despite that my lips were sealed up from within. There was an obvious auditory hallucination evident somewhere within the bedroom. It was the sweet of tweeting from what in terrestrial reality would've been a delicate little bird. It was sounding over and over – looping non-stop. I believe I was supposed to make some kind meaningful connection with that sound. My eyes roved around the crystal-clear hyperreal bedroom. I could not understand what connection I was supposed to make with the ongoing sweet tweeting. Somewhere outside a crow cawed noisily three times. I could somehow sense the entity acknowledged the crow's noisy calls. The hallucinatory tweeting then directed itself toward the unseen crow. But I still could not understand what I was supposed to grasp – if anything at all – by the ongoing tweeting. That heralded the end of the experience. I perceived the extremely rapid departure of the entity from within me. I thought the entity was minded to vacate the location. But it very suddenly made its way back down towards me. I could feel it streaming into my head in a slow, pulsing fashion. The sensation of it pulsing into my head was akin to having the outer surface of my brain massaged. It was not physically pleasurable, but I sensed the perceptible passage of the entity through my brain was somehow helpful and beneficial. As the last portion of the entity transited my head the room suddenly appeared normal again. I then found myself unable to recollect the main part of the experience. I could not recall one single little detail of what had just occurred. I could only remember the very beginning and the very end of the experience. Despite my best efforts, my memory simply could not furnish me with events from mere moments ago. This was exceedingly perplexing. I wondered whether the passage of the entity had somehow wiped that particular memory. A pigeon then flew by the window and the memory of what had just occurred suddenly flooded my mind.

Report: #21

Location: Bedroom (~10:45hrs)

Dose: 28mg

What a Wheeze

The third and final pull found a generous stream of potent vapour. As my head reached the pillows the room filled with a highly energetic, psycho-spiritual medium. The room appeared awash with a strange and turbulent atmosphere. Straightaway that energy increased and continued to increase very rapidly. I barely had time to compute my thoughts when the energy suddenly subsided. I was now in the midst of a spiritual entity which had also secured a portion of itself inside me. The air within the bedroom was absolutely crystal clear. My eyes began wandering around the room. A strange solid presence was evident behind my throat and throughout my upper torso. My inner voice had become divided; a portion had removed from its usual central locale and was operative outside of me. It was also speaking in a foreign accent. Possibly French. But it was vague, indistinct and short-lived. I then heard a voice speaking over by the drawers nearest the window, apparently talking in the same language. I was somehow able to understand the gist of that speech. It was expressing doubt about the ability of the entity to complete the trick that it had in mind. But that speech was apparently been conveyed to an unseen third party on the opposite side of the room. As that speech was taking place, I was subjected to an incredibly robust massage around my temples. This continued after the discarnate speech had concluded. The massage was clearly taking place inside my head and was very soothing and calming. I relaxed and looked at the trees through the bedroom window. Despite the lace curtain, my view of the trees seemed exceptionally clear. The massage continued. I was surprised at the strength of the pressure applied. I perceived movement around the underside of my torso, suggesting something had very smoothly worked its way beneath my back. Now, along with the massage, an incredibly subtle rolling motion was created beneath me. As that subtle rolling motion continued beneath me, I realised my deep and steady nasal breathing had synchronised with the strong and slow massage upon my temples. As I maintained my breathing, the portion of entity inside me increased its physicality. I tried not to entertain any doubt about the expertise of this entity. But it was too late. Uncertainty had taken root in my mind. The physicality around my windpipe (or inside my windpipe) continued to increase. The effect was that each successive breath had to contend with an ever-increasing squeeze upon my windpipe – or an ever-increasing restriction therein. Very soon my breathing sounded rough and wheezing, rasping and croaking, as though I were an old man labouring defiantly with the last few breaths of my life. This was simply too much. I began to doubt the skill of the entity. I was growing extremely scared at my predicament – home alone and at the mercy of an otherworldly entity. And in that very moment, the entity departed. My breathing was no longer rough or troubled. I could still feel the physical presence inside me. But as I opened my mouth and moved my head that strange solidity dissolved. I was emotionally overwhelmed at the mastery of the entity; to take me so skillfully from total tranquillity to genuinely fearing for my life. Now I felt alive! Very much alive! I shook my head in disbelief and wore a big broad smile whilst signalling my appreciation to the absent entity. DMT experiences may not be for everyone. But for those who find such practical otherworldly investigations rewarding, these interactions provide the most profound and life-affirming adventures imaginable.

Report: #22

Location: Bedroom (~09:45hrs)

Dose: 27mg

Man & Ant

Three pulls vacuumed down all available vapour. I reclined while noting the room had become awash with a turbulent, fluid-like medium. As my head sank into the pillows an entity arrived with stupendous immediacy. And immediately that it arrived it imposed its tremendous spiritual strength throughout the bedroom, in the form of a field of exceedingly high frequency vibration. The intensity of energy was simply devastating. It was like nothing else I had ever experienced in any of my previous experiments. This was a different order of magnitude. The frequency grew and grew, higher and higher, with terrific rapidity. I was barely able to communicate to myself that I had just attracted the kind of entity that has no earthly business interacting with humans. The power of the entity was beyond phenomenal. It was simply appalling. I could see the entire bedroom. But my vision was also seeing through the extraordinary psycho-spiritual might of the entity – evident as a palpably seething superdense medium. The inherent power therein and throughout rendered the airspace throughout the bedroom in a dark beige hue. I could not understand how the aged plasterboard walls had remained so silent in containing such a devastating display of power. But this was just the beginning. That tremendous field of living energy then visibly formed itself into an expansive curved membrane, overarching me. I remotely feel the texture of that overarching membrane. But using the word 'texture' feels somehow improper, because my perception of the substance was unique, and the substance itself had such a truly unique feel to it. Its composition was beyond tight; beyond smooth. It really did feel as though it was completely beyond any possibility of ever been penetrated or perforated. As it pressed down upon me from without me, I could feel the phenomenal and immeasurable strength behind it. Very slowly, with great care and purpose, that membrane moved down towards me, just a short distance. But in so doing – and this is where my words will fail to convey that which I wished they could convey – I had an appreciation of the full power that was at the disposal of the entity. And that was a power unlike anything else I have ever experienced in my entire life. It was simply appalling. It was absolutely devastating. It was beyond prodigious. This was a man and ant experience. I was witness to a level of strength and a capacity of power of such magnitude that any attempt on my behalf to detail the possible outcome, should such a power ever be unleashed in an adversarial capacity within the terrestrial realm against mankind, it would render me a doomsayer and scaremonger. I could feel as that membrane (still overarching me) moved slowly over my body. It gradually became broadly focussed over my forehead. And it seemed in doing so, I could much better appreciate the truly frightening power that was behind this entity, as it imposed an immense potential pressure down upon my forehead. I was devastated at the magnitude of power. It was like nothing else I have ever experienced. Just then, a very strong emotional communication became apparent. It convincingly conveyed to me that something of very great importance was occurring outside. The feeling grew and grew within me. All I had to do was stand up and go and take a look through the window. I strongly doubted there would be anything of any significance to behold. But the discarnate emotion was so overwhelmingly powerful that it was enough to spur me into standing up and going over to the bedroom window and looking outside. Despite the houses, and despite the road over to my left, the first thing I beheld was nature. The giant oak trees; the grass verges; the poplars and the firs; a weeping willow; an elm tree and a hawthorn – green and lush, and alive. That was the important thing that I was prompted into beholding. I marvelled at the beauty of nature, interspersed between the suburban houses in a nondescript housing estate. And I marvelled at how skillfully the entity had emotionally prompted me into taking a look outside, and how I had responded to that promoting.

To add some reflective and analytical thoughts. I might reasonably assume the strange turbulent psycho-spiritual energy that initially manifests is some kind of essential energy from me – a psychic energy relating to my mind or my soul. I assume that energy is able to project beyond the bounds of my body to some unknown distance. Secondly, I can assume the entity arrives from its own realm with what appears to be astonishing speed and purpose. I can assume it completely understands the scenario that it encounters, and immediately undergoes some preparatory process to interact with me. In undergoing that preparatory process, it would seem a terrific amount of energy is involved.

To say a little more about my tactile perception of that uniquely formed membranous psycho-spiritual substance, I can add that it was extremely thin; absolutely non-porous; exceptionally smooth but not slippery, and absolutely impenetrable. On that last opinion I could not ever be persuaded to change my view. But in reflecting on that particular characteristic, I have found myself imagining the outcome of that same membranous substance, slowly descending upon the sharpened point of a dependable and sturdy terrestrial knife. At first, I tried to perish the thought, because it seemed far too crazy to entertain. I mean, taking a sharp pointed knife to a spiritual entity that has formed an impossibly taut membranous exterior, backed up by indescribable power, really does smack of ill wisdom. But as a thought exercise, it was difficult to dismiss, and my mind was curious. At the time of the experience, I was absolutely certain that nothing material could ever rupture such a membrane. But now it seems so improbable that such a membrane would ever be able to withstand and remain imperforate against the sharp pointed blade of a cold hardened steel knife. But I know my imagination deceives me. It deceives me because of my familiarity with the hardness of steel, and the sharpness of a fine metal point; whereas my familiarity with the capabilities of those powerful psycho-spiritual entities is extremely limited. And I know only too well that given the same experience, I would harbour not the slightest doubt that such an improbably tightly formed psycho-spiritual membrane would resist the strongest and the sharpest terrestrial steel point without any difficulty; despite the challenge that scenario imposes upon my imagination.

Report: #23

Location: Bedroom (~10:00hrs)

Dose: 31mg

Chiselling Away Quietly

As my head sank down into the pillows, there was a half second delay before the room filled with what I assume to be my own psycho-spiritual energy. That energy quickly increased in intensity. So much so that after just a couple of seconds I was forced to consider the energy was far too intense to be emanating from me alone. But by the third or fourth second, an altogether different magnitude of energy had arrived and imposed itself throughout the bedroom and down into me. I was now at the mercy of a highly energetic spiritual entity. I was able to intuit its character based on previous experiences. I was in the midst of the mind of an Occult Master. I was entirely comfortable. The entity had secured an extensive presence throughout my oral environment; evident from the moment I swallowed. However, I cannot relate the main part of the experience in any great detail. My eyes were open and there was something taking place. It was incredibly hypervivid but I can only recall fleeting visions as they were unfolding so incredibly quickly. Whatever was taking place it somehow related to my cyclical nasal breathing. After a few minutes I began to see parts of the bedroom again. A semi-transparent medium filled the airspace of the bedroom, wherein I saw portions of hypervivid and highly active hallucinatory constructs. There was something of a game taking place between two hallucinatory constructs. It was something like a game of tennis. Something small was evidently passing over me in a back and forth fashion. My head remained completely stationary whilst my eyes flitted left to right, over and over again – completely transfixed on whatever was taking place. The interior of my mouth still felt as though it was coated with the strange psycho-spiritual substance of the entity. But as I opened my mouth and moved my tongue the effect dissolved. The act of opening my mouth and sweeping my tongue around, whilst watching whatever game was taking place in sync with my rhythmical nasal breathing, resulted in my submission to complete wonderment and I fell into a fit of intense gleeful laughter. The hallucinatory constructs slowly faded from my eyes and the feeling of glee subsided. I thought the experience was over, and mostly it was. But I was still very much under the influence of DMT and looking up at the entity, now evident in a much less energetic state – a transparent mass of superdense psycho-spiritual cells. It came down upon me and was soon active inside my head. It was moving around inside my brain. I was entirely at ease with the situation. I could feel it rummaging around inside my brain and moving around behind my eyes. A regular repetitive movement then commenced. It felt like something was gently chiselling away within my brain. This continued for some time before slowly fading from tactile perception.

That short-lived feeling of intense glee was emotionally heavenly. I felt like a little baby whose mother was taking great delight in repeatedly tickling a ticklish spot to send her baby into raptures of ecstasy. There was one other observation that was incredibly interesting. As the entity was withdrawing from me, and the last of the hallucinatory constructs were fading, there was one clearly perceived telepathically verbalised message. A warning of: "Look! There's some broken glass down there!" The warning was directed to a specific location on the bedroom floor. I knew there was no broken glass there and the warning seemed at odds with the overall experience. To what purpose the warning was given I do not know. Upon hearing the warning, I was almost diverted into sitting up and looking for the glass – such was the strength of conviction with which the warning was conveyed. I really don't know what to make of that, other than to suppose it represents something of a dual nature within the entity.

Report: #24

Location: Bedroom (~13:45hrs)

Dose: 33mg

Knock-Knock

I dug deep to find the requisite courage to commit myself and then sat up and inhaled three times. As my head rested down upon the pillows, I implored myself to be highly observant for the emergence of my own psycho-spiritual energy. But in that very moment the room instantaneously filled with an energy that was obviously not my own. And the very instant that energy arrived was the very same instant that its intensity grew and grew and grew – with tremendous rapidity. I have previously used adjectives like "phenomenal" and "prodigious" to describe the intensity of that energy. But this was far beyond all my previous experiences. Its power was absolutely formidable. I could clearly see the visual effect of the increasing intensity and frequency of that energy throughout bedroom. It appeared as though the air throughout the bedroom was resonating to that same frequency. And then, the entity took that energy to a simply impossible frequency. The ascending tone was unmissably audible throughout my head and all around me. It quickly reached a truly impossible pitch, resulting in a paradoxically palpable singular solid mass of impossibly superdense energy that was intangible and all pervasive. My inner voice meekly acknowledged the truly awesome display of power that we had witnessed. Then suddenly, the room appeared as it ordinarily appears. Except I knew it was very far from ordinary. Because a portion of the entity had invested itself inside me. That same entity was also filling the volume of the bedroom at a transparency exactly in harmony with the air. The otherworldly emotion filling the bedroom was absolutely unmistakable. I sensed the entity was preparing to do something. But there was something I was supposed understand about my posture, and I could not quite grasp what it was. My legs were straight and uncrossed, but my hands were over my abdomen with fingers interlocked. Suddenly and unexpectedly, something within my abdomen moved towards where my hands rested. I quickly got the message and put my hands down by my side and the strange movement inside my abdomen ceased. Next there was a very obvious physical movement inside the upper portion of my right arm. I was ready for whatever was about to unfold but a sudden noise outside sounded like someone knocking on my neighbours door.

Immediately that noise manifested there was a palpable wholesale shift of energy throughout the bedroom over in the direction of that noise. After a brief pause, I could feel a psycho-spiritual portion of the entity sliding around the back of my throat. I worried that a long-drawn-out withdrawal process was about to take place. But as I swallowed and opened my mouth, I knew the entity had vacated my physiology. Now it was above me. It overarched me and came down towards me. And then, in the blink of an eye, it was gone.

Report: #25

Location: Bedroom (~10:45hrs)

Dose: 25mg

Transparent Field of Emotion

The room promptly filled with a mildly energetic transparent medium which I supposed had emanated from me. But no sooner had it manifested when it went through several very rapid changes in intensity. A separate energy suddenly arrived. It was very easy to appreciate that energy was not from me. It immediately filled the bedroom and imposed itself to such an extent that the aged plasterboard walls audibly creaked as they subtly flexed under the immense compression. I could both see and feel the exercise of that power from the entity. Indeed, that power was the entity. It was vibrating at an incredibly high frequency which gave the appearance of a dark beige hue; seeming concentrated particularly within the midst of the room. The intensity of that awesome spiritual power thrilled right through me. There was barely any time to feel scared when the energy suddenly subsided and the room appeared normal again. Except it was abundantly clear something had a very strong grip upon my head and my neck – from the inside! It felt like an incredible giant had secured a very powerful clench upon the interior of my cranium and I was totally at its mercy. The interior of my neck felt painlessly swollen from the presence of the entity therein. I assured myself I would survive the experience. There was then a sudden and rapid wholesale shift in that field of emotional energy, over to the east. There were audible hints of voices outside. I supposed the emotional energy was checking for the presence of someone approaching the house. The power of emotion was so incredibly strong that even the oak trees visible through the bedroom window seemed invested with the same emotion. Their entire east facing branches held genuine interest in whatever was occurring far-off in that direction. The unmistakable presence of the entity was still evident inside me – feeling something like a very heavy and incredibly tight-fitting chin and neck compression garment. However, I suspected the entity had actually vacated my physiology. And when I opened my mouth widely and moved my head, the superdense presence dissolved.

Report: #26

Location: Bedroom (~14:30hrs)

Dose: 27mg

Superdense Psycho-Spiritual Foaminess

A huge dense cloud of potent vapour suddenly appeared in the body of the pipe and was drawn deeply into my lungs. As I was making a second pull, the ringing sound in the midst of my head was already very intense and increasing at an alarming rate. A field of seething psychic energy was already visible above me. Except that it didn't feel right. There was something very uncommon about it. For a start, it wasn't filling the entire bedroom, as it usually does. It was very intense but its extent was obviously limited. I decided that I really didn't like it. I sat up, drew my knees close to my chest, clasped my arms around them, and assured myself there was no shame in calling a halt to the experiment. The energy persisted and I continued to feel incredibly uneasy about it. I stood up and walked toward the window. But then I stopped. I thought about turning and exiting the bedroom. But something was not quite right. The already silent bedroom was now abnormally silent. In fact, it was deathly silent. Throughout the entire bedroom there was now the faint hint of a very light beige transparent medium. I sat back down and reassured myself that I was merely scaring myself, and in reality, everything was exactly as it should be. But everything was not exactly as it should be. Everything appeared just the same, but somehow everything also appeared so completely different. Emotionally, the entire bedroom felt very far removed from the land of the living. I could see the trees outside, but regardless of that, I felt totally separated from all living existence outside the confines of the bedroom. It then began to dawn upon me that I was in the midst of a profoundly strange situation. Everything appeared stiff and frozen, fragile and brittle. I looked up at the wall clock and observed the seconds ticking by. I tried to make sense of my situation but could only conclude these were the last few moments of my life. But that didn't feel quite accurate. I then supposed this entire bizarre experience was somehow been recorded and it would be replayed to me in my immediate post-death state. The intensity of the situation was now weighing very heavily upon me. I lay back and as my head sank into the pillows, I realised something. I voiced a heartfelt and despondent: "Oh no!" Instantaneously the bedroom suddenly became wrought in a truly remarkable hypervivid and hyperreal appearance. The colours were simply stupendous. Everything solid appeared densely spongy and enlarged. It was an incredible otherworldly rendering of the bedroom. All at once it appeared far more real than real, and yet far more unreal than the ordinary. I slowly reached out my right arm and gently rapped my knuckles on a drawer of the heavy wooden dresser. It was as solid as it should be. I tugged at the duvet overhanging the foot of the bed and found it to be as soft as it should be. The scenery was so incredible to behold. The air was absolutely crystal clear. Just then, the air gave the appearance of silently shattering into long vertical shards. Such that whatever was observed through the air also appeared shattered into shards. But those breaks would quickly reform back into wholeness, before the same silent shattering effect occurred once again. I then became very aware of a unique feeling that permeated me and the entire room. Everything within the bedroom had an emotional and palpably homogenous relationship to that singular, and singularly strange, omnipresent feeling. Yet accurately describing the characteristics of that feeling is so terribly difficult. My best effort would be to say the bedroom was completely immersed within a synthetic, sweet, psycho-spiritually formed, transparent superdense foaminess. Everything solid exhibited an impossibly hypervivid and hyperreal enlarged foamy appearance. And then, in an instant, the bedroom was back to its ordinary everyday appearance. I was beyond astonished at what had just taken place. I was completely without words. My mouth was agape and my face exhibited sheer disbelief.

Report: #27

Location: Bedroom (~13:30hrs)

Dose: 25mg

Spare Him!

I was steady and calm – capably managing my nerves. Breathing was rhythmic. I emptied the pipe. No sooner had my head settled into the pillows when the room became visibly awash in a turbulent and transparent energy. The moment I made that observation was the very same moment the entity emerged and imposed a truly awesome display of its constitutional power. Stupendous high frequency energy at an insane intensity filled the entire room. As that energy increased and imposed laterally, the plasterboard walls were heard to creak as they flexed under the immense force. That same energy then began to push down upon me. Its strength was phenomenal. Visually I could see everything within the bedroom the way it ordinarily appears. Except now, my eyes were working through a highly energetic psycho-spiritual medium. Above me, the vague visible suggestion of an overarching membrane. It began pushing down upon me. However, I'm certain my tactile perception of the force at play was not sensed solely upon my body. The incredibly taut membrane was actually pushing down upon an unseen field of psycho-spiritual energy that surrounded me; one that was more than likely emanating from me. The imposing energy redoubled its strength and pushed down upon me very powerfully. The effect of that action caused audible sounds from around the room. Those audible sounds of creaking and groaning from the flexing fabric of the bedroom arose in direct proportion to the perceptible forcefulness of the immense otherworldly power. I was been thoroughly imposed upon; trapped beneath a barrier through which I could freely breathe, but on no account would I ever be able to overcome through physical strength. I became acutely aware at just how very calm I was in both my breathing and my mind. But the exact moment I held that thought, the entity imposed a tremendous physicality throughout my cranium, my mouth, and my neck. As my wet tongue parted my dry lips, I perceived the movement of that unique psycho-spiritual substance as it moved through the inside of my mouth to temporarily seal up my lips from within. The physicality of the entity's presence inside my head was particularly solid. It felt tight and inescapable. In dull daylight, I watched as the tree branches outside the bedroom window obeyed the wind. I remained motionless and calm. But the uncommon solidity of the physical presence within my head and throughout my neck forced me to consider the possibility of what would occur if this entity became ill-disposed towards me. What would occur if this entity inadvertently erred in such a way as to diminish the quality of my life, or simply diminish my life? And once I began thinking in that manner my fears quickly mushroomed. So much so that the tree branches dutifully obeying the noisy wind now exhibited genuine emotional concern for me. They seemed conscious of my situation and were silently shouting out to the entity: "Spare him! Spare him! Spare him!" I gulped. I was unsure whether or not the entity was still inside me. I opened my mouth and the strange pseudo-physicality immediately dissolved.

Report: #28

Location: Bedroom (~16:00hrs)

Dose: 25mg

Small Meal

I made three text book inhalations of potent vapour. As my head sank down into the pillows the effects from the substance were already significantly advanced. Without any prior warning a spiritual entity boisterously plunged down into the bedroom. There was no manifestation of intense high frequency energy. It was more like the lower portion of a vast spirit being had suddenly dropped in from the sky in response to my dimethyltryptamine-fuelled psychic signal. The impact from its sudden arrival resulted in minor creaking and groaning sounds from the timber floorboards around me; particularly as its presence forcibly pressed down around me. I was forced to suspect this was something of a heavyweight occult entity. There was a very powerful tactilely perceptible long frequency wavelength. That wavelength felt like it was transmitting vertically down from some considerable distance above the house. Something huge had deigned to investigate my tiny little psychic signal. From the moment it arrived the air throughout the bedroom became wrought in exceptional crystal-clear clarity. Everything within my vision appeared so much cleaner and sharper; far more colourful and altogether more real. My eyes were actually working through a pristine crystal-clear portion of the body of the spiritual entity. I was enveloped within that portion. The lampshade and other miscellaneous items upon the drawers were emotionally appealing upwards to this huge entity, entreating it to venture no further with me. There was an overwhelming sense of a truly gross mismatch between our respective selves. Something very much more higher-minded than myself had found itself investigating something comparably very much lower-minded than itself. Suddenly, the pristine crystal-clear clarity evident throughout the air imperceptibly vanished. I believe the entity had departed from my presence in that very instant. A wave of energy entered into my left temple. I looked up and it was clear a portion of the entity was streaming toward me and into my head. I could feel it moving around inside the left hemisphere of my brain. Its movement was unmissable and surprisingly physical. It repeatedly and briskly began darting in and out of one particular area of my brain. Such purposeful movement put me in mind of a bottom feeding fish that has just found a small meal lodged in a coral crevice. My emotions were finely balanced between self-concern and wonder at the absurdity and profundity of the situation.

Report: #29

Location: Bedroom (~12:00hrs)

Dose: 27mg

Murdering My Ego

In order to prepare myself mentally, I began thinking about what was preventing me from smoking DMT. The notion that I would be metaphorically murdering my own ego came out of the blue. It seemed to perfectly sum up the impasse. I had to knowingly murder my own personality in order to find something deeper within me that was willing to pursue this profound and mysterious research. Upon lying down in readiness for the experiment, I had as good as temporarily murdered my ego. I lay peaceably for around three minutes; listening to the ticking wall clock, my cyclical nasal breathing and the ever-present ringing sound in the midst of my head. I scrutinised the air and wondered whether anything non-corporeal was already in the bedroom, unseen and awaiting me. I sat up and made three perfect inhalations. Upon laying back I implored myself to be observationally astute. A mildly turbulent transparent energy immediately filled the room. But in the very moment I had made that observation an altogether separate and much more intense energy manifested with tremendous rapidity. It palpably descended from ceiling height. And no sooner had that energy fully descended into the bedroom when the very same thing occurred again, and then for a third time. Except with each new descent the intensity of energy increased enormously. Words are simply inadequate to truly convey the subjective experience of witnessing the stupendous and tremendous intensity of that living energy. I could see it filling up the volume of the bedroom. Its seething high frequency created an obvious visibility throughout the entire room, now rendered in an unmissable tan yellow tint. It had occurred within mere seconds. My inner voice acknowledged great surprise at how this energy had imposed itself without causing one little creak or a groan from the fabric of the room. It was overwhelmingly obvious I was in the midst of a very powerful being. My senses were clear. My body felt strangely light. I remember feeling awe at the energy. I could both see it and I could feel it. I remember assuring myself with the knowledge that I was safe and I would survive. Standing atop the wicker drawers to my right, a humanlike like entity representing a young girl was formed of and within that living energy. She was actively playing catch with something to the left of me. I did not pay too much attention to whatever was left of me, because every time my eyes began moving in that direction, the young girl would quickly turn around and moon her rear at me in a most amusing manner; although I never actually caught full sight of her bare bottom. I found that whenever my eyes slowly drifted over to whomever she was playing catch with, she would suddenly moon and my eyes would immediately flit back. But only ever catching less than half a glimpse of what I suspected she was actually doing. It was hugely playful. There was nothing sexual or erotic about it. Indeed, I was always fully conscious of how I was in the midst of an incredibly powerful spiritual entity that was filling the volume of the bedroom. And I knew full well the humanlike female entity and her playmate were both illusory constructs from the mind of that powerful spirit. The experience seemed to go on and on and on, to the extent that I felt surprised at its longevity. The humanlike female entity continued with her playful exploits. There seemed to be a very obvious visual and emotional message conveyed to me; as though the entire experience was encouraging me to come and play far more often with this research. In fact, the message was visually and emotionally unmissable. And such was the sincerity of the message that I felt myself to be completely in agreement with the invitation and the sentiment. Next, in the most unimaginable way, the entity began slowly withdrawing. The very high frequency energy with its tan yellow tint slowly became less and less, and paler and paler. I became aware that I was slowly, and almost imperceptibly, being lowered by a very small distance back down onto the carpeted floor. It was beyond slow, beyond careful, and beyond gentle. Perhaps I should have been surprised at such an occurrence. But I wasn't. I simply maintained my focus in order to confirm the validity of my perception enabling me to report honestly and accurately. The gradual decline of that energy was so very slow as to be almost below the threshold of my perception. The illusory young girl was still playing as she was slowly fading. It all reeked of the unimaginable power and mind-bending magic at the entity's disposal. I swept my tongue around my mouth. It felt as though my mouth was twice its ordinary size and it also felt as though my tongue was sweeping away small smooth pebbles therein. Gradually the room returned to normal. I was left nothing less than absolutely convinced that a mightily powerful entity had deigned to respond to my tiny little psychic signal. And had bidden me to come and play more often.

Report: #30

Location: Bedroom (~13:30hrs)

Dose: 27mg

Capture it in Words

My mind was configured for research. There were no nerves and no fears. I was totally calm and absolutely ready. Three inhalations emptied the pipe, causing my inner sound to increase significantly. As soon as my head sunk into the pillows a tremendous amount of energy filled the room with lightning-like speed. There was simply no time to be scared. I could see the seething high frequency and superdensity of the discarnate living energy. It filled the room and immediately imposed itself upon the walls. It then increased its intensity by several magnitudes, causing the walls to audibly creak from the insane otherworldly pressure. The high frequency medium was clearly visible throughout the bedroom. I could feel it thrilling right through my body. It gave me a distinct sense of my skeletal self. Such was its power that I genuinely feared I had gone too far. I have this notion that one day an experience will take me so far out of my comfort zone that it will profoundly threaten the configuration of my personality. And I thought this was that. Suddenly, the room appeared normal again; all except for a sheer wall of psycho-spiritual energy sweeping up towards me from the front wall. I could not see it, but I had an incredibly strong palpable perception of its presence, and a distinct sense of its width and depth. It moved slowly over me as though scanning me. I could feel it upon me, and I could feel it passing right through me as it smoothly made its way over my body. As it neared my head, I licked my dry lips. And in so doing I could feel as that familiar psycho-spiritual film moved smoothly and quickly through the inside of my mouth, as though in preparation to seal up the opening. I remained stock still. The energy moved up beyond my head. I waited a few brief moments, wondering whether the entity had gone. I tentatively moved my tongue and opened my mouth widely. The unusual psycho-spiritual presence dissolved.

Report: #31

Location: Bedroom (~09:15hrs)

Dose: 25mg

A Spectrum of Emotion & Intellect

I sat up and made three excellent inhalations. A transparent energy suddenly filled the entire bedroom and gave the appearance of jarring back and forth violently with ever-increasing intensity. Mere seconds later, an altogether different order of energy manifested. Either my instinct intuited or my amplified senses perceived that this energy was a limited portion of an altogether very much larger spiritual entity. Its energy was powerful. I could see it as an energetically seething superdense psycho-spiritual medium. And I could also feel it within me and without me. It was forcibly pushing down onto me with tremendous power. It was a magnitude of power I would never wish to fall out with. I would never wish to incur its wrath, even in any small measure. But such was its obvious visibility, such was its density of mind, and such was the force of its pressure pressing down upon me that I genuinely suspected its wrath was what I was about to incur. The longevity of the tremendously powerful seething energy was far greater than I expected. I was genuinely feeling very scared. So scared that I began making silent apologies for any psychic disturbance I may have inadvertently caused. But to no avail. The room remained heavy with intense energy. I silently apologised for having my legs crossed. For some reason I considered having my legs crossed indicated a casual and half-hearted approach to my research. I was so scared that upon uncrossing my legs I faithfully promised to never again cross my legs in this research. The energy was stupendous. The force of its downward pressure was simply impossible to be discounted or overlooked. I silently conveyed that I was writing a book. The energy persisted. And then I noticed something really very obvious but truly remarkable. I noticed I could smell what I perceived to be an effect on the air caused by the incredibly high frequency of the energy. It was strong and very distinct. I was certain it was not the lingering smell of exhaled vapour. I sniffed the air deeply, three times. It was so abundantly perceptible within my nostrils. But what was it? Was it metallic or ozonic? It seemed I was sniffing in the superdense energy of the entity. Upon making that olfactory observation, my fear suddenly dissipated and I felt very much emboldened in my research. Shortly after that the entity vanished. Vacating just quickly as it had arrived.

Report: #32

Location: Bedroom (~13:30hrs)

Dose: 25mg

Praying Peacefully

My nerves became knotted as I drove home from work while contemplating my research. By the time I had entered the main bedroom my wife was in the adjoining bedroom undertaking her Islamic prayers. As I lay down, I wondered if any attending DMT entity would know whether my wife was praying in the adjoining bedroom. After emptying the pipe an exceptionally crystal-clear yet uncommonly dense energy suddenly plunged down into the bedroom from ceiling height. The intensity and frequency of that manifested energy increased hugely. And in so doing the daylight within the bedroom became very much dimmer. The intensity and frequency increased even further as the energy began to sweep over me – passing through my entire body. I could feel it moving through me. It gave me a very strong sense of my bones – especially within my fingers. Unbeknownst to me my wife was vacating the adjoining bedroom. The energy from the entity subsided considerably. Now the room appeared empty of any occult visitor. However, there was still a very strong emotional presence and I focussed my mind upon that. But then I heard my wife moving as the floorboards creaked on the landing. I hollered her not to enter the bedroom and the act of raising my voice completely broke my focus upon the discarnate emotional presence. In that single moment I sensed a deeply mysterious connection between the entity and I had significantly diminished.

Report: #33

Location: Bedroom (~09:45hrs)

Dose: 27mg

What a Substance!

I was home alone and dismissing each and every appeal from my ego to forego this research. I sat up and began. The third inhalation was the vaporous equivalent to a deft left hook delivered by a prime Mike Tyson. It was delivered so swiftly and deeply into my spongy little lungs that my eyes widened significantly upon seeing such a great stream of vapour heading inwards. By the time my head sank down into the pillows an entity manifested with lightning-like speed. Without any hesitation whatsoever it increased its intensity and frequency to a level wholly beyond anyone's capacity to accurately convey through literary means. These energies are living energies! They are beings of hidden nature, exercising the sovereign power of their spiritual constitution! By no measure am I yet capable of creating such an awesome display of power from my own constitution. It is so abundantly obvious what is occurring. And today, it would seem this entity indulged me with a display of power that must surely represent the upper limit of what these beings are capable of. Once again, the walls audibly creaked as they flexed under the mighty force imposing upon them. I could actually see and feel that energy working across a lateral plane as it pressed upon the walls either side of me. What power! What awesome power! Its increase was audible throughout my head. Evident as an ascending high frequency tone that quickly reached a truly impossible pitch. I could actually see the visual effect of that terrific increase in frequency throughout the dense and transparent spiritual medium. The seething transparent atmosphere became tinted in a distinctive yellow. I could also feel the awesome power forcibly pressing down onto me. My perception was made without me; that is, my tactile perception extended outside and beyond my body. A portion of the entity formed an overarching curved feature above me, and then pressed it down toward me with forceful significance. I was now pinned to the floor. I was quite sure I could have moved if I had wished to. But I was in a state of arrested astonishment; completely transfixed by the sheer power on rampant display. Upon licking my dry lips, it became all too evident the entity had secured a psycho-spiritual presence throughout my oral physiology. I could feel it thinly coating my mouth and my throat. In the far upper corner of the bedroom I sensed a discourse was taking place with an unseen presence outside the bedroom window. I could sense communication travelling back and forth between the two locations. I began to wonder whether this was just a misdirecting ruse. There was a strong sense that something was being worked out or decided. Just then, a considerable wall of noise arose as a frenzied mass of children ran out for playtime in the neighbouring school playground. That appeared to dictate a deciding influence upon the interaction as the entity began a very slow process of decreasing its terrific energy. Very slowly the strong yellow tan tint throughout the bedroom became paler and paler. There was very obvious localised movement around my right armpit. It felt as though a very long and very slender tentacular portion of quasi-physical psycho-spiritual substance was slowly withdrawing from me. I raised my arm in a helpful gesture and the strange withdrawal continued. The process of the energy winding down and withdrawing from me was so very slow and so very gradual that I never really discerned any significant change back to ordinary.

Report: #34

Location: Bedroom (~11:30hrs)

Dose: 25mg

Domestic Displacement

Rather than endure a long-drawn-out emotional battle over the necessity to subdue my ego, I simply murdered it. Knowing full well it would soon resurrect and reassert itself. I lay down and welcomed the uncharacteristic calmness imbuing my being. There was no point musing about what may or what may not occur, so I just sat up and made a series of truly excellent inhalations. What occurred next seems almost impossible to write about, because it was so unbelievably extraordinary. I could feel the onset of the substance. And I was conscious the jarring transparent superdense energy filling the room had actually emanated from me. Yet as my head rested back into the pillows, that jarring energy was no longer noticeable. Instead, I witnessed the rapid wholesale descent of an astonishingly crystal-clear medium plunge into the bedroom from ceiling height. Upon reaching the floor it immediately imposed itself in a manner that caused the floorboards beneath the carpet to subtly creak and groan. The otherworldly medium imposed itself even more powerfully. I could feel it forcibly pushing down upon the bedroom floor and I could hear the corresponding sounds as the underlying wooden floorboards creaked with unmissable audibility. I was as astonished as I was scared. The energy then imposed upon the walls. I was able to tactilely sense and visually observe as the strange medium coated each flat wall surface. With that done it steadily increased its unimaginable force upon them to such extent that the plasterboard walls audibly flexed. It had taken mere seconds until it was apparent the entity was completely satisfied with the purchase it had secured throughout the bedroom. The entire bedroom then suddenly exhibited its ordinary everyday appearance. There was no turbulent atmosphere. No seething psycho-spiritual medium. However, there was the unmistakable emotional presence of something very big high above me. Something that was in complete control of what was about to unfold. And what unfolded was that the house began to shake. I could feel as the bedroom shook rapidly back and forth in line with my position. I could easily feel the bedroom floor shaking. I could actually feel the vibrations transmitting through the steel frame that forms the hidden skeletal structure of the house. I could hear that frame continually shaking behind the plasterboard walls. As ridiculous and impossible and insane as this must surely sound, a powerful spiritual entity was forcibly shaking the entire house. I could feel it shaking and I could hear it shaking. It was without any doubt and without question. I was terrified for myself and also worried that my neighbour must be wondering what on earth is going on next door. Thankfully, the shaking stopped. I was aghast. The unmissable density of a powerful discarnate entity remained static above me. It conveyed something to me with complete clarity. My mind could interpret it so very easily: "Do you really want me to come down there?" I was so scared. I said nothing. I simply assumed my fear transmitted upwards. But as that threatening emotion from the entity persisted, it began to transform and took on an almost parental and jovial character. Such that now, despite my ongoing fear, I became cheeky and childlike. Wearing a concealed half-smile, I inwardly voiced: "Oh, come on then!" Suddenly, several loud bangs were heard upon the roof of the house. That was simply too much to bear and I inwardly cried out in frenzied disbelief. The fanned tail of a crow then came into full view over the verge of the roof. Realising the unexpected banging noises were from the crow foraging for food upon the roof tickled me sufficiently to have me fall into a fit of disbelieving laughter. But then I stopped laughing. And I stopped laughing because mere moments ago the house had been vigorously shaken. And I knew why it had been shaken. And I knew I would have to write about that accurately and honestly. And that seemed such a big task. Because reporting on such a thing as that sounds doolally. I was worried about my neighbour. Had he experienced any of those tremors inside his house? Was he home? I listened intently. I could hear him in the adjoining bedroom. He was humming a happy tune. His humming faintly transmitted through the thin wall. That at least was reassuring.

Report: #35

Location: Bedroom (~09:15hrs)

Dose: 25mg

Bursting Forth from Nowhere

I sat up and made three very pleasing inhalations. Each vaporous intake was momentarily imprisoned before release. As my head sank into the pillows the room filled with a turbulent and transparent fluid-like medium. Just as soon as I had made that observation a highly energetic spiritual entity burst forth from nowhere and immediately filled the room. Experiencing the arrival of these entities in such a highly energetic state is never anything less than breathtaking and inconceivable. A seething high frequency medium was now clearly visible throughout the bedroom. It knowingly and purposefully imposed itself upon the bedroom walls either side of me. Upon doing so it further increased its power to such extent that the walls audibly flexed. I could palpably feel the tremendous increase in energy as it powerfully pushed against the walls. It was a stunning display of power and it just did not let up. I was able to invest time observing the impossibly energetic medium. As the frequency increased, I witnessed a countless number of impossibly narrow zigzagging lines along a horizontal plane; each line uniformly representative of the wavelength; each peak moving ever closer to the neighbouring peak; each and every infinitesimal wavelength becoming shorter and shorter and shorter, as the medium became perceptibly tauter and tauter and tauter. I could see the bedroom and I could see the trees through the bedroom window. But my vision was also working through a very highly energetic and very high frequency medium, giving the appearance of a darkened yellow tint. My inner voice acknowledged to itself just how truly unbelievable and stunning the observation was. I beseeched myself to remain super-sharp-eyed. I became acutely aware of the tremendous pressure imposing down upon me from that strange psycho-spiritual energy. It was especially powerful pushing down upon my legs, but far less so upon my upper body. It was obvious the otherworldly pressure was not imposing directly upon my body. It was pushing down upon me from about half the height of the bedroom. And somehow, I could easily perceive the forcefulness of that energy. I was able to feel the energy was pressing down along a horizontal plane. But I could also feel it curved over me at the stated distance. I assumed the entity was actually pushing down upon and forcibly compressing an unseen field of psycho-spiritual energy emanating from me. And if that is so, then I am forced to consider the effect of dimethyltryptamine is to temporarily stimulate such an occurrence – the powerful emanation of constitutional psycho-spiritual energy from within oneself. As I parted my closed lips with the tip of my tongue, it became all too obvious a portion of the entity had invested itself inside my throat and my mouth. It was in the process of coating the walls and the roof of my mouth with that unique and improbably thin psycho-spiritual substance. It was obviously moving towards my mouth opening. I closed my mouth and kept it closed. It felt as though it was being sealed up from within, but I dared not test the integrity of that strange psycho-spiritual seal. Continuing with calm nasal breathing, I looked upon the trees visible through the window. I did not realise it at the time, but the trees appeared to be in fully adorned with lush green leaves. As I watched the trees clothed in full greenery, succumbing to a strong westerly wind, it struck me their appearance seemed more like a memory from a DMT experiment undertaken a year or so ago. I then felt movement within my abdomen and assumed it related to a portion of the entity. A car was heard passing on the nearby road. I sensed the immediate vacation of the entity from within me. I did not quite realise it at the time, but the bedroom had appeared considerably wider, very much brighter, and far more colourful than its ordinary everyday appearance. The trees outside were still heavily adorned with lush green leaves, yielding to the strong westerly wind. I was wholly insensible to the imperceptible changes that were slowly taking place, until it was perplexingly obvious the room had completely returned to its ordinary everyday appearance. It was no longer so wide and it had fallen quite dull. The trees outside were also very different. They were no longer filled with lush green leaves blowing in the wind. The leaves were small and sparse and not particularly green, by virtue of my view being made through a lace curtain. And the breeze was barely bending the branches. But even the very configuration of the branches was very different to how they had appeared just moments ago. The difference between what I had observed moments ago to what I was seeing now was hugely significant and incredibly perplexing. How can the transparent body of a spiritual entity render my view of the ordinary so very extraordinary? How can it create such a vivid difference and render those differences so convincingly real?

Report: #36

Location: Bedroom (~11:30hrs)

Dose: 26mg

Occult Dentistry

Under great self-imposed duress, I joined the pillows on the bedroom floor and then spent five minutes putting myself through a mangle of internal conflict. I knew nothing of any real research significance would play out unless I picked up the pipe. I gathered up my courage and then sat up and got to work before carefully leaning back and sinking my head down into the pillows. The onset of the experience was immediate. But this was a very different energy. It was not seething and it was not turbulent. It was pure and pristine. It was beyond transparent because it rendered the bedroom and everything therein in a truly remarkable hypervivid finish. It was somehow obvious the power behind this particular type of entity was many times greater in strength than those creating that turbulent seething energy. This energy was smooth and effortless. I could feel it passing right through my entire being as though I too was wholly composed of the same psycho-spiritual-stuff. I was genuinely terrified. I assured myself I would never take DMT ever again. And I meant that in all seriousness. I thought I was at the threshold of an experience my mind would not be able to deal with. There was no doubt this entity had invested its presence throughout my body. Although I felt nothing to confirm that suspicion. Upon my cheeks however, I felt the strange firm presence of a very thin and dense psycho-spiritual film, clamping my head tightly in position. I looked out of the window at the trees. They were rendered in a completely hyperreal appearance, even though the lace curtain. My terror subsided. Somehow, the trees outside appeared to move slowly closer and closer toward me. By imperceptible degrees of movement, they seemed to be nearing me. I tried my best to observe their apparent movement, but noted not one little incremental change. How can the trees outside appear so close to me when I am indoors? The same process then occurred in reverse, and once again, I observed not even the slightest little visual change taking place. However, I did note that my body was being very slowly lowered back down onto the carpet from what seemed like a very short distance above it. That was a genuine surprise. The apparent descent was so very slow and exceptionally soft and subtle. But it was also very clear that I was, in reality, being very gradually lowered a short distance onto the carpeted floor. However, what was very odd about this occurrence was that my back was never actually perceived to re-cushion itself into the carpeted floor. It was more the case that whatever had raised me, it had done so with no obvious change in how my back had been originally cushioned by the carpeted floor. I was totally astonished as I continued to perceive myself being lowered. I was even more astonished that I could feel no physical cushioning whatsoever as my back returned to the floor. My inner voice mused upon how nothing seems impossible to these entities. Despite my amazement, I remained calm and relatively emotionless. However, when the entity appeared directly above me, in a visibly transparent low energy state, I transmitted the following words with heartfelt emotion: "You are my ambition!" A portion of the entity descended and entered into my head. I could feel it undertaking some subtle action within my brain. I trusted the entity and its actions implicitly. I could also feel faint movement behind both my eyeballs. The unusual activity within my brain lasted for approximately two minutes. All the while I was able to observe the entity. The potion of entity within me then moved to the back of my nose. It felt as though its presence was filling my ethmoid bone. Its presence in that region felt solid and it gave me a unique sense of the unusual shape of that potion of my olfactory anatomy. That lasted for approximately one minute. Then either by instinct or by acquiescing to a subliminal command or prompting, I opened my mouth very wide, as though I were under the gaze of a dentist. What occurred next was simply astonishing. No sooner had I opened my mouth when the entity set to work on my teeth in a most peculiar fashion. It felt just like a multitude of impossibly miniscule air bubbles were being imploded upon the surface of my teeth. I could feel the bizarre effect as the entity methodically worked its way around my mouth. The sensation was so incredibly strange. It was somewhat similar to the effect of popping candy; except each of the countless implosions – or whatever it was that was taking place – was so exceedingly small and short-lived. The rapidly occurring implosive sensations all felt focussed and targeted. In the space of about three or four minutes I guesstimate thousands of implosive little 'pops' had slowly swept around my teeth. The action had felt like a constant bombardment upon my teeth. It went on and on and on, and although I was certain it was doing me good, the longevity of the exercise began to make me feel somewhat self-conscious about my teeth requiring such extensive occult dentistry. I maintained my mouth in the wide-open position exactly as one would do when visiting an actual dentist. When the activity ceased, I was pleased to be able to close my mouth. Despite the unbelievable nature of what had just occurred I did my best to maintain a calm acceptance of the experience.

Report: #37

Location: Bedroom (~09:15hrs)

Dose: 25mg

Silently & Inwardly Thrice

I was facing a self-imposed dilemma of courage versus cowardice in progressing with my research. How I came to lie down in readiness, with such an awfully strong wind buffeting the house, I simply do not know. I waited for a couple of minutes, silently reassured myself, then sat up and immediately felt at ease as courage permeated my being. The first inhalation was excellent. The second inhalation was disastrous, as I inhaled a small volume of truly awful tasting smoke. The third inhalation was as good as the first. I carefully reclined whilst been conscious of the rapidly rising intensity of high frequency energy in the midst of my head. My head had barely rested into the pillows when a highly energetic entity manifested with astonishing immediacy. Highly active energy visibly filled the bedroom. The already dull daylight suddenly appeared very much dimmer, by virtue of the uncommonly dense medium filling the volume of the room. As the frequency of seething energy rapidly increased ever higher and higher, I silently mused: it really does seem some of these entities are wont to indulge my astonishment of their truly remarkable displays of constitutional power. I could not help myself from assuming such a display of power was purposefully taking me to the very limit of my astonishment. I really wish I could convey in words how devastatingly consuming and phenomenally overwhelming those stupendous displays of energy really are. As the frequency continued to increase, I could see the relative effect within and throughout the seething psycho-spiritual medium. I could also somehow hear the relative increase in frequency throughout my head. I could also somehow feel that energy as it became something like a homogenous and paradoxically solid transparent mass; one that was able to easily permeate all physical objects without hindrance or obstruction. The room was filled with incredibly dense and intensely powerful emotionally intelligent energy. I harboured not the slightest doubt a portion of the entity was invested within me, though I felt nothing. Despite being in the midst of what appeared to be a highly active psycho-spiritual storm, I remained quite calm. From within that terrific field of energy, I sensed an emotional investment within the wall clock to my right, and an emotional investment within the ceiling light to my left. Each was seemingly encouraging the other to engage in a game of throwing something back and forth between themselves, yet I saw nothing moving back and forth. I sensed the encouragement had gone unheeded or ignored. Each request to play then changed and became quite demanding. That startled me slightly. As I moved my mouth to wet my lips the entity made its presence deep within my throat very obvious. There was something of a constriction forming inside my windpipe. I could feel a distinctly gnarled shape forming from that strange quasi-physical psycho-spiritual substance. I was becoming very scared and I knew my options were limited in such a situation. The room appeared as twilight by virtue of the raging occult medium. I felt very alone. Indeed, aside from this entity, I was very much home alone. I demanded calmness and reassured myself I could see this experience out. I told myself all I had to do was to remain calm and be patient. However, the emotions invested within the wall clock and the ceiling light were becoming exceedingly insistent and demanding. I remained calm. But the quasi-physical portion within my throat once again made its presence known to me, as though to remind me of my vulnerability. I was now seriously considering the possibility that this entity could get this interaction very badly wrong. I gave serious credence to the possibility my sudden death may arise from this interaction. As I looked out beyond the bedroom window from my lain position, I felt so completely alone, so unmeaningfully small, so very vulnerable in this isolated adventure. I began thinking about my imminent demise. Three large knotted and gnarled quasi-physical psycho-spiritual nodules suddenly protruded outward from my sternum. I could distinctly feel the shape and the terribly strange composition of the protruding nodules. The quasi-physical presence inside my windpipe further troubled the free flow of air. And that was more than enough to convince me that I would not survive this experience. In genuine fear for my life I cried out aloud: "I'm scared! I'm scared!" And upon doing so, the entity must have immediately fled my body. As soon as I realised it had gone, I felt hugely relieved; and very much to my own surprise, totally calm.

Report: #38

Location: Patio (~02:30hrs)

Dose: 10mg

Freight Night

I returned home from working a nightshift and decided to progress my research with a small dose of DMT, inhaled outdoors in the dark of night. My approach would be to inhale the dose, close my eyes, and just see what happens. Once the kitchen light was switched off, I stepped outside and realised just how dark the night was. I secured myself a garden chair, having narrowly avoided catching my eyes on the washing line. I sat down. All was silent, except for a nearby blackbird singing in the dead of night. I looked up at the cloudless sky, illiberally mottled with stars. Using dim blue light from the flame of my lighter I made my sole inhalation. After just a few seconds I sensed the onset. The inner sound within my head increased in intensity. I closed my eyes but noted nothing of note. The blackbird suddenly stopped singing. I kept my eyes closed and remained as still and as silent and perceptive as possible. I focussed intently on listening to my own inner sound, ringing audibly in the midst of my head. Otherwise, the silence was pristine and absolute. But just then, without any warning whatsoever, and with startling suddenness, a not too distant freight train engaged its horn with two thoroughly loud blasts. My eyes sprang wide open and my eyes bulged out in fright as the loud penetrating sound shredded all of my nerves in an instant. With no aforethought I mouthed out loud as though my response was an involuntary defence mechanism: "FUCKING BASTARD!" The effect of the noise had a hugely significant impact upon me. I felt it through every fibre of my being. I was disgusted at the unforeseeable intrusion. That concluded the experiment.

Report: #39

Location: Rear Garden (~09:30hrs)

Dose: 21mg

Out in the Water see it Swimming

Two crows glided low overhead. I admired their undercarriage. A much smaller bird began singing in the apple tree over to my right. I sat up, emptied the pipe and then laid back. What followed in this experiment represents perhaps one of the most important observations of my research programme. I noted some faint but observable patterning just ahead of me, evidently formed from and within what appeared to be a transparent medium. It seemed that transparent medium was actually emanating from me. As unbelievable as this must sound, it was emanating solely from my left eye. I could clearly see and feel as the psycho-spiritual substance continued to stream out from my left orb and move away from me. As I maintained my observation, it became abundantly evident this was indeed the case. The psycho-spiritual stream continued to exit my left eye, whereupon it expanded into a large crystal-clear sphere, which continued to expand as it moved away from me. The sphere rapidly expanded to at least an arm's length in diameter and I only lost sight of it by virtue of the continuous stream of psycho-spiritual substance continually emanating from my eye. As astonished as I was, I somehow managed to remain calm and expressionless, as I continued observing. Now above me, and apparently higher than the ridge of the roof, I was looking at a great mass of superdense mind-stuff. It was not too difficult to consider this stuff was actually my mind-stuff. My mind did not feel in any way expanded, or even partially externalised. But I was laid looking up at something uncommon that had evidently emanated from me. It really did not feel inappropriate to consider this strange mass represented some portion of my mind. It was so clearly evident. It was above me and overarching me. And I did not doubt that this mass was somehow and somewhere anchored to my body. The depth and density of the central mass of mind-stuff created a very unique and distinct haze; whereas towards the outer portion, it was nearly perfectly transparent. Upon realising the enormity of what I was seeing, my mind was wont to deal with the matter in humorous manner; like when someone smiles or laughs through nervousness. I began to wonder whether I was irretrievably projecting my essential vitality; was I irrecoverably losing a portion of my essential self; would that which was outside of me become lost to me, or would it come back to me? My inner voice was asking its own mind-stuff whether it was okay out there. I then felt a distinct pressure and strange movement beneath the skin of my left cheek. I could see my mind-stuff above me. The movement beneath the skin of my upper left cheek persisted. I assumed this was my externalised mind-stuff making its way back into me. I watched intently as imperceptibly the hazy transparent mass slowly faded in visibility. This was a very significant experiment and a very significant finding for me.

Q. Why would mind-stuff exit solely from my left eye?

A. I consider that perhaps it also emanated and exited from my right eye, if not from my wider physiology. But my sole focus upon the unusual occurrence was made through my left eye. The initial faint patterning was certainly observed by both eyes.

Q. If that mind-stuff really did emanate from me, wouldn't there be some indicator of that?

A. There was! There was a notable increase in that mysterious interior sound within my head, resulting from the increased level of DMT. In addition, as the mind-stuff was streaming out of my left eye, I could feel the skin on my face felt exceptionally tight. Although I was conscious of that, my main focus was upon the strange visual observation. The effect on my face disappeared unnoticeably.

Q. Why do you say its mind-stuff?

A. Because it might be mind-stuff!

Q. What if it's not mind-stuff?

A. Then it's something else!

Report: #40

Location: Thruscross, North Yorkshire (~16:15hrs)

Dose: 30mg

Vacation of Awesomeness

My walk to find a suitable research location felt like a walk to my own funeral. I passed through a farmyard; climbed over a rusty old iron gate, diagonally traversed a grassy field where I counted seven rabbits a running; clambered over a drystone wall and finally entered a grassy field that was to my liking. Several rabbits scampered into a densely wooded copse of pine trees. I sat upon the grass with my back to the sun. The sun was hot but there was a pleasant cool breeze. It took four inhalations to empty the pipe. I was determined to take in as much of the potent substance as possible. By the time my head rested into the grass the intensity of my inner sound was uncommonly high. I spread out my arms in a cruciform manner. My hands tightly grabbed a hold of the lush green grass. A truly huge and densely formed psycho-spiritual sphere was just a few centimetres from my face. It was as incredible as it was unmissable. I could easily discern the sphere contained a strange assortment of psycho-spiritually formed miscellany. The proximity of the base of this huge sphere was so incredibly close to my face. And yet it also appeared to be entirely separate from me. Its proximity and its size were such that whenever I maneuvered my eyes to the left or the right, my view was significantly refracted due to my vision working through the broad base of the huge dense psycho-spiritual sphere. Its visual presence was exceedingly clear and definite. It was absolutely astonishing to behold. I allowed myself to become momentarily overexcited and mouthed aloud several self-encouraging profanities. Upon sitting up, I looked over to my right and observed a great chain length of very large psycho-spiritual spheres, extending well beyond the drystone wall. I looked to my left and witnessed the same sight extending far over to the pine copse. I looked upward. It was clear my sight was working through an extensive psycho-spiritual presence, stretching some great distance above me. The sight was so unbelievably astonishing that my emotions ran high with excitement. I was thoroughly amazed at that which I was seeing and vocalised my feelings with uncaring and profane abandon. Momentarily, I felt absolutely blissfully free from all my terrestrial responsibilities; free from my familial duties and completely unchained from every duty, expectation and social convention

– real or imagined – made upon my person. I felt human, but at a very deep and very profound level. I felt tremendous value in practically pursuing and exploring the mystery of my own being. I felt immense satisfaction at feeling an essential relationship to the natural world, and the wider unseen universe, of which I recognised I am naught but a miniscule mote. In those few short seconds I experienced a vacation of awesomeness. I looked up. The vast psycho-spiritual medium reached high into the sky. Its presence created obvious visual distortions upon passing white clouds. I ruminated on how this potent substance literally expands one's consciousness in manner that is so visually very rewarding.

Report: #41

Location: Rear garden (~17:00hrs)

Dose: 25mg

Crown & Out

I seated myself upon on a plastic garden chair in the midst of the garden and then emptied the pipe in three proficient pulls. By the time I looked skyward all the clouds exhibited significant geometric patterning. I focussed on the detail of one particular patterned cloud, but the brightness of the light blue sky stung my eyes. I dropped my gaze and my head. The very moment I dropped my head something zapped my crown with such forceful rapidity that it rendered me completely limp and insensible. My body lolled forward into a loose lifeless mass. I had a vague understanding of what had just occurred. But I was so shocked by its suddenness. My inner voice bewailed: "Not out here! Not out here!" In parallel with that precise cranial blow, an incredibly high-pitched tone was evident throughout my head and all around me. It wasn't especially loud but its frequency was tremendously high. I barely had the mental capacity to realise I was not in my proper senses. I was sat cross-legged. My upper body was completely slouched forward. My mouth felt indescribably strange. I could feel the crown of my head where something had stunned me. I was vaguely aware of an unusual movement occurring around me. I believed something invisible was creating a sizeable unseen field all around me. After a few moments I had the capacity to sit up from my limp slouch. My surroundings had taken on a spectacular degree of hyperreality. In particular, the greenery of the oak tree canopy blowing in the wind displayed a truly sumptuous velvety appearance. I was still not quite in my full senses but I was becoming sensible enough to know that something had stunned me. I moved my tongue. My mouth began to feel normal again. As my mental senses increased, little by little, I was able to better appreciate that my overall mental state was not especially good. I was still operating largely on incapacity. As my senses slowly returned, I acknowledged that I had underestimated the potency of the crystals. I knew that some powerful but unseen being had just rendered me senseless. As my mental capacities returned to fullness I looked up at the sky. Above me was filled with a vast psycho-spiritual presence. Defiantly, I looked into its midst and grinned hard whilst signalling thumbs-up.

Report: #42

Location: Rear Garden (~10:30hrs)

Dose: 16mg

DIY UFO

The inhalation was faultless. I reclined and awaited the expected. However, things were decidedly different to what I anticipated. Onset was so sudden. Its power took me by complete surprise. The ringing sound in midst of my head was rapidly rising to an incredible high frequency. I could feel the energy oscillating powerfully throughout my head. The physicality of the vibrations was becoming worrying. I then observed as a psycho-spiritual wavefront smoothly and speedily moved outwards from me. The wavefront exhibited a consistent internal patterning – a multitude of adjoined squircles. But what was really surprising was that I could actually feel that energy. I could feel that energy very directly and very palpably. The energy was a bizarre projection of some essential aspect of my otherwise hidden self. The rapidly expanding field of energy was a single unit – a homogenous whole with a paradoxical solidity. From within, I could actually feel that expanding field of energy in its entirety. I even observed its expansion – moving rapidly skyward. I cannot pretend I wasn't scared. Indeed, I was so scared that I sat bolt upright and half jumped off the ground. Such was the magnitude of my surprise at the outwardly projecting manifestation that I mutedly and indigently demanded of the bizarre psychospiritual projection: "What the fuck are you doing?" But moving so suddenly seemed to have changed matters. It appeared the voluminous psycho-spiritual emanation had actually broken free of me. There was no longer any sense that I was the source of that truly strange emanation. I noted how the sky appeared visibly very much bluer than it did before I began the experiment. I was still scared. I was initially scared the expanding field of my own psycho-spiritual energy would attract a very high energy entity. But I was also fearful that I had irretrievably shed some of my essential self. The unnatural clarity and sharp blueness of the sky was simply astounding. I suspected its remarkable appearance was a function of my vision now working through the air and through the still expanding field of my own superdense occult substance. A crow glided low overhead as a gentle southerly breeze blew through the apple tree causing the outermost branches to shimmy. Those shimmying branches seemed to exhibit a conscious yearning to reach higher into the sky they were pointing at. Those branches also seemed aware of my fretful frame of mind. And if that wasn't quite enough, I sensed they were having a private conversation about me with something invisible directly above me. Somewhere nearby, an emergency service siren screamed into action. The pre-recorded words: "Please state the nature of your emergency," sprang up in mind and made me laugh out loud. The laughter was good. It made me feel safer and easier about the bizarreness that was unfolding. I lay back and looked up. The air was filled with psycho-spiritual substance. It was not patterned and it was not composed of spherical cells. It now appeared unfurled, infolding, diaphanous and amorphous. I instinctively felt this was the return of the very same energy that had so powerfully emanated from me. Like a worried parent being cross with a wayward child, I earnestly demanded the substance to: "Get back here right now!" It was abundantly clear that mass of psycho-spiritual substance really was slowly returning to me. I then playfully asked myself: "What if that mind-stuff is not my mind-stuff?" I mean, what if I am unwittingly welcoming a stranger into the house of my mind? What would happen? Would I start to think differently? Would I become aware I am thinking differently? What if conflict arose between me and my occult lodger? Despite enjoying the dastardly dark humour arising from such consideration the starkness of the schizophrenic ramifications really rattled me. The psycho-spiritual substance reduced and diminished to such an extent that it was either absent or simply unobservable. As I was musing over the events, my eyes felt completely compelled to be drawn over to a distant creamy white orb with a distinct haze around it. It was barely moving. Almost involuntarily, I mouthed aloud: "Now that looks interesting!" It was moving at an unrealistically slow pace across the sky. Whatever it was it was in no hurry. I could not take my eyes off it. I scrutinised it intently. Despite its creamy brightness, there was an irregular high reflectance of sunlight from its surface. The reflectance was short-lived but momentarily produced a pronounced dazzling effect. Suddenly, on the other side of the fence, my neighbour started up his noisy lawnmower. But I was simply far too spellbound to be startled. A jet aeroplane at relatively low altitude appeared in the sky, making a skyward ascent. I wondered if the pilot could see what I was seeing. I thought to race indoors and get my phone so I could take a picture of the thing. But for what purpose, I asked myself. What would I do that image? Go to work and show my colleagues? Show them an image of a distant unknown object and invite them to share their honest opinion? That would draw ridicule. And to be fair, I had no way of knowing whether I was making something mundane mysterious, or genuinely observing something highly unusual? The orb continued at an unnaturally slow pace and was gradually lost to sight.

Report: #43

Location: Rear Garden (~14:15hrs)

Dose: 16mg

Occult Complexity of Cloud

My wife gifted me a book edited by Graham Hancock: *The Divine Spark*. Hancock suspects "[The] real breakthroughs in our understanding of consciousness are going to come from psychedelics..." The blurb asks:

> What if psychedelics could open up our understanding of consciousness and powerfully change the way we view our life on this Earth and our relationship to other worlds?

Wearing sunglasses for comfort, I sat up and emptied the pipe in two pulls. The pitch of my inner sound raced upwards at a terrific rate. I remained calm as the frequency rose ever higher. Clouds within my field of vision appeared to undergo a very rapid lateral jarring effect. This persisted for just a few seconds before steadily reducing. The clouds now exhibited a familiar geometric patterning. An aeroplane flew overhead at mid-altitude. There was a truly breathtaking aesthetic quality to the sky, even when factoring in the light filtering properties of the sunglasses. Another aeroplane was flying at very high altitude. I enjoyed the aesthetic beauty of clouds and the dark blue sky beyond. I observed birds passing overhead. I could hear my wife in the kitchen. A low altitude cumulonimbus slowly sailed into view from the west. Its dense grey central mass conveyed a sense of danger and anger. I began to wonder about the occult complexity of the cloud. What was hidden from measurement? What was beyond the limits of my human perception? My next observation was a genuine surprise and one that elicited an incredulous and thrice spoken: "No way! No way! No way!" Beggaring belief, I beheld – at an apparently incredible height – what appeared to be a black orb UFO traversing at a painfully slow pace against a white cloud background. I could hardly believe what I was seeing. I thought to call upon my wife to come and see. But that would mean hollering; and hollering would mean loss of composure; and loss of composure felt like it was against the principles of my approach to this research. And to what end would my wife's observation augment that of my own eyes? I stayed shtum whilst watching the black orb before it inexplicably disappeared. I was astonished. After heading indoors, I felt a strong urge to play music.

Report: #44

Location: Rear Garden (~18:15hrs)

Dose: 16mg

Whimsical Wishes

I exhausted the pipe of all available vapour in two textbook inhalations. The intensity and pitch of my interior sound rapidly increased. But no sooner had that manifested when a really significant vibration began transmitting throughout my entire body. Unusually however, this vibration commenced from the soles of my feet and transmitted upward through my body. A repeat of the very same vibratory energy commenced yet again from the soles of my feet. Just then, a wavefront of psycho-spiritual substance rapidly expanded upwards and outwards from within me. The strange substance – despite its overall transparency – was readily observable. There was consistent patterning contained therein. Suddenly, I felt the magnitude of what I was engaged with, and a tremendous seriousness fell upon me. With great acuity I sensed I was literally putting my occult self 'out there'. I was moved to muse and brooding upon why DMT facilitates such bizarre experiences as it does; what value does it hold for the individual; what impact will it have on wider society? Is DMT a bizarre shock-antidote against the spirit-deadening philosophies of existentialism; against the rigorous inflexibility of traditional science in its unappealing dogmatic guise? My eyes scanned the sky to better appreciate the reach of my own psycho-spiritual substance. And it did seem remarkably extensive. But I supposed it must have a limit. I craned my head as far back as it would stretch until I was looking at a vast area of sky. I could see the extent of my psycho-spiritual output. On no account did it fill the vastness of the big blue yonder. I hoped to have sight of a black orb UFO. I really wanted to see a black orb UFO. But I realised unfulfilled desire would lead to disspaointment. Why would those otherwise unseen entities satisfy my whimsical wishes? I imagined how utterly awesome it would be to have just a momentary glimpse at the full extent of the occult life, filling what appears to be a vast emptiness.

Report: #45

Location: Rear Garden (~16:15hrs)

Dose: 20mg

Jailer of My Own Spirit

I made two very pleasing vaporous inhalations. A significantly powerful vibration originated just beneath my solar plexus. The vibration continued to increase in intensity. Related to that energy, I experience very strong emotions of purposefulness and willfulness. These grew and grew in strength to such an extent that I felt some deeply occult aspect of my being was preparing to break free from my body. Whatever it was, I felt it had a unique and fundamental separateness from my narrating inner voice. I initially felt quite perturbed that some part of me was trying to break free from me. But then, very much to my surprise, I felt great dismay and pity that it had failed in that attempt. I felt a very strange emotion; something like the realisation that I was an unknowing jailer of my own spirit.

Report: #46

Location: Rear Garden (~09:45hrs)

Dose: 25mg

Magnifying Matters Occult

I made three pleasing inhalations and reclined. A faint psycho-spiritual medium rapidly manifested before my eyes. A significant vibratory energy then arose within my upper body. It was active along what felt like a very precise and perfectly straight channel running centrally down the midst of my torso. I could not mistake such significant, centralised interior vibrations. The vigorous movement caused audible popping sounds above the roof of my mouth. As that significant interior vibration continued, I maintained my observation upon the psycho-spiritual medium in front of me. The sudden ballooning of that substance coincided with the sudden cessation of the interior vibration. It was abundantly evident some mysterious aspect of my being had suddenly expanded upwards and outwards – to a very significant distance. I became aware of an uncommon pressure pressing upon either side of my head. I focussed upon that strange pressure and duly called myself an idiot as I reached to remove my sunglasses. I spent the next ten minutes in deep thought whilst watching my own psycho-spiritual substance returning to me. I mused on: why does DMT facilitate the bizarre experiences that it does; does exogenously administered DMT fool my body into thinking death is upon me; does DMT cause my immaterial-self to leapfrog my physical-self – yet only to find it is still very much anchored to a finite physical vehicle; is it by reason and design that DMT is found in relatively high percentages within some particular plants; why should this substance – with its extreme potency into magnifying matters occult – present itself at this particular juncture in the unfolding story of western civilisation?

Report: #47

Location: Rear Garden (~11:45hrs)

Dose: 25mg

Irreparable Pieces

The garden was bathed in bright sunshine. I was huffing and puffing at the prospect of inhaling the latent potency hiding within the pipe. I waited a short while and then decided it would just be better to get on with it. Upon laying back I implored myself not to miss one little detail. I waited for my inner sound to energise and intensify. But it didn't. I waited for a significant vibration to manifest throughout my body. But it didn't. And I waited to see a psycho-spiritual medium with geometric patterning forming in front of my eyes. But it didn't. Instead, an irregular internal vibration quickly travelled up the inside of my lower right leg. No sooner had that occurred, when it ceased. And no sooner had it ceased when the very same effect occurred again and again. I was feeling unnerved. Despite the warmth and the security of the bright summer sunshine, I was unaccountably beginning to develop serious misgivings about my involvement in this particular experiment. There was something complex that was difficult to fathom; a disagreeable negativity was mushrooming inside of me. And I was becoming extremely uncomfortable with it. I tried to remain calm. And to my credit I did remain calm. For a short while. A feeling of intense dolefulness became far too much to bear. I sat up and vocalised sincere exasperation with the prevailing mood I was under. Upon sitting up there was one highly significant observation, and I'll refer to that in a short while. After sitting up and vocalising great discontent, my mind became swamped with strong introspective emotions relating to my research. How would I ever be able to continue experimenting with this substance when it was weighing so disagreeably upon me? I felt as though I was in irreparable pieces. Things did not feel good at all. I then remembered the short-lived observation I had made. Upon sitting up while feeling unreasonably burdened with heavy emotion, I momentarily observed how I was sat within the midst of an absolutely crystal-clear atmosphere. The clarity of that atmosphere was unsurpassable. Ordinary air is clear and transparent. But the crystal-clear clarity of that which I was sat within was incomparable to the air. The significance of that particular observation informed me that I was in the midst of a powerful psychic interaction with a powerful spiritual entity. The further significance of that was to inform me my melancholy emotions were not entirely of my own making. But were, in all likelihood, been squeezed out of my psyche by something far more powerful than me.

Had this entity secured itself a presence within my psyche just before the experiment began? Had it waited for me to commit myself to the DMT before imposing its psychically manipulative capacities? It's not difficult to imagine the presence of discarnate minds; conscious entities; spirit-beings; or whatever term suits you. Hidden kingdoms of nature, containing myriad diverse entities, completely unseen. But only because of the limitations of perception. Entities populating what some describe as a parallel dimension. One could even jocularly anthropomorphise this DMT research scenario. From the perspective of the entities:

Entity #1: [Addressing Entity #2] Over here. Come and look at this. I'm watching one of those humans down here. He's messing about with that DMT.

Entity #2: Oh yeah.

Entity #1: Yeah! I've seen him before. He reckons he's writing a book.

Entity #2: Oh yeah.

Entity #1: Yeah! He was busy earlier this morning, expanding his mind into our dimension.

Entity #2: Oh yeah.

Entity #1: Yeah! He's being messing about outdoors. I've been ignoring him.

Entity #2: Oh yeah.

Entity #1: Yeah! But watch this. I'm gonna anchor myself in his mind, and the moment he's gotten that DMT into him I'm gonna put the terrors on him, and make him sit up and wonder what it's all about.

[Entity #2 observes Entity #1 access psyche of human subject. Entity #2 then observes human subject inhale DMT and momentarily lay down before quickly sitting back up in a state of mental torment.]

Entity #2: [Laughing] Oh my eye! That's too funny!

And perhaps it is quite funny. Then again, perhaps it's insanely ridiculous. But humour aside, if there really are entities that can manipulate the human psyche, that's a very serious matter, isn't it? Or maybe that's just the natural order of things, and we don't realise it. Unseen influences playing with the mechanics of human minds. Something that can really only be understood from an overtly occult philosophical standpoint. It's a notion some may find discomforting, if not downright reprehensible. But surely the notion is worthy of consideration as to its validity. Because if such a notion has any basis in fact, the ramifications of that are far more startling than perhaps we can begin to realise. In Allen Kardec's *The Spirits' Book*, it is stated that spirits who are not incarnated are everywhere "...around us, seeing us, and mixing with us incessantly..." Therein, we learn: "...they constitute an invisible population, constantly moving and busy about us, on every side." Furthermore, the "...communications of spirits with men are either occult or ostensible," they have a much greater influence upon our thoughts and our actions than we suppose. Such thinking lays the foundations for a philosophy that can change the course of culture and evolution. And surely not for the first time!

Report: #48

Location: Rear Garden (~20:15hrs)

Dose: 23mg

The Thick of It

I lay down in the midst of the garden. The sun had dropped behind the shed but the light was still reasonably good. The sky was the most perfect shade of blue to promote clear observation of a mind-expanding experiment. I could hear my two boys splashing about upstairs in the bathtub. Other than that, the air was still and the neighbourhood was peaceful and silent. Two faultless inhalations emptied the pipe of all available vapour. Whilst undertaking the second inhalation, I could not fail to notice the incredible rate of increase in the pitch of my interior cranial sound. Upon perceiving that tremendous increase in pitch, I was forced to acknowledge the experience was going to be memorable. Whilst reclining, I implored myself to be as perceptive and as observant as possible. But the very moment I lay down was the exact same moment something unseen thumped heavily into the ground around me, causing it to shake momentarily. And I knew what it was. And I also knew it was too late to do anything about it. Immediately following that sudden and dramatic arrival, ultra-high frequency energy pushed down onto me and into me. And as it did so, it increased hugely in both intensity and pitch. The forcefulness with which it pushed down onto me and into me was truly prodigious. I could feel it and I could hear it. It gave me a unique sense of my skeletal self; a very strong palpable sense of the frame formed by my bones. The energy pushing down onto me was especially forceful. I could feel the force behind that power was active at approximately one arm's length above me, and one arm's length around me. It was pushing and pushing relentlessly, as though purposefully pinning me down beneath an invisible hemisphere of my own psycho-spiritual energy. I had not expected anything like this at all. It was almost time for dinner. And yet here I was, pinned down by something invisible. Cornered in the midst of the garden. I moved my tongue around. My mouth and my tongue felt enlarged. My tongue felt especially unusual. It was swirling around and around involuntarily, as though hinged at the root to a ball socket. It was so uncomfortably bizarre that I carefully closed my mouth and decided it would be safest to just keep my mouth closed. The unseen and immensely powerful – yet paradoxically tangible – force imposing upon me was becoming gravely concerning. There was an overriding sense that this entity was not particularly playful. Something small and black and physical scurried diagonally over my chest before exiting from my left shoulder. I paid little heed to it. I knew it was just a quasi-physical machination of the powerful entity, trying to spook me. I was genuinely feeling scared. But deep inside, a private part of my psyche wore a tiny little smile. Despite that, my inner voice began making appeals based on my parental responsibilities. I could even hear two little voices giggling away in the bathroom as they splashed. Dense psycho-spiritual portions of the entity were now making their way down towards me. I opened my mouth and directly addressed the entity with three clearly spoken sentences. Upon doing so my confidence grew tremendously, despite the knowledge that I was at the mercy of something exhibiting extreme power. The entity was now evident as an expansive mass of superdense and transparent psycho-spiritual substance. There was a brief moment of something unusual taking place within me. I wondered whether there was some kind of subliminal occult communication taking place; or was the entity freeing itself from my physiology? It remained above me in a clearly visible state. Its energy remained completely palpable. I suspected it was looking into me and reading me. I suspected it thought I was going to jump up and run away.

It seems simply ludicrous to state what I have reported as fact. Feeling a dull heavy thump into the ground around me was totally astonishing. Even as the ground shook around me, I found myself acknowledging the occurrence without question. I recognised such an effect would be easily measurable by vibration monitoring equipment. The effect was equivalent to standing close to a backhoe loader as its thumps soft ground with the rear of its backhoe. But the tremendous increase of energy that followed was quite different and without any terrestrial analogy. I could suppose the relatively soft ground around me was under a degree of compression from the sudden impact; and the huge increase of energy from the entity compressed it even further – resulting in the ever so slight but clearly audible sounds as that force continued to impress upon the ground.

As already stated, that forceful energy was tactilely perceived to be pushing down upon me from approximately one arm's length above me. I could palpably intuit that it was actually pushing down upon and compressing an invisible hemisphere of my own psycho-spiritual output. And that is exactly what I assume was occurring. My own psycho-spiritual energy provided a cushioning effect from that powerfully imposing otherworldly force, but also gave me an interiorly and exteriorly palpable sense of the awesome power that was at play. That is to say, I could easily perceive the truly frightening force imposing down upon me. And yet I was protected – effectively cushioned by my own compressible psycho-spiritual shell. Without that protective shell, I very much doubt my physical self could have withstood such devastating force. Yet I also have to acknowledge, the energy was capable of permeating right through me; to such extent it gave me a unique sense of my bones. But it was the incredible speed of its arrival, and the very obvious force of its powerful impact into the ground around me that immediately told me I really was in the thick of it. But what should one expect when undertaking investigations that engage the user with very highly energetic spiritual entities? And not forgetting the quasi-physical insect-like creature that scurried over my chest so very quickly. Such an occurrence sounds totally outlandish. And yet within the scope of the experience, it was naught but a minor occurrence.

Report: #49

Location: Rear Garden (~09:15hrs)

Dose: 29mg

Revolutionarily Revelatory

The second inhalation emptied the pipe. As soon as I lay down a terrifically energetic interior vibration commenced throughout my upper body. The air above me quickly became awash with a turbulent psycho-spiritual medium. I was astonished. The starkness of the energies that arise when researching the occult side of nature in this manner is so revolutionarily revelatory. But I could not discern whether the energy was solely actually emanating from me, or whether it was actually trying to project into me. Both seemed valid. There was a sudden movement by my right arm. It felt like something was moving beneath the poncho. I moved my arm slightly and the movement ceased. Tremendously turbulent psycho-spiritual energy continued to rage above me. If that was an entity, I was trying to work out whether its energy was benevolent or malevolent. The movement beneath poncho began again, but with a degree more significance. I moved my arm and the movement ceased. The highly active turbulent psycho-spiritual energy changed into a lower energy state – now evident as clearly visible dense mass of see-through psycho-spiritual substance; resembling something like an expansive billowing cloud. I was quite sure the mass was not from me. It was something else. It was from somewhere else. I began to wonder about the nature of the entity. I did not doubt it could easily access my head. But could it also access my mind? And if so, was it able to despoil the contents therein? Perhaps this entity was already influencing my thoughts? Perhaps it wanted me to think that which I was now thinking? The same movement by my right upper arm began again. But to such an outlandish extent that I involuntarily spat out a deific curse and sat bolt upright. The movement had ceased and when I resumed my lain position, I was surprised to find the visibility of the psycho-spiritual medium had decreased to a very significant extent.

Report: #50

Location: Rear Garden (~10:30hrs)

Dose: Endogenous

Life on Earth

I had the all the necessary materials to undertake my research but something was either lacking (courage) or was abundant (nerves). It was thus without any intention to experiment that I headed outdoors to soak up some sunshine. I imagined a totally ridiculous and improbable scenario, wherein a powerful spiritual entity in the same mould as the great Sir David Attenborough was observing me, whilst addressing a small audience of other entities, in an educational capacity:

Entity [in the style of Sir David Attenborough]: "And here we have, the human subject. This particular one here, has slowly begun to expand his spiritual capacities, in a slow and arduous process that will, in all likelihood, take many lifetimes before reaching full maturity. See how he watches the sky. Still unable to behold the vast occult kingdoms of nature from which he has, as yet unknowingly, voluntarily fallen. Look carefully. You can just about make out the slow and steady redevelopment of his psychic capacities. There is even a hint of latent spiritual energy, slowly awakening and beginning to re-establish itself. You can see his innate suspicion of life outside the bond of physical matter. But he cannot yet see it, without resorting to plant-derived spiritual tools."

And it was silly. It was in fact silly enough to make me laugh out loud. An aeroplane made its way high overhead. I marvelled at the machine; marvelled at the stupendous mental effort; the countless man-hours; the technological ingenuity and the raw daredevil courage that has seen these flying machines develop from their earliest inception into the most modern aircraft. I wondered, how such machines are viewed by those powerful DMT entities; those beings of hidden nature; an occult populace residing in a realm unseen. I then wondered whether such entities had an occult involvement in our terrestrial aviation developments. By subliminally instilling the appropriate degree of inspiration in the right individuals at the appropriate time. By rewarding those talented individuals who had toiled year upon year, on solving each and every one of the wide-ranging plethora of problems; challenges requiring understanding and resolution before we could eventually fly such machines. Whilst thinking upon that, I listened to the easily audible and ever-present ringing sound within my head. I wondered whether any unseen discarnate intelligence was presently cognisant of that psychic energy. My eyes felt obliged to look over to the right whereupon they fixed themselves onto an inky matt black orb, slowly traversing the sky at not too great a height. Transfixed, I watched its slow and dead straight motion in a southerly direction. I sprang up onto my feet to maintain eyesight upon the orb and watched its dead straight trajectory continue until it was out of sight.

Report: #51

Location: Rear Garden (~19:15hrs)

Dose: 30mg

Occult Recycling

Upon arriving home from work the garden was quiet and conditions were perfect. I forced myself into preparing a pipe by ignoring and dismissing all my fears, simply in order to get myself into that singular frame of mind that best serves this research. Before heading outdoors, I spoke to my family in order to secure fifteen minutes free from interruption. Before lying down, I strode over to a wheelie bin in order to inspect a rattrap I had primed yesterday, after my boys had reported seeing a very large mouse running around nearby. It was immediately evident the device had delivered death unto a rat. And it had done so with sufficient force as to upturn the trap. Such that I was now looking at the off-white underbelly of a deceased rodent. Four houseflies were busy buzzing around the dead rat. The first intake was long and slow and voluminous. I drew it down deeply and held it therein. The sound within the midst of my head was rising rapidly in pitch and intensity. The second pull was different – a pure white ball of clean dense vapour quickly found its way deep into my lungs. I made for a third pull but the pipe was empty. The sound in my head was now racing upwards at a truly terrific rate. I lay back. But before I had time to gather my thoughts, I realised I was in the midst of an interaction with a very powerful spiritual entity. A very highly defined image powerfully impressed upon my mind's eye. It was so fast and fleeting that I was unable to make out any detail. But it conveyed the character of the entity. This was undoubtedly an Occult Master. There was an overwhelming sense of stupendous high-mindedness, incredible wisdom and great power in abundance. My surroundings were now wrought in a unique and pristine crystal-clear clarity. To my left, I noted a perfectly straight and exceptionally thin vertical line within the crystal-clear medium. Its presence created a bizarre refraction and magnifying effect of the giant trampoline and the rear elevation of the house. I was so surprised to be in the midst of such a powerful entity, whilst laid within the back garden of a small suburban house, when my family were just a short distance away relaxing in the lounge. The stark reality of my situation beggared the entirety of my belief. I was simply too overawed to be scared. I felt I wanted to lick my lips and open my mouth. Upon doing so it was immediately evident the entity had invested a portion of itself throughout my oral physiology. Its unique psycho-spiritual substance was moving up my throat and around my mouth. It was all too obvious my mouth was about to be sealed up from within, by that very same impossibly thin and phenomenally strong substance. I was more in the clutches of this particular entity rather than the subject of its interaction. My nasal breathing was operating at a much faster rate. My chest was rising and falling with great rapidity. The entity was evidently present throughout my head, along a good portion of my spinal region, and deep inside my legs. It was doing something physical within my back and within my legs. Something physical but painless. The strange physicality of its operation was significant and unmistakable. I was greatly concerned about my welfare. A very silly thought arose in my mind. I considered this entity was preparing me in order to take me up into the sky. I genuinely sensed this was actually possible. My mouth was still sealed shut from within and my deep breathing clearly exhibited my emotional state. Whatever this entity was doing to me, it was taking a very long time over it. And whatever it was doing, it felt like it was of such great importance that it must be undertaken and completed without any hindrance whatsoever. Along the lower portion of my spine and throughout much of my legs, I could easily feel a very rapid and repetitive methodical activity; one that I can only really liken to some kind of rapid knitting action. As that action was taking place so very deeply within my physiology, I was very much averse to making any kind of effort to break free from the clutches of this entity. The crystal-clear atmosphere around me had imperceptibly vanished. A sizeable portion of the entity was now above me in a visibly very dense and transparent psycho-spiritual state. It was huge in comparison to my physical self. I knew beyond any doubt I was looking up at the huge mass of a discarnate mind. One that was still very much anchored within me, and undertaking something of apparently great importance; even though I knew not what that something was. I realised there was no point panicking. I told myself to put my trust in whatever was underway and remain calm while letting this entity complete whatever operation it was undertaking. I was surprised at just how quickly I became calm. I then became aware of a very soft massage upon the soles of my feet, or actually within my feet. I sensed my mouth was free to be opened. Slowly and surely the action ceased from my spinal region, and as it progressed down my legs the effect became fainter and fainter. The visibility of the psycho-spiritual mass also became fainter and fainter. Eventually, there was only the slightest hint of a strange swirling motion inside the heel of my right foot. And when that ended the psycho-spiritual mass above me had reached near perfect transparency. My emotional state was deadpan – very matter of fact. I simply lay motionless and looked skyward, whilst thinking about how thoroughly strange this experience had been, and going over and over the possibilities of what had just occurred. After a couple of minutes, I stood up and went over to take one more look at the dead rat. I felt completely sober. I headed indoors, whereupon I loudly announced that I had some very important news to share with the family. Three voices demanded to know what news I had to share with them, so I duly divulged, I had succeeded in killing the rat. My boys raced outside. They were hugely intrigued by the dead rodent. I turned the trap over. The spring-loaded hammer had cleanly sliced partway through the rat's head, in a diagonal fashion. Its right eye was bulging out of its socket. My boys thought that was darkly comical.

An account such as this surely has to be viewed suspiciously by anyone adhering to a belief system with foundations anchored in materialism. I readily admit that such an account not only sounds truly bizarre, but sounds wholly impossible; or simply the imagination of a madman, misrepresenting his own mind under the influence of a very powerful substance. A very powerful psychedelic substance; a hallucinogenic drug; something which creates illusory constructs that have no basis in reality other than within the mind of the one creating or perceiving those hallucinations. Yet anyone harbouring any doubt about the reality of discarnate intelligences would surely express the matter as a fact, after experiencing such an encounter as this. But I am not trying to convince doubters. I am merely researching and reporting on a principle of honesty, while learning a great deal about myself and giving credence to those occult philosophies that posit upon that which is unseen within us and without us.

Report: #52

Location: Rear Garden (~18:00hrs)

Dose: 25mg

Questioning Hygienic Etiquette

I had spent the afternoon tidying the shed. The garden was quiet and my research beckoned. But something was going through my mind. I was conscious I was not particularly clean. My supposedly white t-shirt told its own dirty tale. And that got me wondering whether there was any specific hygienic etiquette to be observed when putting oneself up for interaction with a powerful spiritual entity. Would my unwashed salty patina be anathema to their spiritual highness? Would my dusty trousers and the grime and muck discolouring my t-shirt rule out any such interaction? I considered showering and wearing clean fresh clothes for the explicit purpose of a hygienic approach to my research. But if such a supposition was correct, then I would fail to secure any otherworldly interaction from the experiment. And that cemented my commitment to going into this experiment unwashed. I lay down wearing my sunglasses to filter out brightness from the sky. A couple of workmen were busy working on a nearby roof and intermittently hammering. There would be several loud hammer bangs, followed by faintly audible and indecipherable voices between the two roofers. The noise from the hammer blows made me consider not pursuing the experiment. But I thought it would be interesting to at least test whether or not the sound pressure waves would prevent or even disturb any resulting entity interaction. After making three perfect inhalations I lay back and voiced aloud: "Right! Let's see what happens!" As I looked up there was a really very obvious psycho-spiritual presence that had manifested above the nearside canopy of the apple tree. It seemed evident and without question the entity had been awaiting me. And now it was emerging into fullness and moving over me as my interior psychic sound was reaching peak output. I was really taken aback that this thing had been lying in wait for me; waiting for this moment, waiting for this opportunity. For all I knew, this particular entity may have subliminally prompted me into undertaking this particular experiment. In what seemed like an instant the entity formed a large psycho-spiritual cocoon over me. This improbably dense and transparent cocoon appeared to have a smooth and possibly membranous outer surface. I knew this was an entity of significant power. No sooner had that sizeable cocoon formed over me, when the entity began sending wave after wave of energy throughout the encasing cocoon. I could feel each unique wave of energy penetrating right through me. Each succeeding wave was palpably very much more energetic than the preceding, and correspondingly far more readily permeating. I have experienced similar energies before. But this one really did feel to be the most powerful and the most significant I have ever experienced. Each powerful wave felt imbued with untold esoteric power and purpose; as though covertly carrying arcane occult secrets; holding the keys to a science I could not even begin to imagine. Given the circumstances, I was astonishingly calm. My nasal breathing was steady and rhythmic. Suddenly, the roofers began hammering noisily. Repeatedly striking nail-heads with force and ferocity. It was completely obvious this entity was not in the least bit troubled by those sound pressure waves. It was completely obvious this entity was not in the least bit interested in my state of dress or the extent of my personal hygiene. I puzzled as to how such an obvious and sizeable cocoon of psycho-spiritual energy was interacting with the branches of the apple tree. I did not turn my focus in that direction as I was concentrating on something else. There was some attempt at mental communication taking place. I was supposed to do something or understand something. But I simply could not grasp what it was. I was determined to stay calm. The indecipherable telepathy continued. I became aware of a very strange occurrence. Impossibly taught and invisible, ultra-fine quasi-physical strands that were strung between me and the inside of this psycho-spiritual cocoon began to snap through ever increasing tension. Although I did not suspect it at the time, I now believe this was evidence of the temporary psycho-spiritual bond between the occult entity and I coming to an end. Something must have emotionally overwhelmed me. Because for reasons unknown to me I suddenly sat bolt upright. In doing so, I received the strong emotional sense that something had just gone horribly wrong. I sensed my sitting up so suddenly had actually torn an extensive portion of the psycho-spiritual entity. And now I was sat up, I could see the full extent of this being. It was of absolutely stunning size. Its form resembled that of a vast psycho-spiritual snake, reaching upwards some considerable distance into the sky. Its diameter easily matched my six foot in height. Its presence was not vague or ambiguous. It was unmistakable and clearly observable. But something really did feel as though it had just gone terribly wrong in this interaction. I was certain a portion of the entity had become irreparably torn from its main body by virtue of me sitting up so suddenly. And now I knew that to be so, because I could feel a portion of the entity moving freely around inside me. I was frightfully worried. I looked up at the huge psycho-spiritual serpent-like form and silently made appeals for assistance. With as much mental effort as I could muster, I projected my insistence that these encounters just do not end this way. But regardless of my heartfelt appeals, it quickly became overwhelmingly apparent that this interaction really had gone well and truly, horribly and spectacularly, disastrously wrong. I was stuck with a portion of something occult inside me. Genuine woe and heartfelt sorrow engulfed me. I turned away by rolling onto my side and assuming the fetal position. I closed my eyes and let out a mournful wail of despondent despair. And it was only upon doing so with genuine heartfelt concern and deep pity that I suddenly realised I was been toyed with. I turned over to face the entity. My sudden realisation lit an emotional fuse within me. And as that fuse burned away, I smiled and vigorously shook my head in utter disbelief, whilst looking directly into the extensive psycho-spiritual mass. The full realisation of what just occurred suddenly hit me and my emotions exploded. I turned over and buried my face into the pillows while emitting an unbridled outburst of tears and laughter. I quickly turned to look once again at the great psycho-spiritual mass of the entity. It had accumulated its vastness over the entire garden and was spilling over into the neighbouring garden too. I was beside myself with uncommon emotion. I turned away from the entity once again and punched the ground hard and fast several times, whilst making unintelligible vocal sounds relevant to my state of mind. Upon turning to face the entity once again I gave smiles and nods of appreciation whilst signalling heartfelt applause.

There are definite occult mechanics to these strange interactions. But what the principles of those mechanics are I can really only suppose and guess at. It would seem these entities really are intelligent spiritual entities. They can manifest with such a dense and crystal-clear clarity of mind as to make the ordinary air appear impoverished in transparency. They can manifest as a strange psycho-spiritual substance exhibiting density beyond tangibility. And yet they can modify that psycho-spiritual substance into a density that, under certain circumstances, becomes paradoxically tactilely perceptible.

Report: #53

Location: Rear Garden (~18:30hrs)

Dose: 14mg

Guffawing Madman

I was seated at a picnic bench beneath the apple tree, facing the rear elevation of the house. The single intake of DMT vapour was faultless. I held it down for a good long while before exhaling. I decided to focus my attention on a portion of unkempt earth just ahead of me. My inner psychic sound was racing upwards rapidly in both pitch and intensity. For perhaps just a couple of seconds, my entire visual field became awash with what appeared to be milliards of impossibly minute transparent particles, all vibrating at a truly terrific rate. It was not indefinite – I could easily see and could see right through what appeared to be a very busy psycho-spiritually composed particulate medium. The inner sound within my head was still rising at a truly incredible rate. My visual field began vibrating very rapidly. Maintaining focussed concentration upon the ground ahead of me was now requiring very great mental effort. I realised I would not be able to hold a conversation with anyone except myself. My visual field was jarring at a tremendous rate. I was worried something was about to interact with me – an outcome I was not really setting myself up for in this particular experiment. The jarring soon settled down. The soil now appeared to swaying smoothly and significantly in a very obvious fluidic wavy motion. It was all surprisingly intense. But by far the most difficult aspect was maintaining an unwavering focussed concentration upon the soil ahead of me. The effort of concentration required was unbelievably significant. The mental effort in maintaining that focus was so great that I had not realised my mouth was hung agog and saliva was pooling in my mouth. The soil was still appearing to move with significant wave-like lateral motions. The soil also appeared darker and much more hypervivid in appearance. The effort required to maintain my focus simply became far too great, and I submitted to an outburst of laughter before questioning out loud: "What the fuck am I doing?" With two dilated eyes focussed dead ahead, and a mouth hung agog and full of salvia ready to overflow as drool, my sudden onset of laugher must've made me appear like a guffawing madman. My eyes focussed on an impossibly tiny little insect moving slowly on the outside of a plant pot. It appeared such a weak-bodied little creature, with such an insignificant existence. I could only wonder at its insect level of consciousness, whilst observing it with my human level of consciousness.

Report: #54

Location: Rear Garden (~10:30hrs)

Dose: 27mg

That Thing There

Taking great care to compensate for a slight breeze, I emptied the pipe before dropping sunglasses over my eyes and lying back and looking up. Without any hesitation whatsoever, something began to emerge from the empty air, about three arm's lengths above me. There could be no doubt, this entity had been lying in wait for me. It quickly became very apparent that what was emerging was like nothing else I had ever seen in any of my previous experiments. It was not so much its size – because its size was truly extraordinary – but it was the astonishingly beautiful geometric composition of its vast psycho-spiritual form. The outline shape of its form resembled a huge and spectacular multi-faceted diamond. The underside of the entity tapered down towards me and appeared composed of hundreds if not thousands of consistently sized, lozenge-shaped, overlapping cells. It was stunningly composed; a thing of extraordinary size and extraordinary beauty; complex yet simple; a vast entity embodying stupendous geometric principles throughout its beauteous form. It was so composed that despite its transparency, I never once attempted to see right through its mass, because the detail of its huge outer surface was simply so spectacular. Its psycho-spiritual surface exhibited a very faint iridescent spectral sheen. I knew from simply looking at the entity that this was going to be a very serious interaction. And I had no doubt this phenomenal entity really had been awaiting me. It rapidly descended upon me. I don't recollect it imposing any mesmerising power upon me, but it must have done something because as it completely engulfed me, it also sealed up the opening of my mouth from within. But with such tightness as to make my face feel exceptionally and forcefully gaunt. The inner flesh of my entire jaw was held stiff with stone-like rigidity. There could be no struggle against such an entity. The magnitude of otherworldly emotion being directed upon me was simply tremendous. The interaction felt pre-planned and purposeful. And this was just beginning. A portion of the entity quickly entered into me through the right underside of my torso and immediately began undertaking what felt like hugely significant and extensive work throughout that region. The significance of what was underway – painless though it was – seemed immense. I can only describe the operation as something like a very fast and widespread repetitive knitting action – undertaken in a region to the right side of my spine. It felt like a procedure of profound seriousness and great importance. All the while, I was looking up at the entity and through the entity. The bizarre invasive otherworldly operation continued apace. It was relatively painless. But my word – how gravely serious the situation! The emotional magnitude of the encounter was throwing up all kinds of strange possibilities in my mind. I was genuinely beginning to wonder whether I would remain a terrestrial citizen. As the intrusive operational procedure continued, I gave serious consideration to the possibility that I was being wired up, in order to be taken out into space, or into another dimension, whilst remaining safely ensconced within the midst of the stupendously-formed occult entity. I wondered what the entity would do if my wife came into the garden right now. My mouth was still firmly sealed up from within and there was a distinct resolute strength to the otherworldly grip imposing upon me. I then began to wonder whether the entity was also subliminally controlling my family, in order to prevent the likelihood of any of them coming outside and disturbing the situation. So strange and so serious was this procedure, that I could not shake the thought that I was being prepared to be taken away. And if that was really so, I wondered whether I would ever be returned back home. Would I ever see my family again? I also wondered whether this entity was wiring me up so that I could serve as some kind of terrestrial emissary, to the designs of its otherworldly intelligence. All such things as these, and more besides, were speeding through my mind. Part of me wanted to flee. But it was much too late for that. I really was well and truly in the thick of it. I consciously implored myself to increase my calmness and not give into panic. And more so, I implored myself to ensure I did not make any mistakes or failings with this interaction. A sense of achieving some indefinite purpose, and making sure I fulfilled that indefinite purpose, by avoiding the very real possibility of failure saturated my entire being. As that powerful emotion coursed unstoppably through me, I sensed previous failings – possibly in a similar scenario, or in a past life or past lives. I assured myself that this time I would get it right. I assured myself that this time I would fulfil my duty; no matter what that duty was. I sensed the being had vacated my mouth. I opened my mouth and whispered my gratitude. I psychically transmitted that I would verbally deal with any unwelcome disturbance from my family without moving my body. The strange operation was still ongoing. But it was now becoming slower and fainter. I realised I was not going to be taken away. I realised I was going to survive and would be able to report upon this phenomenal experience. Yet in arriving at that realisation, I felt like a permission had been granted to me. I remained still and calm, until I could no longer see any evidence of the entity. I thought for a short while upon what had just occurred, and then enjoyed a hugely invigorating stretch of my limbs. Just then, from the north, a brilliant white sphere with a halo slowly traversed the sky. Unthinkingly and instinctively, I pointed at it with my right hand and voiced out loud: "That thing there! That thing there! That thing there!" Then my left arm mirrored my right arm and with both hands pointing at the slowly moving radiant white sphere I continued, somewhat methodically: "That thing there! That thing there! I love that thing there!" I headed indoors. Without saying anything and without giving any emotional indication as to what had just occurred, I was very surprised to find my wife exhibited a heightened interest in what had just occurred outside. There are many occasions when she just does not ask; and just as many occasions when I do not volunteer. But on this occasion, the extent of her interest genuinely surprised me.

Report: #55

Location: Rear Garden (~19:30hrs)

Dose: 25mg

Occult Reality

The garden was peaceful. I challenged myself to make progress regardless of my frame of mind. By the time I lay down and exhaled the last pull there was an immediate manifestation of something some three or four arm's lengths above me. Straightaway it imposed a field of energy down upon me. That energy went through three very distinct and very rapid increases in frequency. At its conclusion I was left looking up through a crystal-clear medium of indeterminate size and shape. I noted how passing clouds appeared to quiver and shake. A pigeon flew low overhead – possibly passing straight through the strange crystal-clear medium. It too appeared to quiver momentarily, and produced a brief double image behind itself. A real-life argument between a neighbouring husband and wife ensued. It was not especially loud, but I could hear the male swearing in order to underline that which he was so forcibly expressing. Upon hearing that squabble, there was a discernible shift in focus from the entity. It seemed to direct its attention over towards the argument. There was also a vague visual hint confirming the entity's move in that direction. Soon thereafter, distinct movements began to manifest beneath my right shoulder and my left elbow. I knew this was the entity messing about with me. I psychically conveyed my resolve that I would not to be troubled by such antics. But the spooky movements increased and increased, and further increased, until it became so utterly ridiculous that such movements could actually manifest in this manner. I burst out laughing at the impossibility of the situation. As soon as I laughed the movements ceased. Above me, the crystal-clear entity rapidly vanished. I spent a few moments trying to gauge the extent of my own psycho-spiritual output. An unrecognisable female voice surfaced briefly within my head. She was talking about something mundane. The next voice was the firebrand politician and rousing orator, George Galloway.

Report: #56

Location: Rear Garden (~18:30hrs)

Dose: 15mg

Dangerously Introspective

I decided to smoke a 15mg dose beneath the apple tree whilst staring hard at the granular soil. I suspected my position beneath the branches of the apple tree, and using a relatively conservative dose, would preclude the likelihood of any discarnate intelligence manifesting and interacting with me. I wanted to concentrate solely upon the effects of the substance within me; without any outside interference, so to speak. I suspected looking upon the dark granular soil would provide an excellent background against which to view the outpouring of my own psycho-spiritual substance. I made two really good inhalations and then leant forward. The onset of the substance was very fast indeed. There were a series of very rapid changes evident within and around the periphery of my visual field. My intention was to report upon each and every nuanced little detail. But within seconds I simply gave up trying to fix the sequence of observations in my head. Focussing upon the ground immediately ahead of me was so thoroughly bizarre after the DMT had activated such a truly profound esoteric mechanism within me. In outline, there was a very short-lived appearance of countless and impossibly miniscule psycho-spiritual particles, appearing some two to three arm's lengths ahead of me. But then my visual field began jarring so very strongly that it was exceptionally difficult to maintain concentration and visual focus. There was the vague sense of an unseen presence above me, watching me. Looking down at the ground with such powerful occult energy surging through me felt so incredibly strange. Unsurprisingly, the ground appeared to be jarring in direct proportion to the rapid jarring affecting my visual field. After perhaps a minute, it appeared as though the tap that was dispensing that mysterious flowing energy was suddenly shut off. It was only now, as the ground appeared exactly as it had before the experiment began, that I could better appreciate how very different it had appeared when psycho-spiritual energy was surging from me. I was now in something of a mild trance-like state, whilst still looking down at the ground. My mind was stuck in an introspective loop. A static thought form then developed in my mind. But in actuality, it felt as though it had developed one arm's length over to the right-hand side of my head. It was a cartoonish image of someone on a

BMX. They were wearing colourful BMX race gear and a full-face black helmet. The rider was in the midst of a jump. The image was not of my making. Briefly, partially and peripherally, it was observed. That image caused me to rouse myself from the doleful introspection that was afflicting me. The entire experience reinforced my respect for the profound potency of DMT, even in doses one may consider manageable. Having broken out of that doleful introspective trance I immediately felt huge relief. I can suspect my introspection resulted from forcing myself to stare at the ground. It seemed so unnatural to be looking down at the ground with so much mysterious occult energy surging from my head. Willing myself to maintain that posture and focus surely contributed to putting me into that inward-looking frame of mind. However, that frame of mind seemed hugely exaggerated; to the extent my introspection felt dangerously introspective. Exaggeration of thought and emotion are occasionally characteristic when working with this potent substance.

Report: #57

Location: Rear Garden (~15:00hrs)

Dose: 24mg

Phantom Discourse

It began as a peaceful Sunday morning. The air was still. No noise, no nuisance, no disturbance. I took a short walk. Stillness and silence were in peaceful abundance. A small red car approached with its windows down and its music up. Heavy bass beats thumped through the stillness and silence. I inwardly cursed the driver as he stopped nearby and prepared to park up. A giant of a man exited the small red vehicle. He was very tall with a big round head, big arms and big legs. There was no way I could have physically tackled such a man. And that really wasn't on my mind. Instead, my mind pursued a fictitious interaction between us, which very quickly and unstoppably ran away with itself. I was soon taken aback at just how far my imagination had taken matters. I consciously put a stop to the unsavoury stream of consciousness. I began by imagining the giant of a man had stared at me. And I had duly stared back. He had then asked me what I was looking at. Upon hearing which, the following phantom discourse unfolded within my mind:

Giant Man [aggressively]: What you looking at?

Me [improbably calmly]: You are asking me what I am looking at?

Giant Man: Yeah!

Me: You've got eyes in your head! You're looking directly at me! You can see my eyes are looking directly at you! And yet you're asking me, what I am looking at? Are you fucking stupid?

But my phantom discourse had developed well beyond that point before I stepped in stop it and ask why my mind was engaging so ferociously and violently on a purely imagined scenario. I perished my thoughts. But what in our mind sparks and fuels such low-minded mentality with such propensity toward violent tendency? Is there an esoteric interpretation that can be considered? Could there be an unseen realm that permanently permeates our brain? Could there be an entire kingdom of varying conscious and intelligent hierarchies, some of whom have the capacity or even the desire to prey upon us, and impose upon in such a psychically subtle manner as to qualify as imposing a nefarious subliminal influence?

The following is taken from *The Great Secret,* published in 1922:

> To dismiss the question of infernal spirits: the faithful none the less believed in the existence and intervention of other invisible beings. They were convinced that the world which escapes our senses is far more densely peopled than that which we perceive, and that we are living in the midst of a host of diaphanous yet attentive and active presences, which as a rule affect us without our knowledge but which we can influence in our turn by a special training of the will. These invisible beings were not inhabitants of hell, since for the initiates of the middle ages, almost as certainly for the believers in the great religions in the days when initiation was not yet necessary, hell was not a place of torture and malediction but a state of the soul after death. They were either wandering, disembodied spirits, worth very much what they had been worth during their life on earth, or they were spirits of beings who had not as yet been incarnated. These were known as elementals; they were neutral spirits, indifferent, morally amorphous, devoid of will, doing good or evil according the will of him who had learned to rule them.
>
> [From: <u>The Great Secret</u> (1922) by Maurice Maeterlinck. Page 182]

According to *The Spirits' Book* the classification of spirits is based upon the degree of their advancement, upon the qualities which they have acquired, and upon the imperfections from which they still have to free themselves:

> Another thing that should never be lost sight of is the fact that there are among spirits, as well as among men, some who are very ignorant, and that we cannot be too much on our guard against a tendency to believe that all spirits know everything simply because they are spirits. The work of classification demands method, analysis and a thorough knowledge of the subject investigated.
>
> [From: The Spirits' Book (1996 edition) by Allen Kardec. Page 97]

Writing about *Tenth Class (Impure Spirits)* as part of the wider spiritual categorisation found within that work:

> They are inclined to evil, and make it the object of all their thoughts and activities. As spirits, they give men perfidious counsels, stir up discord and distrust, and assume every sort of mask in order the more effectually to deceive. They beset those whose character is weak enough to lead them to yield to their suggestions, and whom they thus draw aside from the path of progress, rejoicing when they are to retard their advancement by causing them to succumb under the appointed trials of corporeal life. Spirits of this class may be recognized by their language, for the employment of course or trivial expressions by spirits, as by men, is always an indication of moral, if not of intellectual, inferiority. Their communications show the baseness of their inclinations; and though they may try to impose upon us by speaking with an appearance of reason and propriety, they are unable to keep up that false appearance, and end up by betraying their real quality.
>
> [From: The Spirits' Book (1996 edition) by Allen Kardec. Page 97]

After smoking and reclining, I found the frequency and intensity of energy imposing upon me was feeble. There could be no significant interaction. Although it seemed the entity was doing its very best to prove me wrong. A slight but persistent movement began beneath the blanket by my right hand. An amorphous cellular mass was slowly rising skywards away from me. The slight movement near my right hand persisted. I purposefully ignored it and intended to remain ignoring it. But very shortly after holding that thought, a very thin and very physical finger-like form prodded sharply into the side of my hand. My reflexes made me respond like lightning. I sat bolt upright and lifted the blanket, despite knowing I would find nothing. A warm fuzzy feeling surged through me.

Report: #58

Location: Rear Garden (~08:45hrs)

Dose: 20mg

Jaggedly Cellular

The onset of energy from the discarnate entity above me was so immediate I suspected it had been observing me as I prepared myself for this experiment. Its energy was significant and created a jarring underwater-like atmosphere. The longevity of its energetic imposition made realise there could be no significant interaction between us. But because of the unusual longevity of the imposing energy I began to feel spooked. I purposefully shifted my visual focus. But the energy persisted. The energy suddenly became more intense and exhibited a very pronounced visual jaggedness. I was quite certain the entity was attempting to impose its presence within my mouth. That spooked me terribly and I sat halfway up before resting back down and voicing my surprise. The sky was completely overcast. Just then, at a terrific height, a little black orb came into view, apparently from nowhere. I noted it was joined by another small black orb of equal size. They moved about one another very smoothly, circling each other quite closely before disappearing.

Report: #59

Location: Rear Garden (~13:15hrs)

Dose: 27mg

The Most Significant Sandbox

I sat up and made one very long inhalation which completely emptied the pipe. In a matter of seconds my cranial inner sound increased hugely in both pitch and intensity. And it continued, and continued, and continued. It reached such an unprecedented level that I genuinely believed an occult entity had anchored itself in the midst of my head, and was now imposing its own spiritual might with complete abandon. My surroundings had taken on a remarkable crystal-clear clarity. My mouth was closed and my teeth were clamped tightly together. I felt obliged to open my mouth. Upon doing so I found my teeth were momentarily stuck together with what felt like an exceptionally thin and paradoxically dry, gummy film. Having prized my teeth apart I had to make the same effort in unsealing my lips from that same incredibly thin, gummy dry substance. I now sensed a powerful presence of the entity just a few arm's lengths above me. All I could discern visually was a crystal-clear transparency surrounding me. Yet I could somehow sense and even palpably feel the power of the entity; to such extent that my subconscious survival instincts caused my breathing to significantly quicken. I sensed I was been analysed by something not in the business of dealing in foolishness and nonsense. I knew the passing seconds would rule out any really significant interaction between us. There was a sudden change. I was able to observe as well as tangibly perceive the departure of the discarnate intelligence.

There was one really significant aspect of this experience that resulted in long-forgotten childhood memories to flood my conscious mind. But to firstly reiterate my assumption: inhaling DMT in the vaporous causes a significant oscillatory arousal of the pineal gland, which somehow results in the rapid expansive emergence of an otherwise occult (hidden) psycho-spiritual medium from that general region. It is reasonable to suppose the rapid expansive projection of that strange psycho-spiritual medium transmits through one's oral physiology. It is the passage of that uncommon medium through one's mouth that I suspect resulted in the exceedingly thin and dry gummy film to form between my clenched teeth and my closed lips. Upon exerting sufficient force to prize open my mouth – and feeling the tacky nature of that unusual sealant – I immediately recalled experiencing that very same oral experience many times over as a very small boy upon awakening from sleep. It was an experience I had completely forgotten about, until today. As a young child, something had frequently imposed a slight but definite resistance to me parting my clamped teeth and my closed lips upon awakening. With just a little effort, that gummy presence was easily overcome. But nothing remained to evidence the presence of that substance, except perhaps a dryness of mouth and lips. Why as a very young child had I experienced the very same effect that I experienced today, after smoking DMT? The obvious answer has to be because my pineal gland was far more active as a young child. On my esoteric reasoning, the natural action of that young gland whilst I was asleep, would be as a locus for the outward manifestation of that same invisible psycho-spiritual medium. Having volunteered as much, I feel obliged to remind myself that the stranger all of this sounds, the more sense it actually makes to me.

Report: #60

Location: Rear Garden (~08:45hrs)

Dose: 25mg

Ultraterrestrial Agents of Cultural Deconstruction

I had been reading the phenomenally titled: *Cyber-biological Studies of the Imaginal Component in the UFO Contact Experience.* In particular, I was reading Carl Raschke' contribution: *UFOs: Ultraterrestrial Agents of Cultural Deconstruction.* It was fascinating:

> Here then I shall advance a tentative assessment on what UFO's are in point of fact, without straying into the controversy surrounding whether or not they are "interplanetary" conveyances. Our interest in them should center on how the spreading and deepening convictions about them subtly, yet irreversibly, remolds not just perhipheral religious or metaphysical ideas, but entire constellations of culture and social knowledge. In this connection, UFOs can be depicted as what I would call *ultraterrestrial agents of cultural deconstruction.*
>
> [From: Cyber-biological Studies of the Imaginal Component in the UFO Contact Experience (1989) edited by Dennis Stillings]

I sat up and expertly executed three inhalations. Upon lying back, I noted a flat psycho-spiritual plane approximately two arm's length above me, appearing composed of rounded-edged transparent cells. No sooner had I made that observation when it became all too evident that an energetic discarnate presence was emerging. It appeared to fill out those psycho-spiritual cells; giving them depth and quickly occupying the volume of air above me. I could somehow palpably perceive the power of the entity. Something high in the sky then suddenly caught my eye. A high-altitude jet aeroplane was trailing two very thin and perfectly straight white contrails in the cloudless blue sky. The two contrails appeared to very rapidly replicate themselves to the left of the original contrails. I could not help but divert my attention away from the discarnate entity to observe this strange visual effect. It was occurring with such extraordinary lightning-like speed; with extreme suddenness, an exact copy of the contrails moved from the original position before suddenly snapping back into the original position. As I maintained my observation, I heard a helicopter approach. Moments later I observed the familiar livery of a Police helicopter. The discarnate entity above me had now become far more visually evident as an amorphous psycho-spiritual mass – appearing both simple yet complex. A magpie began cackling nearby. I imagined it was complaining about the noisy helicopter. I focussed my eyes upon the psycho-spiritual mass. A very slight tickling sensation was perceived upon the skin of my left temple. This slowly changed into a light tapping sensation in the same region. Those effects persisted and changed between tickling and tapping. I remained emotionless. A low flying biplane flew into view. The magpie continued giving out verbals. A very distinct point source of light then suddenly appeared from nowhere. It was fingertip in size and some three arm's lengths above me. I initially suspected it to be an airborne dandelion head. But as it moved smoothly around, I could see the light had a very distinct halo around it. My eyes were totally transfixed upon the tiny orb of light. It moved around so slowly and serenely. Immediately I computed the light source was a magical machination of the wider discarnate entity that I could now no longer see. And as soon as I made that connection my emotions became highly aroused. I was now like a little child excitedly awakening on Christmas morning. My voice was full of delight and surprise, as I gushed several times in rapid succession: "It's a thing! It's a thing! It's a thing!" And indeed, it was a thing! It was a spherical and radiant little thing, and it was moving smoothly around above me. It then began to slowly make its way towards the neighbouring boundary fence. With great desire and heartfelt sincerity, I repeated my pleas: "Fetch it back! Fetch it back! Fetch it back!" And just before it disappeared out of sight it changed direction and headed back over me. I was uproarious with excitement – hardly able to believe what I was seeing. I watched it intently and with great care. I was mesmerised. And then, it suddenly blinked out right before my eyes and was gone. But my emotions were still rising. I became dewy eyed and gushed forth my softly spoken verbal gratitude – all directed toward that which I could no longer see, but which I suspected could still see me.

Report: #61

Location: Rear Garden (~17:30hrs)

Dose: 32mg

What the Pigeon Saw

After emptying the pipe, I lay back and looked up into the pale blue sky. The ringing sound within my head was rapidly rising. I thought to myself: How utterly extraordinary that something intelligent and unseen manifests so very rapidly and so very obviously during these experiments! I had barely completed that thought when something above me began to emerge out of thin air. The sheer speed of its emergence convinced me this particular entity had been invisibly watching me; waiting for me to commit to the potent substance within the pipe. The outer composition of the entity was simply stupendous: perfectly symmetrical lozenge-shaped geometric cells overlapped to form something resembling a ginormous bulbous disk flower. Its size was astounding. Its stunning beauty instinctively assured me that no harm whatsoever would come to me. This was only mere seconds into the experiment. The occult entity began imposing its stupendous power upon me and right through me in a stepped phase sequence. The sudden impact of otherworldly energy upon the ground around me was easily audible. The highly energetic power behind that impact was easily perceptible upon me, within me, and around me. Each phased increase in power was similarly tactilely perceptible. But to such an extent as to utterly defy and defeat the conditioned rational logic of my western-minded mentality. The rapid display of phased spiritual power was the stuff of speechlessness. As the entity continued imposing its raw yet refined power, I observed that I appeared to be in something of a large bell-jar-shaped environment – formed of that very same incredible psycho-spiritual energy. As the phenomenal display of power ceased it was so obvious that I was within the midst of an incredibly sized and beautifully configured, occult being. A pigeon flying over the roof of the house and towards us must have encountered some problem of ocular perceptive when approaching the entity, because it suddenly braked hard with furious flapping wings and banked sharply in order to avoid flying through the entity. I could feel a portion of the entity invested throughout my mouth my throat and my neck. My lips were sealed tightly shut from within. I felt it was best not to test the integrity of that otherworldly seal. I sensed the entity was planning something. I also sensed it was invested throughout my entire body. A male and female neighbour several houses away began shouting and laughing in a rough and raucous fashion. It had no bearing at all on the entity's interaction with me. Their noise continued. The juxtaposition between their rowdy vocals and that which I was presently engaged in was worlds apart. The very obvious size and power of this entity made me suspect it more than had the capacity to lift me aloft and whisk me away. And yet despite the utter extraordinariness of this profoundly immersive interaction, my mood and my breathing and my heart rate all felt normal. I was calm and dispassionate. The entity suddenly rose up several arm's lengths into the sky. I sensed it was about to begin disengaging from me. And I also sensed its departure had something to do with the limitation of space afforded by the garden. I sincerely wished to be in the middle of a large private garden with this entity. Just so I could better appreciate the full extent of its interactive capabilities. I had quite literally been inside the body-of-the-mind of the entity. And a portion of that entity had quite literally been inside me. It began the slow process of withdrawing from me. Here, I noted something amazing and unexpected. Very smoothly – and without any doubt whatsoever – I was been very slowly lowered by a very short distance back down to the ground. I was hitherto completely unaware that I had even been elevated. As I was smoothly lowered back down – by near imperceptible degrees – there was never any tangible perception of my back re-cushioning itself into the soft ground. And at the conclusion of that bizarre descent, there was a slightly perceptible feeling of something sliding out from beneath my back, but without even the slightest hint of any resistance or friction. The entity commenced withdrawing itself from my physiology in a very slow and very subtle process that felt like some kind of bizarre unknitting process. I sensed it had vacated my mouth and confirmed that. A chattering of starlings suddenly descended upon the apple tree and began a noisy feeding frenzy. The psycho-spiritual mass of the entity was become increasingly transparent. The last portion of its withdrawal was through my shins and the soles of my feet. I stretched out my limbs and felt better for it. The starlings continued making a rare old racket in the apple tree. I clapped my hands together loudly in order to startle them. They ignored me, and so I ignored them.

Report: #62

Location: Rear Garden (~17:45hrs)

Dose: 24mg

Subjectively Heavenly

Beneath a warm and bright blue sky, I exhaled the dose and lay back whilst observing the beautiful sight of my own psycho-spiritual substance overarching me. It momentarily displayed a familiar yet peculiar geometric cellular composition, before rapidly expanding upwards and outwards. Three nearby evergreen trees were busy with starlings noisily chattering amongst themselves. A repetitive and mellifluous song from an unknown bird and the regular sweet chirping from another unknown bird filled the air. Between them, they created a heavenly and hypnotic harmonious chorus of sweet-sounding song. A breeze stirred and rustled the broad canopies of the three mighty oaks, visible over the roofline. For five beautiful minutes a hypnotic avian chorus filled the air that my mind had visibly manifested into. I beseeched myself to fix this subjectively heavenly moment deep within my memory.

Report: #63

Location: Rear Garden (~14:15hrs)

Dose: 27mg

Enlightened Evolution

I lay back and awaited the onset from the substance. But there was hardly any effect, except for an unremarkable increase in the pitch of my cranial interior sound. The numerous windblown clouds were heavily adorned with geometric patterning. It seemed puzzling that the substance could be so obviously active and yet apparently so inactive at the same time. I returned the pipe to my lips. A meagre volume of vapour was duly vacuumed down. I refused to release it until my lungs were desperate for air. Upon exhaling, the entire sky and all the white clouds therein gave every indication of being rendered impossibly unreal. Everything above me felt impossibly dense. Everything appeared foamy. Even the air. Several very obvious four-spoked transparent configurations rotated above me. But only briefly – as though to underline the impossibility of that which already looked so utterly impossible. Concurrent with that bizarre visual effect, a loud and unusual repetitive bird call emanated from somewhere behind me. I held a vague suspicion it was an audible hallucination. For some unknown reason, my mind interpreted the unusual bird call as an invitation to stand up and walk around. But I was so overwhelmed at how abruptly such a small volume of vapour had changed the entire experience that I dared not move. The sky looked so very different. And yet imperceptibly, in just a few short moments, it changed back to having its ordinary appearance.

I can suppose that a high-minded spiritual entity rapidly enveloped me within the volume of its mind and then configured that body-of-mind in such a way as to create the bizarre visual appearance and tactile perception. From within that same spiritual entity, and borne of its own imaginative intelligence, it briefly produced several four-spoked rotating transparent forms; an audible avian hallucination; and an unheeded subliminal prompt for me to stand up.

Report: #64

Location: Rear Garden (~09:00hrs)

Dose: 29mg

Broadband Energy

A small bird was in full song somewhere upon the apple tree. I considered how improbable it seems that something discarnate and intelligent emerges out of thin air and interacts with those using DMT. As I emptied the pipe, I considered once again, how utterly improbable that something living should suddenly emerge from nowhere. Without any warning whatsoever, a very broad band of very strong and heavy transparent energy imposed down across my chest and arms. The bird in the tree stopped singing. The band of energy was perceptible as a perfectly rectangular shaft of energy. I could feel it transmitting down upon me and I could even perceive the angle of its descent. Its heightened clarity of transparency also confirmed its extent and its shape. The band of energy across my chest and arms was really very strong but not quite sufficient to physically pin me down. An unseen portion of the entity then entered into my abdomen. Its movement therein caused me to squirm and giggle and stifle a shriek. In a childlike fashion, I appealed out loud: "Please don't go in there again!" But it did go in there again. Causing me to squirm and giggle and shriek once again. Whilst that was underway, something visually very spectacular but very short-lived kept catching the right side of my visual field. Initially, I suspected it was a mild aberration of eyesight. But then I began to catch sight of what can best described as simulated forked lightning. It was rendered in an absolutely incredible sapphire blue. The speed of this stunning manifestation was completely on par with the magnificent forked lightning of terrestrial nature. At first, I thought the incredible visual effect was taking place on the surface of my cornea. But it was actually occurring in the midst of the air, midway between my position and the nearest branches of the apple tree. Its prevalence appeared to increase after I noticed the effect. I was also trying to maintain my focus above me, in anticipation of what the discarnate intelligence would do next. To my left side, a discernible movement manifested beneath the blanket. It felt like something very thin and very flat was moving toward me. A similar movement occurred by my left hand. It was joyously spooky as I began to wonder whether something was going to touch or grab my left hand. But instead, a very subtle massaging motion began moving up and down the entire underside of my left arm. As that was taking place, I noticed the sapphire blue forked lightning was appearing to discharge randomly along the lengths of the outermost branches of the apple tree. The forking discharges actually appeared to be following the shape of the branches. Watching that amazing effect whilst feeling the soothing massage beneath my left arm had a terrifically relaxing effect upon me. In no time at all I was feeling exquisitely tranquil.

Report: #65

Location: Rear Garden (~11:30hrs)

Dose: 25mg

Under the Weather

Some experiments present an experience so utterly impossible that the thought of reporting upon it produces literary discomfort. This experience was one of those. I prepared the pipe just as the sunny weather turned dull and threatened rain. I kissed my wife before she left the house. She assured me of rain. I stepped outside the kitchen door just as heavy drops of rain began smattering the patio. I headed over to the shed. On something of a whim, I decided to sit upon a plastic garden chair just outside the shed door and conduct my experiment from there. Without much aforethought I inhaled one good pull and held it down. But as I exhaled, it occurred to me that I did not like the dullness of the sky, or my sedentary position. But I also knew it was too late to change my mind. Mere seconds later, there was a very significant increase in the intensity of my inner sound. The sky began to flicker with repetitive horizontal lines – like observing a lower frequency VDU screen on a higher frequency TV. I was unhappy with myself for not properly thinking through my commitment to the experiment. I thought about getting up and lying on the grass, but decided against the idea. I implored myself to sit tight and not panic. Remembering the pipe still had some DMT remaining, I stood up and went to seat myself on the wet grass in the midst of the garden. From there I made one very big and very pleasing inhalation. I lay back, looked up, and exhaled; whereupon I immediately observed a psycho-spiritual entity of such humungous size that I could really only describe it as colossal. Appearing as an incredibly dense billowing cellular mass, it seemed to fill the entire portion of grey sky above me. It certainly spanned the entirety of the garden. A great central portion of its underside tapered down towards me in a somewhat ominous fashion. I spluttered out a heartfelt, "Oh my God!" A pigeon flew right through the transparent psycho-spiritual mass, leaving an improbably long tracer trail behind its wake. A swallow flew right through the same mass at a greater height and also left a long tracer trail. I hoped the entity understood what was catching my attention as a number of other swallows at even greater height flew through the same psycho-spiritual mass and produced distinct tracer trails behind them. Too many seconds had elapsed for there to be any really significant interaction between us. But the sheer size of the thing was so hugely imposing that I had to suspect anything could happen. Something did happen. Something I simply could not explain. Since lying down and looking up, the rain-filled cloud above me appeared to have descended impossibly close to me. But it was only as that same rain-filled cloud appeared to rise slowly up into the sky that I could appreciate just how improbably close it had appeared. As I watched the cloud appearing to rise back to its original altitude, I was aghast at what I was seeing. I was observing something so utterly impossible whilst in a completely lucid frame of mind. I cried out with complete incredulity: "No! No! No!" But there it was. Or so it had appeared. The dull raincloud had somehow been pulled down to an astonishingly low level, before rising back and resuming its original position. I agonised about the impossibility of such an occurrence. I shook my head in great perplexity at the experience. Clouds in the sky simply do reach down to humans on the ground. It then struck me that the configuration of the body of that colossal transparent entity could have created such a magnificent illusory or optical effect. It seemed so obvious. I felt hugely triumphant that I had understood the trickery of the entity. I duly expressed my satisfaction by pointing up to the cloud and stating as much. No sooner had I done that when the cloud suddenly burst and heavy rain began falling. I was now in really high spirits. So high that I lay down and assumed a spreadeagle position. Then, as if by some irrational meteorological magic, the rain suddenly became incredibly heavy and fast. Within seconds I was drenched. My hands repeatedly washed my rain-soaked face and massaged my wet scalp. Not for a very long time had I felt so alive or so truly human; a product of the earth, and a product of the other.

Report: #66

Location: Rear Garden (~02:30hrs)

Dose: 15mg

Superlunacy

My work pattern gave me the opportunity to witness a supermoon and a lunar eclipse from the comfort of the rear garden. The sky was as clear as the air was still and silent. Earth's shadow was already imposing itself over the silvery reflecting surface of the moon. Two inhalations emptied the pipe and after just a couple of seconds there was a sharp rise in the intensity of my spiritual tinnitus. An unfolding kaleidoscopic tunnel-like pattern arose within my mind's eye and gave me the impression that I was moving swiftly through it. I braced myself in anticipation of a higher energy from without, even though I was not really pursuing any interaction in this experiment. I maintained closed eyes for approximately half a minute then opened them and looked directly at the moon. I had to blink a couple of times in order to adjust my sight. The supermoon was approximately 30% partially eclipsed. I believed my eyes were working through my own psycho-spiritual substance that had emanated from me as a result of the DMT. A distant alarm began sounding. I imagined how disturbing that would be for the neighbours. I craned my head back to look up at the stars. A small low passing cloud appeared ghostly and made my insides momentarily shudder with fright. An apple fell from the tree and onto the stone patio but the acuity of my hearing was so sharp as to hear the initial severance of the fruit from the branch. A near neighbours toilet was heard flushing and a moment later my immediate neighbours toilet was flushed. I looked up at the stars and wondered how I would feel if a large black triangle UFO silently passed low overhead and blotted out all the stars. Eventually, totality arrived. The moon appeared much redder than I had expected. It was strange and beautiful. The distant alarm stopped. Another apple divorced itself from the tree before audibly bruising itself upon a flagstone. The moon appeared as singular red eye in the sky.

Blavatsky's *The Secret Doctrine* contains a great many esoteric and occult references to the lunar body; including the earth being the child of the moon; and a strange transfer of life principles from the moon to the earth, which suggests a very central root in our occult ancestry. The following excerpts are taken from Volume I – *Cosmogenesis*:

The moon is *dead* only so far as regards her *inner* "principles" – i.e. *psychically* and *spiritually*, however absurd that statement may seem. Physically, she is only as a semi-paralysed body may seem. She is aptly referred to in Occultism as the "insane mother," the great sidereal *lunatic*.

[From: The Secret Doctrine Volume I (1888) by H. P. Blavatsky. Page 149]

The moon is now the cold residual quantity, the shadow dragged after the new body, into which her living powers and "principles" are transfused. She is now doomed for long ages to be ever pursuing the Earth, to be attracted by and to attract her progeny. Constantly *vampirised* by her child, she revenges herself on it by soaking it through and through with the nefarious, invisible and poisoned influence which emanates from the occult side of her nature. For she is a *dead* yet *living* body.

[Ibid.156]

"The real Sun and the real Moon are as invisible as the real man," says an occult maxim.

[Ibid.179]

In reality the Moon is only the satellite of the Earth in one respect, viz., that physically the Moon revolves around the Earth. But in every other respect it is the Earth which is the satellite of the Moon, and not *vice versa*. Startling as the statement may seem it is not without confirmation from scientific knowledge. It is evidenced by the tides, by the cyclic changes in many forms of disease which coincide with the lunar phases; it can be traced in the growth of plants, and is very marked in the phenomena of human gestation and conception. The importance of the Moon and its influence on Earth were recognized in every ancient religion, notably the Jewish, and have been remarked by many observers of psychical and physical phenomena. But, so far as Science knows, the Earth's action on the Moon is confined to the physical attraction, which causes her to circle in her orbit. And should an objector insist that this fact alone is sufficient evidence that the Moon is Truly the Earth's satellite on other planes of action, one may reply by asking whether a mother, who walks round and round her child's cradle keeping watch over the infant, is the subordinate of her child or dependent upon it; though in one sense she is its satellite, yet she is certainly older and more fully developed than the child she watches.

It is, then, the Moon that plays the largest and most important part, as well as in the formation of the Earth itself, as in the peopling thereof with human beings.

[Ibid.180]

Report: #67

Location: Rear Garden (~02:30hrs)

Dose: 15mg

Stiller Lunar

The moon was exceptionally bright in its Waning Gibbous phase. I sat upon the same chair and in the same position as yesterday. But tonight, felt very different. A blanket of air sat motionless over the estate. There were no extraneous noises whatsoever. The very night felt like it was holding its breath. Every minor movement I made was ripe with potential to disturb the otherwise pristine silence. The brightness of the moon was exceptional. A faint mist gave the appearance of a broad and radiant silvery halo around the lunar circumference. I sat for a few seconds to appreciate the extraordinary silence. Using heat from the whooshing blue flame I emptied the pipe. I decided against closing my eyes and decided to stare hard directly into the face of the moon. I eventually exhaled and stared hard and unblinkingly directly into the face of the bright moon. My high-pitched spiritual tinnitus rapidly rose in intensity. And as it did so, I was able to palpably perceive an expanding sphere of psycho-spiritual energy, rapidly projecting outwards from the core of my being. Immediately upon sensing that uncommon occurrence, the broad silvery halo around the moon appeared to increase notably in both size and brightness. Staring hard and unblinkingly into the bright silver moon, with such an audible increase of psychic energy in the midst of my head, felt like pure preternatural folly. After a minute or two I closed my eyes. No interior visuals were evident at all – making me suspect the DMT was highly active but very far from full potency. I was staring so hard into the face of the moon that it felt as though the moon was staring back at me with equal oomph. I began to wonder: was I absorbing any beneficent or maleficent occult influences whilst fixing my eyeballs so firmly upon the bright lunar orb? My eyes soon tired and I adopted a more relaxed repose. I distinctly felt something discarnate was watching me. The thought did not scare me. I cocked my head back and looked up at the stars. Upon seeing them I thought the silliest thing. I thought they all appeared so very much closer than they did yesterday. I looked back at the moon and realised how totally absurd the thought was. Yet when I looked up once again, it really did seem those pinpricks of light were somehow so very much closer than they were yesterday. I began to imagine how I would react if an illusory figure suddenly appeared from nowhere. The thought frightened me and delighted me in equal measure. Part of me that felt giddy at the thought of something startling and outlandish occurring. The reflective brightness of the moon was simply astonishing. It made the night look more like daylight at half volume.

Report: #68

Location: Rear Garden (~16:00hrs)

Dose: 24mg

Handbag

A freshly filtered and air-dried crystal precipitate of dimethyltryptamine gave a very pleasing plasticky aroma – indicative of high potency. It was evident the smoked substance was causing a very energetic reaction in the midst of my head. I lay down and looked up. Straightway something discarnate imposed its constitutional spiritual strength down upon me with sufficient force as to make its impact and ongoing pressure upon the ground around me both perceptible and audible. I could easily feel its force. Its energy felt like an intense scrutinising ocular gaze. I began breathing quickly. But to my own shameful dismay, I knew I was merely trying to convey fear, rather than actually feeling fear. I psychically projected that my literary pursuits were in respect of these interdimensional occult engagements. And upon doing so the entity changed into an altogether more visually observable psycho-spiritual form. A portion of the entity moved down towards my face whilst intense energy was still imposing down upon me and around me. The entity began streaming into my face. As it was doing so, I could make out the sizeable extent of its psycho-spiritual mass. I wondered what it was doing as it continued to stream into me. Its movement through my physiology caused an audible reaction around my left eardrum. The entity was streaming down into my head and into my torso and was moving around therein with complete freedom. All the while, the psycho-spiritual mass above me was becoming less and less extensive. Its obvious movement inside my torso continued for approximately two minutes. I wondered if it was perhaps checking out my physical health, or refreshing itself with knowledge of the human digestive system. Its movements were so very obvious; it was rummaging around inside me as though I were a lady's handbag and it was trying to locate something difficult to find.

Report: #69

Location: Rear Garden (~11:45hrs)

Dose: 37mg

Complex Polytope in Aspic

I headed into the garden to pick up all the fallen apples. One hundred and one apples filled a rickety toy wheelbarrow. My belly was full of nerves as I sat up and began the first of three excellent inhalations. During the second pull I could feel the highly energetic onset of the substance inside my head. And whilst making the third pull it was evident the substance was highly active within me. I lay back and looked up. A cellular psycho-spiritual presence was easily observable some three arm's lengths above me. No sooner had I made that observation when somehow – apparently from nowhere and in a manner that I am unable to detail – an entity of immense size and beauty emerged above me. The complexity of the geometry characterising the massive discarnate mind was simply flabbergasting. Here was an occult being of truly stunning beauty. Instinct alone informed me its constitutional power was not only beyond my comprehension – it really was none of my business. Something large and powerful had deigned to respond to my tiny little psychic signal. And conversely, something small and mortal was wonderstruck in looking up at something beyond imagining. The constitutional and evolutionary disparity between the two of us was as stark as it possibly could be. A temporary dimethyltryptamine-induced spike in my psychic output had evoked the emergence of a great big discarnate mind. A great big portion of its beautifully simple and geometrically complex form tapered down in close proximity to my face. It was appallingly evident from its sheer size and compositional density that this discarnate mind could impose upon me in ways I simply could not even begin to imagine. I was breathing deeply and with great apprehension whilst taking in as much of the stunning detail as I possibly could. Realising the great chasm of difference between us, I looked directly up at the great entity and outstretched my arms into a cruciform shrug. It was so utterly obvious I was facing something very much more advanced than my physical human condition. And this thing knew full well what I was thinking. And it knew full well that my assumptions were well founded. Hence, I laughed – nervously. And laughter seemed to be the perfect reaction. Because my emotional senses told me the entity enjoyed my response. It appeared that I was laughing alone but it certainly did not feel that way. But beneath the laughter, I knew this was a very serious business. The entity moved down much closer to my face. Within seconds it was streaming through me. And as it was doing so, the geometric complexity of the entity slowly changed into a more amorphous psycho-spiritual mass. It was something like a spiritual wind visibly streaming into me. In just a matter of moments it had gone. Something that was so visibly substantial mere moments ago was now no longer visible at all. I heard a scratching sound from the larchlap fence immediately behind me. I craned my head back and observed a magpie wiping its beak before flying over to the nearest branches of the apple tree. It seemed unconcerned at my presence. Another magpie suddenly flew into the tree. It seemed such an odd occurrence at that very moment. I suspected their business related to courtship or territory. The passage of a third magpie caused the two birds to take to the air in hot pursuit.

I have spent some considerable time trying to work out how best to describe the stupendous form of the impressive occult being. My best effort is to say that it took the form of a very large and bulbous, complex polytope. Its geometry was stunning and perfectly symmetrical. It appeared partially see-through and had an almost physical substantiality; as though the entire entity was formed from translucent aspic jelly. Yet it was a substance that would offer no resistance, viscosity or wetting to the touch. It was one that would, in all likelihood, cause a baffling and bizarre visual refraction should one choose to plunge one's hands into its otherworldly superdense psycho-spiritual body-of-mind.

Report: #70

Location: Bedroom (~10:15hrs)

Dose: 20mg

Shadowy Pom-Poms

The wind was far too imposing for outdoor research. It was time to expand a great volume of my psycho-spiritual substance within the confines of the bedroom. After the third and final pull I lay back. The bedroom appeared so very different to how it had appeared mere seconds ago. Nothing had changed. And yet it all looked so abruptly different. My wonderment was disturbed when the entire bedroom began physically jarring back and forth. I could feel and hear the vibrations borne of the structural movement. This was not what I wanted. My wife was sat downstairs in the lounge, immediately below the bedroom. I was certain she would perceive this movement. I wondered if the entity was doing this purposefully. As a means of providing third party proof of its otherworldly power. There had been none of the usual turbulent energy evident. The room had appeared paradoxically normal and yet so very different. And now the room was audibly and visibly shaking. I knew I was in a DMT experience, but I was puzzling as to why there had been no highly energetic initial phase. And I was totally perplexed at how the bedroom now appeared so imperceptibly at odds with how it had appeared before the experiment began. I was in the midst of an experience that was bamboozling me. And as that feeling grew, I suddenly succumbed to an outburst of belly-borne laughter. Once upon a time those entities would literally squeeze the laughter from me by manipulating my psyche. But today, the manifested entity simply provided the conditions for laughter by its mere presence. I was flooded with the high emotion of joyous laughter and tears. It felt like a warm welcome back from someone that knew me; someone that had awaited my return. I dried my eyes and then beheld with great shock how the room had returned to its ordinary everyday appearance. The contrast of that change was simply spectacular. I jumped up and raced downstairs to ask me wife if she had heard the house shaking. She assured me she had only heard me laughing or shouting, but she had not felt the house shake one little bit.

Report: #71

Location: Landing (~13:00hrs)

Dose: 24mg

Within from Without or Without from Within

My nerves were really significant. I could feel them bunched up in my stomach. Several misguided minutes spent looking at mainstream internet pornography had not made my search for courage any easier. As I sat up my nerves vanished. I made two very slow and steady vaporous inhalations. The onset of the substance was very rapid. By the time my head sank into the pillows the air had filled with a very active transparent energy. I could hear that energy as a high-pitched sound in the midst of my head. And yet it sounded like it was audible all around me; it also seemed strangely perceptible within and without. But no sooner had I acknowledged that when the audible and perceptible energy increased to such a significant level it confirmed beyond any doubt the manifesting presence of highly energetic discarnate intelligence. I wondered whether it would impose any hallucinatory imagery upon my amplified perception from its otherworldly imagination. But instead, the incredibly high frequency energy remained constant. I wished I could see the spiritual entity as it really is. Though I instinctively understood that one would actually have to be spirit to see spirit. The incredible energy continued unabated. There was a growing urge within me to speak out loud. By the third or the fourth minute I was feeling absolutely fascinated with how that energy could continue at that same level. The urge to speak was welling up inside me. I laughed out loud and spoke, something along the lines of feeling genuinely amazed at how these entities can do what they do.

Report: #72

Location: Rear Garden (~08:15hrs)

Dose: 34mg

Superstructure

The immediate neighbours all had their rear bedroom curtains drawn. I quietly prepared my blanket and pillows. With complete impassivity I sat up and began the first of three long and slow pulls. The final inhalation absorbed through my lungs as I lay back and exhaled a pall of superfluous vapour. A horizontal two-dimensional psycho-spiritual presence with rounded-edged cells was already evident some three arm's lengths above me. No sooner had I made that observation when there was a sudden surge of energy down upon me. Its power was significant. I was somehow able to both feel and hear its sudden impact into the soft ground around me as the earth subtly yielded to the strange force imposing from above. The energy then increased massively in intensity and frequency. Although I have commented several times before on what seems to be an impossibly high level of energy, this today was without exception, absolutely off the scale. It reached such high intensity and such ultrasonic frequency as to make it feel like a honed blade of cold fine steel was pressing into my head, precisely incising through an imaginary central line running down the length of my nose. Then I saw it descend upon me – a truly huge psycho-spiritual form resembling the sharp pointed bow of an enormous ship wrought in geometrically stunning complexity. It was simply huge! Colossal! And it entered into me right down the absolute central length of my face and quite possibly the absolute central length of my body. The exceedingly acute angle of its tapered form meant that my right eye was looking upward along its right side while my left eye was looking upward along its left side. And I simply have to repeat myself here, because the scale of this entity was absolutely and stupendously MASSIVE! My eyes stared up with strange impassioned wonder at that which was streaming into me. Instinctively, I felt that such things as these are those things that are behind the UFO phenomenon – occult life forms; spiritual beings; discarnate intelligences; entities of an otherwise hidden nature! The sheer humungous size of this entity totally disabled my ability to maintain an emotionless state. Here was an entity of truly magnificent proportion relative to my biological shell. As the entity continued making its passage through me, I analogised myself to a tiny inflatable dinghy, sat in the path of a huge ocean-going liner, cutting through the water at great speed. The mismatch was stupendous. As the full scale of the immensity of the entity continued to be revealed to me, I realised the seriousness of this encounter. Here was an occult being of incredible magnificence – an intelligence very far removed from physical incarnation. I was dumbstruck and awestruck at witnessing the unbelievable. As the main body of the entity completed its passage through me there was a truly incredible final episode that I can really only liken to becoming caught up in a significant psycho-spiritual backwash that trailed behind the entity as it made its way skywards. I was visibly in the midst of a huge mass of psycho-spiritual substance of such incredible density that it felt impossibly tight all around me. I was caught up in its backwash and as it slowly drew away from me, I was literally being pulled sideways and upwards along with it. I estimate the duration of this particular period of the experience lasted for approximately two minutes. During that time there was an air of very great emotional concern over my welfare. It was just as though the latter end of this entity knew all too well the profound reality-shattering potentiality wrought from me witnessing such a sight. A single outer branch of the apple tree caught my eye. It seemed to be knowingly pointing upward at the departing entity. And it seemed that it too recognised the full enormity of this occurrence. The branch was emotionally beside itself, shrieking uncontrollably: "Look at that thing! Look at that thing! Look at that thing!" I then noticed the neighbouring branch. Its emotion was just the same, except that this branch had a personality noticeably distinguishable to its excited neighbour. This branch was far more startled. It swayed gently in the breeze while pointing upward to the slowly departing gigantic psycho-spiritual mass. The emotional verbal outpourings from this branch included repetitions of: "Oh my God!" and "What the fuck!" all prefixed or suffixed with "Look at that!" Several other branches also appeared to be pointing at the departing entity; each one verbalising its own utter astonishment at the magnificent visitation. The huge psycho-spiritual wake still held me fast and tight in its otherworldly grip and continued to pull me sideways and skywards. Just then, something else commenced; something which seemed to underline the magnitude of this event. Strange sapphire-coloured forked lightning-like discharges began streaking out significantly from the outermost branches of the apple tree – like some bizarre occult version of St Elmo's fire. The duration of each flashing discharge was equal to the forked lightning discharges of electrical storms. It was a truly spectacular sight and underlined the magnificence of that which had preceded it. Realising just how very strange the feeling of been caught up in the bizarre psycho-spiritual backwash, I moved my body slightly. The effect of moving accelerated the conclusion of the experience. And mere moments later, all was back to normal. Except I was stupefied. Never in all my research had I witnessed an entity of such enormous proportion. As the entirety of the experience impacted upon me fully, I reacted. I closed my eyes tight and pressed the heel of my palms over each one. Incredibly active and colourful kaleidoscopic interior imagery was observed. I felt like there should be some sort of emotional response from me. But even my incredulity felt embarrassed upon witnessing such stark visual evidence of such a phenomenal being of occult nature. My eyes were damp. But the static tears felt disingenuous and almost forced, as though for the sake of having or showing a reaction. I was unsure how I should react and nothing felt appropriate. I allowed my attention to be diverted by the interior imagery and began cooing over the kaleidoscopic beauty therein. After a short while I reopened my eyes. Above me was a not insignificantly sized occult entity in a condensed low energy state. Its presence brought the magnitude of the previous encounter crashing down hard upon me. Now my emotions became genuine. It felt like the entity above me was in complete empathy with me. Indeed, I suspected it was checking up on me. I was close to blubbing. But I held it back and began thanking the entity for checking in on me. I mouthed aloud several times, in quick succession, my genuine surprise at just how very big and how absolutely magnificent the sight of the entity had been. Several times over, I asking rhetorically: "Did you see that? Did you see that thing? Did you see that?" The entity descended and passed into me and through me. Its presence had a reassuring effect upon me. Soon after, it too was gone. Once again, the cloudless sky appeared as deceptively empty as it had done at the outset.

Report: #73

Location: Bedroom (~12:45hrs)

Dose: 25mg

Two Ways of Looking at the Same Thing

Almost immediately the room filled with highly active transparent energy and appeared to jar back and forth violently. Straightaway that energy increased very rapidly. The room appeared to be jarring back and forth at a terrific rate. That energetic jarring suddenly ceased and the room appeared exactly the way it ordinarily appears. And yet it also appeared exceedingly different. Apart from the very high-pitched ringing sound in my head and all around me, there was only silence. Occasionally the room would appear to undergo one single sudden jarring motion before appearing still again. I strongly sensed the presence of the entity throughout the bedroom. Yet aside from the aforementioned visual oddity, nothing else happened – even though the room was brimming with emotion and high anticipation. After a short while of patiently waiting, I became more confident. I slowly began blowing through pursed lips, as though impatiently awaiting an outcome. I could distinctly sense the presence of the entity. It was an Occult Master. I am absolutely convinced their capabilities far exceed my imaginative capacity. I waited and waited. But nothing occurred. And the fact that nothing occurred, when the spirit-infused air hung so very heavily with such great expectation, caused me to suddenly laugh out loud. That laughter continued and snowballed. My laughter snowballed to such extent that I was very soon laughing with childlike glee. Strange ecstatic guttural sounds emanated with each exhalation. I was like a little child all over again. Tears fell from my eyes. But what I implicitly understood was this laughter resulted from me sensing the presence of the entity, rather than the entity directly manipulating my psyche. This somehow made the laughter all the more magical and rewarding, because my laughter was borne from me merely recognising the character of the entity. That gleeful outburst signalled the end of the experiment. The entity began withdrawing from me in an unexpected and yet very obvious fashion. A quasi-physical psycho-spiritual clasp – which I was hitherto unaware of – began to slowly retract from the sides and underside of my torso. This had the effect of apparently lowering me a very short distance back down upon the bedroom floor, even though I was completely insensible of my back re-cushioning into the carpet.

Report: #74

Location: Bedroom (~21:00hrs)

Dose: 31mg

Unnerving Tentacular Surprise

I was watching an inane TV comedy drama with my wife. The thought to commit to an experiment kept surfacing in my mind. As the TV programme concluded, a very solemn mood befell me as I slowly and methodically moved to prepare a pipe. The same sombre mood stayed with me. After emptying the pipe, I lay back and my arms fell loosely by my side. I observed the slow swirling motion of exhaled vapour. An unseen yet palpably very obvious presence made one single and very ominous plunge down into the bedroom. I was somehow able to feel the huge weight of its dense bodiless presence as it slammed down hard into room and impacted heavily upon the floor. There was simply no time to be scared. With great immediacy the entity flexed its phenomenal spiritual might. It was a simply devastating display of power. The aged plasterboard walls responded audibly and commensurately over several very intense seconds. At its absolute maximum, the spiritual energy felt like an impossibly dense homogenous solid mass, filling the entire room. It was pushing down upon me with prodigious force. As the walls audibly flexed under the impossible otherworldly pressure, I had the briefest moment to consider whether the entity was purposefully imposing its power to such an incredible extent to alarm me. The audibility from the tremendous pressure being imposed upon the walls was so significant that when I heard my neighbours begin talking in their bedroom, I was quite certain they had heard or sensed something uncommon was taking place. The bedroom was visibly awash with superdense psycho-spiritual energy in a very high frequency state. In the midst of that energy there appeared to be some kind of unique highly transparent presence. I felt that I was under very intense scrutiny. My breathing was hard and heavy. The nerves I had earlier repelled suddenly raced home. This impossibly highly energetic phase lasted for perhaps twenty or thirty seconds. During that time, I could feel what I can only describe as two sizeable psycho-spiritual tentacles slowly snaking their way toward my underarms. This made my breathing very much deeper and caused my nerves to breed and flourish with great vitality. There was a momentary pause as I looked directly into the midst of the strange highly transparent mass in the midst of the bedroom. The two psycho-spiritual tentacles continued snaking their way toward my underarms. It felt so incredibly scary; so very unnerving; and simply impossible to deal with! I hollered out loudly with great self-concern: "Oh! Come on man!" And no sooner had those words left my lips when the entity began retracting from me. And no sooner had the entity begun retracting from me when I realised just how much I regretted allowing my fears to get the better of me. Now it seemed I was been slowly lowered down some very short distance onto the carpeted floor; although there had never been any sense of having being raised above it; and neither was I sensible of my back re-cushioning back into the carpet. The entity vanished in mere seconds. I remained stock still whilst ruing that I had spoken aloud and scuppered the interaction. I realised it was very important how I dealt with that regret.

I found it hugely significant that the entity acted immediately upon my vocal appeal for leniency. It seems both as silly as it seems apt and valid to ask whether the entity had understood my emotion or my speech – or both. As soon as I had made my appeal and realised the entity was vacating, I felt huge regret. I felt I had failed and committed an error of judgement. But at the time those feelings were significantly amplified. The more I thought more about the experiment I began to wonder whether the entity had in fact known I would react in the way I did to its unnerving tentacular surprise. I am of a very ticklish disposition. Perhaps the entity was testing my resolve in what it knew would be a terribly frightful episode for me. If that was the case, then my resolve was found wanting. I really should have placed more trust in the entity. This was clearly an entity capable of incredible high energy. Is there any mileage in holding a suspicion that researching alone – without any trip-sitter accompanying me – may actually facilitate such a devastating display of unbridled power? I ask that simply because when I imagine myself sitting as an observer in such an experiment as this – where an equal degree of occult power is unleashed – it seems wholly improbable that I would not have any perceptive sense of that power whatsoever; especially as that terrific power creates such an obviously audible response from the aged plasterboard walls. It is highly significant that the huge increase in power is palpably commensurate with the audible response from the aged plasterboard walls. I know DMT is a very serious business. But such displays of power as that which I witnessed in this experiment underline the radical revolutionary impact that this substance simply must have on the future and the foundations of the traditional western minded mentality.

Report: #75

Location: Rear Garden (~11:45hrs)

Dose: 33mg

Worthy of Wonder

The first inhalation was dense and slightly harsh to taste but smacked of potency. The third pull pulled nothing. I lay back and looked up. Transparent cellular patterning was already evident in the air above me. Within mere seconds the full power of the DMT took effect. A swirling psycho-spiritual torrent formed of countless geometric cells streamed out from me. It was a truly stunning sight. A bird began chattering mellifluously somewhere nearby. I maintained my focus on the beautiful psycho-spiritual stream emanating from me – spiralling upwards and outwards into the vast sky. I harboured no doubt it reached some considerable distance, which I could not fully appreciate. There was a sudden unexpected movement beneath my right upper arm, as though something was purposefully trying to disturb me. I twitched my arm and the movement ceased but it resumed just as soon as my arm relaxed. Not wanting to remove my eyes from what was occurring directly in front of them I continued to move my right arm in order to stymie whatever minor movement was attempting to distract me. Similar movements manifested beneath my back as though purposefully trying to disturb me. Birds were busy chattering and calling nearby. There was nothing unusual in hearing birdsong, but I wondered whether they were witness to some bizarre magnifying or refraction effect by virtue of the superdense psycho-spiritual medium filling the sky above me. I reached for my sunglasses and that broke my focus. The amazingly configured psycho-spiritual stream appeared to have ceased. Sunglasses did not really augment my observation of the psycho-spiritual mass. I strongly suspected the same dose inhaled within the bedroom would have produced a very different outcome. I wondered about the outline shape of the bizarre psycho-spiritual projection. I playfully likened myself to the thin neck of an hourglass; seeing my psycho-spiritual projection expanding upwards and outwards like some bizarrely over-sized glass bulb relative to my physical shell. It was as silly as it was playful. I stood up and headed indoors. My eldest son asked me what metamorphosis meant. I spoke about caterpillars and butterflies as he searched his dictionary. Metamorphosis is a complete change by a living thing. It made me think about that which had emanated from me only moments ago – my own strange psycho-spiritual stuff that was in all likelihood still slowly and invisibly working its way back to source and baseline latent state.

Report: #76

Location: Bedroom (~09:00hrs)

Dose: 20mg

Psychic Sound

The bedroom was full of bright sunlight. I emptied the pipe in three pulls. Immediately the bedroom appeared to be jarring back and forth. The turbulent energy causing that strange appearance increased and continued to increase. I was quite certain this was my own psycho-spiritual energy. Possibly some of it was transmitting through the walls, the ceiling, the door, the floor and the window. Possibly some of it was rapidly reflecting off those surfaces and back into the room. I urged myself to remain sharp and observant in order to detect the arrival of a discarnate entity – responding to the source of my heightened psychic sound. Unexpectedly, I had a brief moment of absolute clarity, as I realised just how totally and utterly bizarre this undertaking really is. The presence of a discarnate entity became evident as a pressure pushing down upon me from without; periodically pushing down upon my amplified psycho-spiritual energy. I could feel its force outside me, upon me and within me. The energy was relatively moderate. Once again, I experienced a tremendously clear-minded realisation of just how thoroughly bizarre the situation really was; I realised the phenomenal energy was conscious; it was something that was consciously trying interact with me. The insanity of the reality of the situation forced me to question: "Why am I even doing this?" After several seconds it was obvious the entity was unable to secure a temporary mind-to-mind interaction with me. The forceful periodical downward pressure ceased buffeting into me. The room was still visibly jarring with energy, but not nearly as much as it was at the outset.

Report: #77

Location: Rear Garden (~13:15hrs)

Dose: 35mg

Geometrically Patterned Psycho-Spiritual Substance

I sat up and made three vaporous inhalations. Each attempt produced a surprisingly voluminous amount of vapour which was duly vacuumed down and momentarily retained before exhaling. My innate tinnitus responded in proportion to the DMT molecules that found their way to centre of my brain. A curved psycho-spiritual plane exhibiting a cellular structure overarched me. One second later, more DMT molecules arrived at their destination because my psychic sound began amplifying significantly. The psycho-spiritual cells now transformed into a very definite geometrically detailed presence. More DMT molecules must have arrived, further increasing the volume of my psychic sound. The geometrically composed psycho-spiritual substance suddenly projected upwards and outwards in a terrific and torrential radial stream. I was excited at witnessing such a stunning occurrence. It was simply spectacular! I slowly mouthed aloud in an awe and astonishment: "Here we go! Oh my God!" For reasons unknown, I opened my mouth to its widest possible extent and kept it fixed there until I needed to breathe. The sight of my own spiralling psycho-spiritual outpouring was simply astounding to behold. There was a very definite palpable perception of the ongoing projection. The nearside and uppermost branches of the apple tree all seemed to be knowingly pointing to the incredible psycho-spiritual emanation filling the sky, whilst privately uttering astonished whispers between themselves. Beyond the roof the house, the canopies of the three huge oak trees were also knowingly expressing astonishment – albeit with slightly less verve. I was quite certain the chattering birds were also tweeting about the huge psycho-spiritual mass surging high above the garden. A pigeon flying over the larchlap fence behind my head made a sudden sweeping swerve to get away from me. The extensive psycho-spiritual mass now appeared as an amorphous mass of spherical transparent cells, no longer exhibiting the original complex geometric composition. I made an interesting optical observation: a very sharp and surprisingly long-lived afterimage resulted after staring at the apple tree for several seconds and then looking away. I reproduced the same effect three times. Seeing so much of my immaterial outside my body made me feel vulnerable and maternally protective towards the great big psycho-spiritual mass. Without any warning something began moving around beneath the blanket, by my right elbow. It startled me sufficiently to cry out loud: "What the fuck!?" A much more pronounced and far spookier movement then manifested beside my left elbow, causing me to react in the very same way. Soon there were only faint and fading hints of any psycho-spiritual presence. The apple tree and the oak trees had lost the personalities that had somehow projected onto them, and the birds were busy chattering about their own affairs.

Report: #78

Location: Rear Garden (~11:30hrs)

Dose: 23mg

Psychiatrically Crazy Laughter

The second inhalation vacuumed down all that remained. I lay back and dropped sunglasses over my eyes for ocular comfort. My own psycho-spiritual substance began emerging into visibility above me and quickly formed as a very obvious radial geometric form. Within seconds there was a very definite moment where I observed and palpably sensed the projection of that occult substance upwards and outwards into the sky. After just a few seconds, I knew there would be no entity contact. Momentarily I sensed very great vulnerability, as I realised my occult mind-stuff was visibly and extensively outside of me. I realised such concern was now far too late. The upward pointing branches of the apple tree all conveyed silent but significant jubilant acknowledgement of my expanding mind-stuff. Beautiful sapphire-coloured forked lightning appeared to discharge in my right perhipheral vision. I was able to recreate the stunning visual effect by shifting my gaze. I then noted the effect was actually a sharp and perfectly mirrored afterimage of the apple tree branches, wrought in stunning neon sapphire. After reproducing that stunning visual exercise three or four times, I considered I was perhaps becoming overly excited about something that may well already be an established fact in the optical sciences. But immediately that I told myself as much, a visually and emotionally very strong image flashed up in my mind for a mere fraction of a second. The image was seen inside my mind, but it actually felt like it had presented itself outside my head. I could even sense its exact location. The short-lived image was of an innocent young boy. He was with his mum. She was doting on him and stooping over him. The boy held emotional responsibility for the strange visual observations I had just made. And he was now visibly upset that I had made such a sudden dismissal of the uniqueness of the observation. His mum – mindful of my presence but singularly concerned about her child – was comforting him and reassuring him. The scene was evident for a mere fraction of a second. But it was so completely saturated with such emotion that its short-lived occurrence impressed upon me sufficiently to capture and analyse it fully.

Report: #79

Location: Bedroom (~15:00hrs)

Dose: 34mg

Magical Occult Decorator

I sat up and began. The effects from the first inhalation became evident as I began undertaking the second inhalation. The pitch and intensity of my interior psychic sound raced upwards at a truly terrific rate. After the third and final pull I lay back with outstretched arms. The bedroom was actively awash with my own psycho-spiritual energy. There was one single second wherein the room appeared to be jarring and then, with lightning speed, an Occult Master arrived and imposed its almighty power. Over several phenomenally intense seconds I had visible, palpable and audible perception of the huge increase in its power. It was simply stupendous. Its frequency quickly reached such a heightened pitch as to make the energy feel like an all pervading yet impossibly solid psycho-spiritual mass. The room was wrought in awesome hyper-vividity. Colours had impossible depth and saturation. And despite that no bright sunlight was shining into the bedroom, it now appeared brightly illuminated. In short, the bedroom appeared far more real than its ordinary everyday appearance. But it also appeared so very different – as though a magical occult decorator had done a truly spectacular job. I silently acknowledged my incredible calmness given the truly astonishing level of invasive occult energy I had been subjected to. The appearance of the bedroom was stunning to behold. The occult entity had invested a portion of itself inside my cranium. My lips were unsealed but there was a very obvious and very solid presence above the roof of my mouth – giving me a pronounced appreciation of that particular portion of my anatomy. Its presence was especially notable at the back of my throat, as I moved my tongue prior to swallowing. It's possible my psyche was subliminally coaxed into having me exercise my vocal cords. And upon doing so, I found the meaningless guttural sounds emitted from my larynx took on a highly unusual acoustic quality. So much so that I felt obliged to continue making meaningless vocal sounds, simply in order to marvel at the unusual acoustic qualities characterising those sounds. My right hand was positioned beneath a set of heavy wooden drawers, while maintaining a partial grip upon the lighter. My left hand maintained a partial grip upon the small glass pipe. I could feel as the incredibly powerful energy evident throughout the entire bedroom configured itself into a quasi-physical material, around each hand, and duly began working to slowly tease my fingers away from the lighter and the pipe. It was a truly incredible experience. I sensed that this was an incredibly difficult and laborious task for the entity to undertake. Because of the very obvious physicality manipulating my fingers, I could not help but consider that a group of miniaturised physical beings were actually assisting the powerful entity perform this laborious task. There was a mild temptation to take a look at either hand. But I resisted, because concurrent with that activity, something else was taking place; something that had the emotional significance of a very serious medical operation. Throughout the interior length of both arms, a very fast-paced knitting activity was underway. It was painless but absolutely unmistakable. That invasive action felt so incredibly serious that I felt compelled to continue making my vocal sounds purely to divert my attention away from whatever was underway inside my arms. I produced simple melodies and tunes whilst the unusual activity within both arms continued apace. Having figured out the quasi-physical material was trying to rid my fingers of the pipe and the lighter, I helpfully pushed them aside. Upon doing so, the quasi-physical material around both hands dissolved. I assured myself that I would never against retain a grasp on those items longer than was necessary. The emotional seriousness pervading the bedroom was truly terrific. I wondered what the entity was doing with me. I wondered if I was being wired up in some bizarre interdimensional manner. Was this occult entity establishing an invisible occult connection between us that would remain long after this interaction concluded? I continued making melodic vocal sounds as the room imperceptibly changed from extreme hypervividity back to its normal everyday appearance. The strange knitting action gradually reduced until there was just a faint sense of movement midway up my right forearm. This continued even after the room had returned back to its usual everyday appearance. I remained patiently in position until the movement ceased. I thought for a short while about the experience before standing up and vacating the bedroom. I headed downstairs and passed through the lounge whereupon I could not help myself from announcing in relation to DMT, for the benefit of my wife: "That stuff is absolutely unbelievable!"

Report: #80

Location: Rear Garden (~11:15hrs)

Dose: 36mg

Impossibly Proportioned Hourglass

The wind was blustery but I had made up my mind to research outdoors. I was less apprehensive experimenting outside. Having awaited a lull in the wind, I sat up and engaged the flame on its maximum setting. Using every nuance of skill and technique I accurately gauged the position of the flame to secure vapour and avoid smoke. A clean vaporous stream soon became evident and I maintained that position while steadily drawing down all the available vapour. I drew down a great big lung-busting volume of the stuff. And with that done, I lay back and positioned the sunglasses over my eyes whilst retaining the potent cloud deep within my lungs. I eventually exhaled a big billowing cloud of unabsorbed vapour. The onset of the substance was phenomenally powerful. My inner psychic sound began racing upwards with intensity and frequency that I have never before experienced. An incredibly well defined geometrically complex psycho-spiritual presence manifested above me. And as the intensity of my inner psychic sound grew ever stronger, the geometric complexity of the stunning psycho-spiritual presence became ever more intricate. I was now experiencing a level of power that I was wholly unfamiliar with. And no sooner had I acknowledged that, when the power increased even further in magnitude, causing my interior psychic sound to reach a truly frightening pitch. The centre of the geometrically complex psycho-spiritual presence was now displaying a multitude of distinct equidistant points. The whole mass was seething with portentous energy and becoming increasingly complex. It began to swell and bulge and then suddenly, with truly terrifying and terrific energy, it raced upwards and outwards unstoppably. I was absolutely amazed at the stunning beauty of what I was witnessing. My psycho-spiritual self-projecting forth with such tremendous energy as to almost overwhelm me. My mouth must have opened very widely. My tongue was involuntarily sweeping around and around the inside of my mouth; making greatly exaggerated sweeping motions. However, I only recollect becoming conscious of that after it was already well underway. It felt as though my mouth was hinged open at a physically impossible angle. My tongue felt like its length was greatly extended as it continued to involuntarily sweep around and around the inside of my mouth. My field of vision was saturated in hypervividity and hyperreality. There were numerous multicoloured indescribable miscellanies and well-formed three-dimensional psycho-spiritual shapes, whose constant emergence and movement made it appear that the clouds were breaking apart; as though they were mere pieces in an advanced puzzle that was ever forming and collapsing and toppling over. I was barely able to hold onto who I was – or who I thought I was. My psycho-spiritual stuff was still projecting from me in an unstoppable torrent. Only very slowly did I become aware of the sweeping action of my tongue. My saliva lubricated mouth, my swivelling tongue and the bizarre content filling my visual field – along with a mere fraction of operational ego – was all that I was. I had no sense of my body whatsoever. As I became increasingly aware of the bizarre and exaggerated sweeping motion of my tongue, I realised my mouth felt so incredibly unreal and flimsy. It felt like it had great potential to fall apart at any given moment, like a cheaply made plastic toy. Indeed, I was genuinely beginning to consider that such a catastrophe may actually occur. Meanwhile, at the furthest reaches of my mind, something like a post-mesmeric message from an Occult Master – notifying me they had shown me the inevitability of this bizarre oral occurrence during their earlier interactions. It really did feel as though that message had been physically stored at the very back of my head. The message seemed to affirm the capacity of their power; the depth of their knowledge and the extent of their wisdom and high-mindedness. I suspect my ego had remained intact by a mere thread, because that which remained conscious was absolutely overwhelmed by the experience. I was clinging onto sanity and unwittingly flirting with unconsciousness. There was such a finely balanced mental delicacy to this situation; an indeterminable and uncertain final conclusion was impossibly finely balanced. Only very slowly did my familiar mental faculties begin to re-establish themselves. The content of my visual field was still incredibly hypervivid and filled with mysterious hallucinatory content. Strange three-dimensional transparent shapes resembling advanced building blocks were still evident; and evidently formed of and formed within the great mass of psycho-spiritual substance filling the garden. A moment of welcome relief came when the centre of my head felt like it was slowly taking back responsibility for running my senses. The clearly visible and highly dense psycho-spiritual mass ranged high above me was absolutely breathtaking – the garden and a great portion of air above and beyond the garden was thick with an astonishingly expansive amorphous psycho-spiritual mass. I voiced aloud in profound astonishment: "Wow! What the...!?" I had never seen so much of the invisible me so clearly visible outside of me. As that psycho-spiritual substance slowly diminished by returning to its occult baseline state, I began collecting my thoughts. By no measure had I expected such a phenomenal experience. I eventually stood up and noted my eyesight was exceptionally sharp. The garden and the ordinary everyday things within the garden all appeared to exhibit exceptional clarity. In particular, the colours green and red notably stood out. I knew this visual enhancement was caused by my eyes working through the now transparent occult medium still in an amplified state and surrounding around me.

Report: #81

Location: Landing (~10:30hrs)

Dose: 23mg

Neither Shaft nor Head

To what extent can the prevailing weather impose subliminal occult influence upon the human psyche? Outside was deathly still and silent. There was zero air movement. I was filled with an unusual level of apprehension which required a commensurate level of willfulness to overcome, or ignore. The house was dull, quiet and empty. There was something in the air that I simply could not put my finger on. At a very deep level, I thought something was suggesting that I take my research outdoors. But I dismissed whatever my instincts thought they were intuiting and duly insisted upon researching indoors. I made two really excellent pulls but detected no audible increase in my psychic sound. I lay back and looked up at the ceiling. Within a second something occurred. It appeared the entire volume of the setting had suddenly taken on a palpably homogenous emotional weightiness. I could not only feel it but I could actually see it as a uniform turbulence throughout the air. But there was something qualitatively very different about this energy. It was unusual. Something from the same depth of my mind that had urged me to head outside was now urging me to immediately get up from the floor and end this experiment. But the prompting was too faint to be convincing, and so I ignored its appeal. I felt obligated to continue with my research. A moment later I sat up and looked around. The visibility of the uniformly turbulent energy was no longer evident. But I now felt acutely aware of how my occult energies were in a heightened and sensitive state. I felt strangely vulnerable. The stillness and silence inside the house and outside the house only served to amplify that silence and my feelings of vulnerability. I positioned myself on all fours and looked down at the plain beige carpet. It was heavily adorned with typical tryptamine patterning. I stood up and replaced the pillows on the bed. But when I returned to the landing, a gravely dark and very unwelcome thought sprang up in my mind. I acknowledged it and made an effort to shift it. But it seemed to want to linger a little longer. It seemed it wanted to latch itself within my psyche. I decided it was far too dark and unwelcoming to be allowed any longevity, and so I headed downstairs and went outside into the cold air. I decided I must do something active in order to rid myself of the intrusive and persistent dark thought. My first thought was to grab my axe and go and chop some wood. But the thought of Jack Nicholson as Jack Torrance in the "Here's Johnny" scene came to mind. I decided against chopping wood and began picking up twigs and branches that had accumulated on the patio. The activity helped to clear my head and so I decided to sweep the patio. I searched for the yard broom, but despite my best efforts inside the shed and outside the shed, I could not locate the broom anywhere. I wondered whether the broom shaft was missing from the broom head, or whether the broom head was missing from the broom shaft. There was something darkly macabre about making the nonsensical division between the broom shaft and the broom head that made me laugh out loud.

Here is an appropriately dark quote taken from Blavatsky's *Studies in Occultism,* (A Collection of Articles from *Lucifer*, H. P. Blavatsky's magazine, between 1887-1891):

> They laugh at the occult sciences and deride Mesmerism? Yet this century will not have passed away before they have undeniable proofs that the idea of a crime suggested for experiment's sake is not removed by a reversed current of the will as easily as it is inspired. They may learn that if the outward expression of the idea of a misdeed "suggested" may fade out at the will of the operator, the *active living germ* artificially implanted does not disappear with it; that once dropped into the seat of the human – or rather the animal – passions, it may lie dormant there for years sometimes, to become suddenly awakened by some unforeseen circumstance into realization. Crying children frightened into silence by the *suggestion* of a monster, a devil standing in the corner, by a foolish nurse, have been known to become insane twenty or thirty years later on the same subject. There are mysterious, secret drawers, dark nooks and hiding-places in the labyrinth of our memory, still unknown to physiologists, and which only open once, rarely twice, in man's lifetime, and that only under very abnormal and peculiar conditions. But when they do, it is always some heroic deed committed by a person the least calculated for it, or – a terrible crime perpetuated, the reason for which remains for ever a mystery..."

[From: Studies in Occultism (1887 – 1891) by H. P. Blavatsky.

Page 31]

Report: #82

Location: Rear Garden (~12:45hrs)

Dose: 42mg

Thunderbirds Are Go

My youngest son and I were breakfasting while watching a Paranormal Junkie channel on YouTube, entitled: 'Thunderbird Sightings! Do These Mythical Creatures Exist?' Later in the day, I was home alone and decided to make progress with my research. My mood was a mix of apprehension and sober excitement as I imposed my will over my nerves and focussed upon maintaining a workable level of calm. Mundane household items that caught my eye took on profound yet ambiguous significance. Outside on the patio, I noted how the swirling wind had formed a structure from twigs resembling an oversized bird nest. The first pull was voluminous and excellent. The second and third pulls completely emptied the pipe. Upon lying down and looking up, I realised my inner psychic sound was either totally silent or completely absent – despite its clear audibility only a moment ago. As I puzzled over why that was, there was a very sudden and very clear psychic communication within my head, one that readily translated as: "A decision has been made!" It was as though the message had had been imparted to me as an emotion, and my own inner voice had given that emotion the precise wording. No sooner had I received that communication when an entity of truly tremendous proportion and beauty began streaming down into me and through me. I immediately realised what was underway. As it continued to stream into me, I symbolically opened my mouth as wide as I possibly could in order to portray my readiness and willingness to metaphorically drink the living waters of its psycho-spiritual body. As it continued to stream into me, I revised my visual assessment of its size from 'tremendous' to 'vast'. Its superdense transparent body and the intricate geometric detail therein were simply astounding. I began making unspoken appeals to the vast otherworldly entity for assistance with my literary endeavours. But suddenly – unwelcomely and inexplicably – the very same ill-begotten dark thought that had arisen in my mind during the previous experiment manifested once again. I was aghast at what my own mind was furnishing me with. Consequently, I now began making silent appeals for the entity to assist me in ridding my mind of the ill-begotten lagan. As the entity continued streaming into me, I maneuvered my eyes in order to better appreciate the truly awesome extent of this great big psycho-spiritually-robed mind. It was simply colossal in comparison to my physical size. When it had concluded streaming through me it condensed into a vast psycho-spiritual mass above me. It was moving very slowly in an easterly direction; heading over the neighbouring larchlap boundary fence. Its size and the apparent density characterising its central portion were stunning to behold. I was witnessing a truly stupendous being from an otherwise occult existence. I wanted to keep looking upon its otherworldly awesomeness. But something had reached very far down into the depths of my psyche and had dredged up an incredibly powerful emotion of: "Do or die trying!" The emotion was palpably alive within me and without me. I felt as though I had nailed my colours to my mast for the entire universe to see. I unashamed and unabashed at every level of my being. A calm and reflective mood befell me. And then, like a delayed pre-programmed reaction suddenly activating, a long and plaintive wail arose from deep within me. My eyes filled with tears. A swollen bulge stalled achingly between my heart and my throat. I quickly composed myself and looked up at the bright blue sky. Suddenly, at a very great height, my eyes fell upon an uncommonly large bird with an improbable wingspan. It was undertaking a large diameter circular glide. I suspected it was Red Kite, but based on the programme I had seen this morning with my boy – and the apparent huge size of the bird, even at such a terrific height – I could not help myself from indulging in a more esoteric interpretation. It slowly straightened out and began gliding in a perfectly straight line over toward the horizon. Feeling in good-spirits, I headed indoors. However, upon seating myself at my writing desk, I was absolutely aghast when very much to my surprise, my mind fabricated and awfully ill-disposed and ill-motivated thought. I could feel it had arisen in the exact same locale of my psyche as the same unwelcome intrusive thought recorded in the previous experiment. That same dark mental energy of ill-intent then gave a figurative two fingered "fuck off" salute to the large bird I had just witnessed. I was absolutely mortified that my own mind could have allowed such an unwarranted and impolite gesticulation. I headed back outside with a dour ruefulness souring my psyche. I thought to look for the yard broom to make a clean sweep of the patio, but then recollected the yard broom had not been found when I had previously required its services. With genuine concern I began to wonder about my state of mind. I wondered about the darkness that had arisen unbidden from the shadowy depths of my psyche. I felt so much self-disdain. I began to wondering whether my mind was at the outset of a schizophrenic division. I questioned whether amplified dual-mindedness was the price to pay for the rewards of the amazing occult insights I was gaining. I really wanted to just sit down and console myself. My eyes fell upon the crude circular weave of twigs and branches. It seemed synchronous and applicable and so I went and seated myself crossed legged therein; in the midst of the nest-like construct. Maleficent metaphors marred my thinking until I decided enough was enough. I implored myself to pull myself together. I sat bolt upright and redoubled my willful intent to write this report as I lifted myself from the semblance of an oversized bird nest and headed back indoors.

What am I to make of that unexpected and uncharacteristic dark turn of mind? Why had my mind suddenly developed a propensity to act in such a dark and loathsome fashion? The location of that dark thinking was certainly removed from the centre of my consciousness. But it seemed capable of acting independently and autonomously. That mental darkness had a definite physical location within my brain. I could recognise exactly where it was rooted – the lower right-side posterior of my cranium at a superficial depth. But what good is such knowledge when trying to deal with the unwelcome stubbornness of such darkly intrusive stuff?

[Wikipedia: Roc (mythology)]

https://en.wikipedia.org/wiki/Roc_(mythology)

> [Roc] is an enormous legendary bird of prey. [....] According to the Oxford English Dictionary, this word perhaps influenced the word rook, though the chess piece term mainly stems from the Persian...*rukh* or Sanskrit...*rath*, both meaning *chariot*... [...] In the 13th century, Marco Polo (as quoted in Attenborough (1961: 32) stated "It was for all the world like an eagle, but one indeed of enormous size; so big in fact that its quills were twelve paces long and thick in proportion. And it is so strong that it will seize an elephant in its talons and carry him high into the air and drop him so that he is smashed to pieces; having so killed him, the bird swoops down on him and eats him at leisure".
>
> [From Wikipedia, the free encyclopedia]

[Wikipedia: Thunderbird (mythology)]

https://en.wikipedia.org/wiki/Thunderbird_(mythology)

> The thunderbird is a legendary creature in certain North American indigenous peoples' history and culture. It is considered a supernatural bird of power and strength. It is especially important, and frequently depicted, in the art, songs and oral histories of many Pacific Northwest Coast cultures, and is found in various forms among the peoples of the American Southwest, Great Lakes, and Great Plains.

> [From Wikipedia, the free encyclopedia]

[Wikipedia: Thunderbird (cryptozoology)]

https://en.wikipedia.org/wiki/Thunderbird_(cryptozoology)

> Thunderbird is a term used in cryptozoology to describe large, bird-like creatures, generally identified with the Thunderbird of Native American tradition. Similar cryptids reported in the Old World are often called Rocs. Thunderbirds are regarded by a small number of researchers as having lizard features like the extinct pterosaurs such as *Pteranodon*. Reports of Thunderbird sightings go back centuries, and the fossil record does show that giant birds (teratorns) with wingspans between 4 and 5 m (12 and 18 ft) were likely contemporary with early man. Today the creature is generally regarded as a myth.

> [From Wikipedia, the free encyclopedia]

From *The Greenhaven Enyclopedia of World Religions,* under native North American religions:

> ***Totems and Trickster Heroes*** Other distinct or common religious practices among Native American peoples include belief in a celestial spirit known as the thunderbird, believed to be in constant struggle with evil earthly spirits. The thunderbird appears frequently on the totem poles of the tribes of the Pacific Northwest. The totem poles themselves were sacred ritual objects delineating a tribal or family connection with an animal spirit. Many tribal groups also featured stories and moral lessons connected with figures

known generally as tricksters. These tricksters might be heroes, responsible for bringing a particular conflict to a good end or transmitting survival skills. They might also be lazy, stupid, or deceitful. Often they are considered to be divine and eternal in nature, messengers between the gods and humanity.

[From: The Greenhaven Enyclopedia of World Religions (2007) by Jeff Hay. Page 219]

Report: #83

Location: Bedroom (~10:15hrs)

Dose: 35mg

Just a Human

The shaded rear garden was frosty, thus making indoor research an easy choice. I was apprehensive as I prepared the pipe because I was still dealing with what was now proving to be a deeply embedded dastardly notion. Something dark had gotten itself deeply lodged within my conscious mind and I was becoming increasingly uncomfortable with it. I headed for the WC, which starkly reaffirmed the animal side of my human nature. In a self-deprecating plaintive manner, I opined out loud: "I'm just a human!" Even while seated, I experienced a very deep and profound recognition of the complexity and the mystery of the human condition; something unique; something midway between the earthly and the other. I headed downstairs to advise my wife of my intention. She wished me luck. The third pull vacuumed down all that remained. I lay back and looked up. Within one second, I was able to detect something external. But the energy was not what I expected and it had a very strange way of manifesting. It was exactly as though the occult presence had been invisibly present beforehand. And now my smoking DMT had given it licence to emerge and interact with me. It was visible as a see-through medium exhibiting a mildly uniform turbulence throughout its volume. The energy underwent some changes that palpably felt like the entity was trying to become even more energetic. But the increase in energy was only marginal. This was very far from high energy. Without thinking too much, I observed the strange medium within which I was immersed. Immediately I sat upright upon realising how terribly vulnerable I felt to that very same dastardly negativity that had been blighting me. That same dark and deeply embedded influence that had marred my mind over the past couple of days was now revealing its ugliness yet again. Despite the welcome bleached brightness of the warm sunshine, something cold and sinister was active deep within my psyche; arousing the most ill-minded motives from some hidden drawer of darkness down in the core depths of my mind. The potential for a deeply-rooted manifestation of true horror was either sinking into the depths of my mind from without, or was rising up from the depths of my mind from within – or both. Once again, I could feel the physical locality of the unspeakable damned evil deed within my head. I felt thoroughly unnerved and wholly uneasy so I stood up and headed downstairs. I felt obliged to go and see my wife. Vaguely and quickly I delivered the news that my experience was not so good. But it was overwhelmingly abundant within me that I was been economical with the truth. I headed for the kitchen, jumped into my trainers and began hastily loosening the door bolts so as to make rapid exit into the welcome expanse of the outdoors and its autumn coldness. But the thought of standing outside in the cold shade of the rear garden forced a quick change of mind, and so I headed through the front door to stand at the garden gate in the warm sunshine. I was feeling very uneasy with what was going on in my mind. But I was becoming even more uneasy, knowing how that thing in my head was making itself so very persistent – becoming so bold as to make its intentions vocally present to me and doing so at times when I least expected it. Standing all alone by the garden gate and feeling scared for my mental health, I suspected this represented the end of my DMT research programme. I berated myself terribly for not listening to my inner voice on that fateful recent experiment. My inner voice had pleased with me to take the experiment outside. And I had ignored its plea. It had then bidden me to get up from the experiment. And I had ignored that too. And now I was dealing with a most unwelcome and unsavoury idea that had become fixed in my head. How could I know if the idea was borne of a suggestion made to my mind; or was one borne from the dark substance of my own mind? How could I be sure of one over the other? And how could I be sure the two were not working together – in legion, or as a combine? In short – I was dealing with a really terrible bastard motherfucker of an idea that was refusing to budge from inside my head. Something seemed intent on making me see red and acting in rum old manner. I questioned how would I ever deal with this awful nonsense. I came to the very difficult but very honest conclusion that bottling this up would not in any way be helpful. It was on that basis I realised I would need to approach my wife and broach the matter with her. And the sooner I did so the better. Unbeknownst to her, my wife was the focus of those ill-motived machinations that dare not speak plainly. I entered the house and coyly popped my head around the lounge door, while smiling weakly at my wife. I enquired about the possibility of a serious tête-à-tête, outside. My wife was surprised at my request and the seriousness of my invitation. After some back and forth small talk my wife agreed to join me, after she had used the toilet. I headed to make myself a coffee, but upon hearing the kettle as it began to heat the water, I aborted the idea. I headed back outside. Standing between the wooden gate posts – in the absence of a gate – my wife came and joined me. I began by carefully outlining that a really very silly and somewhat unpleasant idea had gotten itself lodged deep inside my head. I continued to explain that this silly and unpleasant idea was best ousted and aired rather than bottled up and confined. I mentioned how the unwelcome thought had really begun to bother me terribly for the last couple of days. Upon outlining all of that, I realised how terribly difficult it would be for me to be absolutely brutally honest and open about the exact details of the thing inside my head. I harked back to the DMT experiment that had resulted in this issue. I hinted at how that experience had somehow resulted in a terribly motivated action becoming instilled deep within my mind; one that kept on popping up when I least wanted it and least expected it; one that was proving immensely difficult to shift or shut out. I gave a broad outline of how yesterday's truly magnificent experience had concluded with that same surprising and unwelcome mental incursion. I was acutely aware of just how very banana's all of this was sounding to my wife. But the potential worst-case scenario of keeping this stuff bottled up was truly heinous. And as such, it really needed saying – whether it was bananas, apples or pears. Cautiously and nervously, I began explaining to my wife how I was trying to shine a direct light onto a gravely dark matter. I explained such an approach was the best way to expose its malevolent nastiness. But how could I possibly string together such words of plain explanation for the benefit of my wife? How could I shine a light on such an evil and diabolical machination of my mind without frightening the life out of her? How could I be absolutely sure that I was acting in the right way; to save rather than despoil our relationship? Tentatively! Cautiously! By outlining and hinting rather than spelling it out starkly and sharply. By watching and feeling my wife's reactions; by listening carefully to her responses; by answering her questions honestly. Rather than keep that kernel of madness loitering and festering inside my mind, I decided to oust its unwelcome wrongness into the cold light of day – to stymie its growth or even better, winkle it out altogether. Lots of things can happen in relationships: good things and bad things. But I never foresaw my having to make such a damn difficult confessional to my wife. I expressed the matter in a way that she could grasp; without me having to resort to a level detail that would derail our relationship. Calmly but with obvious concern she suggested I take a few days break from my research. I had of course already arrived at the very same conclusion. We headed back indoors. And as much as I felt much better for having aired and exposed that dark business, I also knew the impact of my words would prove terribly worrying for my wife. I could only act to reassure her. But I knew she would brood upon what I had said. Later that evening, after arriving home from work, I was taking a hot bath. My wife came and stood in the bathroom and looked down upon my submerged nakedness. Understandably she raised concerns borne of her brooding. I responded honestly and with as much reassurance as I could. I had to concede that for all the amazing sights and insights I was experiencing with this mind manifesting research, the truth was that I was messing about with a very potent substance; one that was quite literally opening up my mind to occult influences. I wondered if I had done the right thing in speaking out. Had speaking out actually resolved the issue? How could I be sure I would evolve with those higher-mined influences, rather than devolve and despoil myself in a lower-minded moment of folly and madness? Talking about it seemed like the correct approach to dealing with it.

From Blavatsky's ISIS Unveiled:

> Although the "magicians" believed as firmly as our spiritualists in a world of invisible spirits, none of them claimed to produce his effects under their control or through their sole help. They knew too well how difficult it is to keep away the elementary creatures when they have once found the door wide open.

> [From: Isis Unveiled (1877) by H. P. Blavatsky. Volume I. Page 66]

> "Shut the door in the face of the daemon," says the *Kabala*, "and he will keep running away from you, as if you pursued him," which means, that you must not give a hold on you to such spirits of obsession by attracting them into an atmosphere of congenial sin. These daemons seek to introduce themselves into the bodies of the simple-minded and idiots, and remain until dislodged therefrom by a powerful and *pure* will.

> [From: Isis Unveiled (1877) by H. P. Blavatsky. Volume I. Page 356]

> Were these God-like men "mediums," as the orthodox spiritualists will have it? By no means, if by the term we understand those "sick-sensitives" who are born with a

peculiar organization, and who in proportion as their powers are developed become more and more subject to the irresistible influence of miscellaneous spirits, purely human, elementary or elemental. Unquestionably so, if we consider every individual a medium in whose magnetic atmosphere the denizens of higher invisible spheres can move, and act, and live. In such a sense every person is a medium. [...] Mediumship is measured by the quality of the aura with which the individual is surrounded. This may be dense, cloudy, noisome, mephitic, nauseating to the pure spirit, and attract only those foul beings who delight in it, as the eel does in turbid waters, or, it may be pure, crystalline, limpid, opalescent as the morning dew. All depends upon the moral character of the medium.

[From: Isis Unveiled (1877) by H. P. Blavatsky. Volume I. Page 486 – 487]

In *The Dark Gods,* Anthony Roberts explains:

The mischievous (and deadly) elementals of the occultist...play dangerous games with those living beings that are sensitive enough to perceive them. The evidence for this is somewhat overwhelming. The 'control force' that lies behind its manifested agents is as much a tormenting mechanism as a revelatory one. As noted above, many of the psychic 'games' perpetrated by this force are highly destructive to both the body and the soul, the forms taken often being conducive to madness, anger and despair. But they all collectively produce an awareness of cosmic perspective in the percipients which *can* be controlled, channelled and understood on an internal and liberating level. In this way what can be termed the 'cosmic balance' is maintained.

As much of the outer 'control force' seems to be wildly paradoxical and banally silly, a well developed sense of humour appears to be one of the most effective of the counter-controlling and defence mechanisms. Remember the old axiom 'the Devil, that proud spirit, cannot bear to be mocked'.

[From: The Dark Gods (1985) by Anthony Roberts *et al.* Page 92 – 93]

In *The Cosmic Pulse of Life,* (first published in 1976), Trevor James Constable has produced a stunningly original if not yet adequately acknowledged or fully appreciated work of occult research. In Chapter Three, *Finding a New Pathway,* Constable writes of his own psychic experience:

> In *They Live in the Sky* I detailed my first psychic experiences and will not therefore repeat them here. Suffice it to say that by persisting with the techniques learned at Giant Rock, I set the stage for an irruption of the unseen worlds into a consciousness – *mine* – not prepared for such an impact. Becoming sensitive suddenly to spectra of vibration with which one is totally unfamiliar can be an unhinging experience. In recent years, the so-called "psychedelic revolution" has exposed untold thousands of persons to the consequences of chemical tampering with consciousness. All such forcing open of doors is destructive of orderly inner development, no matter what the academic qualifications of its advocates.
>
> There was in my case no visions of the unseen worlds or astral phantasmagoria, but I did develop extreme sensitivity to telepathic impulses. I found that I could barely control the situation. In daily business life in the aviation industry, I would hear a sentence psychically before a client ever spoke the words physically. When the telephone rang, I knew who was calling before I picked up the instrument.
>
> A constant struggle soon ensued for control of my physical vehicle – myself against unseen interlopers. I was fighting continually against various forms of automatism. Anyone who doubts the reality of occult things would have no doubt whatever concerning them were they to endure an experience of this order. I emerged from it all with a solid respect for the reality of the occult that I have never subsequently lost.

[From: The Cosmic Pulse of Life (2008 Revised and Updated Fourth Edition) by Trevor James Constable. Page 31]

Report: #84

Location: Rear Garden (~12:30hrs)

Dose: 40mg

Shunned by the Entire School

I was ready for research and keen to secure mind-to-mind interaction with a powerful discarnate intelligence. Whilst undertaking the third pull my inner psychic sound was already ringing with terrific energy. The woolly hat covering my head and my ears seemed to contribute to the extraordinary volume of my tinnitus. The flush of molecules from the particularly voluminous third intake arrived at my brain and further boosted the intensity of my tinnitus. An incredibly busy psycho-spiritual presence appeared above me; composed of a multitude of rounded-edged cells; each cell containing the appearance of a tiny darkened plus sign, centrally therein. I awaited the palpable energetic projection of this highly aroused occult occurrence. But it soon occurred to me that despite the excellence of my inhalations, nothing discarnate had emerged to interact with me. I strongly suspected something was amiss; something about me; something about my research; something about those powerful discarnate entities that usually emerge with untold rapidity. As I watched my occult substance expanding upwards and outwards, I decided I didn't wish to dwell upon why that could be. I tried to shut it out of my mind. But to no avail. My concern was far too deeply rooted to be ignored. I strongly sensed something really was amiss. I felt completely alone – like a little boy without any friends stood all alone in the school playground; shunned by the entire school. Nobody wanted to play with me! And that cut sharply and deeply into my essential self. I was now completely disinterested in the extent of my psycho-spiritually evident occult projection, no matter how high in the sky it had reached. I tried to fathom exactly what the problem was. The most obvious cause was the baleful frame of mind that had recently befallen me. Despite the apparent emptiness of the vast blue sky, I felt I was under the watchful scrutiny of a large albeit unseen audience. My instinct chimed harmoniously with that speculation. But I also knew I did not really know the truth of the matter. Nevertheless, I considered I should offer up an apology. I was all too ready to apologise – mainly through fretting about the possibility of never again securing interdimensional interactions. I began making silently spoken apologies. But they all sounded far too insincere where it mattered most. I then stopped myself upon realising that one really needs to understand what one has done wrong before one can offer up an apology. Could this occult incommunicado have anything to do with me viewing mainstream online pornography, I wondered. But I could really only conclude I was outcast on the basis of having harboured such an awfully baleful machination toward my wife in the dark bowels of my mind. Perhaps those powerful discarnate intelligences were also genuinely concerned about my mental health. Perhaps they were purposefully staying away – and not just for my benefit. I was feeling totally unloved and dejected. Whatever it was, my emotions now carried sufficient weight for me to offer a sincere apology. I made an unspoken apology into what appeared to be a vast and empty sky. I felt I was at least making my apology with some degree of sincerity from that portion of oneself where such things really matter most.

Report: #85

Location: Bedroom (~09:45hrs)

Dose: 37mg

Blowing a Mischief

The third inhalation emptied the pipe. Initially the room appeared no different. But as my head sank down into the pillows it became all too evident something was emerging to share the room with me. The entity appeared to emerge from the midst of the bedroom and quickly filled the room with its jarring energy. Straightaway the room appeared very much lighter and very much brighter – the ceiling appeared lower and the room appeared notably wider. The energy palpably increased which had a proportionate effect upon the rapidly jarring appearance of the bedroom. Seconds later the energy increased even further, resulting in the same proportionate visual effect. The energy was strangely palpable and its turbulent jarring nature was visibly unmissable. Something small and tactile suddenly raced up the outside of my right leg and the outside of my right arm. Whatever it was it felt like it was beneath the fabric of my clothing. It felt like the lightest touch of a fingertip. Both subtle points loved to quickly and delicately trace a line around the outskirts of my body in a continuous circuitous route. The high energy remained constant throughout the bedroom. I suspected the entity was undertaking some obscure occult procedure. I was just happy to have secured its visitation. As I focussed upon the active energy filling the bedroom, I had a sense of the awesome willpower the entity was expending in maintaining this level of energy. I strongly sensed the interaction required a concerted effort of will from the entity. Such realisation made me feel quite special; special in the way that one feels whenever someone you love gives of their time freely. My outline shape continued to be traced by two very small and very delicate quasi-physical projections formed from the entity. Once again, I gained a distinct sense of the significant mental effort required in undertaking this bizarre action. After approximately two minutes the energy began to subside. As it did so, I was genuinely surprised to perceive that I was being very gently lowered some short distance down onto the carpet. It was so slow and so subtle that there was never any sense of my back re-cushioning itself upon the floor. Toward the end of that strange descent, a very much subtler and far more refined lowering action became evident beneath my back and my arms. It was as though something very fine and impossibly thin was very carefully flattening or almost deflating itself, and then very slowly manoeuvering out from beneath me. With that done the room was back to its ordinary everyday appearance, leaving me aghast at how just how bright and just how light it had appeared only moments ago; and how at odds its dimensions had appeared only moments ago. Suspecting that my occult visitor could still see, me and intuit my emotions, I quickly raised both arms and gave a big smile and thumbs up.

Report: #86

Location: Landing (~14:15hrs)

Dose: 30mg

Devastatingly Phenomenal Energy

Slowly and carefully I inhaled most of the dose and retained it before exhaling. There was very little remaining at the second pull. I lay back and remained emotionless and observationally astute. After just a few seconds I began to perceive the expansion of my occult energy. No sooner had I perceived that when a discarnate intelligence began to emerge from nowhere and manifested its powerful spiritual might. As it began to impose its incredible power, I recognised how easily I was able to differentiate between my own amplified occult energy and the energy from the entity. However, that soon became an irrelevant consideration, because over the next thirty or forty seconds the entity smoothly and speedily increased its power to such a level that I simply cannot adequately express it in words. I became utterly mesmerized by the devastatingly phenomenal energy. It was upon me, around me, and within me. It reached an intensity of truly impossible compressive power. And even then – it continued, and it continued, and it continued. It just did not seem reasonable that such an awesome display of power could manifest in the confines of a small suburban bedroom. The sheer power and the mesmeric effect from that power rendered my perception of my surroundings completely out of sorts. My setting had no familiarity with me at all. Was I lying down looking up; standing up looking ahead; or airborne looking down? Each and every position seemed feasible. After the immense power reached its peak, I realised a portion of the occult entity had saturated itself throughout my oral and cranial physiology. A strange rigid stiffness was evident above the roof of my mouth. My head was being held firm and fast from within. I had to recognise the strange constraints affecting the interior of my mouth simply in order to prepare for, and undertake the act of, swallowing. The atmosphere remained incredibly highly charged with discarnate emotional energy even after the devastating display of power had abated. The entity then began the process of vacating from whichever parts of my physiology it had invested itself within. The atmosphere throughout the bedroom was one of utter seriousness. A remote part of my mind wondered about pursuing the option of panic. But no sooner had the thought arisen when the powerful discarnate mind telepathically assured me there was no need for any such action. My mind automatically interpreted the content of that communication from that which was greater than itself. Slowly and surely the high emotional energy subsided, until I was sure the entity had vacated me. But just then, above each elbow, a frantic interior unknitting action commenced. I suspected this was an after-effect upon my nervous system caused by the entity exiting my physiology. As soon as I moved my arms the strange activity ceased. I remained emotionless and speechless. There was no thought to reflect upon the experience and no attempt to regroup my thoughts. I just lay still and silent – unthinkingly accepting that something absolutely incredible had just occurred. I then made some gestures to symbolically direct my gratitude to that which had just interacted with me. Tears welled up in my eyes. I could have so easily have burst into a big blubbing cry. But I wanted to remain calm and in control of my emotions – because I wanted to emulate the mind of the Occult Master. The experience had lasted just a few minutes. And I remained lain for just a few minutes longer.

Report: #87

Location: Rear Garden (~11:30hrs)

Dose: 30mg

Hint of the Other Place

I was really in the mood to commit to my research and was actually looking forward to this experiment. The crystals were fresh and had been looked after with a maternal level of care. With a woolly hat upon my head and sunglasses over my eyes to filter out retinal sting from the white clouds, I lay down. But only to sit straight back up and begin emptying the pipe in two excellent pulls. As I reclined it was immediately evident that a highly complex and geometrically intricate psycho-spiritual presence was above me. It mirrored my length. It was clearly pronounced – absolutely unmissable. It was in fact, visually stunning to behold. I knew I was about to feel the impact from the voluminous final inhalation. And I knew it was going to be significant. The arrival of those final DMT molecules produced an unexpected and significant clicking sound in the midst of my brain. After hearing that, a truly extraordinary silence befell the setting. Had the all-pervading ambient background sounds suddenly ceased at that very moment? A great big geometrically configured stream of very dense crystal-clear psycho-spiritual substance began spiralling out me at a truly terrific rate. It was so profound and so astonishing to see my otherwise invisible constitution; so beautifully configured and so bountifully proportioned; streaming out of me in a vast spiralling torrent. My mouth felt like it was hinged open at one hundred and eighty degrees. My lips, my tongue and my mouth felt composed of warm, wet, soft and slippery puckered rubber. I had a rubbery foreign object inside my mouth. And although my tongue was ever chasing that object, my tongue was ever failing to understand that it was in fact chasing itself. I was aware I was in a DMT experience. But that awareness was so very far from being supported by my usual everyday conscious awareness. The feel of my tongue circling around my heavily salivated mouth was tremendously refreshing. Indeed, that seemed to be the central focus of my limited conscious awareness. I willingly pursued the action of rolling my tongue around and around the inside of my mouth solely for the bizarre oral pleasure it gave. My visual field was terrifically busy with a great mass of incredibly dense and highly active psycho-spiritual substance. There was a great deal of activity within that field. But I simply cannot describe any of that in outline or detail because the content therein was active at a much faster rate than my senses could process. I was not aware the white clouds were providing background whiteness because that whiteness was so heavily saturated. Miscellaneous scenery was moving around in front of me with prodigious energy. An illusory construct suddenly passed my eyes. It was a very highly defined cartoonish gnome-sized gentleman wearing a bright red outfit. He stopped just ahead of me and extended his arm toward me. He was offering me a hat that he appeared to have just picked up from the ground. I immediately understood this hat was supposed to belong to me. It was as though I had unknowingly dropped my hat, and this little man had picked it up as a gesture of good will, and was now helpfully offering its return. All I had to do was extend my right hand and take it from him. It seemed so incredibly real – visually, mentally, emotionally. There was nothing untoward about this small anthropomorphic illusory construct. But in the very back of my mind I was trying to compute who he really was. Was he an aspect of my psyche; something that had formed a degree of autonomous independence from me – and was now wishing to engage in convivial discourse? Despite the genuine friendliness and helpfulness of the little fellow, I was unsure. I was now becoming increasingly aware that my emotional state was one of increasingly deep and sublime beatific contentment. The hat that was not really my hat was still been helpfully held out for me by the highly defined cartoon like little gentleman. I toyed with the notion of extending my right hand and politely taking the hat from him. But some remote part of my cognition realised I was invested with the liberty of choice. I addressed the illusory figure in a very slow and almost drawling manner that represented my highly contented frame of mind: "No! That's okay! I'm good, thanks! I'm really good! You can just drop that hat right there!" I don't remember losing sight of the little fellow, but immediately after concluding that communication my level of emotional contentment heightened immensely. Now, I was in a state of pure bliss. It was perfect and beautiful and it infused my entire being. Only a very remote portion of my cognitive mind realised I was still within a DMT experience. The rest of me felt this blissful experience would last forever. And that portion of me was absolutely happy for this state of blissful contentment to last forever and ever and ever. Unexpectedly, it then seemed that I was floatable. It seemed that I was very slowly and very smoothly drifting over to my left. The sensation was totally dreamy and otherworldly. But no sooner had it begun when it suddenly stopped. But it stopped in such a smooth fashion as to make the movement I had just experienced seem like an incredible magical illusion.

In a dreamy and languid voice, I whispered my complaint: "Oh! I was enjoying that!" Straightway the illusion of movement resumed and once again. It felt that I was smoothly drifting over to my left. It was tactilely divine. My state of bliss was now at peak. The experience felt like it had lasted forever and would continue to last forever. It was heavenly. It was a state of emotional contentment beyond the capacity of my imagination; a state of being that can only ever be experienced and on no account conveyed in this or any other book. By now, I realised that a very high intelligence was powerfully interacting with me. For some unfathomable reason I began to suspect this entity had actually come to my rescue. The sensation of drifting smoothly over to my left continued and was having a terrifically somniferous effect upon me. The entity then began to slowly withdraw an immensely dense portion of itself from my brain. But in a visually very spectacular and tactilely totally stupendous fashion. From the region of my forehead, a drooping crystal-clear cylindrical mass of incredibly dense psycho-spiritual substance stretched out to the greater mass of discarnate mind-stuff engulfing me. Its unique hold upon my brain was profound – it felt so exceptionally tight that it could have been construed as painful. My tactile perception of its dense physicality as it pulled away from my brain made it feel as though the entity had an immensely powerful suction-like hold upon my brain. As it pulled away, I was able to see and palpably perceive as the psycho-spiritual cylindrical mass stretched and drooped. All the while, my state of deep relaxation was becoming deeper and deeper. Until eventually, I was once again all alone, in the small rear garden of a non-descript suburban house, on a cold winter's morning, feeling like I had just been graced with a hint of the other place.

Whatever had created that extraordinary silence it seemed to remain right up until the moment the entity vanished. As the entity was slowly withdrawing itself from this interaction my aural senses realised just how unnaturally quiet the surrounding environment remained. There was no sound whatsoever. It was only after the entity had totally vanished that the birds began to call again. The first was from a bird whose call sounded exactly like the first note of a wolf whistle. Other birdsongs and calls then ensued, creating a great choir of avian chatter. A blackbird swooped down and glided unnaturally close to my face – giving me a ridiculously close-up tracer-trailing view of its fanned tail feathers. It landed on the rainwater gutter at the rear of house and then turned itself around as though to look at me. As improbable as this must surely sound, I could not help but consider the local birds had perceived something uncommon had just occurred within this small garden.

Report: #88

Location: Rear Garden (~17:30hrs)

Dose: 31mg

Losing My Buttons

A crow was cawing noisily and non-stop somewhere nearby. I sat up and made one small inhalation before deciding to reduce the intensity of the flame. Two confident pulls then emptied the pipe. I was certain something was already above me as I lay back. I cannot recollect whether it imposed any power upon me. However, I do recollect it suddenly made itself very apparent. From my limited perspective, it was evidently something geometrically very complex; something incredibly beautiful; and something mind-numbingly vast in size. Its outline form appeared conoidal with the tapered portion immediately in front of my face. My eyes moved to trace the extent of its size by viewing either side of its beautifully configured vast form. Instinctively I recognised this was an entity of such magnificence that it really had no business at all manifesting above me. Part of me felt unworthy that my eyes should behold something of such magnificence. There was no fear evident within me. I was totally calm and at ease. But it was a strange kind of calmness; not quite nonchalant but more of a misguided passivity at what I was witnessing. The crow continued cawing nearby. The vast entity began slowly descending toward me. Upon doing so, the portion nearest me increased remarkably in density, making it appear whitely pearlescent. As that portion engulfed me, I immediately felt the incredible density of the substance. Now I felt privileged. Something visibly vast and so beautifully configured had deigned to reveal itself to me. And now it was slowly streaming into me and through me – a slowly descending big beautiful mass of highly evolved spirit being. But the crow still had my ears. I wanted my focus to be solely upon the magnificence of the entity streaming through me. But the crow's continuous caws had a piece of me. And so, despite the evident highness of the entity, a portion of my mind was invested in comically wringing the crow's neck. The entity streaming through me seemed never ending. Somewhere inside, I recognised the magnificence of this experience. I realised the vast gulf of difference between our respective states of being – the immense disparity between our evolutionary advancement. And some part of me wanted to kill that noisy crow! As the entity streamed through me, I wondered: How many lifetimes (terrestrial and otherworldly) must it take for one to reach such an advanced state of existence? The entity slowed and stopped streaming through me. Its vast psycho-spiritual presence was now unmissably visible above me. I realised I had only a limited view of its complete fullness. The crow ceased cawing. A great portion of the vast spiritual entity remained stable, immediately above me. It was looking at me and looking into me. There was a discomforting silence. It was one of those silences where the greater strength of character imposes upon the lesser character to open up and spill the truth; even unto the very smallest little detail. My mind tried to feed my mouth with words. But those words tried and failed to jump off my tongue. They were banal and pitiful; wholly lacking in the kind of depth and substance I really wished I had within me. I felt beyond silly – beyond foolish. I felt weak and pitiful and empty. I felt excruciatingly immature for allowing my thoughts to focus so balefully upon a noisy crow, when something so literally very high-minded had gracefully granted me sight of its constitutional magnificence. My incarnated humanness weighed heavily upon me. I yearned to be able to say the right thing; to think the right thing; and to feel the right thing. But it was not there. It was simply was not forthcoming. The silent scrutiny from the highly advanced entity made my soul squirm. Something simply had to give. Something simply had to happen. A passion suddenly arose within me; within my chest. With no aforethought whatsoever I grasped each side of my shirt and tore it wide open with all my might. Shirt buttons went flying. I immediately felt hallelujah-like rejoice. I had found the only way to communicate my frustration at my own innate limitations. High emotions surged through me. I verbally vented my satisfaction at having found the perfect way to express myself. With hands still tightly clutching either side of my buttonless shirt I voiced out loud and triumphantly: "That one! That one! That's the one! Right there!" I felt so much better. I felt I had found something of immense value from deep within. I felt I had given a thoroughly good account of myself to that which was above me. The esoteric symbolism of a pelican ripping open its breast fleetingly furnished my mind. I was still in a tremendously heightened emotional state and I was still under the watchful scrutiny of the vast entity. I released the shirt from my talon-like grip and placed my splayed fingers upon my chest, symbolically threatening to rip open my chest and expose my heart for the entity to inspect, right then and right there! It was meant symbolically. But emotionally, there was a brief moment where if I could have done it, I really would have done it. The highly charged emotion was short-lived. Because a puerile portion of my psyche piped-up with an ill-timed and poorly-humoured complaint about the ruined shirt. I felt so appalled with myself that I scornfully shouted down the egoistic and unfunny portion of my psyche, with a great big inwardly hollered: "OH, SHUT UP!" I realised the division within, but felt totally unconcerned by whatever mildly schizophrenic ramifications it may pose. I had recognised an important complexity within; something that told me about my human condition. I didn't focus upon the entity as it departed, as I was too embroiled with my own thoughts and emotions. I was profoundly affected by the interaction; especially by the bizarre emotion it had wrung out of me. The only thing I could really do was to keep on shaking my head, in profound astonishment and disbelief. I felt my commitment to writing about such an experience detracted from the depth and the value of the experience. Writing upon it seemed ultimately, so meaningless. I cried out as though sore from that realisation: "It's about me! It's about me! It's about me; when I die, and they take me apart, and analyse me, and ask me what I've done with my life." Just as I was nearing the end of that plaintive cry, a crow glided diagonally overhead. Without any thought I was diverted to distraction and blurted out loudly and with great depth of feeling: "Oh, that is beautiful!"

[Wikipedia: Pelican]

https://en.wikipedia.org/wiki/Pelican

> Pelicans are a genus of large water birds that makes up the family Pelecanidae. They are characterised by a long beak and a large throat pouch used for catching prey and draining water from the scooped-up contents before swallowing. [...] The pelican (*Henet* in Egyptian) was associated in Ancient Egypt with death and the afterlife. [...] In medieval Europe, the pelican was thought to be particularly attentive to her young, to the point of providing her own blood by wounding her own breast when no other food was available. As a result, the pelican came to symbolise the Passion of Jesus and the Eucharist, and usurped the image of the lamb and the flag. [...] The legends of self-wounding and the provision of blood may have arisen because of the impression a pelican sometimes gives that it is stabbing itself with its bill. In reality, it often presses this onto its chest in order to fully empty the pouch. [...] Pelicans have featured extensively in heraldry, generally using the Christian symbolism of the pelican as a caring and self-sacrificing parent. The image became linked

to the medieval religious feast of Corpus Christi. The universities of Oxford and Cambridge each have colleges named for the religious festival nearest the dates of their establishment, and both Corpus Christi College, Cambridge, and Corpus Christi College, Oxford, feature pelicans on their coats of arms. [...] The symbol of the Irish Blood Transfusion Service is a pelican, and for most of its existence the headquarters of the service was located at Pelican House in Dublin, Ireland. The heraldic pelican also ended up as a pub name and image, though sometimes with the image of the ship *Golden Hind*. Sir Francis Drake's famous ship was initially called *Pelican*, and adorned the British halfpenny coin.

The pelican is the subject of a popular limerick originally composed by Dixon Lanier Merritt in 1910 with several variations by other authors. The original version ran:

A wonderful bird is the pelican,
His bill will hold more than his belican,
He can take in his beak
Food enough for a week,
But I'm damned if I see how the helican.

[From Wikipedia, the free encyclopedia]

Volume I of Blavatsky's *The Secret Doctrine* takes the esoteric symbolism behind the apparently self-harming pelican into much deeper waters; commenting upon a universal glyph that represents the re-awakening of the universe (a perfect Circle with the (root) point in the Centre); explaining, with some criticism, the use of a symbol signifying the pregenetic Kosmos by Christian mystics (a perfect Circle with a cross in the Centre) – "...the great mystery of occult generation, from whence the name – Rosicrucians (Rose Cross)!" And then:

As may be judged, however, from the most important, as the best known of the Rosicrucians' symbols, there is one which has never been hitherto understood even by modern mystics. It is that of the "Pelican" tearing open its breast to feed its seven little ones... [....] As to the strange symbol chosen, it is equally suggestive; the true mystic significance being the idea of a universal matrix, figured by the primordial waters of the "deep," or the opening for the reception, and subsequently for the issue, of that one ray (the Logos), which contains in itself the other seven procreative rays or powers (the logoi or builders). Hence the choice by the Rosecroix of the aquatic fowl – whether swan or pelican, with seven young ones for a symbol, modified and adapted to the religion of every country. Ein-Soph is called the "Fiery Soul of the Pelican" in the Book of Numbers.

[Footnote] Whether the genus of the bird be cygnus, anser, or pelecanus, it is no matter, as it is an aquatic bird floating or moving on the waters like the Spirit, and then issuing from those waters to give birth to other beings. The true significance of the symbol of the Eighteenth Degree of the Rose-Croix is precisely this, though poetised later on into the motherly feeling of the Pelican rending its bosom to feed its seven little ones with its blood.

[From: The Secret Doctrine (1888) by H. P. Blavatsky. Volume I. Pages 19 and 80]

Report: #89

Location: Rear Garden (~14:00hrs)

Dose: 31mg

Armchair Delights

A disused upholstered armchair was retired from the house and placed outside on the patio. With pipe in hand I sat upon that chair in its fully reclined position and made myself comfortable. I decided to commit to the pipe in a somewhat piecemeal and leisurely fashion. Having engaged the flame, I cautiously attempted one moderate inhalation. But before I knew what was what, a substantial dense cloud of potent vapour had jumped through the pipe and had dived down deep into my lungs. I knew what to expect. My interior psychic energy rapidly amplified. I hunkered down into the armchair. The inside of my head was vibrating very powerfully. A strangely detailed transparent glassy medium became evident in front of me. My mouth, my tongue and my lips all felt heavily salivated and rubbery. My tongue began circuitously sweeping around my mouth. It was hugely refreshing. It became evident that a huge mass of psycho-spiritual substance had emanated from me, to a very great distance. An aeroplane flying at a relatively low altitude produced three very pronounced tracer trail images behind itself. I was still only mere seconds into the experience. I was not quite comfortable within the armchair and my mental grasp upon the rapidly unfolding powerful experience was incredibly loose. I cocked my head back and looked up at the clear blue sky. I saw nothing unusual and duly dropped my head back down. The power of the substance was very great. My hold upon my senses was becoming less and less manageable. It quickly reached a point where something had to give. I am not quite sure what part of my psyche gave out. But something must have altered therein because all of a sudden, I commenced with the kind of gurning and guffawing that would have properly befitted a madman. The laughter – despite its maniacal and madcap character – was tremendously medicinal. I decided to go with the flow and submitted myself to wallowing in it with complete psychiatric abandon. The apple tree caught my eye. Its multitude of upward pointing branches and branchlets all appeared knowingly configured into a convoluted anthropomorphic flourish. No sooner had I realised that when laugher spewed forth from my mouth. And it continued to such an extent that I simply had to avert my gaze from the tree. I was enraptured and engulfed by my own laughter. And yet despite that, I knew I would have to look at the apple tree once again, just to be absolutely sure that its anthropomorphic flourish really was as funny as I thought was. Upon doing so, my laugher erupted further and far beyond anything I have ever experienced before. The more and more I looked at the apple tree – still appearing extravagantly configured in an anthropomorphic flourish – the more and more my laugher increased. It reached such heightened intensity that I had to tell myself: this kind of laughter shouldn't exist; this kind of laughter has no right emanating from the mouth of a fully-grown adult male. But as I continued casting my eyes upon the tree, peals of gleeful laugher spewed from me unstoppably. Looking away just did not help. Looking away made me want to look at the tree even more. And that only made the situation worse. But then I thought I heard someone speaking. And that quickly made me realise just how far very removed I was from my conventional self. I listened to the voices. It seemed my eldest son – who was sitting indoors at his homework desk behind the window to my right – was speaking in terms of hoping that he too could laugh like that when he is older. My wife was in the kitchen, stood at the sink behind the window that was to my left. She was speaking vaguely and indistinctly about the extent of my laughter. I believed they were having a conversation between themselves about me. Now, I felt incredibly self-conscious. Not embarrassed. But surprised at just how far my laughter had run away with itself. I tilted my head back and looked up to the sky. A huge tide of my own mind-stuff was slowly making its way down toward me. The visual clarity of the psycho-spiritual substance was truly astonishing. Its width far exceeded the boundary fences on either side of the garden. As I continued looking up at that remarkable substance, I had to accept that its extent appeared endless. The contrast of that psycho-spiritual substance against the pebble-dashed exterior of the house made the substance appear as a slowly descending waterfall of exceptional clarity and exquisite detail. Something small moving through the air at low altitude suddenly caught my eye. It exhibited dazzling radiance. My eyes zoomed to see three slow moving objects. Each object was adorned with a significant halo. A fourth and slightly larger object trailed behind the three. There was some kind of mental connection between us that caused me to voice out loud, in a reassured manner: "That's the one! That's the one!" They moved across the sky from east to west. But no sooner had I spotted them when they increased in speed. I focussed upon them intently in order to satisfy myself that these were uncommon aerial phenomena. I jumped up and tried to maintain my visual focus upon them. But they were soon out of sight. I returned to the armchair. My mood was vibrant and positive. The mild paranoia over whether my family had heard my extreme laughter mattered not a jot. After a few minutes sat in quiet reflection I headed indoors and enquired of my wife whether she'd heard me. She said she had not. I went over to my eldest son and asked him the same question. He said he had not. Both responses sounded sheepishly unconvincing. I asked my wife once again whether she had heard anything at all. She again said she'd heard nothing. But then asked me if I'd been laughing. When I asked why she was asking me that question, she would only volunteer that she guessed I'd been laughing.

Possibly the most mysterious aspect of this experience was the voices I thought I'd heard from my wife and my son. Their approximate distance from me through the glazing and the fabric of the house was inconsiderable. I had been sure they were both discussing my laughter. But both said they heard nothing. This left me wondering whether I had imagined their voices. I am open to considering that my imagination fictionalised the entirety of what I thought was a conversation between my wife and my son. But equally, I am open to considering that my exteriorised mind-stuff was somehow able to intuit and discern the content of their thoughts in relation to my outlandish laughter, in such close proximity to them. Perhaps – as I suspect - they were simply too embarrassed to admit hearing such uncommon laughter from a grown man.

Report: #90

Location: Landing (~12:45hrs)

Dose: 33mg

Lost Recall

Upon emptying the pipe, I assumed my usual recumbent position and was able to see and feel the energetic emergence of a crystal-clear discarnate mind above me. There must have then been a sudden and almighty explosion of incredibly powerful mesmeric energy. I recall hearing the insanely high-pitched sound associated with a powerful entity manifestation. But suddenly, the entire setting appeared entirely ordinary – except for the overwhelming emotional sense of the presence of a powerful Occult Master. My lips remained closed but they were not sealed. My breathing was fast although I did not feel especially scared. The already powerful emotional atmosphere increased, and further increased; to such extent that I felt certain I was supposed to understand something, or do something, or say something. I remained silent and puzzled as to what the prompting was. Until I could no longer hold my tongue and I blurted out unthinkingly: "My god! I don't know how you people do what you do, but it's pure magic!" Straightaway, I felt mildly abashed for referring to the powerful spiritual entity as 'people'. I tried to correct my statement. But in doing so, I realised how very strange my voice sounded upon my ears. And because of that bizarre acoustic effect, I continued speaking, simply in order to hear more and more of my unusual sounding voice. But as I listened intently to my own voice, I couldn't really discern any significant change from how it ordinarily sounds. And yet it certainly sounded so completely at odds with how it ordinarily sounds upon my ears. This only served to magnify my appreciation of the apparent magic I was being subjected to. It then felt like a solid cube had been placed upon my left shoulder. I could clearly perceive its mass and the dimensions of its shape. I reached my right hand over to touch my left shoulder, but there was no such object present. I really wanted the interaction to continue. I really wanted to be exposed to more magic. Rather interestingly, after the high-minded entity had departed, I simply could not recollect any detail whatsoever of what had just occurred after inhaling the dose. I gave up and headed downstairs to make a coffee. Whilst standing by the kitchen sink, I finally recalled perceiving the burst of intense high energy from the entity.

Report: #91

Location: Bedroom (~13:00hrs)

Dose: 25mg

Dense Body-of-Mind

I felt my nervousness and questioned why it was so. Perhaps a better approach to such research would be one of confidence, or emotional rejoice; rejoice at witnessing one's own psycho-spiritual projection; rejoice at the resulting interaction imposed upon one's perception, psyche and physiology by a highly evolved spiritual entity. But it was academic. My mind was too busy endeavouring to overcome genuine fear rather than invest in feeling wonderment. I lay down on the bedroom floor and sat straight back up again to begin the first of three slow and very pleasing inhalations. I lay back but nothing changed. A second or two passed before something discarnate began to emerge in that particularly unique and characteristic way – from out of thin air. There was a sudden palpable perception of a discarnate mental weightiness exerting its presence. There was an unmissable turbulent waviness within the air, at the exact same location where the emergence was taking place. It seemed this manifestation was limited and localised. Over the next two to three seconds it expanded in what appeared as a slow-motion explosion of seething psycho-spiritual energy. Upon filling the room, it then imposed itself, but in something of a unique manner. There was no highly energetic high-powered mightiness; there was no audible sound resulting from any compressive force impinging upon the floor or the walls. It was more the case that a super-high-density fluidic mind had suddenly deigned to pour itself into my bedroom. Rightly or wrongly, my senses informed me that I was perceiving just a limited portion of something that was very much larger. The turbulence affecting the air ceased. The concentrated density of mind that was now visibly ahead of me was simply phenomenal – frighteningly so! Never before have I encountered or experienced such a titanic force of power as was characterised by that presence – mentally and (paradoxically) physically! The density of its psycho-spiritual composition was simply colossal. The appearance of the bedroom had only changed in so far as my eyes were working through a transparent medium of truly phenomenal density. I felt very afraid. Something of such behemothic power had no earthly business revealing itself to me – even in limited proportion. This was a power beyond compare; it was a power that fascinated me and frightened me; but very much more the latter than the former. It made me realise just how exceedingly potent and powerful some of these entities actually are. This was an Occult Master on a grand scale; a very highly evolved entity; a truly magnificent and mighty mind. And right now, this was an experience I was woefully ill-equipped for. Ignoring one's fears is one thing. But having courage of conviction is something entirely different. I said something. But I don't recall what it was. A word, or words, or perhaps just a noise. But all told, it amounted to a cry of "Eek!" The awesome partial manifestation was so incomprehensibly phenomenal that one moment it was there, and the very next moment it was gone. It was visibly and sensibly gone. My relief was immense. That was something far in excess of what I am accustomed to experiencing. But my relief was short-lived and misguided, because something suddenly became active around me; something upon the surface of my skin or beneath the surface of my skin smoothly traced my outline in a strange and repetitive circuitous route. It felt as though I was being measured up for some unknown reason of immense seriousness. I was completely speechless at this continuation of the experience. In a downbeat frame of mind, I resigned myself to the undertaking. It was an undertaking which seemed to have completely ignored the emotional relief I had cherished a mere moment ago. The ongoing repetitive circuitous action reminded me of the snipping action of scissors. It also felt like a very fine thread was drawn laterally beneath the small of my back. There was a very business-like seriousness pervading the entire room. Once my outline had been traced twice or thrice, the entity commenced a very obvious and very invasive action undertaken deep within the tissue of both arms. It was very fast and repetitive. It felt like some kind of bizarre but painless stitching activity was underway deep inside me. My emotion me was one of complete and utter resignation. I knew I was at liberty to stand up and depart the bedroom at any time. But having experienced something of the stupendous nature of this entity, the last thing I wanted to do was act in any way that could be construed as non-compliant. Whilst all this was underway, I could not help myself from thinking that I was undergoing preparation for something far more significant. And if not today, then during in some future research experiment, where things would become clearer or would be made clearer to me. I began thinking deeply about the difference in approaching this research by willfully ignoring my fears, versus approaching this research with investigative courage. The unsettling experience of having witnessed such an impossible density of discarnate mind was having a profoundly introspective effect on me. Whilst the invasive action within my arms was still underway, I began to question whether I really had the requisite calibre of character for such investigations as these. But the enquiry felt like it was made at the level of my soul, rather than my ego. I then questioned the quality of my soul. Was I – the real me – a courageous individual? And what about in past lives? Or had I previously fallen at the final hurdle? Had I previously failed? Not once, not twice, but many times? Success and failure in this particular lifetime both felt like starkly real and genuine possibilities. And the outcome felt like it would be determined by something far deeper than my ego. I questioned myself: Why am I even committing myself to this potent substance? And in committing myself: Am I doing this for the worthiest of reasons? The invasive procedure continued apace for several minutes. And after it had ceased, I spent a few more minutes going over the particulars of the experience before vacating the bedroom.

More may be stated in relation to my tactile perception of that stupendous density of discarnate mind. It is my temporarily aroused – amplified / expanded – psycho-spiritual self that enables such an obvious tactile perception of the density of those insanely powerful discarnate entities. Yet trying to adequately convey my actual tactile perception of that tremendous otherworldly mind-stuff is such a challenge. It is at once transparent and yet impossibly solid and all pervasive. At the time I was experiencing that prodigious mass of occult mind my interior narrative recognised the truly incredible density was: "harder than concrete ... harder than rock ... harder than steel." Visually and tactilely, it seemed a portion of the dense mass of mind had concentrated itself towards the front of the bedroom, and it really did seem that portion was just a small part of a very much greater whole. I distinctly perceived the concentrated density of the mind was in close proximity to my feet and was certainly not directly above my body. I am equally certain such huge compression from that perceived density would've been catastrophic had it been directly above my body. Visually, it appeared to be a perfectly true vertical wall formed of a relatively crystal-clear yet impossibly dense substance. Although I could see reasonably clearly through that mass its incredible density gave it the appearance of sea-weathered glass. In looking for complementary supporting information, I am drawn to Meade Layne's occult derived research, published in: *The Coming of the Guardians – An Interpretation of the Flying Saucers as Given from The Other Side of Life.* First published in 1956, I am finding this work is becoming more and more rewarding each and every time I dip into its heavily esoteric pages:

It is easy to see that there may be (and indeed there are) material worlds – worlds of dense substance all about us, which we are unable to touch because they are too dense, not too rarefied. And some of these objects may at times be touchable but still invisible (colours we cannot see) and make all kinds of sounds which we can't hear. These worlds can interpenetrate with ours, and in turn be interpenetrated by others of still higher density, and our normal senses would never report any of them. If the Aeroforms are to be understood in their true nature as Emergents, it is essential that those elementary ideas be clear in our minds.

[From: The Coming of the Guardians (2009 edition) by Meade Layne. Page 4 – 5]

And:

The importance of this matter of density, to our present inquiry, stems largely from the repeated assertion by the Controls, that the Discs "come out of worlds of substance a hundred thousand times more dense than the matter you perceive with your senses."

[From: The Coming of the Guardians (2009 edition) by Meade Layne. Page 5]

Report: #92

Location: Rear Garden (~14:40hrs)

Dose: 40mg

Cylindrical-Shaped Something

I sat up and ignited the flame. But before I knew what was what I had combusted the entire substance and drawn down the most horrid tasting particulate pollution. I lay back. The sound within my head was significant. It was evident something transparent had projected from me by virtue of the geometric interference patterning appearing upon the clouds. I berated myself for combusting the entire dose. A sharp sounding unfamiliar birdsong filled the air. Other more familiar birdsong caught my ears. The more the unfamiliar birdsong persisted, the more and more I thought about how out of place it sounded. My ears detected the source of the unfamiliar singing had moved closer to me. I looked over to my right and listened intently as my eyes spotted a greenfinch on the far side of the apple tree. Upon returning my gaze skyward something caught my eye. Up at a truly terrific altitude, I observed a short black cylindrical shape with rounded ends. It moved steadily in a northerly direction. I was impressed by what must have been a remarkable size for a phenomenon at such great height. I momentarily lost sight of the thing. But I could at least see that within moments it would pass beneath a cumulus. I caught sight of it again against the blue background. It made what appeared to be a sudden ninety degree turn and then made off in an easterly direction before being lost to my sight. I remained on the ground for a short while longer before heading indoors to prepare my lunch.

Report: #93

Location: Rear Garden (~15:00hrs)

Dose: 39mg

Occult Roughhousing

The crystals had a pleasing smell of potency. Upon sitting down, I perceived my baseline tinnitus was already active at an unusually intense and high pitch. I suspected something was already invisibly present and awaiting me. That suspicion remained as I made four inhalations. The first three were overly cautious so as to avoid combustion. However, the fourth pull took in a great dense bomb of clean white vapour and completely emptied the pipe. I held it down for a good long while then lay back and exhaled. I was now beneath an overarching canopy of dense psycho-spiritual substance. Throughout the extent of that canopy I observed the appearance of hundreds of very small, dark equidistant points. I knew it had not projected from me. For a very brief moment, I felt a degree of self-satisfaction with my hunch that something really had been awaiting me. But then, over the space of mere seconds, the entity imposed a truly formidable level of power down upon me and around me, and right through me. I could both feel and hear its otherworldly impact into the poncho covering the soft ground beneath me. The energy rapidly increased to a truly astonishingly level. Whilst inside that powerful field of incredibly dense conscious energy, I observed visual changes to my surroundings. However, I was far more concerned with my safety than whatever strange visual changes were underway. Within mere seconds of experiencing the power of that tremendous living energy, I was very forcibly and very vigorously manhandled by that very same energy. It was like nothing else I have ever experienced. It was very fast and very rough. It smacked of forcefulness and decisiveness and effectively conveyed an attitude of: "No messing about now! Come here you!" The sheer level of brusque physicality imposed upon me; the speed with which I was been handled; and the powerful no nonsense emotion underpinning just how irrepressibly I was being processed made me certain that I would not return to life as I knew it. The entity had invested a very strong and very powerful presence throughout my head, my mouth, and my throat; making me feel as though I was securely locked into place, whether I liked it or not. Very quickly, very deeply and very powerfully – and seemingly with little or no care for me – an invasive deep tissue operation commenced throughout both my arms.

It did not matter that it was painless; the very rough and rapid manner in which I was been worked upon convinced me there was no way I could survive this. Inside the house, I could hear my two little boys excited by a computer game they were playing. Outside the house, I was engulfed in something so incredibly intense and so absolutely immersive as to make me feel that what remained of my life was limited to mere seconds. I wondered why I had ever gotten myself mixed up with pursuing such research. I thought of my wife. She was in the house and no real distance from me. I realised just how much I was missing her now that I would never see her again. And yet despite fretting about never seeing my family ever again, I remained paradoxically and almost perversely remarkably calm. Something red suddenly caught my eye. It seemed infused with personality. It was watching me and was speaking about me to something alongside it that was equally infused with personality. The red thing was commenting about me to the other thing, saying: "Look at him! Oh, he's really getting it now!" And the thing next to the red thing was agreeing and passing similar opinion. They both enjoyed laughing at my plight. However, I was far too involved with what was underway to feel too concerned about what they were saying to each other. I looked away briefly and upon returning my gaze I noted both things were actually clothes hanging out to dry on the washing line. I thought about bolting. But I knew I was totally captive to a level of force that was completely off the scale to anything I had hitherto experienced. Realising this predicament, I urged myself to remain focussed on what was underway; perchance the opportunity to continue with my ordinary life presented itself. The intense invasive work on my arms concluded, but was immediately followed with an equally bizarre and only marginally less forceful binding action. I was now being very tightly wrapped and bound in an unseen psycho-spiritual wrap; one that kept on tightly wrapping around me over and over again. Thoughts that I may yet survive the experience took root in my mind and quickly developed. As those thoughts grew the powerful entity slowly began to release me from its extraordinarily powerful grip. It now seemed I was been lowered to the ground some short distance. I took care of my emotional welfare by hyperventilating, simply in order to manage my emotions and to feed into my genuine relief that I was to remain alive. The entity was visibly unfurling from me and making its way skywards toward the continuous grey cloud. My relief was immense. I wanted to run indoors and hug my wife. But instead, looking up at the superdense psycho-spiritual mass leaving me, I bared my teeth and forced a deadpan grin of respectful defiance while signalling thumbs up. I then felt compelled to look up to a particular potion of the sky and noted there was now a hole in the otherwise continuous and uniform cloud cover. The perfect circle forming that hole displayed beautiful light blue sky beyond. Without really thinking why, I wished I could disappear through that same hole. I then questioned why the hole was there, as I had not noted its presence moments earlier. It seemed so uncannily out of place in the dense and continuous cloud cover. The obvious supposition was that the departing entity had just punched a hole through the cloud during its rapid skyward passage. And as I watched, the hole began to quickly vanish as the cloud closed in around it. Within moments it had completely closed. But I noted with great interest how the cloud filling that hole took on the semblance of something resembling a grey-coloured radial sphincter, replete with striated lines. I remained on the ground for several minutes while going over each and every little detail and feeling truly amazed at what I had just experienced.

On careful reflection – and desirous to choose the best words to accurately convey what occurred in this experience – I am satisfied in saying I was subjected to a truly extraordinary level of occult roughhousing. If this were my first ever experience with DMT, I would not only never again conduct such research, but I would earnestly entreat anyone thinking to make such explorations to leave well alone. I was manhandled and roughhoused by an entity the likes of which I have never encountered before. The emotion emanating from that being was one of singular resolute seriousness: very strict in the administration of its strength; totally prodigious in its power; willful with driven purpose to level far exceeding anything else I have ever experienced. And yet it does not really matter how accurately I choose my words, and how well I may manage to string a few sentences together, because I simply cannot convey the genuine turmoil and terror I experienced as something invisible yet visible, physical yet non-physical, grabbed a hold of me and handled me in such a rapid and forceful manner. The only valid terrestrial analogy I can bring to mind is that of a spirited dog playfully but violently wragging a soft toy.

Report: #94

Location: Bedroom (~13:15hrs)

Dose: 37mg

Open-Eyed REM

After preparing the pipe and heading outside I realised the wind was far too breezy. Indoors, my residual fears became many times enlarged. It seems far less demanding upon my nerves when I research outside. The bedroom was beautifully sunlit. Sitting up was a willful exercise in ignoring my fears. I made three textbook inhalations and then lay back. Almost straightaway, I had visual and tactile perception of something discarnate emerging out of thin air. Very rapidly it imposed its constitutional might. In an instant – and while still imposing its awesome power – the room appeared so very different: larger, cleaner and brighter, with a beige tinge evident throughout the air. With lips closed I hawked a small frog from the back of my throat. In that very instant there was a very obvious change throughout the volume of conscious energy. It was as though in that very instant the experience I was just about to be subjected had suddenly changed. After that I have no recollection of any further increase in energy. I recall considering whether to try running from the bedroom, because at some conscious level it was so obvious that I was in the midst of a power that was very far in advance of human consciousness. However, I am quite sure there was a hugely terrific increase in power, because mere seconds later the room was rendered in a truly majestic and stunningly brilliant illuminated finish. The room now appeared totally at odds with its ordinary everyday appearance; it appeared nothing at all like an ordinary terrestrial bedroom. It was enlarged. It was wrought in pristine whiteness. It was spic and span to a heavenly standard of housekeeping and cleanliness. It was simply breathtaking. But despite the otherworldly beauty, I was feeling so scared. My breathing was short and fast; my eyes were flitting around the room as though I was experiencing open-eyed REM – looking for the source of the magic and not realising I was actually immersed within the mind producing the magic. A portion of the entity was active behind the top of my head but its actions were so subtle as to be on the threshold of my tactile perception. I sensed I was been subtly coaxed into looking dead ahead, through the bedroom window. I focussed my sight on branches of the oaks. My breathing was short and rapid. I worked very hard at calming my breathing whilst resisting the temptation to allow my eyes to rove around the room. The appearance of the bedroom in its dazzling otherworldly radiance did not fully register with me until the entity began to slowly depart. That departure became evident as the dazzle decreased and the radiance slowly reduced. This occurred so very slowly and so very subtly. But it soon registered that the visual alteration had been one of truly astounding proportion. Even when I thought the transformation back to the ordinary everyday appearance was complete, I was genuinely shocked to see that it was still undergoing very significant changes back to its ordinary everyday mundane appearance. As the dense invisible mind-stuff continued to diminish and depart, I felt so astonished by the entire experience; I felt profoundly unsettled at a very fundamental level of my being. So much so that for some considerable time I simply did not trust that the ordinary everyday appearance of the bedroom was in fact its ordinary everyday appearance. The possibility of there been one final significant twist in the experience felt so real that I dare not move or assume anything. I just kept looking and breathing and breathing and looking. The weather had changed from bright sunshine to incredible dullness. A change which contrasted the visual differences by several orders of magnitude. The emotional impact from the encounter was considerable. It began by me railing against pursuing authorship on such matters. Inwardly, I vented: "This is not about a book! This is not about a book! This is about me!" I felt so profoundly shaken by the depth of personal insight into myself. I felt totally terrified of my fears succeeding, and I felt woefully weak about the ability of my courage to triumph. All options seemed open. I felt pivoted on a finely balanced fulcrum between my soul succeeding triumphantly and my soul failing miserably. The introspection was as painfully sore as it was reassuringly rewardingly. It was frightening and informative, helpful and insightful. As my mind worked through that business, I began to consider the differences between our respective consciousness: man contrasted against powerful DMT entity. My tongue suddenly and rather unexpectedly made a comical gesture in extensively projecting outwards. The action totally intrigued me. It was such a simple gesture. But it was one that told me so much about the human condition without one word uttered. I sat up and leant back against the cupboard door; raised my knees and hugged my shins. I became vexed at my inner voice for narrating as though I were writing. My reaction to the experience in that very moment felt as though it held very profound and very far reaching relevance to who I actually was – at a very deep level. I encouraged myself with repetitive and positive verbal outbursts, then stood up and walked over to the bedroom window and briefly looked outside before resuming the same position in the same location. Something caught my eye. An ant was working hard to negotiate the carpet fibres and numerous strands of my wife's long dark hair. I maneuvered onto my front such that I was now facing the little ant. As I watched it negotiating the apparently difficult terrain, I appreciated how it was operating on ant-specific instructions. Looking at the ant and knowing the chasm of difference between us, and knowing the ant could not see me in the same way that I could see it, I felt strangely empowered. Was I in a position not too dissimilar to the powerful discarnate DMT entity that had just interacted with me? I opened my mouth wide and from the back of my throat I exhaled my breath upon the ant. It stopped in its tracks, briefly, and then continued along a different route. It stopped again, reconsidered its route, turned around and began heading back the way it came.

Report: #95

Location: Rear Garden (~12:30hrs)

Dose: 40mg

Lacking the Requisite Full-Blown Madness

The school sports field fell totally silent. I sat up and began the first of three pulls. The first was voluminous, the second was especially voluminous, and the third found very little. I lay back and looked up. I can't say I was mindful of any significant increase in my tinnitus, but I had no doubt whatsoever the crystals were potent. Approximately eight arm's lengths above me, something glassily crystal-clear began to slowly emerge into visibility. It appeared to quiver, which put me in mind of the membrane forming a very large soap bubble buffeted in a gentle breeze. But the more and more the full extent of the occult entity became discernible, the more and more I realised I was looking up at the underside of something that was – without any exaggeration whatsoever – a colossal ship-sized entity. As my eyes and my mind began to comprehend the sheer impossible size of the thing, I realised I was looking upon something that was truly immense. I noted countless very small dark equidistant points throughout. Sighting such a level of detail brought to mind the occult being that had recently roughhoused me. But this entity really was of an entirely different order of magnitude. This really was a ship-sized entity. And this experiment was now becoming less of an experience and more of an event. There was simply no way I could have any form of mind-to-mind interaction with something on such a gargantuan scale as this titanic thing. I knew that and I felt that with every fibre and at every level of my being. My hands waved about vigorously, signalling my desire to proceed no further. Similarly, I shook my head from side to side, signalling the very same negatory stance. And to avoid any doubt about what I was physically communicating, my mouth adamantly streamed out: "No, no, no, no, no, no, no, no!" This colossus was well and truly beyond anything else that has ever deigned to reveal itself to me. From the outset of realising the ginormous size of this entity, my mind computed: "This thing is like a ship!" For the first few moments – based on the monstrous size of the entity – I was terribly fearful. And I remained terribly fearful. Yet after just a short while, curiosity and intrigue stirred within me. I focused on a mass of the glassily crystal-clear substance that had descended into the garden and down toward me. Much to my own surprise, it seemed I was acting on instinct when I raised my head and opened my mouth as wide as possible so that my lungs could greedily inhale the very air within which the glassy crystal-clear medium was subsumed. I was conscious the action was very strange even as I was undertaking it. But there was something within me that seemed almost hard-wired to act in such a way. It seemed an instinctive reaction in the presence of something of such immensity and advanced spiritual evolution. What underpinned my next action I am not so sure, but I extended my right arm and immersed my fist into the glassy crystal-clear substance. My fist and my wrist refracted significantly therein. A sudden and unexpected sudden sharp bang emanating from inside the shed totally startled me. I sat upright and noted the shed door was wide open, just as I had left it, but I saw a little robin fluttering around inside. I looked back up to see the entity. But instead, over in the direction of the school sports field, and stretching very high into the sky, I beheld an unforgettable and totally magnificent sight. I had to suppose the colossal body of the entity had moved skywards, because I was now looking at a very broad and crystal clear, oblong-shaped, telescopic vertical projection of magnificent proportion. That one sight alone was without any doubt one of the most remarkable sights I have ever seen in my entire life. The entire experiment and experience felt far more like an event of immense significance. My emotions were not only hugely heightened but were pared right back to depths of my heart. My fingers acting like talons wanted to tear open my chest and rip out my heart and offer it up to the entity. I symbolically went through those actions as best I could with complete and utter conviction. I was beside myself to a level I have never before experienced. I was frenzied in disbelief. The robin continued flapping about in the shed in a dishevelled state, causing me to voice out loud that I was going from one drama to another. As I prepared to stand up to help the little bird, I noted it had landed atop a bicycle tyre. It was now at the threshold of the wide-open door. All it had to do was fly outside. Indeed, such a scenario seemed inevitable. But instead, the robin flew back into the shed. Perplexed, I stood up and approached the shed whereupon the little bird made its exit, flying right by my left ear. I returned to my position. Choked with high emotion, I laid on my front and pressed my face hard into the cushions. I raised myself onto all fours and began punching the soft earth beneath the blanket with all my might because I realised, I would have to write about something I could hardly even come to terms with myself. The magnitude of the event was still sinking into me. And it was about to thoroughly shred all of my emotions. After turning over onto my back, I curled up fetally and collapsed over to my left side. The magnitude of the sighting; the sheer size of the thing; and the sheer impossibility that such a thing as that could even exist, momentarily ruined me. I burst into blubber and bawl. My eyes were tightly scrunched up and wringing wet. The pain of my astonishment completely ruled out any feelings of fascination. I thrust the fingers of my right hand into my mouth and bit down hard. I wanted to champ them to the bone, but I lacked the requisite full-blown madness. The magnitude of the event kept on washing over me, piquing me and poking at my raw emotions, driving me to tears and anger. I analysed exactly how I was feeling and determined with absolute exactitude that I wanted to turn myself inside out. This event was without any doubt the most stunning, the most revealing, and the most overpowering of my research thus far. I looked up at the sky with a solid lump of raw emotion swollen in the back of my throat.

I can assume the little robin's sight was affected by the strange and glassily apparent superdense substance filling the garden. I can only guess at how confusing the environment must have appeared to its little eyes. I must suppose the strange substance created bizarre visual changes to its otherwise familiar habitat. There is not much more I can add about my sighting of that gigantic ship-sized entity. I was still shaking my head about the sighting several days after the event. I can only wonder when thinking about what such an entity as that does with its existence; how it came to be; how it came to be so big; what challenges it faces on its own evolutionary path. Later in the day, I began to wish I had stood up and immersed my upper body in the great mass of the crystal-clear substance. I wished I could have observed the stunning visual effects of looking through something so strange and spectacular. I also began to wish I could have gone right inside the midst of the huge entity in a travelling capacity – a terrestrial passenger embarking on a strange occult voyage. In thinking upon such a scenario, my mind began singing on a non-stop loop, Wanda Dee's lyric from The KLF's 1991 hit single, *Last Train to Trancentral*: "Come on boy, d'ya wanna ride? Come on boy, d'ya wanna ride?" Despite the magnificence of both the appearance and the size of the entity, what made this event so totally overwhelmingly magnificent was the style of its departure – that very broad and crystal-clear, oblong shaped, vertical telescopic extension – reaching so high into the sky. The telescopic configuration made it appear the tremendous form had ascended smoothly upwards in stages. The evident intelligence and beauty behind its mode of departure had a tremendous impact upon me. But what was perhaps far less obvious to my conscious sensibilities at the time, was that something so maddeningly large could descend so very low over a housing estate and a school, and yet go totally undetected by anyone other than myself, by virtue of my temporarily highly aroused occult senses.

Report: #96

Location: Bedroom (~14:00hrs)

Dose: 36mg

One Magic Little Cloud

My fears were significant. It would have been easier not to undertake the experiment than to commit to it. Indeed, I had to force the issue, knowing that if I put it off today it would be much harder to commit myself tomorrow. The bedroom was brightly sunlit. I sat up and began. There was a sudden inhalation of clean white vapour. I tried for a second pull while the substance was acting very quickly upon me. Within mere seconds my psychic sound was ringing high and loud and my crystal-clear psycho-spiritual self was already in the process of energetically projecting. It soon became evident the entire dose had been inhaled in one magic little cloud. I lay back and a discarnate intelligence emerged with tremendous rapidity. After filling the room with truly terrific speed it then imposed a phenomenal intensity of ever-increasing high frequency penetrative energy. Whilst that highly mesmeric energetic increase was underway, I briefly had time to inwardly ask myself: "Oh my god! Why am I even doing this?" The frequency of energy quickly approached a rate which made its wholesale composition feel impossibly taut and impossibly solid. My mind questioned what kind of frequency I was experiencing, and without giving the matter any real thought volunteered the answer: "A divine frequency!" The frequency of that energy reached an impossibly stupendous peak level which thoroughly mesmerised me. The room now appeared very highly defined; very colourful; larger; cleaner; brighter – and was emotionally brimful with a discarnate mind intent on fast-paced playfulness. One or two Illusory constructs moved around the room with such lightning-like speed that I was barely able to maintain a level of perception upon them that would serve my memory well. It felt like my lips were sealed up from within. The entity had indeed invested a portion of itself within my cranial physiology. There was a single sudden banging noise from somewhere outside. I suspected a near neighbour had just closed a car door. With no hesitation whatsoever, as soon as the sound pressure wave from that noise arrived, the discarnate mind – or a portion therefrom – raced over in that same direction. As it did so, I distinctly felt its sudden surging motion in that direction. The entity perceptibly tore itself away after having temporarily melded its psycho-spiritual substance into my dimethyltryptamine-amplified psycho-spiritual substance. Even stranger was that I visually observed the sudden and rapid surge of the entity in the direction of the noise. The experience was greatly diminished, but it did continue. My mouth was agape and I was consciously moving my lower jaw left and right repeatedly, because I sensed the movement was somehow in unison with the impossibly rapid movements of the illusory figures darting around the room. The emotion was evidently one of very fast-paced playfulness. I wanted it to go on and on and on. I was completely mesmerised by the speed of the strange movements throughout the bedroom – they were so captivating. The withdrawal of the experience was so very subtle that I was never aware of any visual or emotional diminishment. During that phase, I felt something being inserted into me – somewhere in the region of my left shoulder blade. I thought it was just another machination of the discarnate entity and so I remained calm and motionless whilst wondering what was actually underway. A few seconds later I could really feel something was active deep inside that portion of my physiology. And whilst it wasn't painful, it was arousing some concern. It continued even after I was sure the entity had departed, making me wonder whether the strange effect was some kind of nervous spasm caused by the exit of the entity from that region of my physiology. When I moved the effect immediately ceased. At 14:00hrs the room was back to normal, albeit noticeably duller in the absence of bright sunlight. The presence of significant tracer trails behind the slow movement of my hands confirmed the continuing presence of my own transparent and exteriorised occult self. I remained prone for a few more minutes in a somewhat sombre and relatively emotionless state of mind.

The single intake of vapour deserves some additional comment. I imagine other researchers have experienced the unusual occurrence wherein the entire dose forms into one single little cloud of potent vapour. I playfully considered whether or not the pipe had been subject to some kind of occult subterfuge by the same entity – though I am quite certain that was not the case. I found it hugely interesting in how the discarnate entity responded to that sudden noise from outside; and how I was able to tactilely and visually perceive its sudden surge in that direction. For me, that raised fascinating questions about the extent of the field of consciousness of that particular entity. I am forced to assume its focus was entirely upon me, and that it was unknowing of what was occurring in the immediate environment outside the bedroom. I must also assume it was both sensible and sensitive to the sound pressure wave. But from its response, it appeared that whilst some of the discarnate mind had surged in the direction of the noise, some of it also remained with me and continued to commit itself to fast-paced playfulness. Finally, it was really obvious those fast-paced visual hallucinations were indeed illusory constructs formed within the dense mind-stuff of the occult entity. In addition, there were equally fast-paced bizarre refractions of the ordinary reality of the bedroom. I suggest the effect was caused by the superdense mind-stuff moving in a cyclical motion.

Report: #97

Location: Bedroom (~11:30hrs)

Dose: 36mg

The Proper Response

This was an occasion where my courage was really tested. I questioned whether or not I had the requisite mettle to undertake the experiment. Could I overcome a very significant level of fear? More importantly, did I have what was required to commit myself to this experiment inside the house rather than outside the house? The dose represented the entirety of available crystals. After a welcome kiss from my wife she headed for work. I agonised over whether I could commit to this experiment indoors. I willfully forced the issue by dropping two pillows onto the floor and joining them. I cannot recall ever feeling so scared about committing myself to an experiment. I was so absolutely certain something was already invisibly present and watching me – just waiting for me to give it the necessary occult licence to impose powerfully upon me. My nerves got the better as my bowels beckoned for a second visit to the WC. Back in the bedroom, I stood at the window and huffed and puffed and sighed heavily several times before lying down. Immediately, I sat straight back up and made three absolutely perfect vaporous inhalations. Midway through that process, I realised there was a complete absence of any audible or perceptible effect resulting from the substance. I discarded the pipe and lighter either side of me and then lay back and exhaled the final inhalation. With no hesitation whatsoever an entity rapidly emerged out of nowhere. It instantly filled the bedroom with truly tremendous forcefulness of mind. That energy then began to increase in both intensity and frequency. And it simply would not stop. It was a totally devastating display of power. The energy imposing upon the plasterboard walls caused them to audibly flex from the ever-increasing compressive force impinging upon them. The effect was very pronounced and the energy was still increasing. I could hear it and I could feel it – within me and without me. It was such unbelievably powerful energy; and the willfulness of mind behind that force was simply stupendous. The house began shaking. I could feel it and I could hear it. It was without question. The house was shaking as though it were a washing machine on its final spin cycle. It was not short-lived. It continued and continued and I was totally sensible of the perceptible increases in the frequency of vibrations. Whilst the house was shaking, I realised such an obvious physical occurrence could not go unnoticed by my neighbour. I listened out for a shout of surprise, but none came. I imagined my neighbour making a telephone call to the British Geological Survey, stating with great alarm that he was experiencing local tremors. The vibrations continued. The power was immense. The room was brimful with a very powerful and very dense discarnate mind. I was now in the midst of an experience of truly astonishing proportion. The vibrational decrease in that phenomenal energy was tactilely and audibly perceptible; the dense transparent medium filling the room smoothly changed from a faint pearlescent hue to exceptional crystal-clear clarity – somehow making the room seem much deeper than usual. The power of the discarnate presence was overwhelming and I was fearful of what would follow. From my heart, but via my mouth, I volunteered a meek and harrowing plaintive wail; partly in recognition of the mind-boggling power that engulfed me; but mostly, it was an appeal for mercy. Just then – very much to my surprise and fascination – I poked my tongue right out, after which I began hyperventilating, simply in order to manage my emotional state at having witnessed something so devastatingly powerful. The rapid deep breathing was really helpful. My eyes observed how the room seemed so very much deeper than usual. I was absolutely determined my eyes would observe the changes as it reverted back to its ordinary appearance. Except that they didn't. By imperceptible degrees the room changed back to its ordinary dimension of depth. Equally, my perception of the discarnate presence also diminished gradually and by imperceptible degrees. For a short while I remained completely still and emotionless. The magnitude of what I had just witnessed then began to sink in. And it emotionally ruined me. I turned over and buried my head into the pillows. Emotions were rising like magma in the belly of a swollen volcano. They suddenly erupted. I sank my teeth into the pillow and bit down hard with all my might before wragging it around like a demented dog. My astonishment was paining me. Tear ducts were swollen. A coarse lump of raw emotion sat stuck and stalled at the back of my throat. I banged my right hand hard and fast into the pillows. I turned my head to the left and noted a little hole in the plasterboard wall. I wanted to hide inside that little hole. I wanted to live inside that little hole and ignore whatever was occurring outside. Upon realising I would have to honour my commitment to writing honestly about what had just occurred, another emotional explosion erupted. I burst into a frenzied highly energetic state. I began beating and biting at the pillows and wailing noisily before slumping down back down and staring upon and into the same little hole in the wall. I then mustered sufficient mental capacity to analyse my present state of being. And without any need to think things through I cried out loudly, over and over: "This is the proper response! This is the proper response! This is the proper response!" And I was satisfied that was so. Biting hard into the pillow and wragging it around was the proper response; feeling painfully sore with amazement was the proper response; indeed, each and every aspect of my reaction was the proper response in such a circumstance as this. Despite much shaking of my head, I managed to partially compose myself. I stood up and replaced the pillows on the bed. But I was still deeply affected by the experience. I began dry heaving, as though I was about to be sick. I did not feel physically sick, but the action seemed somehow comforting. The more it continued the more and more it seemed both calming and strangely appropriate. I questioned why the action felt so appropriate and duly realised I felt bilious with madness; not the disastrous or dolorous state of mind that qualifies as true psychiatric madness, but a madness more in keeping with the stark realisation that one had just experienced an occult occurrence of stupendous magnitude whilst in complete lucid sensibility. Sat at my writing desk a short while later, a surge of emotion rushed through me once again; I was writing as I was crying, and crying as I was writing; my tongue lolled repeatedly in and out of my mouth, making childlike high pitch crazy sounds, which subconsciously and then consciously, soothed my soul.

Report: #98

Location: Bedroom (~15:00hrs)

Dose: 46mg

Boohoo

Even after all this time, it just does not seem possible or even plausible that what occurs after I inhale the potent vapour, actually does occur. And yet that which does not seem possible or plausible, after inhaling the potent vapour, all too suddenly becomes all too evident. This dose represented the entirety of what I had available as fresh crystals. I was home alone. After washing my hands and spitting out mouthwash into the basin I voiced aloud, several times: "Boohoo time has come! Boohoo time has come! Boohoo time has come!" I positioned two pillows on the floor, joined them, and decided it was best to just get on with business. The third and final pull was by far the most voluminous. I lay back and noted the room appeared no different. Just one second later, something psycho-spiritual and incredibly weighty began to emerge and manifest. In what seemed like an instant the bedroom became awash with uniformly seething energy that felt as solid as rock. Its palpable solidity and weightiness were truly startling. This was energy of mind the likes of which I had never experienced before during my indoor research. This was a mind not given to nonsense and a mind that would not suffer foolishness. And I was very scared. I was scared because I could see the seething atmosphere caused by its presence; and I was scared because I could palpably feel the frighteningly weighty willfulness of its overwhelming otherworldly presence. This was an entity mighty in strength; full of unstoppable drive and determined purpose. I communicated my fear with a lamentable and lengthy wail and slowly shook my head slowly from side to side. I knew my fear was within me, and under the circumstances, I knew it was also without me. There was no doubt that I was now in something of an occult pickle. The energy visibly and palpably changed. It centred its focus solely upon me – principally upon my head and my torso. The energy was imposing forcibly and directionally down upon me and into me. It seems factually inaccurate to say the energy significantly increased, even though it did so. It is far more accurate to say the force and the weight of that discarnate mind knowingly and willfully pressed down hard upon me, and drove right into me with purposefulness and forcefulness. I heard something from the region of my sternum: a faint audible response from the uncommon compression upon the soft tissue. But I was far more concerned at how this entity was really putting it on me. I was underneath a very powerful occult cosh and desperate for mercy. A region at the very back of my mind began whispering that the passing seconds would preclude any really significant interaction between us. And whilst I knew there was some truth in that, the thing above me felt like it was capable of miraculous things that I could not even begin to imagine. The incredible force kept on imposing down upon me and into me. Occasional pulsing increases in its power made it feel as though I was being shouted at or stared down hard, almost as an alternative to being thoroughly roughhoused. After several seconds and feeling a degree more comfortable knowing that any really significant interaction was now unlikely, I raised my hands upwards and earnestly asked aloud: "How do I become like you?" But no sooner had that question leaped from my lips when I realised it sounded wholly out of place and totally inappropriate. The concerned half smile upon my lips was equally misplaced and I quickly removed it. I sensed this entity could sense my weaknesses at the level of my ego and my soul. I closed my eyes. Perhaps I was hoping the entity would communicate with my mind in clear spoken English; or possibly I felt embarrassed and afraid, and completely out of my depth. The entity departed swiftly and the room returned to normal. Except that mentally and emotionally I was now in a very different place. I felt perturbed that something like that could exist. I felt regret that I had acted as I had. And I felt grave concern knowing I may have to face something of a similar stature at a future date. For several minutes I remained on the floor in a state of vexed shock.

I was greatly affected by this encounter. It made me question what level of courage I really had within me. Yet I was warily fascinated by the nature of the discarnate intelligence. I wondered: What does a being like that do with itself? What qualities would define its existence within a hierarchical scheme of occult taxonomy? I am quite certain the entity in this experiment was of the very same nature as the one that gave me occult roughhousing. They seem to have a very different nature to those I have termed Occult Masters. The latter seem to exhibit compassion, understanding, patience, great power and wisdom in abundance. Whereas that which I experienced today was far more forcefully singular in its drive and willfulness; immensely powerful but in a very different manner; there seems to be an absence of humour and compassion; just an immensely powerful drive to progress in a purely willful evolutionary manner. I cannot imagine anything could stand in the way of such prodigious willfulness. And when I consider what other high-ranking entities exist in the occult otherworld, I feel that unless one can progress beyond these incredibly willful beings, one may never find out. Rightly or wrongly, I can suspect this particular type of entity operates in the capacity of powerful gatekeeper to higher realms. I can only wonder at the configuration of human consciousness required to engage courageously with such entities. I can only wonder at the personality we would witness in a human imbued with that very same quality of singular willful determined drive.

Report: #99

Location: Rear Garden (~10:30hrs)

Dose: 26mg & 33mg

Inactively Spectacular

I suspected the crystals had lost much of their potency. A welcome cessation of wind facilitated two excellent vaporous inhalations from the 26mg pipe and a third pull emptied the pipe. Midway through the process I could feel the strange effect within my head, indicative of the amplification and exteriorisation of my occult self. I lay back and looked up. But something was not quite right. An incredible and almost overwhelming sense was growing within me that something was on the cusp of exploding outwards with tremendous energy. But it didn't. My inner sound was now eerily and unaccountably silent. That interior silence created a most surreal and bizarre effect, which seemed compounded by the dramatic billowing white clouds and the deep blue sky. My inner sound is always audible to me; always, always, always! And now there was the most bizarre and eerie silence in the midst of my head. It was an astonishingly eerie effect and it felt like an unknown drama of truly bizarre proportion was about to spectacularly unfold, either upon me or from me. For a few moments I wondered if I was actually already in the midst of a truly bizarre interaction with an occult entity; one whose invisible presence had somehow purposefully silenced my inner psychic sound, just to create the impossibly eerie silence I was now experiencing. And even though I suspected that was not the case, I could not help myself from divulging more and more into the immense eerie surrealism that I was now steeped in. My temporarily aroused occult self was easily visible as an expansive and glassily apparent psycho-spiritual mass ranged far and wide above me. Tracer trails behind my hand movements were significant. An unusual mental image began to increasingly impose upon my conscious mind. It was the facial image of a large middle-aged woman. She was stuffing a pastry into her mouth. The image was poised between hilarity and tragedy. I could see the image very clearly in my mind. But the image was felt to be outside me – over on my right side – and of a considerable size; perhaps six foot in height. I was now feeling genuinely surprised at just how incredibly dramatic and terribly enjoyable this experience was, despite my misgivings about the potency of the crystals. My mind turned its attention to the 33mg pipe, sat upstairs in my writing office. I purposefully passed through the lounge to collect the pipe. In high spirits, I assured my wife that my otherwise invisible self was elastically attached to me yet outside ranged high above the garden. She smiled. I raced upstairs and obtained the pipe. Back outside, the wind was significant. I sat up and managed one reasonably good pull. Upon laying back I found the midst of my head remained eerily silent; but in such a way that made the effect feel so incredibly eerie, both within and without. A dark coloured bird flew low overhead. Its appearance was all wrong. It appeared like a straight-edged origami construction with isosceles triangle-shaped wings that appeared joined to the body at the vertex point. The manner in which it furiously flapped its wings made it appear as an amazing mechanistic clockwork invention. Its appearance and its manner of flight was so totally out of the ordinary that I could not help reacting; in a hushed holler, I cried: "That's not a real bird! That's not a real bird! I'm telling you!" The sighting perplexed me. Was it a real bird or was something discarnate engulfing me and purposefully creating an illusory avian form from within its mind? The wind died down and I managed another reasonably good pull before resuming my lain position. Now, something really was up above me. I could see it. A great mass of adjoined crystal-clear spherical cells of varying sizes at about seven to eight arms lengths above me. I was sure this was not my mind-stuff, but was something discarnate, watching me. I decided to empty the pipe but there was very little remaining. Yet upon laying back and looking up, I was overwhelmed by the immensity of emotion charging the air. Not only was something present, but it was poised and ready to overwhelm me with its occult energy. The power of the emotion was simply overwhelming. It felt like the sky was about to crash down upon me. My hands grabbed and gripped the blanket tightly. The level of drama was well beyond the order of being on the edge-of-one's-seat. Even the clouds – loosely shaped in the style of a large Hindu swastika – seem purposefully configured to impose an immense level of emotion upon me. The level drama was so great I felt I was starring in a movie – a dramatic thriller of unparalleled intensity. I also realised and relished how much I was enjoying this entire experience. My grip on the blanket remained as I observed the approach of a large dark grey cloud. My mood suddenly changed as same bird as before, or one very much like it, suddenly flew along the exact same route as before. It now appeared more like a regular bird, even though the strange origami-like appearance and mechanistic manner of flight were evident. Now I was doubly perplexed. I was perplexed because either it was a real bird, or it was not a real bird – and between the two I could not be sure what kind of bird I was observing. The dark grey cloud blotted out the sun, and with that my mood within me and without me underwent a change. Now I could feel the damp cold wind. Once again, I acknowledged just how much I was enjoying this experiment when the very same bird, or one just like it, flew by in the exact same direction as before. This time it looked more like a regular bird. I spoke out loud in judgement of the experience, because I simply could not help myself from doing so, and I felt it keenly: "That was fucking spectacular!"

Report: #100

Location: Rear Garden (~11:30hrs & ~17:30hrs)

Dose: 54mg

Soporificker

I sat down wearing sunglasses and took great care to produce vapour. The breeze was a factor. Following a couple of light inhalations, I became blissfully unaware that I was drawing heavily upon the pipe. After realising I had drawn down a great volume of vapour I paused, set the pipe aside, then commenced a slow exhale. I'd taken in such a great volume of vapour that I was able draw some of it back down for further absorption before recommencing another slow exhale. Upon reclining and looking up it was immediately evident a huge mass of very dense mind-stuff was above me. Its energy was evident as a very deep and slow cyclical vibration of terrific intensity.   Throughout the massive psycho-spiritual form, I noted a great number of equidistantly spaced small dark points. I consciously feigned fright for fear of being subjected to unrelentingly powerful and imposing energy. But the strange cyclical energy was having a very calming effect upon my mind, and I soon realised it was in fact, putting me into a state of deep relaxation. From my left side a pigeon flew into the dense mass of mind-stuff. I noted it suddenly headed groundward over to my right. I then heard the pigeon crash into the ground. My state of mesmeric relaxation was so advanced there was simply no thought to look over and see the poor crash-landed pigeon. As I was slowly going deeper and deeper into this deeply soporific state, I could hear the pigeon flapping around on the ground, in what sounded like an effort to recover. I then felt I wanted to close my eyes. Or I could not resist an unspoken prompting to close my eyelids. I closed my eyelids and beheld a very highly saturated red-coloured simple mandala. It was very beautiful to behold, but I was simply far too relaxed to feel any excitement about it. The highly defined red-coloured mandala slowly spun clockwise. And the more and more it spun, the sleepier and sleepier I became. I heard the pigeon flapping furiously and then flying off as I went even deeper into a soporific state. As the bright red imagery spun ever faster and faster it put me on the cusp of falling asleep, until I strained to willfully overcome the imposing sleepiness. I opened my eyes and burst out laughing to acknowledge my surprise at just how close I had been to actually falling sleep. I headed indoors. Whilst stood looking out of the kitchen window, I observed a pigeon land on the larchlap fence, just behind the blanket I had laid upon. It turned its head and appeared to look down intently toward where I had lain. I burst into laughter once again, having convinced myself that was the very same pigeon that had audibly crash-landed only moments ago.

Report: #101

Location: Rear Garden (~19:15hrs)

Dose: 28mg & 38mg

Menacing Calmness

With sunglasses on I sat up and produced four moderate pulls. Within seconds of lying back it was visually and tactilely evident that a discarnate emergent was some four to five arm's lengths above me. I could see its broad and psycho-spiritually obvious presence. Over my entire body – but especially focussed upon the midst of my chest – I could feel a deep and cyclical vibration associated with its presence. After just a few seconds, I realised there would be no significant interaction between us. I felt disappointed. The entity diminished without me really paying much attention to it. I waited a short while before heading indoors to prepare another pipe. Back outside I sat down and made one very long and very voluminous inhalation. I held it down before slowly exhaling and allowing my mouth to play around with the unabsorbed vapour. I made for a second attempt but the pipe was empty. Upon lying back and looking up, I observed the slow emergence of something sizeable and glasslike in appearance. It had a broad and relatively flat underside which appeared as a quivering membranous exterior. Within seconds I discerned I was actually looking at something resembling a beautifully crystal-clear cylindrical shaped entity. There appeared to be a great deal more activity going on above and beyond the cylindrical form, but I could not make it out. I quickly became enamoured by the energy emitted from the entity. Its energy was very powerful but not in a raging or a forceful manner. Quite the opposite. Its tremendous power was explicitly calm and yet at the same time, it was a power I would not willingly approach. There was just far too much of a mismatch between what it was and what I was, for me to even begin contemplating such a thing. My mind and my breathing were both racing. I began wondering why I no longer see the highly defined and overwhelmingly vivid hallucinations that these entities used to impose upon me. But based on the awesome sight in front of me right now, despite its truly menacing level of calmness, I was very fortunate to be observing what must surely come to be regarded as one of the most awesome sights of nature – the observation of an impressive occult lifeform defined in truly stunning crystal-clear clarity. The entity came down very close toward me, briefly shrouded me, and then was gone.

Report: #102

Location: Rear Garden (~19:30hrs)

Dose: 18mg

Sometimes It's What You Make of It

From inside the house, the continuous white cloud hanging low in the sky made the early evening appear dull and cold. A decision made on a whim to conduct DMT research before dinner saw me race to prepare the pipe. I pulled myself into a tatty old turquoise coloured mountain jacket and pulled a woolly hat over my head. The wind was blowing briskly. I decided to seat myself upon the redundant armchair. Whilst patiently factoring in the wind speed and wind direction, I found the perfect convection currents to produce vapour. After two very pleasing pulls I sat back and felt the powerful onset of the substance. At approximately three arm's lengths above me a cellular psycho-spiritual presence indicative of my own psycho-spiritual projection began to emerge with exceptional clarity. I felt I had perhaps underestimated the potency of the substance – I could feel that same psycho-spiritual emergence vibrating with remarkable intensity within and without me. The wind was now beginning to blow really quite hard, and it was becoming noisy; which was beginning to make this experiment feel terribly uncomfortable. However, it appeared I was relatively sheltered in something of a microclimate – a small pocket of peace and calm positioned close to the rear of the house and beneath the overhang of a tall evergreen. Ahead of me, it was evident the low white cloud and the spring green leaves of the apple tree were at the mercy of a significant and persistent strong wind. The sound from which as it blew through the apple tree was substantial. As I watched my psycho-spiritual self-expanding upwards and outwards into the moody sky, two ducks with outstretched necks flew low overhead, quacking in quick succession as though making complaint against the weather. Their passage seemed to serve as a prelude the immense challenge I was about to face in navigating this experience. I needed to manage myself and so decided I should allow my mind to cavort fancifully, in whatever way it wanted to entertain me. From the comfort of the redundant armchair, when the wind increased in force, I fancied I was the captain of an old wooden sailing ship; clinging tightly to the wheel in the midst of a terrible storm; except instead of gripping a wheel, I was gripping the arms of the armchair, and gurning in defiance at the storm that was clearly intent on capsizing my ship. The unexpected sight of a large bumble bee battling bravely against the wind presented itself. I imagined that bumble bee was a sailor fallen overboard – doomed to drown in the stormy waters of the vast ocean. I gurned harder while committing myself fully to the ongoing nautical nonsensical make-believe. The sudden arrival of a small robin in the midst of the garden quickly wiped the nonsense from my face. The robin was looking to make its dinner from a few grains of cooked rice that my wife had thrown out. In a voice modified to sound anything but sane I acknowledged the robin's presence and the purpose of its visit. The strong gusting wind hindered the flight of yet another large bumble bee, and once again I imagined another sailor had gone overboard. I began to holler in a thick Scottish accent: "We're doomed! We're doomed! We're all doomed!" A grossly extended gargantuan yawn threatened to test the hinged integrity of my jaw. I duly interpreted that yawn as some kind of test upon the integrity of my ship's timbers; as an unwelcome attempt to rend my vessel asunder. I increased my already tight grip upon the armchair and gurned fiercely and forcefully. Then I addressed the windblown clouds, calling out: "Is there anything up there? Is there anything up there?" I then fancied I heard an alien voice inside my head. It was strange and high pitched. It was a wailing and warbling voice – wholly indecipherable in content. But I could definitely hear something! Its presence was without doubt! But what was it doing inside my head? I then realised I was hearing my eldest boy sat inside the house playing his computer games. He was in high spirits. And so was I. I playfully interpreted his high-pitched warbling as strange alien communication from above. Another huge yawn threatened to capsize my vessel. I clung onto the chair even tighter and gurned ever more forcefully at storm, in complete defiance of its power. I was conscious this complete and utter nonsense was making this experiment into be a truly memorable and thoroughly enjoyable undertaking. More gurning; another bumble bee; zipping up my jacket to the top; hunkering deeper into the armchair; comical vocal expressions of doom; the onset of large drops of rain; the robin taking a second helping of cooked rice; another yawn testing the integrity of my timbers! And then, something impossibly subtle made me feel obligated to look upwards, whereupon I observed a small black orb with a halo around it. It hung stationary in the air just below the fast-moving windswept cloud. Immediately, I clasped my open palms together as though in sudden prayer, to exhibit my sheer delight. An emotion of joy cascaded through me. The black orb began to move very slowly in a north easterly direction. My smile was now on full beam as I gave thumbs up and further signalled my pleasure. I was delighted and watched intently as the orb increased its distance and diminished in size until eventually, my eyes could no longer see it.

Report: #103

Location: Rear Garden (~18:30hrs)

Dose: 36mg

Kaa

The weather was dull and still and silent. It would have been far easier to forgo any practical occult research but I wanted to maintain some continuity. After manoeuvering myself for comfort I sat up commenced emptying the pipe. As I lay back and looked up something was already in the process of emerging. It appeared to be about five arm's lengths above me. But as the emergence reached fullness, I simply could not believe the extent of what I was seeing. Every portion of sky was visible only when looking through the extensive psycho-spiritual mass that ranged far beyond the boundary of the garden. It was speckled throughout with hundreds if not thousands of equidistant small shaded points – making my observation of its extent easy and unambiguous. I had time to check in all directions. In each and every direction the sky was visible only when looking through the immense form filled with tiny little shaded points. I even had time to double check. Over to my left – the psycho-spiritual form covered the entirety of my view. Over to my right – the psycho-spiritual form covered the entirety of my view. Ahead of me – where the visible portion of sky was by far the greatest – the psycho-spiritual form completely covered the entirety of my view. And as I lifted my eyes and craned my head back, the very same form extended completely over the larchlap boundary fence. Throughout those observations two other things were perceptible. There was a deep pulsating energy evident all around me. Its wavelength was very low but its intensity was significant and weighty. Secondly, the apparent high density of the presence seemed to serve as indication of the magnitude of its constitutional spiritual power. I decided to attempt to convey by means of thought transference that I was writing a book. But no sooner had the thought arisen when I innately understood, based on my assessment of what was above me, that the otherworldly entity was very far in advance of my little life ambitions. The overarching psycho-spiritual entity was simply stunning to behold. From its central portion immediately above me, a dense projection of the mind-stuff slowly made its way down toward me. That sight was simply incredible to witness. Amazing hallucinations and otherworldly visions are one thing, but this was unbelievably spectacular. I implicitly understood that I was supposed to look directly into the approaching mass as it passed down over me and passed right through me. I stared hard into its descending psycho-spiritual vortex. Two crows sped through the midst of the being – one chasing the other. Disney's animated *The Jungle Book* came to mind; the scene where Kaa the serpent uses his spiralling hypnotic eyes to entrance Mowgli. The effect of staring so hard into the strange psycho-spiritual form descending into me was so odd that it soon felt as though both my eyes had merged into one and were operating as one singular eyeball. The visual content filling my perhipheral vision gradually lessened until it was absent. I clean forgot that I was looking skyward in a half-hypnotised state. I was feeling profoundly relaxed. After a short while the entity began to depart from the location and appeared to change its form as it moved very slowly skywards. The change of appearance and the very slow departure of the entity all served to highlight its incredible size. In the latter period of its departure, its form had changed into a psycho-spiritual mass comprising an apparent jumble of numerous long straight edges and portions of partial cuboid forms, incorporating a pale-yellow hue throughout.

Report: #104

Location: Rear Garden (~19:00hrs)

Dose: 81mg

Remote Rapport

Upon arriving home from work, I immediately set about preparing the pipe with fresh crystals then donned my sunglasses and headed outside. After adjustments for comfort I sat up and began. The first inhalation produced an almighty stream of dense vapour which I retained within whilst feeling completely confident with what I was doing. The second inhalation also produced an almighty volume of vapour. I retained it within my lungs before allowing my mouth to slowly play around with the unabsorbed vapour exiting my mouth. The third inhalation was in the same mould as the first two. I had never before drawn down so much vapour in one single experiment. As I lay back and looked up something arrived with tremendous rapidity. It was circular – about the same diameter as the ten-foot trampoline – and exceptionally crystal-clear. It was approximately five arm's lengths above me. I could feel its energy passing down through me. That energy made my entire body feel as though its physical matter was relatively empty of itself and within itself. As that energy continued transmitting through me there was a really strange feeling that made the interior of my torso feel totally empty. But there was something else. The underside of my shirt buttons was sliding along the surface of my skin in unison with my breathing. But it felt so very pronounced and so incredibly strange. Something faint touched me two or three times on the outside of my left arm. For some reason I suspected my sunglasses were a hindrance to seeing clearly, and so I used my right hand to lift them and hold them above my eyes. However, the brief and discomforting exposure to bright sunlight forced me to quickly reposition them. I was feeling quite unimpressed with the experience considering juts how much vapour I had just taken in. But then I became aware of something else. Something invisible was threading a very long psycho-spiritual thread around different parts of my physique; as though something very large was undertaking an occult needlework exercise around my physiology. I realised the experience was far from over. I spoke out aloud but immediately regretted my choice of words. The bizarre psycho-spiritual thread continued to weave in and around my entire physique. I was quite sure that thought transference was taking place. The entity was communicating something about doing something with my back. I was cool and calm about the bizarre proceedings that now were well underway. However, as I was trying to interpret the exact content of the thought transference, my eyes caught sight of a large dark insect in flight over to my right. And for some unknown and bizarre reason, its presence convinced me that I was being requested to turn over onto my front so the entity could undertake its work far more easily. I duly turned over onto my front and buried my face down into the cushions. But it immediately dawned on me the loss of mind-to-mind focus between the entity and I would not readily facilitate our interaction. I turned back over, fearing I had just made a critical mistake. At first it seemed my surroundings were just as they were before I began the experiment. But then I questioned why a great portion of the partially cloudy blue sky appeared so unnaturally close to the ground. As I studied that area of sky, and how ridiculously close to the ground it appeared, my jaw dropped as I observed a truly vast crystal-clear disc-shaped entity moving purposefully and stealthily skywards. As that improbably wide crystal-clear disc moved skyward, a humungous cone-shaped portion hung down from its centre. It exhibited incredible psycho-spiritual density and detail therein. The crystal-clear disc was soon out of sight. I was aghast. My gaping mouth remained agog in testament to the shock I was feeling at witnessing such an incredible sight. I realised that by turning over I had gotten this interaction completely wrong. Regret was now mushrooming inside me. I wished I could communicate to the entity and convince it to come back and resume the interaction. But that was not going to happen. I knew I would now need to capably manage my growing regret. But I also knew I had just witnessed a sight that was jaw-dropping. Indeed, I now had complete experiential understating of the reasoning behind that idiom – jaw-dropping! I remained lain for a long time while going over the experience and assuaging myself of regret.

I can assume the experience in its fullness would have been a continuation of the bizarre occult threading within and around my physiology. Possibly this was nothing more than a simple trick for the entity to undertake; one that it knew would greatly startle and surprise me. But could it be something stranger? Something deeper? Could it be the entity was psycho-spiritual knitting a small portion of its vast mind into my tiny little human frame? Undertaking a profound occult technique aimed at establishing an occult and remote rapport between us? Perhaps it was subtly snaring my soul. Such that upon my death, that very same entity will reel in the immaterial me in something of an occult fishing exercise? Such speculations are as bizarre as they are imaginative. But the nature of these experiences is so very much out of kilter with consensus reality that the interpretative possibilities seem endless.

Report: #105

Location: Rear Garden (~11:15hrs)

Dose: 47mg

Great Mass of Mind

The weather was windy. The pipe contained a mix of gooey waxy globules and pure white dimethyltryptamine crystals. I made one moderate inhalation which soon began to exteriorise my otherwise invisible self. The wind picked up significantly, impeding further efforts at producing vapour. Despite my best efforts it was no use and so eventually, I lay back. But I really wanted to establish contact with something occult, so I sat straight back up again and after moving the lighter this way and that I found the sweet spot, and drew down an almighty stream of vapour that soon emptied the pipe. Knowing the difficulty experienced in producing that vapour I refused to exhale what I had just vacuumed down. I lay back and eventually exhaled a cloud of unabsorbed vapour. I don't recall the emergence of the entity above me. It seemed it was suddenly just there. It transmitted low frequency but very intense energy that was palpable across my entire being. It is no exaggeration when I report that it filled the entire portion of visible sky. I was able to check and double check by moving my eyes around as the palpable energy continued to impose upon me. A great big massive discarnate mind overarched the entire garden. The continuous white cloud seen through its transparent body-of-mind appeared to be rippling. It was clearly something of stunning beauty; complex yet simple, with a multitude of equidistant small shaded points throughout. It clearly spanned the rear elevation of the house and the entire footprint of the garden. The central portion tapered down toward me. Its energy continued. I was neither bold nor scared. I was just intrigued and amazed at what I was seeing. Something tactile began subtly exploiting a sensitive area around my upper right arm, but ceased every time I flinched. I did not want to break my stare. The entire entity then began to slowly move upwards and depart in a south easterly direction. A significant portion of its tapered form remained for just a short while longer, but became increasingly faint and vague.

Report: #106

Location: Rear Garden (~20:45hrs)

Dose: 20mg and 26mg

It Should Be!

My mood was cold and steely after a family trip into the city ended in a farcical falling out with my wife over table space at a fast food restaurant. As a consequence, I made my way home alone. Once home I headed out with my bike for some solace at the skatepark. Upon returning home I found my wife and children outside the house awaiting me. My wife had not taken her house keys with her. Thus, an already fraught situation increased further toward fragility. I forced myself into action and headed outside where I convinced myself to press ahead with my research. The dreary uniform white cloud was perfect for sighting a small black orb. And that was really all I wanted – something to acknowledge me. Not least because I was forecasting at least three or four days before my wife and I would be back on agreeable terms. I sat up and managed a moderate stream of vapour. The DMT molecules quickly began to take effect whilst I was drawing a second stream of vapour deep down into my lungs. I lay back and looked up and observed the incredible detail of my psycho-spiritual outpouring. The weather was starting to feel raw. I zipped up my jacket and pulled down hard on my woolly hat. I admonished myself for not preparing a larger dose and duly arose and headed indoors to prepare a second pipe. I wondered if anything invisible was mindful of what I was doing; was something occult watching me at that very moment? Back in the garden I sat up and made one lung-filling inhalation which completely emptied the pipe. High frequency energy directed down upon me. Something very visible and yet highly transparent began to emerge some five arm's lengths above me. It exhibited uncharacteristic straight-edged geometric patterning throughout its amorphous form. The frequency of its psychic energy audibly increased around me and within me, and as it did so the stunning interior geometry of the entity increased in complexity as it continued to emerge, seemingly from out of thin air. It soon became abundantly clear this entity was very different to anything I had ever seen in any of my previous experiments. Within seconds a vast and slowly spiralling transparent psycho-spiritual vortex had mesmerised my eyes. Its interior exhibited unimaginable geometric complexity. I stared hard and unblinkingly into the heart of its stunning kaleidoscopic geometry as it spiraled down and engulfed me. I was able to see the stupendous detail as thousands upon thousands of small and perfectly formed geometric cells joined to form thousands upon thousands of larger geometric cells – which in turn joined to form countless larger geometric cells. The beauty of this seemingly inexhaustible spiralling form was simply mind-numbing. As I looked straight ahead, I was totally entranced by its beauty. Its beauty was its power. A feeling of calm and wonder held me completely spellbound. But there was something inexplicable. There was something much deeper than can ever be expressed or conveyed through words. As the beauteous spiralling vortex continued to engulf me, I wondered whether the entity was subliminally transmitting something deep into my psyche. As I looked carefully into its intrinsic interior detail, I was truly amazed at the geometry within the geometry within the geometry. This was an experience well beyond hallucinations and illusory imagery. This felt purposeful. This felt like a very rare glimpse of something immense; something that was cognisant I was writing upon such matters; something that knew I would dutifully report such a sighting. As its beautiful spiralling descent continually engulfed me, my mind earnestly demanded to know: "What is this? What is this? What is this? Is it a God? If it isn't, it should be!" The geometric cells engulfing me began to change. Slowly they became larger and more rounded in shape and I realised the descent was slowing. The encounter was coming to a close and I knew this giant mind would now make its way back to wherever such things as that reside. It eventually became evident that descent had given way to ascent. Although I was unable to see the main portion of the great mind that had just departed my presence, the garden was filled with a glassy psycho-spiritual backflow which departed very slowly. I did not know quite how to react. My frame of mind was one of profound astonishment. I felt like I should blub, and indeed I found myself on the verge of doing so. But to commit to tears would have felt forced. All I could do was shake my head, and keep on shaking my head as a means making myself believe that I had just witnessed something unbelievable; as a means of coming to terms with what I had just experienced. I thrust the knuckles of my fist into my mouth and bit down. What on earth could compare to that magnificent entity that had just graced me with such a spectacular view of its beauteous and divine mind?

Report: #107

Location: Rear Garden (~12noon)

Dose: 46mg

A Funnel Thing Happened

I picked up the lighter and the pipe in preparation to proceed whilst huffing and puffing and troubling myself with overly exaggerated sighs. The experience that followed my inhalations was so utterly bizarre that immediately following the experience I was troubled at the thought of having to write about such a sighting. My attempt at vaporising and inhaling the dose was one of the most difficult I have ever experienced. I don't recall exactly how many minor wispy little pulls I clocked-up, but it went on and on and on. It became such a prolonged and longwinded operation that I even took to focussing on the diaphanous shadow of the convection currents, cast upon the cerise blanket, in order to try and gauge the most favourable position of pipe-to-lighter. Wisp after wisp after wisp of potent vapour was drawn down. Eventually it became evident the substance was active in exteriorizing my otherwise invisible self. But it was equally evident that I was becoming exhausted and breathless at the ongoing efforts to empty the pipe. After several more attempts and wispy little intakes, my breath was well and truly spent. Exhausted, I lay back and looked up at the partially cloudy bright blue sky. Nothing happened. But then I noted there was something vast and crystal-clear filling a great portion of the sky immediately above me. And a great big portion of that crystal-clear thing was visibly descending down toward me. It was a truly astonishing sight. My chest still laboured with breathlessness. But it soon became evident that a vast funnel-like crystal-clear appendage was slowly descending from an indeterminate height. The mouth of that funnel was extremely broad and was slowly making its way down toward me. I was absolutely astounded at what I was witnessing. A huge crystal-clear nozzle was slowly and purposefully descending down toward me. The incredibly flimsy psycho-spiritual substance forming that otherworldly funnel quivered and wobbled as it made its slow descent. It was soon evident the huge opening was actually configuring itself to completely swallow me. The impossibly thin crystal-clear quivering membrane was knowingly manoeuvering itself. I clearly observed as the large funnel subtly engineered itself into a position where I would very soon be completely in the midst of its wide-open mouth. And as that eventuality played out, I found myself in its mouth, looking up through an incredibly long funnel, with an ever-decreasing diameter that reached high into the sky. My emotions were highly aroused. I was in a state of high astonishment. I was inside the broad mouth of long crystal-clear funnel that had descended from the sky. Humorously, I began to imagine this was the nozzle a giant occult vacuum cleaner; about to suck me up into the sky. With heartfelt sincerity I beseeched the occult operator of the giant vacuum cleaner: "Take me up! Take me up! Take me up!" This sight was sufficiently phenomenal to exceed all my previous dimethyltryptamine-borne astonishments. My fists tightly gripped the blanket. My back was arched and stiff. And my mouth voiced in a hushed manner over and over, with tremendous incredulity: "What?! What!? No Way! No Way! No Way! Oh my God! No Way!" I was aghast at what I was seeing, and how it had formed. And then, it was gone. But my emotions were ignited, to such extent that I began beating my clenched fists hard into the soft ground, almost in protest against at what I had just witnessed. After much shaking of my head and signalling thumbs up to the sky I considered I had just witnessed a monumental experience.

Report: #108

Location: Rear Garden (~19:15hrs)

Dose: 15mg

Occult Incursion

I thought I would leave off from my research today. I had spent three highly energetic hours riding my bike at the local skatepark. My body felt ruined from the physical exertion. A playful enquiry for matters amorous was rebuffed by my wife on the basis of menstruation. I opened a letter of reply from my local MP in response to comments I had made about the new Psychoactive Substances Act. The letter stated exactly what I expected it would state. After a cup of tea, I vacuumed the carpet. An internal debate then began about my commitment to my research. I questioned whether or not I should betake myself to the garden, with a small manageable dose. Perhaps a little black orb would manifest terrestrially. The weather was heavy and close – as though the sky was laboriously going through the motions of accumulating a critical threshold of moisture for heavy rain. I lay upon the grass. There was an overwhelming sense that something invisible was already awaiting me. In fact, it really did feel like something had waited very patiently for this moment to arrive. I sat up and deftly drew down a long stream of vapour which was retained within my lungs for several seconds. The second inhalation drew down a surprisingly large volume of vapour. I lay back. With no hesitation whatsoever something emerged into fullness some five arm's lengths above me. Its immediate emergence gave me no reason to suspect it had not positioned itself there, just waiting for me to exteriorise my occult self. I had only seconds to sense and observe the nature of the entity. Instinctively, I understood it was going to descend upon me. It rapidly descended and entered a portion of itself into my head. There was no messing about. It moved so quickly and so purposefully. And I was so unquestioningly compliant. My inner voice even acknowledged: "It's going in there to do what it has to do!" Within seconds it had done exactly what it wanted to do and had exited my head in rapid fashion before zipping away diagonally in a south westerly direction. I was speechless and puzzled as I tried to come to terms with what had just occurred. The experience was over in mere seconds. My mind began racing at what had just occurred. There was an overwhelming sense I had just being subjected to an occult incursion; a violation of person and mind. It all seemed so pre-planned and purposeful – and so well executed. It really did seem that something had exercised great stealth and great patience in achieving its aim. I couldn't help myself from considering I had been subliminally influenced into undertaking the experiment. It certainly felt that way. It felt as though I had exercised unthinking irrationality in committing myself to an experiment when I had in fact told myself that I would leave my research well alone. It felt as though I had just fallen into a trap – an occult trap. My mind was racing considering the possibilities of what had just occurred. Had something just been planted deep within my mind? Not something physical, but some kind of occult mind technology; something that would lie dormant in the depths of my psyche awaiting remote activation at some unspecified future date. Such a possibility felt gravely real. And if it was real, what was it? What would it do? When would it do it? Would I even know when whatever it is activates? Would I be able to resist whatever it was? And if I wanted to winkle that thing out from my mind, how would I do that? Who or what could help me to do that? My mind was busy analysing the darker and more distasteful permutations arising from the shadowy side of my psyche; a region of mind that given the opportunity is all too ready to volunteer the dastardliest notions into full consciousness. I remained lain upon the grass feeling greatly perturbed as infrequent spots of rain spat down upon me. The dark content running through my mind was in no way assuaged by the nature of the entity that had just accosted me. Its nature was quite unlike anything else I have ever encountered. Its appearance and its presence – despite being psycho-spiritual and transparent – was visually and palpably very strong. Its outermost appearance displayed a composite of perfectly interlocked units; long psycho-spiritual strips, each overlapping one another in an orderly fashion as though it were a constructible puzzle. As a portion of that entity entered into my head, I could see and I could feel those units composing the whole. There was a definite character and a definite consistency to its form and composition. Although my tactile perception of its unique nature was very strong, trying to express that clearly in words presents such a challenge. I would have to say the form really did feel like a composite construction made from units of psycho-spiritual material. After several minutes fretting about whether I had been infected with a manipulative occult mind parasite, I got up and headed indoors. I continued fretting whilst taking a hot bath and continued to fret after having taken that bath. Some three hours later, after eating dinner and taking more time to reflect, I felt much less violated and far less suspicious about the actions and the motives of the entity. At the time the experiment concluded, just after the entity had rapidly zipped away, I was adamant this was the singularly most unnerving experience of my research programme. But now, I suspect the action of the entity was purposefully designed to put me into that fretful and fearful frame of mind.

This type of entity is a very different mind to those I have termed Occult Masters. These seem far less benevolent and far more inclined to operate by instilling fear or fright into the researcher. In some strange and indecipherable manner, I suspect these uncommon entities may be of a higher order than the Occult Masters. I find it hugely interesting that this entity appeared distinctly disc-shaped.

Report: #109

Location: Rear Garden (~10:45hrs)

Dose: 45mg

Brimming with Living Invisibleness

I sat up wearing sunglasses and made two moderate inhalations. Upon reclining I immediately sensed the presence of an entity above me. Seconds later it projected a deep and intense energy onto me and around me. I was intrigued as to how the entity could become present so very rapidly. It was exactly as though the entity had been invisibly present above the garden before I had even begun my experiment. After a few seconds spent observing the entity and feeling its power I sat up and drew more potent vapour from the pipe. After exhaling and lying back, I found the energy had completely ceased but the entity remained visible in an expansive low energy state. A dark grey cloud immediately behind the entity provided visually striking background. After taking another moderate pull from the pipe it felt like the sky immediately above me was bristling with latent occult potential. The feeling within me and without me was so very powerful that I could really only conclude something with tremendous latent power was primed and ready to impose upon me and engulf me within its mind. The sky was visually striking. The dark grey cloud had passed. A sizeable portion of the bright blue sky contained numerous billowing white clouds and storm clouds exhibiting varying shades of moodiness. Another attempt on the pipe pulled down a great volume of vapour. There was now an overwhelming sensation that the entire sky was bursting and brimming with living invisibleness. An impossibly intense feeling of high drama was evident within me and without me; it was tremendously exciting and profoundly enjoyable. Distant low rumbles of thunder added the perfect soundtrack to such delightful high drama. And then, for just a few brief moments, it appeared that everything had stopped moving. There was no air movement whatsoever. The magnificent billowing clouds all appeared static and completely still. Everything appeared completely motionless. The immense beauty of what I was seeing coupled with the surrealism of immobility created a very convincing cartoonish reality. The intense beauty of such a dramatic sky felt emotionally wedded to my memory. This was highly enjoyable research. I chanced to look over to my left and immediately cried out with astonishment as I beheld the stunning deep velvety greenness of the sunlit oak tree leaves. My wife caught my eye through the kitchen window. I stared at her for a few seconds. She raised her head and retuned my smile. I tried the pipe again but it was hardly worth the trouble. Upon reclining the sky seemed so very different. It had become completely covered with white and off-white cloud without me really noticing. I was really pleased with the experiment, but I sensed there was more to come. After just a few minutes spent deep in thought, an irregular-shaped inky black mass appeared low in the sky some considerable distance ahead of me. It was a really impressive sight and moved very slowly in a northerly direction. I thought it would be good for my wife to come and take a look. I beckoned her to come outside. She exited the house followed by our two boys. I pointed over to the slow moving inky black mass and beckoned them to: "Look at that!" The initial response from all three greatly surprised me. They all began asking in an inquisitive and puzzled tone: "What? Look at what? What? Where?" I could not believe my ears. My inner voice began rhetorically hollering: "What the hell is wrong with these people?" I just could not believe how they could fail to see the very obvious inky black mass moving so very slowly against the white and off-white background of sky. Its presence was so plainly obvious. But then I supposed: What if they really cannot see it? Possibly it was only visible to me as the research percipient of the experiment? But I knew they could see it. It was as plain as day. Somewhat perplexed by my family's reaction, I addressed them in a mildly incredulous tone: "You see that black thing over there, against the clouds, moving slowly?" My wife responded first and dumbfounded me even further when she queried: "That black balloon?" I just could not believe my ears and immediately retorted: "That's not a black balloon! Look at it! It's not even balloon-shaped! And see how slowly it's moving!" My boys then chimed in and expressed their opinion that it was a black balloon. I realised my mood was finely balanced between taking the matter far too seriously and taking a genuine interest in my family's responses to the thing in the sky. There was a brief uncomfortable silence. Eventually my youngest boy volunteered, in a very loud and excited manner: "It's a UFO! It's a UFO! It's a UFO!" I asked my wife if she really thought it was a balloon. She looked at it thoughtfully and said she thought that it was. The black mass seemed to stop moving. My youngest boy shouted out, far too loudly: "It's levitating! It's levitating!" I felt I had made a mistake by calling my family outside. The peace was shattered. And that which I held to be highly condensed psycho-spiritual energy formed into an irregularly-shaped inky black mass, they all held to be a black balloon.

Report: #110

Location: Rear Garden (~17:20hrs)

Dose: 44mg

Probably Won't

I sat up wearing sunglasses beneath a near uniform overcast white sky and made three excellent inhalations. My inner psychic sound began to rise rapidly in pitch after the first pull. Further increases were rapid and obvious. As soon as I lay back and looked up, I was bathed in a familiar energy. It was deep and strong. I could see the cellular composition of the transparent entity above me, displaying numerous dark shaded points throughout. The power of its energy was such that I was breathing deeply and heavily. Possibly my subconscious mind was dutifully acting out a self-preservation response. The entity then expanded its body such that it impressively spanned and overarched the entire garden. I moved my head and my eyes all around to confirm the entity was in fact covering every portion of sky visible to me. It was such an incredibly impressive sight. I gave a big broad smile and signalled my pleasure. A few moments later it transformed into a great mass of low energy psycho-spiritual mind-stuff, filling the air above the garden. There were strange movements throughout portions of the psycho-spiritual mass; movements that I could see and also tactilely perceive. Tubular lengths were uniformly writhing around and creating what appeared to be impossible objects, over and over again. As I observed what was underway, my own mind began formulating the same writhing and looping actions; forming the same shape over and over again, like tying a knot that somehow never managed to become tied. There was something about this shared action that was not only entrancing but seemed to also convey the personality of the entity. The psycho-spiritual presence gradually faded from sight. I turned my attention to watching windswept leaves falling diagonally over the roof of the house from the giant oak trees at the front. The differences in size and colour; the different rates of spiralling spin and zigzagging descent, all seemed to infuse each and every leaf with a different personality. One leaf landed close by. I picked it up and examined it. It was astonishing how leaf litter could be infused with so much personality. After just a few seconds of examination I tossed it aside, but immediately felt the need to utter my apology to the leaf for disposing of it in such an offhand manner.

Report: #111

Location: Rear Garden (~19:00hrs)

Dose: 23mg & 66mg

Suprascapular

I was feeling washed out after a day at work and my courage was not in abundance. I sat up from the ground. The sky was empty except for one or two cotton wool clouds and the wind was stronger than expected. Trouble with the lighter resulted in one less than moderate intake and then suddenly, I drew down a great stream of vapour which completely emptied the pipe. I reclined and waited with great anticipation to feel the energetic surge from the second inhalation. But there was nothing. There was no discernible effect whatsoever. For a few brief moments I wondered if something was already interacting with me; interacting with me in such a way that completely nullified the audibility of my psychic output. But there was no feeling of any discarnate presence whatsoever. Feeling completely frustrated, I headed indoors and prepared a second pipe. The second pull from that pipe was incredibly voluminous. My confidence was so high that during the third pull I drew down an even greater volume of vapour and completely emptied the pipe. I lay back and exhaled what had not soaked through my lungs. A powerful and deep energy projected down onto me. I was unable to verify the full extent of the intricately detailed geometry now above me. It was not that the deep blue sky seen through the dense and transparent mind of the entity was a hindrance to seeing it clearly. It was more that I sensed the entity was purposefully attempting to cloak itself from my view. Its deep energy was no longer perceptible. Something began manoeuvering behind my left shoulder blade. Initially I flinched, but then realising what was underway I decided to remain as calm and as still as possible. Over the next several minutes it felt like a powerful psycho-spiritual auger was slowly twisting and drilling into me. I would not say it was particularly painful, but I told myself I would not pay for such an experience as part of a therapeutic massage. It continued and felt like it was slowly reaching deeper and deeper into my tissue. It then felt like there was some kind of localised occult engineering taking place in that region. The psycho-spiritual form was steadily diminishing from my sight. I was feeling perplexed at what exactly was underway in my body, but remained completely calm. I slowly raised my right arm in order to sweep my hand out in front of me. But just as soon as I raised my right hand the strange physical sensation around left shoulder blade ceased.

The apparent invasive nature of the experience was so strange that I must be forgiven for thinking the most outlandish of possibilities. Was the entity fixing or limiting a physical ailment that had yet to manifest within that region? Was the entity was implanting something that would sit there undetected and undetectable; something that could or would affect my mind or my body? There has to be an answer as to what exactly was underway. Possibly the entity was exploiting some aspect of my nervous system which it knew suspected would mystify me. An internet search identifies the suprascapular nerve in that region.

Report: #112

Location: Rear Garden (~11:00hrs)

Dose: 42mg

Lower Mesoglea of a Jellyfish

I prepared the pipe using waxy yellow crystals and took great care with all three inhalations, noting with satisfaction the significant increase in audibility of my psychic sound. I imagined the transmission of that energy was psychically audible in a realm beyond the capacity of my ocular vision. As I lay back and looked up there was an immediate palpable sense of something above me. Within a couple of seconds, I was looking at a psycho-spiritual presence of indeterminable size but clearly exhibiting a great many equidistant tiny shaded points throughout its form. Concurrent with that emergence, very high frequency energy became audible all around me and within me. The frequency of that energy grew higher, and higher, and higher. In some strange way I could actually feel the changing amplitude throughout the entire volume energy – as though one single wavelength was representative of the whole energetic mass. Its frequency and intensity went well beyond what I considered possible. My astonishment made me smile even as my mouth hung agog. The energy continued towards an ever-higher pitch. I wondered where exactly that energy was audible to me. It would be inaccurate to say the energy was audible within my ears. It would be more accurate to say the energy was 'palpably audible' in the midst of my head and all around me. As the entity transformed into a lower energy state, I sensed it was trying to communicate something to me but I could not grasp what it was. A small garment of clothing drying on the washing line caught my eye and it too seemed to be conveying something. As I was trying to work that out, I observed a remarkable sight. The lower and outer portion of the entity distinctly resembled something like the lower mesoglea of an oversized jelly fish. It was visible as a quivering and highly crystal-clear psycho-spiritually-formed skirt, and clearly demarked the presence of the otherworldly occult entity in terrestrial reality. I could not take my eyes away from it. Slowly it ascended a short distance and became increasingly invisible as it did so.

Report: #113

Location: Rear Garden (~12:35hrs)

Dose: 48mg

Nuanced State of Mind

I lay upon the blanket made my position comfortable then sat up and began. Midway through the first pull I could hear my spiritual tinnitus amplifying at a truly terrific rate. The second pull was dense and substantial and had an incredible effect – like a sudden upward change in gear and the application of high revs. From that moment I knew this was going to be an experience to remember. The third pull emptied the pipe as the high-pitched sound in my head was still actively rising. I leant across to place my lighter on the patio rather than the wet grass. I was feeling incredibly woozy as I maneuvered myself into position. Above me, emerging and raging with incredibly intense energy, an entity far wider than I am tall and displaying a front face like the business end of giant tunnel boring machine – proudly displaying hundreds of jaggedly sharp saw-teeth. I knew I had gone too far and I knew from my awkward posture I was woefully ill-prepared for this interaction. For a fraction of a second, I rued my commitment to this research; I felt I was incapable of dealing with such a thing; I felt this was far beyond the capacity of my courage. But just then, something unexpected occurred. Over in the school playground a sudden uproar of noise ensued as hundreds of young children rushed out for playtime. It was a totally raucous level of noise. Fascinatingly, the entity above me stalled and remained static for just a second. The final inhalation was now beginning to impose itself upon my already highly aroused and significantly exteriorised occult constitution. The immense wall of noise continued and it was soon apparent the entity was unable to ignore the astonishing level of sound energy. I could see and feel its rapid departure in the direction of that noise. Its departure must have coincided with the DMT reaching peak level within my brain. I acknowledged how the timing of that uproarious noise had saved me from an occult being whose size and saw-tooth complexity looked far more frightening than I could contend with. But now, none of that mattered. Because now, so much of my psycho-spiritual self was quite literally so far outside of me that what remained within my physical shell was operating on pure bliss. I was well and truly, blissed-out. The ongoing cacophonous wall of noise from the school children now sounded like nothing less than the end of the world.

Indeed, its influence upon the little bit of my mind that was still operating consciously forced me to suspect the world around me was in a state of chaotic disarray. And yet I was feeling completely detached from it all, serene and safe; in complete and utter bliss as the wheels were coming off the world all around me. My predominant sense was how truly blissful I was feeling. And I was feeling absolutely heavenly. I was completely aloof from the surrounding chaos visiting my ears. I was completely motionless and silent, even though all around me sounded like the worst kind of disaster. I was in an exalted state; a privileged position; I felt completely lordly and totally untouchable. Only very slowly did I begin to realise that something was actually taking very good care of me whilst I was in this blissfully incapacitated state. As my visual and mental senses slowly increased, it became abundantly clear that an absolutely immense entity was operating to carefully shepherd the great mass of my exteriorised mind-stuff back into my body. The blissfully serene state continued, as did the wall of noise from the school. But I was in a truly magical state of mind; one that was typified by an unshakable superior calm aloofness; a heavenly mentality that made me feel as though I had risen far above the physical coarseness of my human existence. The sudden passage of two squabbling pigeons directly overhead did not flap my nerves one little bit. Without moving my head one iota, my eyes languidly moved leftward to see the two pigeons beating their wings furiously as they battled it out along the rainwater gutter. Through my nose, I inhaled an insubstantial volume of air, and then nasally exhaled a slightly larger volume of air. That minor action was absolutely steeped in tremendously deep communicative meaning. Despite acknowledging the presence of the fighting pigeons, I was so very far removed from their feathered nonsense. My mind was in such an incredibly aloof and lofty state. Minor facial movements and the subtlest changes in my breathing all harboured such incredibly profound and mysterious meaning – each one indicative of my nuanced state of mind. As my ordinary senses slowly retuned, it was clear the entity that cared for me was filling a vast portion of the sky above me. In the same serene state, I listened detachedly to the incredible roaring and rumbling sound as an aeroplane passed somewhere overhead. Once again, a haughty little nasal sniff spoke volumes about my frame of mind. My ordinary senses were returning to fullness – but only very slowly. I began to realise the magnitude of the experience. Even as I continued feeling serene and blissful, I realised the state of mind experienced in this experiment really stood out within my research. Indeed, whilst in the midst of that serenely calm and absolutely heavenly frame of mind – when all around me sounded like utter chaos – deep within my heart, I hoped the ever-unknowable thing behind the absolute entirety of everything that was, is, and ever will be, was cognisant of what was underway in this little garden. Because what was underway felt like it was of nothing less than of universal import.

Report: #114

Location: Rear Garden (~20:30hrs)

Dose: 49mg

Psycho-Spiritual Porcelain

I had to force myself into this experiment, but ultimately managed to exhaust the pipe in four pleasing pulls before reclining. My recollection of the emergence of the entity is scant. I recall a significant display of audible and perceptible power as it willfully extended itself to cover the entire footprint of the garden. It was an incredibly impressive sight, but I could not help but wonder how its psycho-spiritual body circumvented or negotiated the apple tree – it seemed such a hindrance. My eyes began darting around the garden to observe the extent of the entity covering the garden as a strange psycho-spiritual dome. Afterimages of the apple tree rendered the leaves in striking bright silver. I still could not work out how the entity had negotiated the apple tree. Its overarching domed configuration over the garden was large and impressive, but its height appeared insufficient to encompass the apple tree. The personality of the entity was totally intriguing. Its character seemed directly related to its appearance. This seemed to be an entity with lots of power, but a very narrowly defined mind. It was projecting its power down onto me with great anger, as though it wanted me to be scared of that power. But it was empty anger; it was power without personality; and as it continued projecting, I realised it did not know how to stop itself. In fact, I sensed it knew very little other than what was within its very narrowly defined limits. Its psycho-spiritual form felt like it was fashioned from constructible pieces and amazingly, there were areas above me with visible and strangely tangible interlocking units displaying distinct saw-toothed edges. The feel of its mind to my own exteriorised mind-stuff was really unusual – it felt almost brittle; almost like psycho-spiritual porcelain. Its energetic anger continued on and on and on without cessation. Eventually, I lowered my eyes and raised my hands to wave it away. Upon looking back, the entity was departing and vanishing in an easterly direction. But now there was something else. I now felt completely open and vulnerable. Not in a small measure – but very much so; completely open; worryingly vulnerable and at risk. It was an awfully destabilising feeling. I felt something had a watchful eye upon me. Something was watching me and it knew what I was engaged with. And that something was patiently biding its time. I gulped, and that's when I saw what I saw. I spoke slowly and cautiously, saying: "I see you! I see you!" It completely filled the air above the garden; it filled the air above the neighbours garden to my right; and appeared to extend far over into the school sports field over to my left. A great big mass of mind-stuff. I felt terribly uneasy and refused to keep my eyes focussed on any particular portion of its massive otherworldly form. I looked this way and that way. I sat up but felt obliged to lay straight back down. I then cried out in alarm as two pigeons furiously beat their wings to abandon landing in the garden.

Report: #115

Location: Large grassy field (~17:00hrs)

Dose: 55mg

Long Grass Game

I loaded up a pipe and headed out on foot to some nearby farm fields. One particular field was heavily overgrown with wild grasses up to shoulder height. I waded through looking warily around to make sure no one was eyeing me with suspicion. After wading in a good long way, I cleared a small circular area by bending over the high grasses with my foot and then lay down. The overhanging grass beautifully framed my view of the perfect blue sky. My biggest fear was not the substance, but the lighter. The twin flames remain lit for several seconds after the ignition trigger has been released, and this grass was sufficiently dry to take flame. With sunglasses on I sat up and made four very pleasing inhalations in the hope I would attract an occult visitor. I could soon hear and feel my psychic energy as it rapidly intensified. After exhaling the fourth and final lungful there was an incredibly eerie silence. My mind was functioning with crystal-clear clarity as psycho-spiritual substance rapidly emanated from me like an expanding hemisphere of crystal-clear consciousness. Within seconds I realised there would be no interdimensional visitation, and so I settled down into enjoying the experience – murmuring with guttural contentment. With each and every contented murmur, the overhanging grass would bend and nod in agreement; and as I continued with my contented guttural murmurings, the overhanging grass continued to bow and bend and nod, making me feel quite kingly and making the grass appear obligingly subservient. Everything was peaceful. Everything was good. Everything was going so very swimmingly, when all of a sudden, I was forced cry out with great alarm: "What the fuck!", as a nearby pheasant furiously beat its wings to retreat from my unwelcome presence. I quickly composed myself with several deep breaths. There were occasional quivers and minor ripples throughout the crystal-clear medium emanating from me. I realised I was now beginning to hear distant road traffic. The contrast of hearing that now with the astonishingly eerie silence experienced at the outset was truly remarkable.

Report: #116

Location: Rear Garden (~21:00hrs)

Dose: 25mg

Remotely Feeling Feathers

Three pulls emptied the pipe and as soon as my head rested into the cushions an entity began to emerge. It seemed as though the entity had been invisibly present the whole time. There was no suggestion of any sudden arrival. It was just there – as though it had invisibly settled itself above this small suburban garden in readiness for me to amplify my consciousness with DMT. It was about five arm's lengths above me and as its emergence continued it soon became evident that this was a mind-numbingly vast entity relative to my physical size. It covered the entirety of the garden and beyond. Throughout its transparent form the appearance of thousands of equidistant small shaded points. I was taken aback by both its size and its apparent prior invisible presence above the garden. There was no energy of any note, and I suspect that lack of otherwise palpable energy made me question the nature of the entity – was it well-meaning or contrarily disposed? That uncertainty quickly formed into doubt. And that doubt quickly manufactured mistrust. It was likely misplaced, but I momentarily averted my gaze. Except there wasn't really anywhere else to look because I was as good as blanketed beneath its widespread otherworldly form. I wondered if I should just get up and abandon the experiment by walking away, but good manners prevented me from doing so. I sensed the entity sensed that all was not well with me and indeed, I was having a hard time maintaining my composure. I outstretched my arms as though to indicate to the entity my genuine surprise at its vast size. But then, very much to my surprise, I suddenly welled up as though on the verge of exploding into tears. And although some of that emotion did manifest, I was still working very hard at maintaining composure. The entity began to vacate by very slowly moving skywards and diminishing in visibility. I felt abashed, and somewhat stupidly began to imagine the entity had been bedding itself down over our garden for the night. And I had come along with DMT and disturbed its peace. And although I knew the idea of an entity bedding down above the garden was a very silly notion, I could not help myself from considering it was such. All I could really intuit was the entity did not wish to spook me or see me in any emotional turmoil. The air above me was really thick with my own psycho-spiritual output. A crow flew directly overhead at about twelve arm's lengths distance. I could clearly hear the steady beating of its wings. But far more surprisingly, I had a very strange and unique tactile perception of the oily dryness of its feathers – especially its wing feathers. It really was very peculiar and I could only wonder how my exteriorised mind-stuff had enabled me to have that tactile perception.

How does one classify and catalogue these remarkable occult entities? This one appeared noticeably different to those astonishingly magnificent entities I have termed Occult Masters. But asking how one classifies and catalogues these occult entities feels something not unlike an ambitious dog asking itself how to go about classifying and cataloguing humankind. My thought that this entity was bedding down for the night seems silly. But I cannot really be sure what it was or was not doing beforehand. Perhaps it is more reasonable to suppose this entity was attracted to my presence because I had lain in the garden watching the sky for half an hour before committing to the experiment. Is it unreasonable to consider that one's baseline psychic output can attract the attention of an occult entity in such circumstances? Possibly – unbeknownst to me – this small garden has become something of an occult hotspot for those entities seeking opportunity to interact with a human intent on undertaking dimethyltryptamine-fuelled occult investigations. But what was really intriguing about this encounter was the obvious response of the entity to my emotions. As soon as it realised that I was struggling with its overwhelming presence, it respectfully departed. On that basis it would seem reasonable to assume its emotional intelligence is at least on par with my own, if not considerably greater.

Report: #117

Location: Rear Garden (~08:50hrs)

Dose: 7mg

The Darker Quarters

This was a really fascinating experiment. The 7mg dose was all that I had available from a very displeasing low yield freeze precipitation. I took in a single and surprisingly voluminous inhalation and held it down within my lungs. A relatively sizeable portion of the air, some few arm's lengths above me, began vibrating very rapidly. Within mere seconds, something visibly and tactilely emerged above me, as though investigating my heightened psychic output. It appeared as a horizontal psycho-spiritual film covering the entire garden and exhibiting a multitude of very small and dark, equidistantly spaced points. Its energy was palpable and audible. There was a sudden change in that energy which I cannot detail any further, but I palpably sensed a short-lived pattern had formed therein. Seconds later, I was unaccountably beset with the most awful baleful machinations of mind against my wife. The thoughts seemed concentrated and focussed. And just as much as they were heinous and unwelcome in content they were equally discomforting in their persistence. I shook my head vigorously as though to rid my mind of such awfulness. I addressed the apple tree and the shed, each in turn, in a plaintive tone as though beseeching their help, or appealing for their understanding: "Mr Tree? Mr Shed?" Addressing them was certainly a welcome diversion from the horribleness despoiling my head; a horribleness intent on maintaining centre stage. I began to wonder whether such a mindset might qualify as treading on the path to schizophrenia – even if only lightly and upon tiptoes. I tried to transform my bad thoughts by substituting them with more agreeable matters of mind. I then tried to recollect how and why I came to be experiencing such a disagreeable mindset, but accurate recollection seemed surprisingly difficult. I persevered in racking my brain whilst still contending with unwelcome horribleness filling my head, until at last I recalled that I had smoked DMT. The recollection resulted in a muted and painfully prolonged eureka moment, as I now suspected the entity had knowingly amplified the dastardliest thoughts from the deepest darkest recesses of my psyche. Having reasoned along those lines and feeling I had made satisfactorily incisive analysis of what had just occurred, I immediately felt much better. As much as this had been worryingly wretched experience, the wider significance behind such analysis became increasingly evident to me as I realised, I was dealing with a suspicion of immense profundity.

It's difficult to know where to begin, but a valid line of enquiry is to ask whether the entity purposefully exploited practical working knowledge of the human psyche. Did that entity know just what to do and just how to do it, in order to momentarily mire my mind with maleficent machinations dredged from the darkest depths of my psyche? I contend that it did. But another valid line of enquiry is to ask why an entity would impose upon my mind so nefariously. Here, I don't think the answer is straightforward. It would be an all too easy cry the entity was demonic. But that really doesn't benefit our knowledge or understanding sufficient to demand cessation or discontinuation in furthering such research.

Report: #118

Location: Rear Garden (~14:15hrs)

Dose: 40mg

Latent Occult Locale

It was sunny. I inhaled three times and then lay back. An entity was soon upon me. Its energy was fiercely analytical. I could feel it upon me and all around me. The ground seemed to shake in response to that energy. I realised how this would've been a hugely unnerving experience were my research still in its infancy. But this was not the first time I had been subjected to such a fiercely analytical gaze. I calmly looked into the entity as its high frequency analytical energy continued to impose upon me. And after a few seconds, it felt like the entity acknowledged the position I was taking and it transformed into a far less energetic state. It now appeared the entity was composed of a large amorphous mass of spherical psycho-spiritual cells. The fiercely analytical energy dissipated. The entity then streamed into my head, through my face. I insisted upon staying calm and resolute. I could easily feel the uncommonly dense psycho-spiritual substance passing through my face. Its extraordinary density created a tactile perception of coolness. The psycho-spiritual mass continued streaming into my head, but as I could feel no movement inside my cranium, I assumed the entity was just passing straight through me. After a short while there was no more entity-stuff above me. The air appeared empty and the sky was cloudless. But then there was a sudden bizarre inflation-like bulge within my back, that made me feel as though I had risen off the ground ever so slightly. I was so surprised by this that I sat bolt upright and tucked my knees tight into my chest. Was the entity inside me? I assured myself that although such an entity could be inside my body, it could not take full operational control of my mind. I resumed my prone position once again but the same inflation-like bulge emanated once again. I was not overly concerned by this, as I assumed the entity was merely playing with me.

Report: #119

Location: Rear Garden (~19:45hrs)

Dose: 25mg

Wrong Person Wrong Place Wrong Time

These were fresh crystals and their aroma spoke highly of latent potency. I was not long home from an energetic bike ride at the local skatepark. Sweat had evapourated leaving a salty patina upon my skin. I sat up and inhaled the dose in three. As soon as my head sank into the cushions, I immediately felt the presence of a discarnate mind some five or six arm's lengths above me. It was visibly evident as a very obvious crystal-clear medium. Straightway the entity imposed a very dull and very heavy pulsating energy down upon me. That energy then increased rapidly in its intensity, and as it did so, the size of the entity increased proportionally. Intense energy was cyclical thudding into me and all around me. Its weightiness grew and grew and grew, unstoppably, and quickly became a cause for great concern. I had never experienced anything like this before. The intensity of power behind that thudding weightiness was devastatingly serious. Not only was I very scared, I was far too scared to move. This was the occult equivalent of an industrial power hammer and was more than enough to underline the humungous mismatch between my own nature and the devastatingly powerful nature of the thing above me. The thing above me expanded its psycho-spiritual self to such an extent that it was visibly taking up a great portion of the garden and appeared to extend to a considerable height relative to the house. The perceptible impact from the cyclical hammering was more than sufficient to convince me that I was not really cut out for investigations such as this. This was far too much! I had gone far too far! I was well and truly outside my comfort zone! Suddenly, the energy changed. It went from an impossibly strong and tremendously weighty cyclical hammering, into a rapidly rising high-pitched frequency. Before I knew what was what, my surroundings became wrought in such stupendous high definition that the ordinary reality of the garden had completely changed. A lot of activity was going on all around me, at the behest of this powerful entity, but I cannot report anything about that because I simply cannot recollect what it was. I remember two things about the apple tree. The first thing was that its canopy appeared unnaturally square. And the second thing was that as the leaves moved up and down in unison with the wind, the movement made it seem as though apple tree was communicating to me, on behalf of the entity, something to the effect: "Oh, you're getting it now! Now you're really getting an experience!" And indeed, I was. But my mind was so incapable of taking in what was actually occurring that I had already begun to assure myself this would eventually end. My pants felt as though I had just pissed myself – even though I knew I hadn't. But I realised my midsection also felt very damp. It was such a certain feeling that I moved my hand to feel the bottom of my t-shirt. It was indeed damp to the touch. I could not understand how or why my t-shirt was feeling so damp. While looking directly ahead in a mesmerised state of mind – at what I don't recall – I continued to feel my t-shirt by rubbing it between a thumb and finger. There was no doubting it felt very damp indeed. The intensity of the experience made me pine for ordinary everyday reality. The intensity of the experience gradually subsidised, but I cannot provide any great detail of that occurring. I recall moving my arms and my body just a little. But that was more to convey my discomfort at the intensity of the experience. As I observed a great mass of psycho-spiritual mind-stuff filling the garden and the air high above me, I settled down, because I realised the experiment was coming to an end. I muttered an assurance to myself about staying calm and remaining still and everything will be okay. But the entity then commenced an invasive deep tissue knitting activity in my left forearm. Humorously, I imagined this strange action was the occult equivalent of a cub scout earning an achievement award. I remained calm whilst looking up at the mass of psycho-spiritual substance filling the air. The action in my left forearm went on and on and on. After the psycho-spiritual stuff in the air had become vague, I moved my arm and the action ceased. Its cessation in that manner made it seem as though my muscles had been suffering from significant spasm. A small bird flew overhead at eaves height but dipped down toward me as it passed. The bird and its passage at that very moment seemed infused with mysterious significance. I remained in position for several minutes more while continually shaking my head in astonishment and recollecting as much detail as I possibly could.

Oh my God! That power! The intensity and the heaviness of that power was like nothing else I have experienced in my research! Unleashed and out of control all hell would break loose with that kind of power running amok in the terrestrial realm. It was more than enough to convince me I was the wrong person in the wrong place at the wrong time. Exactly like the sound energy and vibrations that result from industrial hammering – impacting cyclically with stupendous force – the occult energy experienced in this encounter had a consistent cycle and a truly forceful intensity. From the outset, that sharp rise in intensity over mere seconds convinced me I was beneath something of untold power. Perhaps the entity intuited my fright. Perhaps that was the exact moment when the unconquerable energy suddenly changed to a very high frequency. Because up until then, that energy seemed like it was threatening to run rampant over me. If that entity was an Occult Master – and there were certain elements of the experience that made it seem so – then this was a stark introduction to another side of their nature; and an awesomely powerful and frightening one at that!

Report: #120

Location: Rear Garden (~10:45hrs)

Dose: 40mg

Absence of Fight or Flight

I was home alone and absolutely forcing myself to make progress. During a second sedentary visit to the WC, I tried to find the positivity needed to commit to a DMT experiment. I wondered whether anything invisible had prior knowledge of my growing intention to commit to an experiment. After washing my hands, I removed an oversized thermal blanket from the bathtub and wrestled its sodden weight downstairs and outside over the washing line. Anything waiting for me to commit to the pipe would just have to be patient. With feet facing west and sunglasses over my eyes I sat up and began the first of three inhalations. I was now feeling courageous. The third pull took in a vast volume of vapour and emptied the pipe. I lay back and waited a while before exhaling. Very high frequency energy immediately imposed down upon me, and with very great rapidity it increased in pitch to untold enormity. I do not believe I will ever again experience a frequency higher than that which I experienced today. Indeed, I am quite certain that as far as incarnate human consciousness is concerned, this was surely the absolute upper limit of what is tolerable. I didn't even have the time to properly perceive the extent of my terror. I could go on and on and on writing; trying to convey in words the sheer impossibility of the high frequency of that energy. It was all-pervading; unbelievably singular; and over several very intense seconds it reached an audible and palpable flatline frequency that words simply cannot adequately convey. As it reached its stupendous maximum, I realised I was very far from ready for this. Indeed, I regretted that I had committed myself. This was too much! This was too much by far! But it was also far too late! I tried to open my lips, but they were securely sealed shut. Before I knew what was what, I found myself inside a very unusual, very colourful, and very highly defined environment; one that defies any detailed explanation, simply because I was whisked from one scene to another scene before I could deliver my vocal remonstration to stop the experience. I then realised I was able to open my mouth. I had the capacity to verbally call a halt to the experience and decided I should do just that. I wanted to derail the entire experience. I did not care that there would be a protracted withdrawal of the powerful entity from my physiology. And I did not care there would be a long and uncomfortable silence as that withdrawal process was underway. I just wanted to remove myself from this impossible experience. I wanted this overwhelmingly fast-paced experience to stop, and I wanted it to stop right now! But just as each and every opportunity to shout out became available, I was suddenly whisked off into another scene. And that would make me think twice about shouting out, because once the scene had changed, I tried to convince myself I had the capacity to remain calm, and the fortitude of character to see this experience through to the end. Nevertheless, my survival instinct decided otherwise. My deepest preservation instincts wanted what was best for me. And what was the best for me was derailing this experience by hollering for immediate cessation. But each and every time, just as I was about to holler, I was whisked away – again and again and again. I could feel the swollen physicality of my emotions bulging painfully inside my chest. The substance of that raw emotion would rise and fall with each and every failed attempt at shouting out. With each and every failed attempt I would endeavour to convince myself that I could see this thing through. Brief moments of shaky courage were continually transforming into doubts and misgivings. This turbulent pendulum between my raw emotions and my survival instincts soon had me in state approaching helplessness and hopelessness. I wanted so badly to cry out loud and demand the experience stop. But the experience was too fast-paced, and the scenery was strange and ever changing. Each time I was about to shout out I was rapidly whisked away into yet another scene; and each new scene gave me the briefest opportunity to gather up my courage and regain my composure. But it was very quickly becoming too much to bear, and this time around I really was about to cry out loud with all the might I could muster. I had taken just as much as I could bear and I could not bear any more. And then all of a sudden, that strange environment spat me out onto the ground, right where I began the experiment. A feeling of relief and surprise surged through me as I recognised the garden and realised, I had been released. But the experience was not yet concluded. Because now, a series of emotional outbursts and physical responses were sequentially wrung out from my psyche and my physiology – one after another, in rapid fashion. I cannot recall the exact order, but there was a dry-heave; a cry of profound astonishment; "Ooh's" and "Aah's"; a remonstration at the manipulation of my voice; a burst of tears; and a plea for my dear old mum. The magnitude of this phase of the experience was only marginally less intense than that which preceded it. The extent to which the entity was able to manipulate me was truly remarkable. To my limited understanding, this phase of the experience seemed purposefully designed to show me some of the emotional characteristics that define the human psyche. There was no doubt about it – I was being expertly manipulated by a powerful Occult Master; and manipulated in such a manner that showed me some of the emotional landscape of my psyche. And then the entity was gone. There was no hanging around. Its departure was no less speedy than its arrival was rapid. I was speechless – utterly dumbfounded! All I could do was shake my head in utter astonishment. And after a while, I smiled at the sky. But that did not feel like anywhere near appropriate or adequate. After much more shaking of my head, I signalled thumbs up and gave a big broad smile. But that felt relevant and appropriate only to some small degree, if at all. Nothing I could say and nothing I could do felt like it could adequately encompass an emotional or spiritual recognition of the magnitude of that which I had just experienced. I turned over onto my front – intending to bury my face into the cushions. But instead, I turned my head to the side and looked over the tops of the countless blades of grass. I then turned onto my back and placed a cushion over most of my face. Bemusedly and cautiously, from beneath the cushion, I looked up at the blue sky whilst feeling complete wonder for that which is hidden. I clasped my right hand over my mouth and recommenced shaking my head. I was in a state of heightened astonishment and feeling a tremendous amount of incredulity at what I had just experienced. Just as I was about to get up, two very little birds flew across the garden. Their flight and their flight path seemed exaggeratedly fluttery and undulating.

This was an unexpectedly intense experience. But really, with DMT, that is exactly what I should have been expecting. I cannot help myself from considering this particular occult entity knew of my intention to undertake this experiment. But I can only suppose. I cannot know for sure whether the entity had any influence upon me prior to undertaking the experiment. There is not much more I can say about the incredible intensity and the phenomenal frequency of that living spiritual energy. Over several seconds it reached a state wherein the representative wavelengths had completely flattened; they were pulled to an impossible tautness – making the energy feel impossibly solid and yet all pervading. What kind of a mind has such power at its disposal? It absolutely beggars belief! And yet the nature of the interaction gives some indication as to the nature of the mind. Clearly, they have practical working knowledge of the emotional configuration of the human psyche. The entity was able to manipulate my emotions much like a puppet master manipulates a marionette. The questions borne by such an occurrence are weighty indeed. And yet it was much more than just an adroit manipulation of my emotions. It went much deeper than that. It was like been in a fight or flight situation. Except that neither option was actually available. On no account could I fight the mighty intelligence - it was manipulating my psyche and repeatedly and capably frustrating my efforts to end the experience. I was in a truly impossible situation. And the consequence of being in that truly impossible situation was that I gained a qualitative glimpse into the character of my soul. Indeed, that particular insight actually seemed to be the central point of the experience – an opportunity to sense the state of something so absolutely central to my existence. And yet in gaining that sense of the character of my soul, I also came to realise how evolutionarily lowly it was; how immeasurably distant it was from the degree of advancement to that which was both edifying me and toying with me.

There were other minor but noteworthy perceptions and observations towards the latter stages of the experience – when the entity was sequentially wringing profound emotional and physical reactions from me. When I was vocalising my astonishment, there was a very subtle sense the entity was subtly suggesting that I temper my outbursts, as though to avoid attracting unwanted attention from neighbours. For all I know a nearby neighbour may have been busy hanging out their washing, or sat in deckchair enjoying the sunshine and having a smoke. And when I was just about to cry out to the heavens, but instead cried out for my dear old mum, I distinctly sensed the entity's delight at that response. I could've cried out profanities, or cried out to God. However, I really sensed the entity's delight over the choice of my emotional appeal. As that latter episode was drawing to a close, I was aware of a very fine vertical thread somewhere over on my left, in close proximity to me. I could vaguely see it and could feel its presence. It had some definite connection with what had been underway and what was still underway. A remote part of my cognition was very mindful of that thread, in terms of fretting not to damage it. The two fluttering birds were wrens.

[Wikipedia: Wren]

https://en.wikipedia.org/wiki/Wren

> Most wrens are small and rather inconspicuous, except for their loud and often complex songs. [...] Wrens have short wings that are barred in most species, and they often hold their tails upright. [...] The wren is also known as *kuningilin*

"kinglet" in Old High German, a name associated with the fable of the election of the "king of birds". The bird that could fly to the highest altitude would be made king. The eagle outflew all other birds, but he was beaten by a small bird that had hidden in his plumage. This fable is already known to Aristotle (*Historia Animalium* 9.11) and Pliny (*Naturalis Historia* 10.74), and was taken up by medieval authors such as Johann Geiler von Kaisersberg, but it concerns *Regulus*, and is apparently motivated by the yellow "crown" sported by these birds...[...]. In modern German, the name is *Zaunkönig*, king of the fence (or hedge). In Dutch, the name is *winterkoninkje* (little winter king). The family name Troglodytidae is derived from troglodyte, which means "cave-dweller", and the wrens get their scientific name from the tendency of some species to forage in dark crevices. [...] No sexual dimorphism is seen in the plumage of wrens, and little difference exists between young birds and adults. [...] Wrens have loud and often complex songs, sometimes given in duet by a pair. The song of members of the genera *Cyphorhinus* and *Microcerculus* have been considered especially pleasant to the human ear, leading to common names such as song wren, musician wren, flutist wren, and southern nightingale-wren. [...] Wrens build dome-shaped nests, and may be either monogamous or polygamous, depending on species. [...] The wren features prominently in culture. The Eurasian wren has been long considered "the king of birds" in Europe. Killing one or harassing its nest is associated with bad luck—broken bones, lightning strikes on homes, injury to cattle. Wren Day, celebrated in parts of Ireland on St. Stephen's Day (26 December), features a fake wren being paraded around town on a decorative pole; up to the 20th century, real birds were hunted for this purpose. A possible origin for the tradition is revenge for the betrayal of Saint Stephen by a noisy wren when he was trying to hide from enemies in a bush.

[From Wikipedia, the free encyclopedia]

Report: #121

Location: Rear Garden (~12:45hrs)

Dose: 33mg

Vulnerability

The sky was covered with thin cloud. My fears and nerves were terrifically heightened. I thought it was best just to get on with it. After sitting up I took in an unexpectedly great volume of vapour and kept it within my lungs for a good while. I lay back and within seconds sensed the emergence of an entity. Its transparent appearance reminded me of the mouth of an improbably oversized lamprey. It quickly emerged more fully and exhibited a multitude of equidistant small shaded points. Within seconds, a sizeable conical portion reached down toward me. The conical portion focussed on my solar plexus. I could feel a strange energy in that region. Overall though, it was evident the energy within this interaction was insufficient. I maintained my emotionless state. The entity was visibly diminishing from my setting. Different voices in my head clamoured for the opportunity to be given centre stage. A work colleague with a nasally spoken London accent was speaking unmemorable content. An unknown male with a ghetto-style of speaking took over but the content of his speech was also unmemorable. I was surprised at just how potent the substance was. The garden and the immediate sky were awash with my own psychic substance. I felt a real sense of the danger involved in this research, and I felt it keenly. There is no security. No insurance. I have only my mind. Anything can emerge from that unseen and unseeable realm. Willpower and courage are essential. But there is more, I am sure. Known and unknown voices continued to clamour for airtime in my mind. It was as though they were trying to climb under or over or through my own interior narrative, in order to assert themselves and make themselves heard. Despite my fears I told myself I would have to finish the pipe, because if I did not finish the pipe then I may as well withdraw myself from any further research. The great mass of my own psycho-spiritual substance above me convinced me that unseen entities were observing me. I sat up and made two further pulls which emptied the pipe. I lay back and felt an impossibly heightened sense of impending high drama. The level of anticipation felt within me and without me was truly remarkable.

Report: #122

Location: Rear Garden (~20:15hrs)

Dose: 25mg

Disproportionate Emergence

I was not long back home from work. My wife was busy in the kitchen. I briefly confided in her how I felt about undertaking an experiment. My mood was a mix of sombreness and trepidation. I lay upon the grass and told myself there was no way I was going to inhale the entirety of this dose. I simply lacked the requisite degree of courage or the appropriate level of recklessness. I decided I would inhale lightly and infrequently. I sat up and procured one insubstantial vaporous inhalation. I held it down for a while. Very much to my surprise, as lay back and exhaled, it immediately became apparent something had commenced emerging a short distance above me. The only reasonable conclusion I could deduce from this, was either the entity had prior knowledge of my intention to commit to an experiment, or it had simply been watching me and waiting for me to commit to the pipe. Above the garden, a countless and rapidly growing number of equidistant small shaded points became evident throughout an ever-growing mass of psycho-spiritual substance that had emerged from nowhere. I observed as it quickly enveloped the entire garden, rising upwards as it did so. It was phenomenal. And as I observed the ever-increasing extent of its growing psycho-spiritual presence, I was absolutely aghast that such an occurrence could be secured from such a low volume inhalation. Within seconds, the air above the entire garden was completely covered with a perfectly stable and perfectly flat superdense otherworldly substance, full of countless equidistant small shaded points. This was very much more than I had expected. This was wholly out of proportion to the insubstantial single inhalation. Something rather queer and unexpected then occurred throughout that superdense psycho-spiritual substance, in that it momentarily darkened and took on an almost mercurial finish – not in its colour, but in its nature. Areas of its surface shimmered and rippled in such a way as to make it really obvious this was a very unusual substance. The ripples and the peaks of each induvial ripple were exceedingly narrow. I am quite certain water could not produce anywhere near the same effect. In that single moment the substance had taken on something of an almost physical appearance. All this was far more than enough to convince me that I was beneath a power of unfathomable proportion. I could somehow feel the magnitude of phenomenal power at the disposal of this high intelligence. I sensed it was readying itself to impose upon me greatly. But I was far from ready for this. Consequently, my reaction was to shake my head vigorously, and mutedly cry out several very determined negatory phrases. I wanted to get up and run inside the house, where I imagined hiding behind my wife as she stood defensively in the kitchen. I then transformed that image; imagining myself lying nonchalantly on the sofa, watching TV, whilst pretending none of this DMT stuff had ever happened – that none of this profound occult business had any truth. But it was happening. And it was true. And I was giving serious thought to beating a retreat. But something became evident. This entity was apparently having private discourse with an unseen third party. I could sense the exact location of where that discourse was taking place – over in the far-right corner of the garden, and above the unmissably visible mercurial substance. I could even sense the gist of that discourse. The phenomenally-configured entity above me was questioning another entity about some kind of assurance that had been given; some kind of assurance about me being a reliable individual for these interactions. At the exact same time that discourse concluded, a real-life terrestrial squabble immediately commenced in a nearby neighbours garden. Whilst the verbal melee was underway, the entity above me underwent a transformation. I was still feeling very scared and was still giving serious consideration to jumping up and running indoors. As the terrestrial argument continued, a great portion of air bedside the canopy of the apple tree became filled with a very complex psycho-spiritual presence. Now, upon realising there'd be no significant interaction taking place, I began to regret my negatory reaction. A strange feeling of failure filled me; as though I had failed by some small yet significant degree in an ongoing initiatory endeavour – the knowledge of which was far beyond my human level of comprehension. Except that this experience was far from finished. The terrestrial dispute died down. My visual perspective made it appear as though I had sunken partially into the ground. A very long and very thin quasi-physical tentacle palpably worked its way towards me. Other movements began to manipulate me and manhandle me from beneath my back. Something invasive was underway. The manner in which certain areas of my back and my thighs were lifted aloft was absolutely startling. It was just as though air cushions were suddenly inflating and raising portions of my physiology by small degrees before deflating to lower me. I was quite comfortable with the procedure despite the profound feeling of absolute seriousness that accompanied it. The invasive maneuvers beneath my back continued as an impressive mass of psycho-spiritual substance rose high into the sky above me. I remained calm and within a couple of minutes the mass of mind-stuff was no longer visible. A repetitive spasm was evident in my upper arms – possibly an after-effect caused by the interaction. The spasms ceased when I moved my arms. I felt so unsettled that something so very significant could arise from such a small intake of vapour. I knew there was more potent substance remaining inside the pipe, and I thought about sitting up and hitting it again. But that thought seemed like the craziest idea in the world. I can't deny, I feared that very same entity returning with frightening haste. But my mind made the matter of hitting the pipe again one of principal, and dare. I sat up and pulled once on the pipe before lying back and exhaling through my nostrils. My feeling was one of defiance. How dare that occult entity emerge so greatly out of proportion to that which I had inhaled. But nothing happened. There was no heightened emotion, and no sense of any foreboding high drama suddenly imposing upon me. I realised my action was equivalent to shaking my fist at the sky long after the high drama had vanished.

Report: #123

Location: Rear Garden (~12:15hrs)

Dose: 34mg

Quasi-Physical Sensation

I had to force myself into committing to my research. I had to change my thinking into a more positive and courageous mindset, because as things were, I was pretty much forcing myself into this experiment and simply hoping for the best. As I was making the third inhalation, I realised just how very peculiar it was to feel my consciousness undergoing intense and rapid expansion. I lay back and observed the beginnings of an energetic-entity emergence. But at that exact same time, a noise over by the shed became apparent. It sounded like someone dropping a small pebble into an empty plastic bucket, over and over and again. But it seemed so very loud that I had to work really hard at consciously dismissing its annoyance. The power of the entity rapidly increased and imposed forcefully down upon me. Its powerful and forceful energy melded into my exteriorised mind-stuff, thereby making itself perceptible upon me, within me, and without me. Quickly and impressively the entity expanded a great portion of its psycho-spiritual mass upwards, creating the appearance a high-reaching psycho-spiritual canopy, spanning a sizeable portion of the garden and extending upwards to a height equal to the pitch of the roof, if not a little higher. The entity now resembled something like a very large triangular pyramid, with me beneath its base. But what had been especially impressive, was my very obvious tactile perception of the elasticity of the psycho-spiritual substance, as it had stretched itself during expansion. The speed and strangeness of what was underway held me mildly bemused and transfixed. But that annoying noise sounding like a pebble repeatedly being dropped into plastic bucket was becoming increasingly difficult to ignore. The visual clarity of the presence of the entity was exceptionally good. And the tactile perceptibility of its highly energetic presence was no less impressive. In fact, it was unmissable and seemed to be forcefully making its power known by tightly pulling upon my own exteriorised mind-stuff. My partially mesmerised mind was racing making analyses. But I was unable to determine exactly what the intelligence was intending to achieve by displaying its power this way. Because of that uncertainly, and because the ongoing noise emanating from somewhere near the shed, I began to invest my focus upon the noise and questioned what was causing it. I tried to imagine myself comically throttling the source of that noise. I suddenly sat bolt upright and tried to focus my eyes upon where the noise was emanating from, but the noise sudden ceased. I resumed my lain position. The energy from the interaction with the occult intelligence had now greatly diminished. The noise resumed – albeit with much reduced intensity – causing me to sit bolt upright once again. I scanned the area ahead of me until I heard the noise once again. Its intensity was now very much reduced and after a short while I was able to deduce the noise was nothing more than the plastic rainwater gutter expanding in the heat of the sun. But the significant diminishment in perceived loudness was so absolutely remarkable. I can only conclude the uncommon density of that psycho-spiritual substance – especially when temporarily melded into the psycho-spiritual substance of a discarnate entity – exhibits the expected acoustic characteristics for sound transmission.

Report: #124

Location: Nearby Farmland (~17:30hrs)

Dose: 64mg

Purposefully Perpetuating Bewilderment

This pipe was pre-prepared with gooey and waxy DMT. On the short walk through the housing estate I passed two adult males, busy at roadside repairing a white van. I imagined stopping and engaging them in convivial conversation; explaining the content of the pipe in such a way that they would nod wisely with unquestioning understanding. From the foot of a very large hill I followed a well-trodden winding pathway. The wild grass was short and stubbly, having recently been reaped. Three quarters of the way up the hillside, I diverted from the path and found a good spot where I could position myself with the sun behind me. The view stretched out impressively – overlooking the Surrey Hills in the far distance. Not that the view mattered any, because my eyes would soon be directed skywards. I removed my jumper from around my waist and fashioned it into a makeshift cushion before lying back and making myself comfortable. I placed my phone beside me and decided to press ahead. My first inhalation was pleasing and voluminous. I was feeling very confident. I held it down for a good long while before releasing what had not soaked through my lungs. I then waited just a seconds before commencing the second inhalation, which was equally as voluminous. My psychic sound was now racing upwards in pitch and intensity. The third pull found very little vapour remaining, but I persevered to ensure the pipe really was empty before I lay back. My right-hand kept hold of the pipe. Unthinkingly, I kept my sunglasses shading my eyes. It was immediately perceptible that something had found me. A sizeable swirling psycho-spiritual mass exhibiting multitude saw-toothed zigzagging lines descended down upon me. My inner voice reassured me: "Whatever happens happens!" The substance was peaking, leaving me feeling quite strange and disorientated. The short stubbly grass put me in mind of a bed of nails; my skewed angle upon the hillside greatly exacerbated my feeling of disorientation. I also realised my view through the sunglasses was surprisingly dimmed, and quite out of sorts. It appeared the lenses were almost pressing up against my eyeballs. My mouth felt as though there was a small foreign object therein, which despite my best efforts, I could not catch with my tongue and neither could I spit it out. I was quite out of my senses. I knew who I was, and I knew where I was and what I was doing. But those considerations were very much secondary to the sharp discomforting stubble beneath me; my feeling so lop-sided; the unusual dimness of my sunglasses; the proximity of the lenses to my eyes; and whatever my tongue was chasing around inside my mouth. I came to understand the sunglasses were a hindrance to the experiment because the entity had communicated that exact sentiment to me – but in multiple variations on the theme of that sentiment. Manifold communications about the unhelpfulness of the sunglasses bombarded my mind. I removed the sunglasses and beheld an incredible sight – a vast mass of psycho-spiritual mind-stuff comprising extremely large spheres; each one approximately five arm's length in diameter. It was a truly astonishing sight; completely see-through and unambiguously observable. A red kite glided around directly above. My senses were still skewed and my tongue was still chasing something around inside my mouth. I began to hawk, as a means of expelling whatever was inside my mouth. My tongue continued to sweep around and around my mouth. It felt so abundantly refreshing and my mouth felt so incredibly well salivated. At that point, I realised something quite interesting. I realised that to some degree, I was purposefully maintaining my unusual state of mind and my actions; as though purposefully perpetuating my state of bewilderment; or half-consciously hamming up my skewed state of mind for some inexplicable reason relating to the presence of the occult intelligence. I then began to wonder whether the vast psycho-spiritual mass of impressively sized spheres was actually my own exteriorised mind-stuff. But upon thinking that, there was one further very clear communication from the entity, telling me not to forget my belongings. The location of that communication even had a palpable presence – exactly where my belongings rested beside me. The communication was so explicitly clear I unthinkingly voiced my thanks and gave assurance I would not forget my items. Some thirty seconds later, that vast mass of psycho-spiritual spheres had totally vanished. I sat up and enjoyed the beauty of the view for a short while before lying back and going over the details of the experience. Several male and female voices – all with very strong Scottish accents – were vying to take centre stage of my interior narrative. Each spoke short snippets of speech which was never interesting, but was only banal because there was no real standalone subject matter. They were simply using words commonly used to give structure to meaningful speech. After a few minutes I got up, tied my jumper around my waist and picked up my belongings before setting off down the hill. Several strides in, I realised I had forgotten to pick up my lighter and duly about-turned to locate the device.

It's absolutely amazing to contrast lying upon the ground looking up at the sky in an ordinary frame of mind, with lying on the ground looking up at the sky as some mysterious aspect of one's being becomes sufficiently aroused to rapidly expand and thereby attract the attention of a discarnate entity of occult nature. Something previously unseeable emerges and appears to emerge from nowhere. The validity of such an occurrence and the actuality of such experience begs ontological question after ontological question. Is it really the case that something immaterial, or relatively non-physical, rapidly expands and projects outward from one, in response to a boost of dimethyltryptamine molecules? It seems reasonable to assume that same immaterial something ordinarily resides within us (and quite possibly without us) at a steady baseline state. And the arousal caused by exogenously administered DMT, is one that results in its rapid expansion far beyond its ordinary latent state. Possibly that mysterious psycho-spiritual stuff latently rests within the microtubules of our brain; within every living cell of our body? That same mysterious psycho-spiritual stuff also quite likely resides in a parallel occult kingdom; a realm not so much hidden from our sight, as merely existing outside of the range of our perceptive capacities at this stage in our evolution. But should we begin to entertain the notion that some of these occult beings can impose upon our minds, and thereby purposefully or inadvertently influence our ideas, or vicariously drive our actions? Is it possible the prevailing state of one's own mindset has the potential to attract – on a like-for-like basis – those intelligences most in tune with one's general mode of mentation? If one becomes aware of those influences, then that is perception of occult influence. The view across west London and beyond was incredible. I wondered how far that strange psycho-spiritual stuff could stretch under the influence of DMT. I thought about the fast-pace of central London life. Numerous individuals, each with their own unseen occult atmosphere anchored within them and around them. Such a field must vary from individual to individual. There must be variations in intensities, densities and frequencies. Not to mention hidden qualities relating to the actual nature of the individual at the root of soul. Those qualities must manifest and there must be common everyday examples of such manifestations. Sometimes we meet a stranger, and immediately develop strong rapport; whereas at other times, we may feel a strong dislike or aversion to a stranger, without even realising why.

Report: #125

Location: Burnsall, Yorkshire Dales (~11:45hrs)

Dose: 18mg

A Day in the Dales

This was the first full day of a short family holiday. We arrived at our location – a large grass meadow beside the meandering river Wharfe situated below the imposing Burnsall Fell. The field was not too busy as we parked our vehicle up against a large stone wall, forming an abutment to the bridge spanning the river. Our boys raced to the river to catch trout fry in fishing nets. My wife and I set up our picnic a short distance from the vehicle, beneath a small tree adorned with dark purple leaves. The thought to chance a research experiment came to mind. There were only four of five other cars nearby, but nobody in close proximity to us. I made my decision and informed my wife. With my pre-prepared pipe in hand I sat beside the vehicle with my back resting against the stone abutment. Ahead of me rose the impressive Burnsall Fell, and the merciless sun in a completely cloudless sky. I felt obliged to turn my head to the right, whereupon I noted a Jack Russell terrier, tethered to the spot and watching me intently. I skillfully drew down the entire dose in one deft pull. The volume of vapour was so great that I was quite literally chewing it and swallowing it down. I really wanted to get the absolute maximum potential from this dose, and so I retained it within my lungs for as long as I possibly could; only exhaling when I felt the onset of the substance and noting with great satisfaction, very little superfluous vapour exiting my mouth. The strength of the substance rapidly imposed itself. My inner psychic sound increased terrifically and quickly became phenomenally intense. My inner voice appealed to itself – begging to know what I had just done. But it was far too late for that now. The purple leafed tree underwent wholesale pixilation. The energy inside my head was skyrocketing. It was much too much to handle, and I needed to lay down flat. But in making that attempt I dashed the back of my head against the stonework and slumbered discomfortingly and diagonally against the wall. This was not good. This was ill-thought out research. The sun was now unbearably hot and the impressive radiance around its disc was undergoing strange pixilation for just about as long as I could bear glancing upon its fierce face. A woman walked past ahead of me. Her profile extended significantly ahead of her and behind her in a time-lapse manner, but swirled in a pattern that reminded me of decorative featherings upon a cake. I was now convinced this was my worst ever research decision. The woman suddenly began making childlike noises by way of greeting the dog. I imagined the dog wagging its tail and shaking its back end vigorously as it went through the motions of readying itself to pounce upon her with loyalty and affection. My wife was stood a short distance ahead of me, beneath the shade of the tree, unpacking picnic items. Something about her posture piqued me into sudden self- realisation about our relative positions; she there standing all alone beneath the shade of the tree preparing a picnic; me awkwardly positioned and psychedelically struggling whilst the sun was imposing heavily upon me. I got to figuring we must look like we've argued. Immediately, paranoia set in. I struggled to sit myself upright. I then called my wife. She came and leant against the side of the vehicle and looked over me. I was in a psychedelically dishevelled state and it was not pretty. I tried to stand up, but my limbs were not functioning. This was not pretty at all. But I could not help myself from having a little laugh over this farcical situation. The laughter was not shared. I could not stand up no matter how hard I tried, and so I gave up trying. When I eventually found the capacity to stand erect, I walked gingerly over to the picnic blanket and positioned myself comfortably upon it. Straightaway I sensed the presence of something above me and looked up to see a large psycho-spiritual form, several arms lengths above me. It resembled a huge pillow in its outline form and its internal appearance reminded me of the parallel raised chambers on an inflatable lilo. I raised my hands in a gesture indicating apology and false alarm. My wife joined me on the ground and I disclosed that something was above us and observing me. But no sooner had I said as much when I sensed how ridiculous that must've sounded to her ears. I continued with my hand gestures a few seconds longer and then began to compose myself in between bouts of laughter at my own stupidity for racing into research so unthinkingly.

Report: #126

Location: South Beach, Blackpool (~21:00hrs)

Dose: 32mg

Blackpool Revisited

This was a day at Blackpool on a hot summer's day. After enjoying a day at the theme park, we retired to a quiet part of the beach in the early evening and set up our picnic. After eating we made our way down toward the incoming tide. The water was expectedly cold. I resolved to keep my gonads dry, but the paddle slowly turned into an ever-deepening wade; and feeling obliged to set a brave example before my boys, I waded out further and further until the bottom half of my thighs were submerged in cold seawater. My wife was determined she would immerse herself in the sea but was struggling to take the plunge. After securing my families attention I placed my hands behind my head and proceeded to fall backwards beneath the murky seawater. After some splashing about we strode back up the shore while collecting driftwood for a fire. After a hot tea, I questioned my worthiness as a researcher and questioned my readiness and my courage. The clear twilight sky atmospherically magnified the brilliant full moon above the sand dunes. I decided to force the issue and ventured atop the dunes to find myself a secluded spot, overlooking the inconsiderable Blackpool airport. The rotors of a nearby grounded helicopter were noisily chopping the air. I was quite certain the outcome of this experiment would be nothing more than the impressive visual expansion of my psycho-spiritual self. The entire dose was vacuumed down in two voluminous attempts. Upon lying back into the sand, it became immediately evident something very large was rapidly emerging from out of the air. Its psycho-spiritually transparent form was easily evident as a multitude of small, lozenge-shaped cells; each cell was clearly defined by a very thin shaded border; giving the entire mass the appearance of being an extensive psycho-spiritual net. With great immediacy, the extent of that presence increased well beyond anything I thought possible. From my perspective, it appeared the entire area above the sand dunes was completely blanketed beneath this impossibly extensive psycho-spiritual mass. In my astonishment, I began repeating: "No, no, no, no, no!" one after another, many times over, while giving serious thought to fleeing the scene. But the thing above me was having none of that. Within seconds the portion directly above me descended toward my face – purposefully tapering down toward me as though to take a much closer look at me. The cells forming this tapered portion were visibly stretched. The atmosphere was impossibly intense. This entity was as good as demanding to know who or what exactly had made so much psychic noise on these sand dunes. I was completely blanketed beneath the untold breadth of a vast and impressive occult entity. The helicopter's engine and rotor blades were terrifically noisy. The incredible intensity and discomforting proximity of this vast psycho-spiritual being effectively held me under the cosh of its presence. This was an encounter well beyond anything I was expecting. I innately understood the tapered portion of this entity could see me; it could sense me, it could analyse me. Its extensive blanketing form exhibited countless geometrically perfect cells. It was nothing less than spectacular and beautiful. But I was not really in the mindset to properly appreciate its beauty. I was face-to-face with something vast and highly unusual; and something in no mood to reduce the intensity of its energy. But after many seconds had passed, I began to realise nothing much else was going to happen, despite the ongoing intensity of its presence. My confidence increased as my apprehension decreased. I suddenly voiced an unexpected profane laden outburst; and then began voicing my amazement at the truly extraordinary size of the thing; and how totally unexpected its emergence had been. My voice steadily increased in volume and incredulity, until eventually I gave into nervous laughter. Then, unable to bear any more intensity from this thing, I sat bolt upright. Everything suddenly appeared normal. I spat out vehemently and loudly, several times over: "Fuck, fuck, fuck, fuck, fuck, fuck, fuck!" I grabbed the pipe and my lighter and quickly stood up. I was flabbergasted and stood rooted to the spot. I shook my head in disbelief then made my way back to the picnic, whilst continuing to shake my head. My wife observed the shock on my face. Our boys ran off to play in the dunes. I sat down by the fireside and begged for a cup of tea. I thought about what had just occurred and shook my head a good while longer whilst looking deep into the flames of the fire.

Report: #127

Location: Birkin, North Yorkshire (~20:15hrs)

Dose: 38mg

The Old Eye

I am no fan of fishing as a hobby, but my youngest boy had expressed an interest. This was me making good on a fatherly promise. There's a small spring-fed pond in the countryside outside my hometown, known locally as *The Old Eye*. The weather was damp with a low grey cloud precipitating rain – conditions were grim and gloomy. Beneath an oak tree aside the pond, I exercised great patience in slowly setting up two junior fishing rods. One boy stood silently watching me whilst the succumbed to bouts of fidgeting through disinterest. Patience eventually paid off and after priming each hook with a prawn, I set my boys at different positions and watched them cast their first line. I instructed them in basic rod operations and explained the need to maintain a watchful eye on the floats. Having advised them that patience was essential for fishing, and feeling quite satisfied I had made good on my fatherly promise, I wished them luck and advised I required a period of privacy and solace. I made my way towards a wheat field and waded in before sitting down and removing my pipe and lighter from a small plastic container. My mood had changed. I was serious. My lungs vacuumed down a great volume of vapour and retained it for a while. I began the second inhalation as the onset of the substance began to take effect. I had sufficient pneumonic capacity to empty the pipe of all available vapour, and did just that. I then lay back and nestled my head upon the flattened wet wheat as my psychic sound continued to amplify greatly. It was immediately obvious and palpably evident that something occult was investigating my psychic output. With terrific immediacy, a multitude of large and concentrically-configured saw-toothed circles emerged and descended upon me. I wondered what the hell such a thing as that was doing out here in the middle of nowhere. But then realised such a thing as that may well be wondering the same of me. Its appearance had so much potential to be terrifying – appearing like the enlarged mouth of an otherworldly monster, based on the oral characteristics of an improbably oversized lamprey. It engulfed me before I had any time to contemplate remonstrating. Its energy was relatively subdued in comparison to other encounters. As soon as the entity emerged, rainfall suddenly increased. It seemed so strange in an environment so remote from human habitation, with such truly awful weather producing such dismal conditions, that an entity would actually emerge. But this entity just did not seem to have much personality about it. I wondered whether the entity was the protector of this particular wheat field, without really knowing what I meant by that. The rain became heavier and faster. Large drops frequently spattered my face. I extended my right arm and swept it through the melded mind-stuff. Impressive trailer trails resulted and I continued slowly sweeping my arm through the dense psycho-spiritual stuff so that I could marvel at the unusual visual effect. Thoughts of my two boys came to mind. I pictured them standing quietly beside the pond in the grim and increasingly inclement weather; clutching their rod while hoping to catch the same pike who had, in all likelihood, retired to the depths. I gave it a moment longer and then sat upright and surveyed the wheat field. There was incredible beauty; countless heads of wheat stretched out below my eyeline; the uniformity of their height indicated a gentle countered depression of the field. There was no sign of the entity. I endeavoured to spring upwards into a standing position. The rain was now very heavy and conditions were well and truly miserable. Realising my senses were somewhat awry I forced myself to focus on priorities. I felt my trouser pocket in order to verify my car keys were exactly where they should be. I set off towards the pond but stopped upon realising I was headed in the wrong direction. The heavy rain really had put a different complexion on things. Upon arriving back at the pond two little fishermen stood dutifully alert. But with no sign of a bite on either hook. I questioned my eldest boy and sought honest answer as to whether he liked fishing. He said that he did but understood it required patience. I strode off and left him standing in the heavy rain. I then questioned my youngest by asking if he was enjoying himself. He said that he was. Now I regretted leaving my experiment prematurely when I could have had a few more minutes with the wheat-field-entity. But the weather was truly horrible and the already grim light was fading fast. As I put my hood over my head, I realised these conditions were far from favourable for two young boys without their jackets. I marched the short distance to and fro from one boy to the other, making enquiries about welfare, enjoyment, and whether or not the float had moved. Out of earshot from my youngest boy I confided in his brother exactly how I felt about fishing. Upon hearing which his earlier stance underwent something of a radical revision and he agreed it would be a good idea to pack up and leave. I approached my youngest boy again. I would have so loved for him to have gotten a bite on his line. He said he was sure he had seen a pike or two swimming near to his float. I coaxed him into calling it a day, which was not too difficult in such wretched weather.

Report: #128

Location: Rear Garden (~13:45hrs)

Dose: 37mg

Joyous & Agreeable

There was simply no way I could commit myself fully to this pipe. My level of apprehension was far too high. The thought of inhaling a sufficient dose to facilitate interaction with a powerful spiritual entity seemed like the craziest idea in the world. The sky was completely cloudless. It's difficult to explain what came over me as I began the first inhalation, but I progressed onto a second pull and a third pull which emptied the pipe. I palpably perceived the presence of something above me but momentarily questioned whether I had sufficient mettle to commit fully to this encounter. No intense or high frequency energy imposed down upon me. Yet I sensed some strange connection or familiarity with the entity above me. No sooner had that realisation occurred when I suddenly burst into heartfelt boisterous laughter. I remained completely conscious of my residential surroundings but really wanted to laugh out loud with complete abandon. But I knew that doing so would potentially raise eyebrows and attract unwanted neighbourly attention. And all the while, in the very back of my mind and whilst I was still laughing, I realised something really profound – this entity had moved me to this state merely by my sensing its presence and intuiting its character. And yet I also sensed I was being expertly puppeteered by the entity. And that made my ongoing laughter all the more joyous and agreeable. But what followed next only served to underline the power of the puppeteer, as my oral environment and my emotions were subject to a degree of manipulation completely out of keeping for an interaction so obviously characterised by the absence of any energetic melding of our mental energies. From my perspective, the entity exhibited a capacity that made it seem it was completely my own choice to open my mouth to its fullest openable extent. A sequence of noises relating to a series of emotions were progressively squeezed out of my psyche: gleeful laughter; a cry of surprise; and sounds indicative of absolute wonderment. And in the midst of all that, the entity had engineered something quasi-physical in the back of my throat whilst my mouth was agape. It momentarily made me gag and then cough, but in a really comical way. And once that sequence of actions and emotions had completed, it would start all over again. But as it did so, I could feel a dense psycho-spiritual sphere, slightly larger in size than a tennis ball, slowly rolling up my chest from my sternum. And whilst all that was underway, the back of my mind busied itself with feelings of wonder and awe that so much could occur when I was expecting so very little in the absence of the usual initial highly energetic initial phase. As those enjoyable manipulations upon my psyche came to a close, I remained calm and still – suspecting I was still in something of a partially mesmerised state from the encounter. The entity then manifested into a vast and beautiful psycho-spiritual form – clearly visible to my eyes. It remained present above me and seemed to have a definite interest in me. I sensed there was something of a nurturing and maternal element to its character. A portion of its strange and otherworldly form descended down upon me. I tried my best to scrutinise its strange beauty, but my eyes had become sensitive to the daylight brightness and no matter how hard I tried to refresh them through repeated blinking, they were stinging. I could feel the psycho-spiritual presence upon me. Its unusual otherworldly density created the illusion of a cooling effect upon my left side. I was quite sure the entity was doing something invasively inside my left arm, and I was completely comfortable with that. After a couple of minutes there was no longer any visible sign of the entity. I looked directly up at the otherwise cloudless sky and observed vague but definite evidence of a cloud forming directly above me at an indeterminable height. I observed the cloud as it moved at a very slow pace in a north-easterly direction. It was so very vague that its presence could have so easily been missed or overlooked. But for some reason, I thought the observation was noteworthy.

This was evidently an entity I have come to term as an Occult Master. It seems valid to ask: Was the Occult Master able to sense my pre-experimental apprehension? And if so, might I assume it tailored the experience accordingly, to take account of that apprehension? It's an interesting notion; as is the concept of being puppeteered by an otherwise unseeable body-of-mind. What was really interesting for me is that in the build- up to the experiment, I was absolutely adamant that I would not commit fully to the pipe. Indeed, to commit fully seemed like folly – the craziest thing in the world. It felt positively impossible. And that remained the case right up until the moment I sat upright and began inhaling. And then something changed within me, without me realising that any change had actually occurred. If I can suppose I was puppeteered during the experiment, should I also suppose I was subliminally puppeteered immediately before inhaling the potent substance? Should I even go so far as to suppose I was subliminally coaxed into the decision to pursue this experiment? I find such questions hugely intriguing. But it is hard to deny that such suppositions also come with potentially discomforting corollaries.

Report: #129

Location: Rear Garden (~19:40hrs)

Dose: 42mg

Crisis of Confidence

I was experiencing a crisis in confidence without being able to pinpoint exactly why. There was simply no way on earth I had sufficient confidence to empty the pipe in three successive pulls. This experiment was me forcing myself forward merely to maintain continuity in my research. The air was eerily still and silent. The sky was a low hanging cloudy white blanket, creating a muggy closeness and a feeling of dense atmospheric heaviness. I sat up and slowly drew down one voluminous inhalation. Upon resting back, I straightway sensed the presence of something above me. The immediacy of its presence suggested it had been watching me and awaiting me. It emerged more fully – evident as a crystal-clear psycho-spiritual mass filling the air above me. A low intensity but palpably very heavy energy impinged upon me. There was a no nonsense feeling to that energy. My breathing quickened. There was an overwhelming sense that at any moment this entity would significantly increase its energy and thereby mesmerically overwhelm my dimethyltryptamine-amplified psychic output. I was nervous and I suspected the entity could sense my nervousness. Its energy was especially heavy over the lower half of my legs, where it felt like an impossibly tight band forcibly pressing down upon me. I soon began to feel far more comfortable with my situation and began to feel that I could resign myself to a high energy interaction. But it was far too late for that now. Movements beneath my right and left arm became evident. The movements felt as though they were made from beneath the blanket. The movement beneath my left arm in particular felt like something spindly was poking at my skin. Its physicality was so surprising. It continued until I suddenly sat up and lifted the blanket – even though I knew I would find nothing there. I lay back and appealed aloud with earnest sincerity to the entity: "How do you even do that?" But visually and palpably it appeared my occult visitor had departed. I waited for a few minutes while busy with deep thoughts and then sat up and made another pull on the pipe. I expected a heightened sense of anticipation. But as I resumed my recumbent posture the level of anticipation and expectation was so phenomenal my stomach felt as though it was curdling. Something began to slowly emerge above me. Visually it was spectacular. But with my crisis of confidence it was simply too overbearing and frightening – a vast psycho-spiritual mass exhibiting a multitude of concentric zigzagging lines. There were long psycho-spiritual shards and strangely configured curvatures therein, all making up one very large and very imposing otherworldly form. I had no doubt whatsoever it was looking at me. I could feel the energy of its gaze as it stared at me and into me. The weight of its stare indicated the tremendous latent occult power at its disposal. This entity was as good as warning me with what awaited me should I continue to amplify my psychic signal. The stillness of the air was absolute. My nasal breathing was operating slow and shallow. Not one single leaf or blade of grass dared to even move. But the silence was paradoxical. It was absolute to my ears, and yet the high-pitched psychic sound within me and without me was all too audible to my mind. My perception of the stillness and the silence of the heavy air was heightened and augmented by the presence of the interdimensional entity above me. A need to lubricate my dry lips with my tongue was undertaken carefully and slowly. The audibility of sound resulting from that oral action was extraordinary. A mere moment later, the sound of furiously beating wings from a surprised pigeon were loud and noisy as the bird made a forceful effort to flee from me. I was certain the entity sensed my fear. Very slowly and very purposefully it began to maneuver; appearing to slowly turn around as though to face away from me; evidently departing and diminishing. At the back of my mind I pictured myself sitting up in defiance and grabbing hold of the pipe to inhale what little that remained; as good as calling upon the entity: "Come on then! Give me what you've got!" And somewhere within me, I really wanted to do just that. How I wished I had the necessary courage to do just that; to bravely and defiantly grab the pipe; to give it one almighty vacuuming pull and then submit to whatever consequence may follow. But I was scared. This is a very different scenario to dealing with the counterpart of my species. Did I really want to venture into foolhardy provocation with a powerful interdimensional intelligence? Just as much as I was able to imagine myself exhibiting that courage, it simply was not there in substance. Not today, at least! A large dark moth flew quickly overhead. Its manner of flight seemed perplexed. My inner voice observed reflexively: "I didn't know moths could fly that fast."

Report: #130

Location: Rear Garden (~13:15hrs)

Dose: 31mg

Psycho-Correction Techniques

My wife was not yet home. An investigative sniff of the pipe indicated potency. I sat up and insisted on having courage and confidence as I emptied the pipe. Straightaway it was palpably evident something of significance was above me. Latent potential of very great power was all too evident. I could see the crystal-clear medium defining the discarnate mind. But that which I could see suggested a cuboid presence. Over in the schoolground a large pile-boring augur rumbled away and periodically emitted an alarm that sounded like a car horn. None of that seemed to be of any concern to the entity. My courage and confidence momentarily quivered. I then felt movement beneath my right arm. Knowing what was about to take place I moved both arms nearer to my side in what I considered to be a helpful gesture. A strong quasi-physical movement began directly beneath both shoulder blades and a very obvious invasive operation then commenced. It felt like something was being screwed very tightly deep within me; in similar manner to how someone uses a ratchet wrench. I was unsure how I felt about this. The lack of any initial high energy made me suspicious about the character of the entity. The physicality of what was underway was very pronounced and was undertaken in a serious and no-nonsense manner. I began debating whether or not I should remain lain; or whether or not I should demand cessation; or whether or not I should just jump up and flee. In one sense I felt relief there had been no intensely energetic temporary melding of our minds. But in another sense, the lack of that phase really heightened my suspicion as to what I was being dealt. The crystal-clear clarity of the entity went some way to assuage my concern; such pronounced clarity conveyed a character of highness. Nevertheless, I continued in an undecided frame of mind until the invasive movement ceased. It was evident that whatever had been underway it was now complete, and it appeared I was alone once again. I stretched out my limbs and realised how good I felt – mentally and physically. I felt full of vim and confidence, but could not work out whether that related to the strange interaction I had just experienced. Whilst musing deep in thought upon the esoteric interpretation of 'overshadowing', I told myself: "Overshadowing is one thing. But being wired up is quite something else!" For around the next hour I could distinctly feel the two areas where the invasive activity had taken place.

In occult parlance, 'overshadowing' seems preferable to 'possession', which is usually more familiar when preceded by 'demonic'. Searching for a comprehensive definition of overshadowing proved more difficult than I imagined. I decided to e-mail John of the Gentiles, the author of *The False Prophet Azazel*. He very kindly replied, drawing reference to the late Theosophist Annie Besant, who it seemed coined the term in question:

> The use of the term Overshadowing comes from Theosophical Society president Annie Besant:
>
> To the Theosophist, such demonic possession is known by the pseudo-scientific designation of Overshadowing (as we learn from Annie Besant in Superhuman Men in History and in Religion circa. 1913 A.D.): "Overshadowing is the dominating of consciousness for a time by the Superhuman Helper (by the angel). The consciousness of the man is dominated (likely through the employment of low frequency infrasound acoustic psycho-correction techniques), not stimulated. The idea (implanted by the angel) dominates his thought, and becomes to him apparently his own (thought). Many a one (a human) is overshadowed by a Higher Being (an angel) who is not conscious of the source of the thoughts that come into his mind... these are breathed out from a higher consciousness (the angel) to a lower (a human), and they dominate the lower (human) and become its ideal. Ideals, those fixed ideas that guide and control conduct (which control the actions of an individual), constantly come from the overshadowing power..." (the word 'power' is synonymous with the word 'angel.' The 'thought' on which the person acts is conveyed to the human [via ELF wave information/data transfer] by the angel—the individual thereby serving as an avatar of sorts).
>
> [Quote provided by: John of the Gentiles]
>
> [ELF denotes: extremely low frequency]

Report: #131

Location: Rear Garden (~10:00hrs)

Dose: 25mg

What's Your Emergency?

I was feeling very confident. I emptied the pipe in three pulls. It immediately became palpably evident that something was above me. With near equal immediacy, that very same something suddenly emerged into stunning visibility several arms lengths above me. It appeared as a perfect flat plane with a multitude of equidistant small shaded points throughout. It covered the entire footprint of the garden. The small shaded points rapidly developed into small, uniformly-sized symmetrical shapes. I don't recall whether any significant energy imposed upon me or around me. However, it was somehow very obvious that a truly tremendous amount of power was at the disposal of this intelligence. Thoughts from a previous experience where I was unable to fight or flee flashed through my mind. I felt I was about to succumb to a similar situation and my courage and confidence suddenly forsook me. I began shaking my head and waving my hands and blowing hard through pursed lips before making vocally negatory remonstrations. This was far more than I had expected – even though that is exactly what I should have expected. This is what I should have been prepared for. Except that now, I wasn't. It seemed I was hopelessly ill-equipped with the requisite fortitude for this endeavour. Interestingly, there was a distinct moment where I sensed the entity had stalled. It seemed to hold itself static for just a second or two. And during that very brief moment I realised this experience would progress no further. I then suffered indomitable regret. Weighty thoughts raced through my mind as I felt the game was up. I felt I had reached the end of the line. I felt my entire research programme had derailed and ended prematurely, right here and now. I felt I would have to write this report as my very last report. I would have to come clean by confessing that I had gone as far as I could go and I could not go any further than I had already gone. The regret weighed heavily upon me. There was no comfort whatsoever. But whilst all that was going through my mind, I could not work out why it felt as though my entire body was comfortably sunken halfway down into the ground; and why it felt as though I was moving smoothly and diagonally backwards. Those strange and inexplicable effects continued, and although they were so obvious that they could not be ignored, I was still dealing with feelings of failure and regret. The powerful entity then began to visibly emerge in a low energy and visibly very obvious psycho-spiritual state. It was only then that I was able to fully appreciate what had investigated my amplified psychic signal. It was a most amazing and remarkable sight – a psycho-spiritual occult entity of vast stature; curving upwards and away from me high into the sky; gradually broadening out as it did so. I no longer felt my regret so acutely. Here was a sight that was simply impossible not to be captured and retained deep within my memory. Here was a sight so richly rewarding to my research. And here was a sight showing me the size of the subject I was dealing with. The strange otherworldly detail throughout its internal form was simply spectacular: strange curves; twists and folds of a beauteous nature. It curved upwards and away from me; taking a wide berth away from the rear corner of the house and extended upwards far beyond the height of the house and beyond the height of the massive oak trees at the front of the house. My human mind – hardwired to anthropomorphic interpretations – likened the form to the occult equivalent of a huge arm extending its hand down toward the earth's surface. Indeed, because I was still feeling strangely and comfortably half-sunken into the ground, whilst at the same time smoothly gliding diagonally backwards, it really did feel as though I was in the process of being released from the otherworldly clench of the impressive entity. Even visually, it appeared as though I was in the process of actually being delivered to the garden by the strange grasp of this vast occult form. My instinctive reaction upon seeing the impressive fullness of the entity was to place my splayed fingers over my chest, as though in readiness to tear it open. But I also felt the entity was purposefully revealing itself to me, knowing full well that I would have a strong emotional to the sighting. After a minute or two the entity was no longer visible. I tried to come to terms with my failing and my regret. I lifted my fingers from off my chest and closed them into tightly clenched fists and shook them tensely. But then realised it was far better to remain calm, level-headed, balanced and composed. This was not the end of the world. And my failing to commit fully to this interaction had given me a truly stunning visual encounter; showing me the incredible extent of the occult entity. And I was determined this would not be my final experiment. I headed indoors and outlined to my wife what had just occurred. Her gentle reassurance was welcome. I made a mug of tea and headed upstairs. My youngest boy was fresh out of bed and complaining of stomach ache in the bathroom. His mum joined him and suddenly shrieked out my name with great alarm. I turned to see my youngest boy crumpling lifelessly towards the bathroom floor. My wife was doing her best to prevent him from crashing down by hugging him tightly from behind. His weight overcame her strength and he was soon laid out and looking lifeless. For a moment I half panicked through dithering over whether to phone the emergency services or stay with the boy. My wife's choice to stay with him made my choice easier. I tore down the staircase and dialled the emergency services. In a clear spoken but raised voice I demanded an ambulance. My ears could not fail to detect the mild panic and near faltering delivery of my voice. My eldest boy was sat on the sofa glaring down hard into his tablet. I told him not to panic. He looked up and told me he did not know what was happening and then resumed his gaming. But despite his apparent nonchalance, I strongly sensed the distraction of his tablet was helping him deal with that which he was learning, as I outlined my emergency to the capable and calm operator. After answering several questions by way of relaying information hollered down to me from my wife, and racing upstairs and downstairs in order to convey the findings of my own visual assessment, it seemed an ambulance was no longer required, as he fully revived from his swoon.

Report: #132

Location: Rear Garden (~19:00hrs)

Dose: 63mg

Good Housekeeping

Earlier in the afternoon I was at work and seated at my desk looking out of an upper storey window. Countless grey shaded houses interspersed with countless green shaded trees filled my view. While surveying the considerable swathe of drab urban expanse, I pictured myself in the garden at home, undertaking a research experiment and observing the energetic emergence of an occult entity. But the actuality of such a thing seemed so preposterous when considered against the scene of urban civilisation spread before me. But when I looked at the vast and apparently empty blue sky, it didn't seem quite so outlandish. I arrived home to an empty house. There was an unmistakable smell of tryptamine potency coming from the crystals in the pipe. I headed outside. My emotional state was mixed. I was dealing with high anxiety and trying to transform my fear into a clear-cut drive of courageous determination. I sat up and made two insubstantial inhalations before changing the lighter from one hand to the other. A third inhalation took in a healthy volume of vapour which I retained before exhaling. The immediate palpability of an invisible presence several arms lengths above me convinced me the thing had been watching me all along. A vaguely visible energetic medium of no great power and with a mild cyclical pulse imposed upon me. The energy was mostly perceptible over my legs. The sensation was like feeling pressure from a fluid – a dry fluid. I wondered why the sensation was limited to my legs. I began to question my courage and commitment to this research. That question quickly developed and I began daring myself to pick up the pipe. A series of mixed emotions began to trouble me deeply before I suddenly sat bolt upright and began drawing vapour from the pipe, with careful application of heat from the flame. I lay back feeling great trepidation while constantly reassuring myself that I would survive. I expected the entity was going to surge down upon me and into me while wreaking its unfathomable power upon my body and mind. But it wasn't quite like that. In fact, it was nothing like that because nothing happened. There was no incredibly heightened sense of anticipation; no sense of any impending high drama; no intense feeling that something was about to descend upon me thunderously with lightning-like rapidity. I knew there was more to be had from the pipe.

Except now, I really did sense something. I was under observation. Something was watching me. I could not see it but I could certainly sense it. There was no doubt about it. The same argument as before entered my head: did I have the necessary courage to commit to that pipe? But this time the matter felt very different. The strength of the argument inexplicably developed an unbelievable intensity. As ridiculous as this must sound, it felt like the future fate of the entire universe hinged upon whether or not I had the fortitude to recommit myself to the pipe. But it was psychologically painful and an absolute extremity of burden. It was far more than I wanted to be dealing with. I cried out aloud with worry and distress: "Don't do this to me!" But the intensity of what was at stake was simply overwhelming. And the expectation to make good was simply overpowering. The future fate of the entire universe rested upon me sitting up and hitting that pipe hard. And I didn't want to. I was too scared. I didn't want to be in this position. I wanted to jump up and run indoors and hide behind my wife. I did not wish to play any part whatsoever in the future fate of the universe. I didn't have it in me. But thoughts of the pain from failing in such an immense responsibility could not be ignored. No matter what – this simply had to be obliged. On no account could it be allowed to fail. The existence of absolutely everything felt like it rested solely with me. It was horrible – horrible and harrowing. It was unspeakable; unutterable; unimaginable. With the passion of a venomous curse that deserved to be vehemently spat out I sat bolt upright and defiantly sucked down a great stream of potent vapour. I lay back, held it down, waited a second more, then exhaled and realised absolutely everything had completely stopped. Everything was completely still and silent. It was beyond eerie. There was an overwhelming sensation without me that readily translated within me to: "You've really gone and done it this time!" There was absolutely no wind and not even a whisper of breeze. Not one single leaf fluttered and not one single little blade of grass dared to move. The silence was impossible. And as I carefully studied the sky, my eyes could only conclude that it too was fixed and frozen in time. The sense of stoppage was unearthly. My senses were communicating the impossible. My senses were telling me the laws of motion had, in one single moment, silently stalled. Absolutely everything apart from my eyes and my heartbeat, my mind and my shallow breathing had ceased motion. And then suddenly something was there. Something truly stunning to behold. The incredible detail of its form indicated intelligence and power far beyond my capacity to imagine and understand. It was so stunning it seemed to completely nullify the surprise that it should have justified. A visually very obvious and very dense psycho-spiritual form with an outer surface composed of thousands upon thousands of overlapping lozenge-shaped cells, projecting outward and downward from what appeared as a visually very obvious flat plane, spanning the air high above the garden. It was a stunningly configured occult lifeform. The flat psycho-spiritual plane surrounding that mind-blowing protrusion contained a multitude of equidistantly spaced small shaded points. But there was other patterning throughout that flat plane surface that appeared to be undergoing change after change after change. The power of the entity was without question. It was totally overwhelming in appearance alone. In the seconds that followed my mind was certain this was going to be the ultimate experience. Nothing could ever or would ever be able to exceed whatever this thing was about to do me. And I was hopelessly ill-prepared. I had no doubt whatsoever that this thing could take me apart and put me back together again. It was about to transmit its untold energy down upon me and into me, and do whatever it willed with me. But I baulked through fear and the entity sensed my misgiving. Yet it still wanted to impose upon me. Thoughts of the future fate of the universe once again squeezed my most essential emotions. My courage was hiding somewhere inside me and I simply could not find it. My courage had made itself small. My courage simply did not want to know about the very big thing above me, let alone the fate of the universe. My courage had deserted me; leaving just me; the raw me; the scared me; the me that knew myself all too well and the me that knew myself not at all. The compulsion upon my psyche was beyond tremendous, as this theme of acting to save the universe sharply poked away at something somewhere very deep within. I was experiencing a force majeure and it was one which I simply could not oblige or obey. I wanted to run indoors. I didn't want this. This was too much. But the ache of failing crippled me where it hurt the most. I had to act. I simply had to act. Even against my own will I knew that I had to act. I simply had to submit myself to this all-powerful presence; this majestic looking humungously massive thing. There was simply too much at stake not to. And knowing that I must do that which I did not want to do, and feeling under great duress to do that thing, my mind made its decision and my body reacted accordingly. A sudden outburst of rage or madness saw me viscously tearing up sods of grass in each hand as I prepared to submit myself against my will. And having done that, I suddenly began to think: "Perhaps this experience won't be quite what I imagined it would be." And it wasn't. Because now, the breathtakingly impressive entity, and every obvious trace of its presence, had in that single moment vacated and vanished. It had all occurred in just a few seconds and now the entity was gone. Or so I thought. Because then, in the crown of my head, a very obvious invasive knitting action became palpably evident. It continued for perhaps one minute. It wasn't painful, but the action felt like it was of profound importance. I remained calm as the activity continued while my mind began to go over and over the entire experience, to harvest as many factual details as possible.

I knew that toying about with this substance was like playing with fire. I had pictured myself undertaking piecemeal puffs on the pipe and observing the passage of a little black orb. But instead, something near unspeakable was able to make it appear utterly convincing that the laws of motions had been put on hold. That same something – having revealed its awesome magnificence – was then able to convince me the future fate of the entire universe rested upon my full commitment to this experiment. That same something was an occult being whose configuration was as stunningly beautiful as it was powerfully frightening to both my terrestrial and occult senses. I beheld its presence for just a few short seconds – a few short seconds filled with intense mental and emotional pressure.

There was one additional observation that I later considered to be of immense significance. A fleeting observation made after reclining for the second time. As I had lay back and settled, something psycho-spiritual and of a similar size and outline shape to me had sped toward me with incredible rapidity. But I had observed it, and I had observed enough to recognise and recall its detail. There were shapes within that form and shapes within those shapes. But its descent toward me was so very rapid. For just a fraction of a second it was there. And then it was no longer there. There was the subtlest of movements behind me – certainly enough for me to inwardly observe the me-shaped psycho-spiritual thingy had gotten itself either behind me or inside me; quite possibly inside my mind; to a depth that would allow it some degree of manipulation over my psyche.

Report: #133

Location: Rear Garden (~10:00hrs)

Dose: 32mg

Hundreds & Thousands

The rear garden was experiencing a beautiful sunny interval. I managed one voluminous inhalation before the lighter ran out of fuel. I lay back and looked up as my psychic sound increased markedly in volume. It was equally audible all around me. I was palpably perceiving my own invisibly exteriorised occult substance. Birds chattered a pleasant avian chorus from high in the giant oak trees. I eventually stood up and headed indoors to refuel the lighter. Upon resuming my prone position, I experienced a very obvious palpable sense that something was above me. I sat up and completely emptied the pipe in one voluminous pull and then lay back. Fretfulness and amplified trepidation welled up throughout my entire torso. If I had not worked so hard to maintain my courage, they would have so easily overwhelmed me. I sensed the entity above me had suddenly and rapidly vacated the setting. Above me, I now observed a truly impressive sight: a sizeable mass of my own psycho-spiritual mind-stuff. It exhibited a distinct haziness by virtue of its depth and density. The central portion of that mass was easily evident, but gradually diminished away from the centre. By moving my eyes around the outskirts of the dense psycho-spiritual mass, I was able to observe its impressive extent by contrasting against the light blue sky. I wondered whether my psycho-spiritual mind-stuff would eventually become conscious and active in a higher occult kingdom, free of terrestrial incarnations. Lace curtain hanging in the rear bedroom window suddenly caught my eye. I imagined how terribly creepy it would be to observe a stranger's face peering down upon me from behind. The thought made me burst into gleeful, nervous laughter. I realised just how very much I was enjoying myself in this tame experiment. A neighbours dog began yapping noisily, which caused me to imagine playfully strangling the critter into silence. But that seemed a tad extreme, so I transformed the mental imagery into me pouring sticky treacle all over its coat. The dog suddenly ceased its yapping, thereby giving the impression it had received some semblance of my thinking. A crow glided slow and low overhead, causing me to voice out loud with surprise and delight: "Wow! I love that crow!" But when a starling made its sudden exit from the apple tree, by furiously flapping its small wings, I considered it exhibited a distinct lack of grace. My fingers involuntarily signalled that sentiment by splayed stiffly outwards in the direction of the bird's flight. I headed indoors. My wife was in the kitchen. I could still feel mild effects from the substance and announced aloud with heartfelt emotion: "I love that stuff!"

Report: #134

Location: Rear Garden (~09:00hrs)

Dose: 38mg

Field of Limitation

There was a pleasantly potent tryptamine aroma as I carefully pre-melted the crystals into the pipe. On the short walk home from dropping my boys at school I absolutely refused to worry about the impending experiment. Back at home I headed outside with willful determination and made a start. The first pull was really good. The second was average. And the third took in a great big volume of vapour. Very quickly something began to emerge some distance above me. A passing parakeet left a long tracer trail visible in its wake. A large crystal-clear medium displaying small shaded equidistant points therein merged into visibility. Very quickly its energy amplified tremendously. It was deep and cyclical – almost like thumping bass notes from a large bass drum – and psychically very unsettling. As its energy amplified the still emerging entity transformed from displaying small equidistant points into a beautifully patterned crystal-clear psycho-spiritual mass, emitting unnervingly powerful psychic waves. A particular portion of the entity appeared perfectly flat and rectangular – almost like a smooth and highly polished glass door. There was a moment, just a fraction of fraction a second, where I was on the cusp of fleeing the location in order to escape the prodigious energy. But I determinedly redoubled my willfulness. And in so doing, it suddenly felt as though I was directing my own willful energies upwards and outwards – projecting them towards the powerful entity. Several young hens – new pets for my boys – all began cheeping from beneath the giant trampoline. I wondered whether they had some small sense of something uncommon occurring. My adrenaline was pumping and my breathing was fast. The entity seemed full of pomp and power, and my determination to face it squarely made it feel like a battle was developing – albeit with something I simply could not physically fight. And then the entity, and all of its prodigious power, was simply no longer there. It had vanished. I realised just how fast my breathing was and allowed it to continue with my chest heaving up and down before I suddenly exhaled fully and held my lungs static, while consciously working to relax my post-adrenaline state. There was an immediate and beautiful silence that was near absolute. It seemed in that very moment the low and pervading background noise had suddenly ceased. The only noise marring that silence was the passage of a high-altitude aeroplane directly overhead. I resumed my breathing in a more relaxed state. The sky was full of my own glassy psycho-spiritual mind-stuff. Altocumulus clouds exhibited extensive snowflake patterning. I spent a couple of minutes in silent thought and reflection before heading indoors.

What I found really very interesting about this experience was consciously exercising and actually feeling my willpower projecting outward. In doing so, I felt a very strong commonality with the mind of the discarnate entity; a commonality separated more by degrees rather than by character. This apparent projection of my will totally fascinated me. I began thinking about how the immateriality of one's mind relates to one's genetic makeup. Does one's DNA determine the quality of one's willpower? Or does one's willpower determine a specific sequence of genes that give rise to one's sense of having willpower? That led me to thinking about whether occult beings such as the one encountered today have their own occult equivalent of our DNA. But that seemed intuitively preposterous and downright ridiculous.

[Wikipedia: Will (philosophy)]

https://en.wikipedia.org/wiki/Will_(philosophy)

> The Will, generally, is that faculty of the mind which selects, at the moment of decision, the strongest desire from among the various desires present. Will does not refer to any particular desire, but rather to the capacity to act decisively on one's desires. Within philosophy the will is important as one of the distinct parts of the mind, along with reason and understanding. It is considered important in ethics because of its central role in enabling a person to act deliberately. One of the recurring questions discussed in the Western philosophical tradition is that of free will - and the related but more general notion of fate - which asks how the will can be truly free if a person's actions have natural or divine causes which determine them. This in turn is directly connected to discussions on the nature of freedom itself and also the problem of evil. [...] Virtue and vice according to Aristotle are "up to us". This means that although no one is willingly unhappy, vice by definition always involves actions which were decided upon willingly. Vice comes from bad habits and

aiming at the wrong things, not deliberately aiming to be unhappy. The vices then, are voluntary just as the virtues are. He states that people would have to be unconscious not to realize the importance of allowing themselves to live badly, and he dismisses any idea that different people have different innate visions of what is good. [...] Psychologists also deal with issues of will and "willpower" the ability to affect will in behavior; some people are highly intrinsically motivated and do whatever seems best to them, while others are "weak-willed" and easily suggestible (extrinsically motivated) by society or outward inducement. Apparent failures of the will and volition have also been reported associated with a number of mental and neurological disorders.

[From Wikipedia, the free encyclopedia]

Turning to more esoteric references, Volume I of Blavatsky's *Isis Unveiled* makes the same enquiry, and elucidates very briefly on the universal:

What is the WILL? Can "exact science" tell? What is the nature of that intelligent, intangible, and powerful something which reigns supreme over all inert matter? The great Universal Idea willed, and the cosmos sprang into existence. I *will*, and my limbs obey. I *will*, and, my thought traversing space, which does not exist for it, envelops the body of another individual who is not part of myself, penetrates through his pores, and, superseding his own faculties, if they are weaker, forces him to a predetermined action. It acts like the fluid of a galvanic battery on the limbs of a corpse. The mysterious effects of attraction and repulsion are the *unconscious* agents of that will...

[From: Isis Unveiled (1877) by H. P. Blavatsky. Vol. I Page 144]

In *The Theosophical Glossary* we are given a fuller and rather fascinating occult definition, using quotes from the Flemish chemist, Jan Baptist van Helmont (1580 – 1644), and the great Paracelsus:

Will. In metaphysics and occult philosophy, Will is that which governs the manifested universes in eternity. *Will* is the one

318

and sole principle of abstract eternal MOTION, or its ensouling essence. "The will", says Van Helmont, "is the first of all powers....The will is the property of all spiritual beings and displays itself in them the more actively the more they are freed from matter." And Paracelsus teaches that "determined will is the beginning of all magical operations. It is because men do not perfectly imagine and believe the result, that (occult) arts are so uncertain, while they might be perfectly certain." Like all the rest, the Will is *septenary* in its degrees of manifestation. Emanating from the one, eternal, abstract and purely quiescent Will (Âtmâ in Layam), it becomes Buddhi in its Alaya state, descends lower as Mahat (Manas), and runs down the ladder of degrees until the divine Eros becomes, in its lower, animal manifestation, erotic desire. Will as an eternal principle is neither spirit nor substance but everlasting ideation. As well expressed by Schopenhauer in his *Pererga*, "in sober reality there is neither *matter* nor *spirit*. The tendency to gravitation in a stone is as unexplainable as thought in the human brain...If matter can – no one knows why – fall to the ground, then it can also – no one knows why – think....As soon, even in mechanics, as we trespass beyond the purely mathematical, as soon as we reach the inscrutable adhesion, gravitation, and so on, we are faced by phenomena which are to our senses as mysterious as the WILL."

[From: The Theosophical Glossary (1892) by H. P. Blavatsky. Page 342]

In *Studies in Occultism*, also by Blavatsky, we learn more about the role of the eye, relative to one's own Will, or to the Will of another, through hypnotism:

As the rate of vibrations (molecular motions) in metals, woods, crystals, etc., alters under the effect of heat, cold, etc., so do the cerebral molecules change their rate, in the same way: *i.e.*, their rate is raised or lowered. And this is really what takes place in the phenomena of hypnotism. In the case of gazing, it is the eye – the chief agent of the Will of the active operator, but a slave and traitor when this Will is dormant – that, unconsciously to the patient or *subject*, attunes the oscillations of his cerebral nervous centers to the rate of the vibrations of the object gazed at by catching the rhythm of the latter and passing it onto the brain. But in the case of direct passes, it is the Will of the operator radiating through his eye that produces the required unison between his will and the will of the person operated upon.

[From: Studies in Occultism (1887 – 1891) by H. P. Blavatsky. Page 21]

From the same work, Blavatsky has more to say on the topic of the immateriality of the mind, and man's Will:

The study of the "Physiology" of the Soul, of the Will in man and of his *higher Consciousness* from the standpoint of genius and its manifesting faculties, can never be summarized into a system of general ideas represented by brief formulae; no more than the *psychology of material nature* can have its manifold mysteries solved by the mere analysis of its physical phenomena. *There is no special organ of will*, any more than there is a *physical basis* for the activities of self-consciousness.

[Ibid. Page 39]

Report: #135

Location: Rear Garden (~10:15hrs)

Dose: 32mg

Earth Lights

My first pull was vaporous and voluminous but beyond that I struggled to find more. The effect of that single inhalation quickly became evident as my psychic sound sharply shouted out its highly energetic arousal and my psycho-spiritual stuff rapidly expanded. I was sure something was already above me. A large crystal-clear medium was obvious. Within just a few seconds I realised nothing would be interacting with me, which made me feel despondent. A high-altitude aeroplane heading east appeared to be travelling at a surprisingly fast speed. The sky appeared filled with thick and visually very obvious glassy mind-stuff. Just then, coming through the sparse clouds, a really very obvious and strange looking whitish sphere came into view. It was travelling in the same general direction as the clouds but with a little more pace and pursuing a curved path. Its appearance immediately transformed my mood. My arms shot upwards and my fingers pointing directly at the sphere. My emotions became excited and childlike. Its appearance was something like a large dullish white football, with a light glow and a distinct halo. My eyes continued to keep pace with the path of the object as it momentarily became obscured by clouds. It suddenly reappeared and continued to traverse the sky before eventually moving out of visual range behind the canopy of the oak trees. My mood was buoyant. A short while later I was back indoors, vacuuming the carpet and admiring the suction capacity of the appliance.

Emotionally, the appearance of what I have assumed to be an occult lifeform seemed to serve as acknowledgement of the fact that I had just terrifically expanded my mind-stuff, and that had not gone unnoticed in the occult realm. The surface of the form appeared dull white interspersed irregularly throughout with differing shades, making the contrast obvious. Although I am satisfied in saying it was an occult entity, and although I am certain that its presence related to my research experiment, there are other possibilities; such as earth lights:

http://inamidst.com/lights/earth

Earth lights are a rare anomalous light phenomenon,

mistaken throughout history as dragons, UFOs, and ball lightning before being recognised as a separate category. One leading theory is that they are produced by tectonic strain in minor fault lines, so that they are literally generated by the earth. In America they've been called "spooklights" or "ghost lights" since at least the 1950s, but Persinger and Lafrenière were the first scientists to recognise the phenomenon, in the late 1970s. The lights were renamed and brought to wider public attention by Paul Devereux in 1982 with his publication "Earth Lights". They appear in many colours, shapes, and sizes, though the basketball-sized globular orange variety seems most common. Most sightings occur at night, when some lights can be seen from miles around. They're reported to be able to move against the wind and reach extraordinary speeds. Their terrestrial nature means that though many sightings are sporadic, there are some locations where they appear relatively often. It's through studying these hotspots, such as Hessdalen in Norway and the English Pennines, that their characteristics become evident.

From: http://inamidst.com/lights/earth

Paul Devereux is an author, researcher and broadcaster with specific interest in general consciousness studies and a number of fields which can be loosely termed as earth mysteries. The following quote is taken from the Earth Lights portion his website. It is abstracted from a presentation given at the Science Museum in London in 2003:

What are earth lights? Well they certainly have electrical and magnetic attributes, and some form of plasma is assumed. Modern witnesses who come close to earth lights typically report hallucinatory episodes – suggesting magnetic fields that are known to be able to affect parts of the brain. One thing that has struck me in poring over witness reports from different periods of time and parts of the world is the similarity of descriptions stating that earth lights sometimes behave as if they have a rudimentary intelligence, like inquisitive animals.

[From: Paul Devereux (2003)

http://www.pauldevereux.co.uk

Report: #136

Location: Landing (~13:45hrs)

Dose: 17mg, 17mg, 24mg, approx. 25mg

Lacking Wholeness in its Appropriateness

I was home alone and decided to forge ahead with an experiment despite being filled with an unconscionable degree of nerves and anxiety. I set about preparing a pipe but found I only had 17mg worth of courage. With the pipe prepared my body demanded a second sedentary visit to the WC. A sudden surge of unwelcome noise filled the environment as a lawnmower tractor began mowing the neighbouring school sports field. With the bathroom visit behind me, I was feeling fear beyond all reason. I looked through the landing window and noted another groundsman preparing a petrol strimmer. More noise was inevitable. Regardless, I sat up, sighed heavily, and began. The dose was inhaled in one voluminous pull. I lay back and straightway wished I'd used a larger dose. The petrol-powered strimmer announced its readiness for work with a great deal of noise A palpable sense of something slowly emerging above me was without question. In the sense of undertaking practical research, I find these threshold emergences absolutely fascinating. The strange palpability in sensing the emergence of an occult presence into one's immediate setting is highly mysterious and absolutely astonishing. The noise from the strimmer was incredible. The back and forth passage of the lawnmower produced a significant Doppler Effect. But the unwelcome noise seemed to have no influence whatsoever on the partially emerged entity. I knew my effort was nowhere near good enough and so under self-imposed duress, I stood up and strode to my desk. Gazing at my reflection in the mirror, the power of the substance was all too evident – a very strong and very clean psychedelic. As I began preparing the second pipe, I felt a warm and emotional pleasance descending down into me. I could actuality feel the density of presence of the invisible entity inside my head. Yet despite feeling the pleasance of its presence, my courage at the scales extended no further than another 17mg dose. As I carefully pre-melted the crystals into the pipe my bowels began turning over as though in need of more WC. I ignored them and worked hard at trying not to think too ill of groundsman driving the noisy lawnmower back and forth. Back in position, I sat up and sighed heavily before emptying the pipe in two attempts. This time the emergence was far more pronounced. The invisible energy felt incredibly solid. I could feel a slow and cyclical vertical motion throughout the energy. The palpably very obvious cyclical motion felt like it was spanning the height of the setting. Rightly or wrongly, I believed the entity was purposefully providing me with ample opportunity to analyse and observe what was underway in this usually very rapid phase. It was indulging me in my occult inquiries. But the benefit of that extra time was sufficient only for me to conclude the perception of its emergence was at once both very obvious and very highly mysterious. To my expanded psycho-spiritual stuff, its presence was palpably very obvious. Its density was perceived or interpreted as solidity. The cyclical vertical motion therein was unambiguous. The strimmer and the tractor noise were of no obvious concern to the entity. Its energy soon diminished. And again, I questioned whether I was willing to leave the experiment at that. Part of me wanted to leave it at that, but another part of me knew there was no valid excuse not to pursue more. I returned to my desk and settled for 24mg. As I prepared the pipe my lower constitution began making strenuous appeals for the WC. I ignored the rectal hectoring, resumed my position on the floor, then sat up and emptied the pipe in two pulls. I lay back knowing full well the entity was watching and waiting for me to give it sufficient licence to temporarily meld its mind into my mind. The energy from the entity was very different this time; one I have experienced many times before. But on this occasion, that energy was purposefully restrained and very long-lasting. I was able to tactilely perceive that the energy imposing upon me and around me was descending from a great height. I was easily able to tactilely perceive as that energy repeatedly rebounded between the floor and the same great height somewhere above the roof of the house. This was the exact same character of energy that enables the entity to secure an invasive presence within one's physiology. The nature of that energy was so very obvious that I willingly held my breath and remained absolutely motionless, as though to facilitate unhindered entry into my physiology. Once again, its muted power seemed purposeful for the benefit of my research inquiry, rather than to secure itself an invasive presence inside my body. The entity remained unfazed by the noise of the tractor and the strimmer. The energy slowly diminished and then faded. Now I was faced with the exact same dilemma as before. Did I call it a day or did I press ahead with further inquiry? That dilemma caused angst-ridden frustration to proliferate within. I felt my courage versus my cowardice was under a scrutinising analytical spotlight. The tractor and the strimmer both suddenly fell silent which seemed to focus upon and magnify the significance of my decision making. Deep down I knew there was only one valid option. I quickly stood up and made for my desk despite feeling a cloak of duress dragging behind me. In something of a huff and a puff, I dispensed with seating myself at the desk and grabbed my wrap of crystals before reseating myself on the landing floor. Using the tip of a knife blade, I scooped out two small mounds of the potent crystals, gently pre-melted them into the pipe, ignited the lighter and began a long and slow pneumonic pull. The vapour stream began to enter into lungs and kept on going, and going, and going – on and on and on. And it continued beyond all reason; making me suspect a cache of crystals from the previous three experiments had become surreptitiously retained within the pipe for this very moment. With my lungs filled to capacity the stream of vapour finally ceased. I momentarily paused while placing the pipe and the lighter on the floor either side of me, before resting my head down into the pillows and exhaling. I strongly suspecting something intense would immediately prevail over me. My mind began to feel really very strange indeed. My visual field began to take on a very mystical and woozy appearance exhibiting pronounced fluidic movement and sparkly effects. I quickly convinced myself this was a prelude to something far greater. And as a consequence of that suspicion my courage momentarily squirmed. I now was between jumping up through fear and committing myself to whatever followed. The decision seemed so impossibly finely balanced, yet upon deciding to submit myself, the mystical sparkly effects and the fluidity affecting my visual field suddenly ceased. The location returned to its normal everyday appearance and my mind felt remarkably clear and lucid. Except something prompted me to speak out loud. And upon doing so, my voice sounded so very strange in my ears. So strange that I felt obliged to vocalise a series of "La, la, la", just to hear how strange my voice really sounded. I then began looping: "La, la, la, all day long, la, la, la, all day long." The addition of "all day long" made me laugh out loud with tremendous glee. And that caused me realise I was now undergoing a familiar sequence of psychic manipulation at the behest of the entity. I could somehow feel it. I could feel that I was about to undergo a sequence of extreme emotions. My laughter suddenly transformed into tears, which quickly became extreme. I scrunched my eyes tight and wailed as a young child wails for its mother. A mere moment later a great intake of breath was a precursor to a powerful surge of profound incredulity and exasperated astonishment, followed by much shaking of my head. Respect and reverence for what I assumed was a divine entity meddling with my mind swelled inside my chest. I wanted to give gratitude. I felt obligated to do so. But nothing was appropriate. If one word or one action was partially appropriate, it was also lacking wholeness in its appropriateness. Flummoxed by this impasse, I breathed in deeply through my nostrils and held my breath for a short while before exhaling. And strangely, that was it! That very action was somehow the perfect conveyance of my gratitude. Not just the act of breathing in and out; but in recognising my terrestrial life is principally sustained through that very act. The recognition was at once obvious and yet filled with a depth of profundity that felt universal in breadth. The entity was now palpably disengaging from my left shoulder with what felt like a partially painful unknitting procedure. There was also an incredibly faint and barely tactile line being drawn up one side of my back, across my shoulders, and then down the other side of my back. I shook my head many times. All words and most gestures still felt severely limited in conveying my astonishment. But breathing, and breathing deeply, and breathing consciously seemed to convey what my heart wanted to say.

Report: #137

Location: Rear Garden (~09:00hrs)

Dose: 29mg

Can a Number & Unit ever Convey such a Contrast

Are dreams solely the machination of one's own mind, or can the content of dreams sometimes be influenced by an occult entity, naturally interacting with one's mind during sleep? Upon awakening this morning, I questioned why in my dream I had found myself inside a large room within a castle with a funny looking dodo chick with off-white feathers trying to find a way to escape. The dream sequence continued with me clambering up the wall and finding a partially ajar sash window. The dream then suddenly changed and I was living in a house with a group of strangers and an improbably oversized straw-coloured snake of uncertain intent. The snake had a cage for its habitation but was seldom inside it. And while ever it was roaming the house, there was palpable unease and uncertainty. I soon found myself eyeball to eyeball with that snake, whilst the greater part of its body was inside the cage. I could glean nothing at all from its eyes. On something of a whim, I made a move to batter its head with a baseball bat. But the violent action was only ever implied. I do not recollect actually undertaking the action. Straightway there was a very strong feeling of deep remorse, as though I had actually committed the act but without knowing the intention of the snake. The dream was incredibly realistic and highly defined which left me feeling I had been subject to some natural yet mysterious interaction from the hidden side of nature during my slumber.

On the short walk home after dropping my boys off at school the potential for unmanageable high anxiety was peripherally evident. I headed outside. The weather was cold. I sat up and emptied the pipe in three pneumonic pulls. Upon reclining, something with a strong energy began to emerge some five or six arms lengths above me. I believed it was going to energetically meld its mind into my own energised and exteriorised mind. But from somewhere inside, my emotions momentarily conveyed fright. And that one single little hiccup possibly changed the outcome of the experiment. Over the next several seconds, the entity began to emerge more fully. And in doing so, it presented my eyes with a most unbelievable sight. As more and more of its psycho-spiritual body emerged into visibility, the more and more I became absolutely aghast at its incredible size. An extraordinary number of beautifully symmetric psycho-spiritual cells were all in the process of expanding. The perceived density of the substance forming the vast body-of-mind was absolutely astonishing. Even though it was only halfway through its unfolding expansion, I could not help myself from crying out with astonished incredulity: "What on earth?!" As its size and perceived density continued to increase, my eyes scanned to measure its breadth. I raised my head by a small degree to see ahead of me, and craned my head back in an effort to see what was behind me. Its overall expansion was clearly related to the unfolding expansion of each and every individual cell – in a great multitude of psycho-spiritual cells. Its density was visually evident by viewing its outer surface and seeing into and through its midst. The entity was soon apparent in what I assumed was its absolute fullness. It was an absolutely unbelievable and extraordinary sight. But there was something distinctly unique about this entity. The cells comprising its outer surface were rough and gnarled. Each cell was roughly square and approximate in size to the span of my hand. But each cell was so obviously rough and gnarled. It reminded me of bark on the trunk of an aged tree. Initially, I thought I was looking at the stuff of nightmares. I tried to intuit the character of the entity. But all I could intuit was its rough looking outer surface appeared rubbery; and in some strangely perceptible way it also felt rubbery to my expanded mind. This entity appeared old and hoary. I felt its neutral indifference towards me and my presence, and I felt the chasm of difference between our respective evolutionary states. It was not that it gave me any reason to fear it – it simply gave me nothing at all. Its dense outer surface – rough and gnarled as it was – exhibited a very faint iridescent sheen. I wanted the entity to descend and allow me to slowly sweep my hand through the lower portion of its body, so that I could observe what I knew would be very impressive tracer trails. Several birds flew overhead and their wings alternated strikingly between light and dark. The brief distraction of looking at the birds caused a significant diminishment in the visual obviousness of the entity above me. And soon after, it was no longer evident at all.

Later in the day, as I reflected upon what I had witnessed, I wondered the age of the entity. The usual unanswerable questions queued to populate my mind: where did that entity come from; how did that entity come into being; how old was the entity relative to my age; why was its outer surface so gnarly? Its outer surface really did appear very old; hoary and wizened – like an occult husk ready for sloughing. I also wondered how the volume and content of the entity's mind would compare to the volume and content of my mind. That made me wonder – in a ludicrously abstract sense –

whether any attempt at transferring the contents of its mind into my mind would irreparably ruin my mental vessel. From that, I came to question how the capacity or the limitation of a human mind – or indeed any mind – could be measured. Would it be by: volume; density; data storage capacity; or some other simple or abstract measure? By what meaningful measure could my human mind be contrasted against the mind of the entity I witnessed this morning? And can a number and a unit ever convey such a contrast?

Report: #138

Location: Bedroom (~09:30hrs)

Dose: 28mg

What's it Going to Be

The pipe was emptied in three slow and steady inhalations. The first two pulls were meagre and the third was spectacularly voluminous. Two or three seconds passed before I palpably sensed something emerging into the bright sunlit bedroom. And for just one fraction of a second, as it was doing so, there was a very peculiar and very fleeting moment wherein it felt like the entire room had momentarily filled with absolutely stiff and impossibly solid invasive energy. If I had really experienced such an occurrence – and I was quite sure that I had – it was now completely absent. The same emerging energy continued apace, rapidly increasing in its strength and palpability. My courage began to drain from the pit of my stomach – I could feel it. I tried to plug the hole but it was too late. The entity that now completely filled the volume of the bedroom had recognised my murmur of doubt. My sudden lapse in courage had steered this experiment away from the usual highly energetic liaison. The bedroom looked just the same, but it also appeared very different. The height from floor to ceiling appeared reduced; daylight was notably dimmer; and there was an air of great expectation pervading the entire room, as good as asking me: "So what's it going to be?" There were no words as such. Just an air of great expectation weighing very heavily upon me. Wanting me to speak or respond in some manner. The words of the question were clearly evident in my mind: "So what's it going to be?" I shrugged and laughed and responded out loud, in an equally enquiring manner, as though I didn't quite know the answer myself: "That is the thing!" An unexpected burst of laugher became impossibly infectious. I went to laugh again and found myself laughing almost ecstatically. I recognised my psyche was now under the vicarious influence of the entity and that entity was an Occult Master. But even recognising that fact only served to hugely increase my surprise and my laughter. A few seconds later my laughter gave way to a strange oral action, stereotypically typifying the emotion of craziness, as I rapidly and repeatedly flicked the front of my tongue over my upper front teeth and lips – creating a sound not too dissimilar to a turkey gobbling rapidly nonstop. That these actions were at the behest of psychic influence or mind manipulation was overwhelming; sufficient enough for me to half sit up and repeatedly punch my right fist hard into my left palm, as though to convey the extent of my astonishment. I lay back and observed how the room still appeared to be so very different. My emotions were a mixture of happiness from the laughter and dismay from the murmur of doubt I had experienced. There was no sense of triumphalism. Where the sunlight was not too dazzling, I watched the trees beyond the white lace curtain succumbing to the wind. Imperceptibly, the room returned to its ordinary appearance, making the contrast with what it had been when filled with the occult mind all the more obvious.

Report: #139

Location: Bedroom (~10:30hrs)

Dose: 21mg

About Learning

At the prospect of undertaking an experiment my stomach palpably became an airless void undergoing slow and unstoppable disintegration. I was with dread. A second visit to the WC was without question. But even with that behind me, my bowels appealed for more of the same. I sat up and began carefully emptying the pipe. I quickly felt the effects in the midst of my head as something very mysterious became sufficiently aroused to audibly increase and rapidly expand. An Occult Master emerged with such rapidity one could only conclude it had observed me making my final pull on the pipe. I had forgotten just how frighteningly awesome their power is. It filled the room in an instant and began to seriously increase its power. How can something physically intangible feel so impossibly solid? In a near instant its palpable solidity became such that I could not help but feel a small degree of fear. It seemed the Occult Master also perceived my fear as it quickly reduced its energy. That energy was still sufficiently intense to be both palpable and visible. Its pervasive presence significantly dimmed the brightness of daylight in the bedroom and strangely altered the appearance of the bedroom. I was breathing deep and hard and continued to do so, even as I realised the entity had somehow synchronised itself with my breathing. By changing the pattern of my breathing, I observed the highly active energy throughout the bedroom responding to that change. I began to breathe in and out very deeply and very slowly. And upon doing so, the volume of energy filling the bedroom responded in unison – visibly and palpably contracting and expanding with every exhale and with every inhale. I could see as the energy moved toward the wall with each inhalation, and moved away from the wall with every exhalation. It was so obvious. I was supposed to understand something by this. It seemed all too evident. I vocalised my sentiment: "Breathing is related to willpower!" Just as the last of those words formed in my mouth uncontrollable laughter spewed out from my mouth. The laughter was so unexpected and so totally overpowering that I became absolutely infected by it. Laughter engulfed me and swirled around me; it overtook me; I was beside myself with so much rapturous laughter. And even as I laughed, I knew what would come next. But even knowing what would come next could not stop my laughter. As my tongue projected from my mouth, I implicitly understood I was at the mercy of an Occult Master. Tears hanging from my eyes were nowhere near sufficient to convey the depth of my joy and heartfelt emotion.

Report: #140

Location: Rear Garden (~13:45hrs)

Dose: 34mg

Swathes & Swathes

The cold light blue sky was cloudless. I sat up and began inhaling. A familiar sound in the midst of my head quickly manifested as I continued emptying the pipe with great purpose – determined that I conduct myself in a professional manner. I focussed my eyes upon the flame and the pipe. The rising energy within my head suddenly became far more intense and continued to intensify while sounding like it was all around me. I began feeling really worried about what was underway as a tremendous sense of fear surrounded me. It felt as though an invisible field of fear was pushing down onto me from without me. But above me there was nothing visible except for sky. Hens were audibly pecking away at the ground around me. My fear was quickly becoming intense and intolerable; forcing me to wish I was no longer in this experience. But that same fear also prevented me from getting up. It had all become very unpleasant rather very quickly. Just then, some short distance above me, something began emerging into visibility. It took just seconds for me to recognise something incredibly impressive was slowly revealing itself to me. A beautifully complex form composed of a countless multitude of stunningly configured geometric cells began to appear from nowhere. Each cell was either expanding or undergoing a strange process of unfolding as it continued to emerge. Within moments I was observing something of incredible geometric complexity, exhibiting breathtaking beauty and symmetry. It spanned the air above the garden and tapered down toward me from its centre. The apparent density of this transparent body-of-mind was truly remarkable. Something very big indeed had deigned to emerge and look upon something rather small. My breathing was hard and fast – proportionally representative of my fear. I could still hear the hens pecking away at the ground around me without a single little care in the world. But I had not yet seen half of this entity. My breathing continued hard and fast. The jaw droppingly impressive entity had fully emerged; or had emerged as fully as it chose to emerge. My fear was tangible within me. I knew the vast impressive form tapering down toward me could see me. On willful whim of self-determination, I consciously dissolved all my fear and made my breathing slow and calm. I fixed my eyes hard upon the vast thing ranged above me and drilled my gaze directly into eyeballing the tapered portion facing me. I was now full of willful determination. But I did not yet have a full appreciation of the enormous size of my occult visitor. The entity quickly responded to my willful display of impertinence. In a bizarre and difficult-to-describe manner, more and more of the entity somehow emerged from somewhere. It then appeared the entity was preparing to undertake a slow and cumbersome about-turn maneuver. And in so doing, vast psycho-spiritual swathes of the entity began to bunch up in slow and purposeful rippling actions right in front of me. I was looking at a curved portion of an improbably oversized gigantic snake-like entity – an occult entity of unthinkable proportion. The bizarre rippling maneuvers continued along the huge curvature of its form. My initial observation of that particular action was more than enough to convince me that I had totally underestimated the vastness of this thing. Swathe after swathe of the same slow rippling maneuvers continued along the vast bend in the impossibly dense cylindrical mass of the being. To be observing such an occurrence in otherwise consensus reality was absolutely mind-blowing. After each series of ripples had bunched up sufficiently, the entity would then very slowly and very purposefully unfurl those ripples further along its length, as it slowly and purposefully projected itself skyward; behind which, another dense psycho-spiritual mass of creped ripples would bunch up before undergoing the very same slow and purposeful procedure. This was now more of a momentous event rather than an experience. The hens audibly pecked away at the ground either side of my head, totally oblivious to the unfolding magnificence above the garden. There was something uniquely peculiar the psycho-spiritual substance composing this particular entity – visually and tactilely. My own mind-stuff could perceive that peculiarity. It was like an incredibly plush velvety substance – but uniquely so. And somewhere deep within, related to that apparent texture, there was a very strong reminiscence of something I knew; or something I had experienced before; but I could not quite bring it to the forefront of my mind. By now I knew exactly how this event would conclude. And I was waiting for that moment to arrive. But something significant was lacking within me. There was complete absence of awe. It should have been there. It really should have been there. But it wasn't. And so, I tried to force the emotional response that I thought I should be experiencing. But forcing such sincerity was completely bogus. The beginning of the end arrived. The entity had acted in such a way as to give me ample indication of its humungous size. And now, I knew the last remaining portion of that vast entity was going to take a very close look at me. And that is exactly what it did. My hands were already tightly gripping the half open front of my tatty old turquoise mountain jacket, in a gesture meant to convey readiness to tear open my chest. The gesture was sincere. But not completely so. And so, I gripped the front of my jumper, in a gesture meant to convey that same readiness to tear open my chest. But realising my strength was insufficient to trouble the woollen jumper, the same insincerity befell me. The huge portion of entity that remained continued to gaze down upon me and I could feel the terrific weight of its otherworldly stare. I felt there was simply nothing I could do that would properly convey my recognition, my respect and awe for that which had just revealed itself to me. Until at last, I turned my head ninety degrees to the right. A chicken stopped pecking the ground and looked inquiringly at me. I raised my left hand and symbolically shielded the left side of my face. It was all that I could think of that felt genuinely sincere – an action designed to hide my insincere stare from the watchful eye of the gigantic entity. And after just a few seconds, when I looked back up, the vast entity had completely vanished. My emotional reaction to what I had just witnessed – though still relatively muted – slowly came creeping up on me. With much shaking of my head I re-entered the house whilst expressing passionate and energetic incredulity at that which I had just witnessed.

There was one other observation made towards the latter end of this experiment that I did not recall until much later. After great swathes of the entity had magnificently rippled skywards, and it was in the process of readying itself to look directly at me, something caught my eye. It appeared to be an unusually large jet-black bug zigzagging around in the midst of the entity's psycho-spiritual body. But something about it that caught my eye. It seemed strangely out of place; unusually spherical, and had a small halo surrounding its form. It zipped around rapidly in long zigzagging lines and then inexplicably disappeared whilst under my watchful observation. A moment later it was evident again and undertaking the very same maneuvers. But once again, as my eyes became fixed upon its movements, it suddenly and inexplicably disappeared. On reflection, I cannot really say it was anything other than a bug. Indeed, if it looks like a bug, moves like a bug and behaves like a bug – then in all probability it very likely is a bug. But by the same argument, it something looks like an occult entity, moves like an occult entity, and behaves like an occult entity – then in all probability it very likely is an occult entity.

Report: #141

Location: Rear Garden (~11:45hrs)

Dose: 33mg

Full Piloerection

The chamber of the pipe smelled pleasingly potent. I sat up and began the first of three pulls. The first effort audibly increased the pitch and intensity of my spiritual tinnitus. After vacuuming down the third pull I reclined into the cushions. There was absolutely no palpable energy from the large discarnate entity visible some several arm's lengths above me. That complete absence of energy created a tremendously eerie feeling within me. There was an uncanny silence around me – even though I could hear the sound of the wind blowing. The presence of the entity was without question: a large circular crystal-clear presence. The clouds seen through its transparent body took on the same symmetrical patterning evident throughout the visually obvious medium. The lack of any palpable energy transmitting down upon me was tremendously unnerving. In order to bolster my confidence, I assured myself we both had the exact same willpower, differing only be degrees. With that in mind, I fixed myself into staring hard at the impressive entity, and continued to do so even as one of the hens began making soft chirping noises beside my head. I wondered if the presence of the hens was any cause for the entity not to project its energy down onto me. My gaze remained willfully fixed upon the entity, which appeared static and stable. But then a hen unexpectedly pecked one of the fingers which totally undid my trance-like state. I sat upright to verbally scorn the offending hen. But the hen did not appear to understand my emotional outburst and carried on pecking the ground. I lay back and looked up but my resolute state of mind had burst like a bubble. Another hen began pecking the sole of my footwear. The entity moved steadily skywards. Its ascension made it appear as though the clouds seen through its crystal-clear body were also impressively ascending. It was soon absent from sight. My own expansive mind-stuff remained clearly visible high above me. I wondered in general terms about my research. It is tempting to suppose the actual size and the actual form taken by these entities as they appear in the terrestrial realm is the actual size and the actual form they naturally take within their own kingdom. I am, however, instinctively disinclined to believe that's the truth of the matter. I wondered whether the characteristics of their appearance in this realm held any relation to the qualities of their individual evolutionary advancement. Qualities relating to: wisdom and understanding; strength and mercy; ambition and compassion – things of that nature. I raised my head in readiness to stand up, but found myself staring directly at a decrepit old pigeon. It was standing just beyond my feet with its feathers fluffed up in full piloerection. Its head was hunkered low and snug, giving it the appearance of wearing a muffler to keep out the cold. It didn't move a muscle, despite my direct eyeballing. Three hens were in close proximity to the pigeon. They all appeared quite nonchalant about the old pigeon until one began to extend its neck menacingly and strutted purposefully forwards. The old aged pigeon stooped low, turned around and hobbled away, using its terribly lopsided right wing as something of a walking stick. But the hen continued its charge, and the other two hens followed suit, causing the pigeon to take flight. I verbally berated the three hens. But as pets, they are neither cat nor dog, and my words of admonishment proved worthless.

The question about the actual true form of such entities is one that I find absolutely intriguing. In Allen Kardec's *The Spirits' Book,* it is asserted therein that spirits envelope themselves in a so-called perispirit – a semi-material envelope drawn from the universal fluid of the globe that enables them to move around in our world. When asked: *Does the semi-material envelope of the spirit assume determinate forms, and can it become perceptible for us?* The communicated answer is:

> Yes; it can assume any form that the spirit may choose to give it. It is thus that a spirit is able sometimes to make himself visible to you, whether in dreams or in your waking state, and can take a form that may be visible, and even palpable, for your senses.

> [From: The Spirits' Book (1996 edition) by Allan Kardec. Page 92]

Report: #142

Location: Rear Garden (~11:45hrs)

Dose: 37mg

So What?

My approach to this was very much along the lines of: "This is my research and I'll do what I like." Since midmorning I had been seated at my writing desk undertaking online research for a literary project. Despite a good night's sleep, and despite a stimulating mug of coffee, an unaccountable lethargy was slowly imposing upon me. I began to entertain the notion that perhaps the idea I was researching was taking me in the wrong direction; possibly an invisible overshadowing mind was communicating its displeasure at my line of research. The more and more lethargic I became, the more and more the supposition seemed both apt and reasonable. Minutes later, I surrendered to impossibly heavy lethargy and headed for bed. Whilst resting, I ruminated on what I had been researching and contrasted it against other priorities. After just a few minutes I realised I was nowhere near to sleep and sprang out of bed completely free of the intolerable lethargy. I headed outside. With the pipe at my mouth I drew down a reasonably good volume of vapour and retained it within my lungs as I lay back. I understood the single inhalation would have signalled my presence to unseen entities in an unseen realm. I sat up and made a cautious pull on the pipe, based on the cowardly excuse of suffering a sore throat. I knew what to expect as I exhaled the second inhalation – the sudden onset of overbearing apprehension in anticipation of something highly energetic and overwhelmingly dramatic. Just as expected, there were several seconds of impossibly intense apprehension, followed by paradoxical disspaointment at the absence of any significant occult visitation. The air high above me was awash with my own psycho-spiritual-mind-stuff. The wind picked up. I was quite sure something was above me and watching me. The soft appearance of the blue sky and the passing white clouds was visually pleasing. It was either a lull in the wind or something subliminal that prompted me to sit up. I was now feeling determined to empty the pipe. I drew down a great big stream of vapour until there was nothing left in the pipe. I struggled to retain it within my lungs and my throat winced as unabsorbed vapour subtly rasped over its swollen sore rawness. I immediately realised that had I not exhaled so suddenly, then the great big discarnate mind now clearly visible above me would have energetically interacted with me. I could feel the weight of its presence, the energy of its poise, and its readiness to powerfully impose upon me. I stared at the impressive transparent mass of mind and observed the truly incredible number of small individual cells that contributed to making up its amorphous whole. A striking Arctic blueness was widespread throughout its midst. It was such an incredibly stunning sight that my mind could not stop from narrating: "Oh my God! Look at that thing! Look at that thing! I can't believe I am seeing these things! I can't believe I am actually seeing these things and writing about these things!" The wind picked up considerably without the slightest consequence to the static mass of mind above me. Windswept leaves transited through its voluminous immaterial body leaving long tracer trails in their wake. I continued to stare at the entity while wondering why such beings are obligated to respond to a dimethyltryptamine-induced spike of psychic energy. Despite its beautiful icy blue transparency, I knew full well that I was playing with fire. The entity remained static and in full visibility. And then, it was no longer there. To say it vanished seems inappropriate, and to say it disappeared also seems somehow inaccurate. It was simply there, and then it was simply no longer there. The presence of my own mind-stuff with the entity absent was now easily contrastable. I remained watching the clouds for a while longer before heading indoors. Sometime after lunch my wife and enjoyed some private time together, after which I showered and dressed before hurrying to collect our boys from school. I observed my reflection in the bedroom mirror and realised I appeared exactly like someone who had just enjoyed the pleasure of sex. I sought my wife's opinion as she showered. She peered from behind the shower curtain and tittered at my glowing facial pinkness. I strode to school quite certain I was advertising sexual depletion. Did I hold my head high with eyes glassy and bright, or hang my head low with eyes glazed and sunken? With great positivity and purpose, I marched onwards and avoided all instances of potential eye contact. The playground was full of adults waiting to see cheerful young familiar faces. Across the playground and the school sports field I could see our home and the general area above the garden where the occult entity had emerged during the experiment. From this distance, and with the wider perspective, things appeared a little different. But different in a "so what" kind of way. Like, so what if spirits really do exist? It's not really such a big deal, is it? If the great library at Alexandria had not being burned down three times then perhaps this stuff would not need reporting as being so novel. I imagined striking up conversation with the male standing beside me. I imagined pointing over to the house where I lived and then telling him: "See that house? I smoke brain chemical in the back garden of that house over there and see spirit beings emerge out of thin air." It seemed so ludicrous. I mean one cannot really say that without expecting to feel acute discomfort at the expected reaction. But as I looked over toward the house and thought about my research, with the sky looking so impossibly vast, the consideration of the actual existence of powerful spiritual beings did not seem outlandish or even unreasonable.

Report: #143

Location: Bedroom (~09:00hrs)

Dose: 25mg

Sounds Doolally

The bright sunlit bedroom was the obvious choice. I sat up and inhaled three times to empty the pipe. After just a couple of seconds the palpability of something slowly emerging from nowhere became perceptible to my energised mind. It was unusual in that the emerging entity actually seemed to be descending into the room from above. As the palpability of its presence slowly increased, it was obvious there was truly tremendous latent power behind the low frequency psychic vibrations. Those low frequency psychic vibrations had an unusual pulsing solidity, giving unquestionable indication of immense power. There was something about this occult entity. It had a deeply rooted familiarity within my mind. Against all expectations, I was suddenly moved to gleeful childlike laughter. I was genuinely surprised at the laughter but that surprise only fed into my laughter more and more, until my eyes were wet and glistening with tears. I opened my mouth and flicked my tongue rapidly over my top teeth whilst making a fast-paced doolally sound: "loll-loll-loll-loll-loll-loll-loll." It did not matter that I had volunteered the action. It only served to move me deeper and deeper into more and more laughter. And as I tried to control that laughter, I sensed the moment the room had emptied of the impressive occult entity. I was soon able to reign in my gleeful laughter and adopt a far more serious research-minded mentality. I gazed through the dazzling bleached sunshine whiteness of the lace curtain; looking beyond the windblown oak trees to the light blue sky beyond. The contrast between my mood now and my mood mere moments ago was stark. I had enjoyed the laughter immensely. Indeed, it seemed bodily and soulfully medicinal. But now my mood was intensely serious; serious about my research and serious about my analysis of this experience. As much as I welcomed and enjoyed the laugher, I felt such experiences were limited in furthering my research. The thought of undertaking similarly dosed experiments in the same setting, and obtaining the same outcome over and over again seemed positively banal; like repeating a highly enjoyable but ultimately unenlightening ecstasy. But there was more to it than that. I suspected something had actually changed within me – in respect of my response to the substance. Once upon a time the inhalation of such a dose indoors would have resulted in the room appearing to jar back and forth violently. But that no longer occurs. And there has to be a reason for that. I could suspect the quality of crystals I am now using is inferior to those I used earlier in my research programme. And that may well be the true and could well be the only viable answer. But I suspect something else has changed. I strongly suspect research of this nature is progressive and initiatory. And whilst I can suspect I have made some worthwhile progress along such a path; I can equally suspect I have unearthed some innately limiting factors within my own psyche. Indeed, I feel that in order to progress further, those limiting factors will need to be transformed and overcome. I can also suspect that whilst some of those entities exhibit great patience, I can also suspect the progress of a research percipient along such a path is commensurate with a number of relevant factors. And if such suppositions have any basis in fact, then I must also suspect some of those entities have the innate ability to intuit a considerable amount of information about the individual and their progress as a research percipient.

Report: #144

Location: Rear Garden (~09:15hrs)

Dose: 29mg

In Other News

The pipe was emptied in three pulls, the first and the second of which captured the main volume of available vapour. Upon lying back something was immediately palpable at approximately four arm's lengths above me. The energy quickly became visually perceptible as an area of mild turbulence. It was somehow perceptibly evident the rapidly pulsating energy was operating at a level many times below what was available. I suspected it was going to impose some of that power down upon me with great immediacy. But I could hear one of the hens pecking the ground very close to the left side of my head. I wondered whether the presence of the hen was a hindrance to such an outcome. The turbulent energy descended closer and slowly transformed to reveal itself as a large tapering cone, composed of small transparent cells, all in the process of unfurling and steadily expanding. My eyes flitted around to gauge the extent of its ever-growing size; very soon I was whispering my disbelief as its impressive size soon did justice to its perceptible latent energy. But even as I mouthed my astonished admiration, there was a lack of sincerity somewhere deep within me, and I wondered whether the occult entity could sense that. Nevertheless, I continued with my whispered astonishment and intuitively reasoned it would perhaps appreciate the apparent adoration. The broad tapered portion of the large mind neared my head and remained there for a couple of minutes. I was unsure whether it was undertaking an invasive action at the forefront of my brain, but had a vague suspicion something like that was underway.

Report: #145

Location: Rear Garden (~09:00hrs)

Dose: 40mg

That's Just Crazy

At 08:30hrs, I was seated upon the WC and reading *The Ringmakers of Saturn,* by Norman R Bergrun. At 08:45hrs I left the house to walk my boys to school. On the short walk home angst and doubt were kicking away at the wall of my stomach. This is a mental pursuit; a pursuit of managing emotions and giving them no truck, whilst remaining as willful and courageous as possible. Upon arriving home, it was self-evident I was operating in something of a self-imposed trancelike state, simply in order to get myself ready to undertake the experiment. With everything prepared and ready, my lower abdominals began making appeals for a second sedentary visit to the WC. I stood motionless at the bathroom door in order to gauge the validity of the appeal. Having determined it carried no weight I headed back outside. Subdued fears arose in my mind based on unsettling thoughts and feelings from previous experiments. I began asking myself: what if this happens and what if that happens? Keeping a lid on such speculations, I sat up and emptied the pipe in three pulls. Straightaway upon lying back, something began to visibly emerge approximately one arm's length above me; giving me the distinct impression it had been watching me and waiting for me to complete the final inhalation. There was something unusual about this emergence. The entity initially appeared something like an unfolding rosebud. Except the analogy was not quite accurate. The entity continued to rapidly emerge. My mind suddenly became furnished with the memory of yesterday's energetic emergence. The memory was so complete that I realised I had significantly underrepresented the strength and the power of that which I had experienced; as though a mass of very important detail had been overlooked and left unstated. But now there was something very unusual about this unfolding emergence. There was simply no perceptible energy and no audible energy associated with its presence. None whatsoever. The cold frosty morning, the cloudless light blue sky and a complete absence of any air movement created a stillness and silent peacefulness that was near absolute. But the complete lack of any palpable or audible energy from this entity heightened that stillness and peacefulness severalfold. Within mere seconds of emerging the entity began to unfold

346

far more expansively, and soon clearly exhibited an impressive size as it spanned the garden. But its size did not matter, because I realised something else. I realised I was completely and utterly at ease. Completely relaxed. I was absolutely comfortable in the presence of this visitor. Indeed, it felt like I was with an old friend; a friend in whose presence there was nothing but openness and honesty and complete ease of being. The nearest portion of its dense transparent body slowly descended toward my head. I looked directly at and into the otherworldly substance, noting distinct patterning formed by great multitudes of very small adjoining psycho-spiritual cells. I fixed my eyes forward unblinkingly as the substance descended into my eyes and my head. I wondered whether anything subliminal could or would take place. The experience was charged with high mystery and seemed to have purpose. I gazed with wide open eyes at the descending substance, and could only wonder and marvel at what I was observing. The peacefulness was incredible. There was no air movement; no bird song; no noise from the hens; no discernible background noise whatsoever. The departure of the entity was uneventful. It just slowly rose into the air and became increasingly less visible as it did so. Five or six pigeons flew overhead. Their flapping wings appeared to alternate between jet black and dazzling white in the bright sunlight. It seemed strangely apt and made the silence all the more remarkable. Just then, in one single perplexingly coincidental moment, the sound of a nearby emergency siren screamed into life, at exactly the same time as a nearby pneumatic drill began noisily breaking hard ground. Such a coincident occurrence at the end of an experiment noted for peacefulness and silence seemed absolutely beyond belief. I reacted by raising my arms and splaying my fingers in a gesture of complete disbelief while mouthing aloud with great incredulity: "That's just crazy!"

Report: #146

Location: Rear Garden (~11:30hrs)

Dose: 34mg

The God of Fuel Indicator Needles

Lying back after three good pulls a discarnate entity began to visibly and palpably emerge above me. It appeared as a smooth and glassy flat plane approximately four arms lengths above me and exhibited small equidistant surface dimples throughout. Its energy palpably modified, increasing slightly in intensity as though analysing me. After several seconds the energy subtly diminished in power and the psycho-spiritual presence also steadily diminished in visibility as it moved away from me. I thought about how incredible such a sighting actually is. But also, how very mundane this particular experience was. Before the experiment, I was busy vacuuming out the rear of my vehicle. While using a small kitchen knife to dislodge a plastic cover I managed to stab the underside of a middle finger. The tip of the blade pierced right through the skin creating an open wound right along the junction with my palm. It was not painful but blood was flowing freely. My youngest boy was with me. When I stretched opened my hand, the wound opened up further, making the blood erupt in cyclical pulses. Absolute horror and frozen panic filled my boy's face, far beyond anything I had expected. I had just returned home from the local tip where I had discarded an old sofa. A couple of days earlier my wife and I had hired a hired truck and drove a couple of hundred miles to collect a sofa that was to my wife's liking. The tank full of diesel took us to our destination with ease. And initially it looked like it would also get us back home. However, with the digital display indicating thirty-four available miles, when we had fifty miles to cover, it was really unwise of me to drive past a motorway service station. Especially when my bladder was begging to be emptied. But the hire truck had to be returned by a certain hour, and I was fretting about the loss of a sizeable deposit that I could ill afford to lose. With a range of thirty miles displayed I confided in my wife the genuine possibility that we may run out of fuel. I modified my driving to a far more conservative speed. We decided to remain positive and hopeful. With twenty-five miles available the road sign for the next available motorway services read thirty-two miles. With a mere twenty miles of diesel-distance remaining I beseeched my wife to commence prayers, despite knowing she'd already begun. My own prayer was more of a silent but sincere appeal for anything;

anything at all to get us to the next service station. But the fuel indicator needle was already covering the ride line denoting an empty tank. I was quietly becoming desperate and willing the impossible: can anything invisible help us; can anything invisible push the vehicle just to take the pressure off the engine; just to help us cover the last few miles? It was nonsense! I knew it was nonsense! But I simply did not know whether the god of fuel indicator needles was a thing. As the available miles counted down our worries and our prayers ramped up. An exit road gave us the choice of staying on the motorway or exiting the motorway. But there was nothing but fields either side of the motorway. The digitally displayed mileage was quickly counting down. With less than ten miles of range remaining it was looking impossible that we would not run out of fuel before the next available services. With seven miles of range remaining I realised something that boosted our hopes. Our homeward exit from the motorway was coming up. And I knew that some short distance from that exit there was a service station. It was now just a matter of driving the few remaining miles with what was in the tank. I began shouting at the vehicle whilst slapping my hand hard upon the steering wheel: "Come on baby! Come on baby! You can do this!" Wherever possible I disengaged the gears and commenced coasting. The loss of speed was both worrisome and vexing. Upon re-engaging the gears, the range of six miles had reduced to zero miles. On the last mile to the exit road the engine began to stutter and splutter. I began shouting louder and hitting the steering wheel with greater force as the engine began to lose power with increasing frequency. We made it to the slip road and the traffic lights serving the roundabout were in our favour. We had one more mile to go for fuel. I was bouncing up and down in the seat and shouting loudly: "Come on baby! Come on baby! You can do this!" I was now banging the steering wheel with great force as a means of drowning out the sound of the poor engine as it thirsted for fuel. On approach to the second set of traffic lights, the vehicle died of thirst and rolled to a stop. I engaged the hazard warning lights. Two or three attempts at reignition proved useless. We were stuck and the clock was ticking. We needed to reach home, offload the sofa, and return the vehicle to the rental company with a full tank of diesel before deadline. It was time to act. The petrol station was just a mile away. Leaving my wife behind with assurance that this would end well, I jumped out of the vehicle and began running. My mind was a mix of half-sentence prayers and insistence on remaining positive no matter what the outcome. I stopped running upon realising I had underestimated the distance. But walking felt like failing. Upon spotting my intended destination I resumed running. But it didn't matter. Because my positivity took a major hit when I found the petrol filling station closed and advertising apology for inconvenience due to closure. For nine or ten years that place had never been closed. And yet today, when I needed it the most, it was closed for refurbishment. I phoned my wife to give her the news but to also give assurance that I had another plan. But plans were thin. And this was looking like I'd be making a call to the emergency breakdown service with a late return of the hire vehicle and painful loss of substantial deposit. I ran across the busy road. Two cars were parked in a nearby lay-by. The first car was very small and red, but the paintwork had lost most of its gloss and turned milky pink through prolonged exposure to sunlight. The second vehicle was a brand new shiny black Mercedes jeep. A large man with a black beard was sat at the wheel looking intently into his phone. I looked toward him as I approached and he soon looked up. I signalled that I wished to speak to him and he lowered his window. My lungs were heaving. My appeal was delivered between gasps for air as I felt sweat pushing out from the pores of my forehead. He listened and looked at me for a few short seconds before telling me to get in. His son was in the back seat. He was about eight years old. I told him his father was a hero and a smile filled his face. He drove several miles to a filling station where I purchased a jerry can and filled it full of diesel. Carefully and politely, I wrapped the jerry can inside my tatty old jacket and placed it inside the cleanly upholstered footwell. Once again, I told the boy his father was a hero and promised I would say so for a third and final time before departing. The hero told me he was supposed to be picking up his wife from the airport. I immediately apologised for having inconvenienced him. He continued by saying things were not so good between him and her. He then told me I was incredibly lucky because he had only just pulled into that lay-by to read a text message. I knew just how lucky I was. He dropped me behind the thirsty truck and I asked him to wait one moment. My wife had the fright of her life as I flung open the passenger door. I demanded the £8.02 she had earlier counted from her purse. I returned to the hero and stuck my head through the passenger side window. I knew he would refuse the money and so I thrust it into his son's hand and assured him with great sincerity that his dad really was a hero, and one that I would never forget. We got home and we got the truck back with no loss of deposit. I later came to figure that a boy of his age, hearing someone convincingly convey his dad being a real-life hero, was worth a lot more than the coins I had tipped into his young hands.

Report: #147

Location: Landing (~12:30hrs)

Dose: 36mg

Cross-Eyedness

I had an unaccountable urge to commit to research but chose to busy myself with miscellaneous matters whilst wondering whether something conscious and invisible was subliminally trying to coax me into smoking DMT. It was time to make progress. Two voluminous pulls emptied the pipe. As I lay back it was immediately obvious that an invisible yet palpably evident entity was not only filling the location, but had been present all along. I expected an overwhelming wave of mesmeric psychic energy to impose down upon me. But this was not that. This was different. The presence of the entity was without question to my amplified mind. But visually, there was only the subtlest hint of a transparent medium with density and clarity greater than air. My eyes suddenly felt like they were being forced out of focus. I consciously reset them, but once again it felt like my ocular orbs were being forced into cross-eyedness with subsequent loss of clear and singular vision. I quickly realised the bizarre effect was being caused by the entity manipulating my amplified field of consciousness. I could actually feel the subtle lateral movements being made within that field. It was an astonishing experience. It mattered not that I reset my gaze. The lateral movements imposing upon my amplified mind caused my eyes to physically skew and that, of course, severely affected my vision. Another subtle lateral movement was then imposed which had the strange effect of making my lower jaw move very slowly to one side. I was so surprised I cried out in disbelief. But upon crying out I immediately felt terribly unprofessional. I imposed silence and perceptive astuteness upon myself. The very same manipulation of my lower jaw occurred once again. The subtle yet perceptible lateral movement imposing upon my amplified mind was effectively moving my lower jaw to one side. What made this all the more surprising was the air throughout the location appeared totally ordinary with no visible hint of any entity whatsoever. The palpable energy then began undertaking some activity behind my head. There was a really obvious movement, but I could not work out what was underway. The movement kept recurring as though patiently waiting for me to understand what it was. I then realised the ends of the pillow immediately behind my head were slowly being pushed up some small distance. Just as soon as I realised that there was another change. A very obvious and very soothing massage commenced along my upper back and shoulders. I was actually being given a really very soothing massaging manipulation by the capable occult entity. That something so very palpable could be occurring with such a complete absence of any obvious energy was truly remarkable. Even more remarkable, there was no longer any palpable perception of the entity above me. Its palpable presence was focussed solely upon massaging my upper back and shoulders. And if that wasn't quite enough, there was a very obvious perception of me being very slowly and very comfortably lowered a very short distance down onto the carpeted floor – which only made already profound matters seem absolutely impossible. That such a very obvious occurrence could take place even as the massage continued should have called into question the entirety of my credulity. But the subtle descent and the soothing massage were so very obvious and so absolutely unquestionable that I simply had to accept what was occurring. The massage gradually became lighter and lighter. It was physically pleasing and tremendously relaxing. The massage gradually petered out, and although I could no longer feel or sense any presence of the entity, I did not doubt it was still very much present and wholly cognisant of my emotions. I remained calm yet astonished. The truth was I would've willingly stayed engaged with that entity all day long in that relaxed manner, given half a chance. I carefully recounted what had just occurred. Then after a good long while of being locked in thought, I concluded in three cautious and uncertain whispers: "You're much closer than we suspect! You're right next to us! You shape our minds!"

Report: #148

Location: Bedroom (~10:15hrs)

Dose: 33mg

Swelling Within My Chest

I remained professionally calm in the build up to the experiment and maintained that calmness as I sat up and inhaled a smidgen of vapour; just enough to post notice of my intended undertaking. I then proceeded to empty the pipe in two successive pulls before laying back. I remained calm as something otherwise occult began emerging from elsewhere. I remained calm as it rapidly filled the bedroom and increased its intensity. I felt sure there was a subtle change associated with the wall clock. The energy rapidly changed. It became sufficiently dense and stiff as to operate invasively which caused audible and perceptible physical movement around the region of my left ear drum. I remained calm. The energy was truly remarkable. I realised how unusually calm I was feeling. The tremendous energy filling the bedroom subtly and imperceptibly diminished. As it did so there was a single moment wherein it suddenly became apparent the ticking from the wall clock was noticeably much quieter. Or rather, in that moment, the heightened audibility of its ticking had just returned to normal. Initially unperceived, the inference was that its audibility had somehow increased when the room was awash with superdense occult energy. I remained relaxed and calm and assumed the entity had returned to elsewhere. But for all I knew it was still invisibly and impalpably filling the volume of the bedroom. There was no sense of its presence. I thought deeply for a short while before standing up and heading downstairs.

Report: #149

Location: Landing (~13:15hrs)

Dose: 30mg

Mooning

The pipe was emptied of all available vapour in three successive pulls. I lay back and immediately felt the paradoxical tangible solidity of an occult presence throughout the location. I was absolutely certain it had been awaiting me. The highly audible psychic sound associated with its presence was ringing with such incredible intensity that my mind automatically assigned the power as: "Almighty!" The energy seemed intent on interacting with me but there also seemed to be some difficulty that it could not overcome. There was a perceptible pulling sensation in the midst of the air that somehow made the ceiling appear higher than usual. The sun-bleached blue concertina light shade caught my eye. It seemed to be conveying anger. It had not changed in its appearance but seemed to be conveying anger on behalf of the entity. There was something really remarkable about the psychic audibility and conscious palpability of the entity's energy. It sounded so very well rounded, and it tactilely felt so very well rounded. It seemed to signal a characteristic prestige and propensity for resoluteness and finality. Yet despite its power, the passing seconds ruled out any significant interaction between us. But no sooner had that thought occurred to me when the lightshade suddenly became the central focus for the manifestation of an irreverent image of a diminutive cartoonish man, adorned in bright red clothes and mooning as he looked back at me, whilst conveying a facial expression totally befitting such cheeky action. The cartoonish image was not seen upon the lightshade or around the lightshade. But somehow and somewhere in the direction of my gaze, a very small and very highly defined cartoonish individual was visibly mooning at me in order to make the parting feelings of the entity known to me. I was left feeling completely perplexed at the peculiarity of the experience.

Report: #150

Location: Bedroom (~13:15hrs)

Dose: 27mg

Not Such A Merry Christmas

It was Christmas day. My boys were busy playing with toys and I'd driven to the local skatepark to ride my bike in the grey winter conditions. The roads and pavements were understandably empty, and although I expected the skatepark to be deserted, there was a woman seated upon the single wooden bench. A dark blue winter coat with a faux fur-lined hood covered her bowed head to keep out the cold wind and light drizzle. I assumed she was the mother of the two young boys busy scampering around on foot. After a brief stint riding, I headed home and took a hot shower before forcing myself to prepare a pipe. I headed downstairs to inform my wife of my intention and to instruct my boys to endeavour in remaining vocally subdued for the next ten or fifteen minutes. Assurances were given. I pulled on a black woollen jumper and headed upstairs. With the bedroom light switched on, I positioned two pillows on the bedroom floor and joined them. Having checked the clock, I sat up and began pulling vapour from the pipe. I strongly suspected the widespread ambient silence of Christmas day would make the occult sound of my psychic signal stand out like a sore thumb. After the third and final pull I was all too aware the substance was significantly expanding my consciousness. The action of reclining appeared unusual in the midst of my own superdense and crystal-clear psycho-spiritual substance. I have no specific recollection of the entity emerging. It was suddenly there and with such highly energetic intent that my calmness immediately evaporated. I gave serious consideration to bolting. But the speed with which the energy increased in power was totally mesmeric. Slight creaking sounds from the fabric of the bedroom walls were in direct proportion and response to the huge increase in energy. The floor and the walls audibly creaked, and I was quite certain the partially ajar cupboard door behind my head had just slammed shut. It was a truly incredible display of power and I was completely at its mercy. The sheer density of mind gave the appearance of seeing through a dark beige transparent medium, filling the room. The incredible density of that mental body was evident by its unique appearance: appearing very smooth; appearing very highly defined and completely imperforate without any hint of dimple, pore or blemish. My appeal for peace and quiet from my two young boys had clearly fallen on deaf ears. A cacophony of argy-bargy ensued from the room directly below me. The juxtaposition between them having fun and me at the complete mercy of this immense power was striking. But then I realised I had left the bedroom door wide open. I was completely intrigued to know how the transparent dark beige atmosphere was interacting with that opening. But my state of mind was so mesmerised I seemed unwilling or unable to consciously move any part of my body other than my eyes. And even then, as I tried to direct my gaze over to my right, my eyes were wont to flit around the room as though programmed to operate in REM mode. But with each and every brief view over to my right, I observed the dense body-of-mind was not filling that side of the bedroom. There, it appeared to exhibit a clearly defined border through which I was able to contrast the ordinary air. Noise from my boys continued, even as their mum began shouting at them. Once again, the contrast between what was occurring upstairs and what was occurring immediately downstairs was so remarkable given the separation by distance. Each and every time my eyes caught sight of the illuminated light bulb, pronounced afterimages would persist in the super-dense medium of mind. It soon became evident this impressive field of powerful energy was shrinking. Something began to manhandle the underside of my upper right arm. Extraordinarily and unbelievably, the left side of my upper body was very slowly raised, such that I was very gently and ever so slightly tilted over to my right side. This position seemed to facilitate a very obvious and very physical invasive operation in the underside of each upper arm. As ridiculous as this must surely sound, it felt like a row of bolts were being turned and tightened very quickly in unison, deep within my muscle tissue. It was painless but very physical and very obvious. Whatever was underway it felt like it was bone-deep. By now I was completely resigned to the experience and whatever was underway inside my limbs. I was in highly observant and emotionless state. The discarnate mind imperceptibly shrank and the invasive operation deep inside my arms came to an end. There was a distinct moment where it was somehow obvious the occult entity had left the room. I remained calm and emotionless going over and over the entire experience. Eventually my thoughts returned to the woman I had seen while riding at my bike at the local skatepark. There was no reason for her to have taken any interest in me and indeed, she hadn't. Occasionally she would stand up and go and check on her young boys before sitting herself back down. Her posture had indicated patience in anguish. She appeared uncomfortably out of place; sat in an otherwise deserted skatepark on a desolate and grey

Christmas morning. Clearly, her children's pleasure was her motive. But they appeared blissfully unaware of their mother's obvious isolation and quiet stoicism. I analysed the situation intently; wondering why she would take her children to a deserted concrete skatepark on a cold and miserable Christmas morning. The answer seemed self-evident. I began questioning myself and my empathy; should I have gone over and wished her a merry Christmas? The answer came back in an instant: What if it was not such a merry Christmas?

Report: #151

Location: Bedroom (~10:30hrs)

Dose: 19mg

Preposterously Weighty Notions

The very thought of preparing a pipe was sufficient to seat me upon the WC. 19mg was a manageable dose. Interestingly, even after all this time, there are moments when entity interaction just does not seem like it should be at all possible. I was experiencing that today. I took great care, stretching my inhalations over three successive pulls before reclining. My inner voice narrated: "Everything is normal! Everything is normal! Uh oh! Something is happening! I can feel something happening!" A limited portion of a large discarnate mind energetically emerged within the bedroom and energetically engaged with my highly amplified consciousness. This was palpable within me and without me, and was visible as an active turbulence throughout the air, characterised by a multitude of impossibly narrow lines representing the wavelength along a horizontal plane. Momentarily, it felt as though a large mass of a much larger mind was flowing down into the bedroom. That energy visibly and palpably increased and strengthened significantly. I was certain it was analysing me. I remained calm in my posture and breathing. After several seconds that intensive field of energy reverted back to its original intensity. It remained easily palpable and continued to exhibit numerous wavy lines representative of the frequency of psycho-spiritual energy. A very smooth vertically aligned energy then swept slowly up my body, starting from my feet. I could feel the energy moving through me. And I could feel that it was indeed a portion of something very much larger. As that energy slowly moved through my lower limbs, I could hear and feel very slight physical movements within my left and right inner ear. The energy sweeping up my body stopped as it reached the midst of my chest. The perceptible energy then suddenly ceased. My interior narrative was speaking with a distinct male voice that was not my own. I consciously dismissed the voice and reverted to my own interior narrative. Up ahead and clearly visible to my mind, but not visible to my eyes, the easily recognisable face of a female celebrity I had recently seen on TV. Her face was perfectly morphed into a female anime character. There was a short-lived emotional scene with an anime male pulling away from her, like two lovers about to be separated by distance. The image was very clear and very dreamlike. As the image vanished, I began thinking very deeply about the experience. It was without question, a limited portion of something far larger than was appreciable within the dimensions of the bedroom had emerged and undertaken some form of analysis of me before departing. I thought deeply about the role of such an entity in nature: do such entities have any role in human lives; in our post-death state? It was absolutely obvious the entity had analysed me in order to determine why I had made so much psychic sound above ordinary baseline level. And finding me alive and well, it chose to engage with me no further. That made me wonder about these interactive experiences. Could it be those discarnate entities I have termed Occult Masters are themselves limited to a prescribed level of consciousness commensurate with and applicable to their own evolutionary stage of advancement? Could it be that their more energetic mind-to-mind interactions with DMT researchers is nothing more than them fulfilling a specific function relevant to their nature? Possibly acting in a manner that would otherwise soberly usher the immaterial constitution of a dying human from this realm over into an etheric realm, an astral realm, and beyond? I understood I was considering preposterously weighty notions. But I also considered that I was perhaps being unreasonably critical of the intellectual capacity of those mightily powerful beings. Such thoughts felt almost dangerous. Not because they smacked of untruth or fantasy, but rather because somewhere within me, somewhere very deep and impossibly remote within me, something infinitesimally small had an inkling that the human constitution houses something latent that is equal unto or even greater than them. Such thoughts felt so terribly weighty and so terribly discomforting that I found myself blowing hard through pursed lips, and shaking my head from side to side as though to shake those very thoughts from my mind.

Report: #152

Location: Bedroom (approx. noon)

Dose: 27mg

The Forming of a New Connection

I ascended the stairs while huffing and puffing with anxiety. After sinking my head comfortably into the pillows, I immediately sat straight back up again and made two excellent inhalations. Even as the first pull was still soaking through my lungs, I could audibly and perceptibly perceive the onset of the substance from the midst of my head. Whilst retaining the second inhalation, I could feel those same effects amplifying significantly. I lay back and implored myself not to miss one little trick. For a second or two it was evident the crystal-clear energy actively filling the room was my own. I assumed the jarring appearance of the bedroom resulted from some of that energy reflecting off hard surfaces. An entity arrived. One moment it was not there, and then in an instant it filled the entire bedroom. Visually, it was very obvious – the room was seething with a paradoxically turbulent yet uniform energy. But it was the emotional and the mental sense that another mind had just manifested in my immediate setting that was so overwhelming. No sooner had it arrived and no sooner had I sensed its arrival when it underwent a series of rapid changes. At the time, I was fully cognisant of all those changes, and was sure I could report upon them accurately and in detail. However, at the conclusion of that short-lived and highly energetic phase, my frame of mind had somehow become subtly different. The ceiling appeared remarkably higher. Rightly or wrongly, I had the distinct impression that this entity was calling upon another of its kind to come and assist. That made me edgy, but I remained still whilst my eyes scanned the room. The unspoken appeals for assistance continued. My eyes flitted up towards the wall clock, which caused the character of the interaction to change. The entity ceased its silent calls for assistance. The wall clock appeared to repeatedly and rapidly flit far across the wall before snapping back into position with terrific rapidity. It now felt as though my attention was purposefully being directed toward the wall clock. Occasionally I would glimpse at the unusual appearance of the bedroom and its illusorily reconfigured height. A distinct moment arose wherein the situation felt quite comical. Concurrent with that, I experienced a vague perception of the character of the entity, but could not determine whether it was incredibly simple and naïve or terrifically high-minded, and I was now serving in the capacity of its plaything. Either way I suddenly burst out laughing, and the more I thought upon those two possibilities, whilst the wall clock continued to dart rapidly back and forth at terrific speed, the more and more I laughed out loud. The unusual effects slowly and imperceptibly diminished as my laughter eventually subsided.

The speed with which these entities emerge – apparently from nowhere – is simply stupendous. My perception of its emergence today was really excellent. However, no sooner had I experienced that emergence when that conscious energy underwent a series of very highly energetic transformations. Within mere seconds, that had resulted in temporarily and subtly transforming my state mind. In short, it had mesmerised me. My body was still very much at my own command. But it lay still and static because my mind was so utterly transfixed upon the discarnate mind that had somehow temporarily arrested my attention. At the conclusion of that opening mesmeric phase, when the seething energy had transformed into a completely transparent and notably crystal-clear medium, I wondered about the qualitative nature of that incredibly potent mesmeric power.

[Wikipedia: Animal Magnetism]

https://en.wikipedia.org/wiki/Animal_magnetism

Animal magnetism, also known as mesmerism, was the name given by the German doctor Franz Mesmer in the 18th century to what he believed to be an invisible natural force exerted by animals. He believed that the force could have physical effects, including healing. He tried persistently but without success to achieve scientific recognition of his theories. [...] Today it is almost entirely forgotten.

During the Romantic period, mesmerism produced enthusiasm and inspired horror in the spiritual and religious context. Though discredited as a credible medical practice by many, mesmerism created a venue for spiritual healing. Some animal magnetists advertised their practices by stressing the "spiritual rather than physical benefits to be gained from animal magnetism" and were able to gather a good clientele from among the spiritually inspired population.

[From Wikipedia, the free encyclopedia]

Except that mesmerism was never actually forgotten; it was merely re-baptized as hypnotism. In occult lore, however, the two are very different. Generally speaking, with hypnosis, all hypnosis is self-hypnosis – that is, one cannot be hypnotised unless one acquiesces one's self and thereby one's will to hypnosis. Mesmerism, however, is the power to fascinate someone; it is the quality of being fascinated, enchanted, captivated, spellbound, enthralled, charmed, enraptured, beguiled, transfixed, entranced, ravished, compelled or absorbed. But before taking a closer look into the occult accounts of what mesmerism actually is, and what it is not, it would not be inappropriate to take a much closer look into what Mesmer himself meant by the term – Animal Magnetism. The following is taken from Israel Regardie's, *The Philosophers Stone*:

> Franz Anton Mesmer was born in Austria in 1734, and in 1766 in Vienna he became an M.D. His inaugural address maintained that the sun, moon and stars affect each other and cause tides, not only in the ocean and sea, but in the atmosphere too. It was his theory that they affect in a similar way all organized bodies, through the medium of a subtle and mobile fluid which he conceived to pervade and permeate the universe, and to associate all things together in material intercourse and harmony. His theory further included the idea that all things soever in Nature possess a peculiar power which manifests itself by special action upon other bodies. That is to say, it is a physical and dynamic power acting exteriorly, without any chemical union, or without being introduced physically into the interior of the organization. Mesmer also contemplated the idea that all organic bodies, animals, plants, trees, metals, might be magnetized. By this he meant they could be charged or impregnated with a flow or current of vital energy. This cosmic vitality or animal magnetism could be transmitted, he claimed, by direct contact with a body already magnetized, or by means of the hand, the look, or even the will.

[From: The Philosophers Stone (2013) by Israel Regardie. Page 114 - 115]

Turning our inquiring gaze toward the occult interpretation of mesmerism produces some quite fascinating literary returns. Starting with a brief outline definition from Blavatsky's *The Key to Theosophy*:

Mesmerism the term comes from Mesmer, who rediscovered this magnetic force and its practical application toward the year 1775, at Vienna. It is a vital current that one person may transfer to another; and through which he induces an abnormal state of the nervous system that permits him to have a direct influence upon the mind and will of the subject or mesmerized person.

[From: The Key to Theosophy (1889) by H. P. Blavatsky. Page 162]

In *Isis Unveiled*, Blavatsky states:

The phenomena of mesmerism are explicable upon no other hypothesis than the projection of a current of force from the operator into the subject. If a man can project this force by an exercise of the will, what prevents his attracting it toward himself by reversing the current? Unless, indeed, it be urged that the force is generated within his body and cannot be attracted from any supply without. But even under such a hypothesis, if he can generate a superabundant supply to saturate another person, or even an inanimate object by his will, why cannot he generate it in excess for self-saturation?

[From: Isis Unveiled. Vol. I (1877) by H. P. Blavatsky. Page 500]

And in her *Studies in Occultism*, we find an article concerned with 'Hypnotism and Its Relation to Other Modes of Fascination'. This takes a question and answer approach; and in answer to what hypnotism is and how it differs to mesmerism, we learn that some (at that time) believed hypnotism to be an artificially produced condition likened to another mode of sleep; whereas others designated it as a self-induced stupor, produced chiefly by imagination. Mesmerism, however, we are told, differs in that "...it is the human will – whether conscious or otherwise – of the operator himself, that acts upon the nervous system of the patient." And, rather intriguingly:

Q. *In both (hypnotism and animal magnetism) there is an act of will in the operator, a transit of something from him to his patient, an effect upon the patient. What is the "something" transmitted in both cases?*

ANS. That which is transmitted has no name in European languages, and if we simply describe it as *will*, it loses all its meaning. The old and very much tabooed words, "enchantment," "fascination," "glamour," and "spell," and especially the verb "to bewitch," expressed far more suggestively the real action that took place during the process of such a *transmission,* than the modern and meaningless terms "psychologize" and "biologize." Occultism calls the force transmitted, the "auric *fluid,*" to distinguish it from the "auric *light*"; the "fluid" being a correlation of atoms on a higher plane, and a descent to this lower one, in the shape of impalpable and invisible plastic Substances, generated and directed by the potential Will...

[From: Studies in Occultism (1887-1891) by H. P. Blavatsky. Page 18]

In *Sepharial's, A Manual of Occultism*, published in 1914, we find a chapter dedicated to Hypnotism and Mesmerism:

Mesmerism may be distinguished in a popular manner from Hypnotism in that it presumes the existence of an effluvium which is in the nature of a subtle essence capable of being transmitted from one body to another under the direction of Will. Paracelsus calls it the Archeus or Liquor Vitae. "The Archeus is an essence," he says, "which is distributed equally in all parts of the body if the latter is in a healthy condition; it is the invisible nutriment from which the body draws its strength, and the qualities of its parts correspond to the nature of the physical parts which contain it. . . . The Archeus is of a magnetic nature and attracts or repels other forces belonging to the same plane.

The Mesmerists, or those who believe in the transmission of animal magnetism, whether we regard it as the Archeus of Paracelsus or the Odyle of Reichenbach, affirm that the emanation is most active through certain channels – *e.g.* the eyes, the lips, and the finger-tips.

The nervous fluid not only follows the direction of the will, but is moreover impressed with our individuality, both physical and mental. It bears the signature of our thought, it carries the healthy or diseased tendencies of our body, it is moved by our will and coloured by our desires and passions.

Baron Du Potet, in his *Manual de l'Etudiant Magnetiseur*, says: ...What you call nervous fluid or magnetism the men of old called occult force, the power of the soul, subjection, magic!

[From: A Manual of Occultism (1914) by Sepharial. Pages 193 – 200]

Teasing such esoteric excerpts from their original publication and reinterpreting and applying them in the context of DMT-fuelled interactions with powerful occult beings of hidden nature provides, in my opinion, an incredibly worthwhile and insightful analysis of the esoteric mechanics at play. The foregoing references refer to the projection of a current, force, subtle essence or effluvium from the operator into the subject. We have heard it named *Archeus,* or *Liquor Vitae* by the great Paracelsus, and *Auric Fluid* in other occult parlance – a correlation of atoms from a higher plane descended to our lower plane, in the shape of impalpable and invisible plastic substance. A connection here can be made with my own DMT-induced superdense psycho-spiritual projection, which exhibits impalpability and varying degrees of transparency. That mesmerists affirm such an emanation is most active through the eyes, the lips and the finger-tips, also seems to have some relevancy to my research. But of particular importance, and giving credence to that which I have previously suspected and suggested, is that the mysterious nervous fluid carries an occult signature of our self – both physical and mental. In the majority of my DMT-induced interactions with occult entities, it has become all too evident that I am subject to the will of the entity. That for me is where matters literally and metaphorically become truly fascinating, for it seems to me the mesmeric effects induced upon me by the occult intelligences are achieved by dint of will. And yet we have seen that merely describing that which is transmitted as will, does not truly account for what actually takes place. And so "fascination," and a host of other descriptive words are far more akin to describing the actual mechanics of the mind-to-mind interaction that takes place between the research percipient and the attending occult intelligence. And matters could quite satisfactorily be left at that. Except in keeping with the nature of Occult lore, matters can always be taken a little deeper. To do so, we are back with Blavatsky and her *Studies on Occultism,* wherein we read that there is an abyss of difference between the two states of mesmerism and hypnotism:

That one is beneficent, the other maleficent, as it evidently must be; since, according to both Occultism and modern Psychology, *hypnotism is produced by the withdrawal of the nervous fluid from the capillary nerves,* which being, so to say, the sentries that keep the doors of our senses opened, getting *anaesthetized* under hypnotic conditions, allow these to get closed. A. H. Simonin reveals many a wholesome truth in his excellent work, *"Solution du probleme de la suggestion hypnotique."* Thus, he shows that while "in Magnetism (mesmerism) there occurs in the *subject* a great development of moral faculties"; that his thoughts and feelings "become loftier, and the senses acquire an abnormal acuteness"; in hypnotism, on the contrary, "the subject becomes *a simple mirror."* It is Suggestion which is the true motor of every action in the hypnotic: and if, occasionally, "seemingly marvellous actions are produced, these are due to the hypnotizer, not to the subject." Again.... "In hypnotism instinct, i.e. the *animal,* reaches its greatest development; so much so, indeed, that the aphorism 'extremes meet' can never receive a better application than to magnetism and hypnotism." How true these words, also, as to the difference between the mesmerized and the hypnotized subjects. "In one, his ideal nature, his moral self – the reflection of his divine nature – are carried to their extreme limits, and the subject becomes almost a celestial being (*un ange*). In the other, it is his *instincts* which develop in a most surprising fashion. The hypnotic lowers himself to the level of the animal. From a physiological standpoint, magnetism (Mesmerism) is comforting and curative, and hypnotism, which is but the result of an unbalanced state, is – most dangerous."

[From: Studies in Occultism (1887-1891) by H. P. Blavatsky. Page 27]

PART 3

There is a sound on the other side of this wall

A bird is singing on the other side of this glass

Footsteps

Concealed

Silence is preserving a voice

UNDERWORLD, *Juanita : Kiteless : To Dream of Love*

Do you begin to see

As your third eye opens

Do you begin to see

Even more clearly

SANDALS, *Here Comes the Sign*

They're justified and they're ancient

And they like to roam the land

They're justified and they're ancient

I hope you understand

They don't want to upset the apple cart

And they don't want to cause any harm

But if you don't like what they're going to do

You better not stop them 'cause they're coming through

THE KLF, *Justified and Ancient ("The White Room" version)*

As with the preceding edition, I maintain this is a work of serious scientific inquiry with just as much validity as any present-day research into matters mysterious, profound or unseen. To state my research succinctly, I have undertaken practical investigations into hidden nature through inhalation of a potent mind manifesting substance and have adopted an occult-influenced interpretation of my subjective findings. Investigating what actually occurs after smoking DMT, taking my research outdoors proved hugely informative and tremendously rewarding. Indeed, I cannot overstate just how beneficial outdoor research was to my investigative programme.

Nothing in these remaining experiments from my research has detracted from the conclusions drawn following my first year of documented research. If anything, I believe I have augmented my earlier research and have added to the arguments that favour an occult analysis of the DMT experience. In my opinion, the most insightful and meaningful way to report upon practical mind manifesting research with DMT is through adopting an occultly interpretative analysis. If traditional science remains uncomfortable with the central thesis for the existence of hidden spirit – incarnate or discarnate – then one can reasonably suspect the discipline has either become uncomfortable with adhering to its investigatory principles or has succumbed to some influence wishing to maintain the materialist status quo.

To restate my reason for taking these mind manifesting experiments outside, experiment #34 detailed a bedroom-based experiment where the imposing force of the manifesting entity literally shook the house. It still sounds totally daft and completely off the wall to state as fact that an entity plunged into the bedroom, and imposed its enormous power upon the walls, to such extent that they audibly flexed under the tremendous otherworldly force powerfully imposing upon their surfaces. One can really only marvel at the tremendous power some of these entities have at their disposal. But it was what followed that justifiably alarmed me. The entity having so obviously secured its purchase throughout the bedroom, was then able to make that room shake back and forth with apparent ease. The entire room was experiencing significant movement. It was without doubt. Not only were the vibrations physically perceptible but the sounds of the house shaking were clearly audible and commensurate with the movement. I could distinctly hear the increased frequency as the final vibrations travelled up the steel skeletal frame hidden behind the walls. The experience was as perceptively astonishing as it was emotionally terrifying.

Taking my research outdoors greatly benefitted my understanding of the occult occurrences at play during these life-changing encounters. Without the restriction of interior walls, I gained a much better appreciation of my dimethyltryptamine-amplified occult constitution. Boosting my endogenous level of DMT facilitated the most extraordinary observation of my own powerfully projected psycho-spiritual substance; evident as an uncommonly dense and transparent expansive projection. It was only after heading outdoors that I could really observe the improbable extent of my occult self, following its arousal into expansion under the influence of the powerful tryptamine molecules. But that arousal and projection did not always manifest consistently.

In experiment #39, my psycho-spiritual substance appeared to emanate via a most peculiar route. In that particular experiment, my left eye was both an instrument of observation and evidently the route of emanation for a continuous stream of my own psycho-spiritual substance. As that substance streamed out from my left eye, it rapidly expanded into a large mass of superdense transparent cells above me and above the garden. The key question to ask: What exactly is that substance? Is it evidence of my otherwise immaterial consciousness; can it be rightly considered as 'mind-stuff' or 'psycho-spiritual substance'? Is that substance evidence of my spirit or my soul, expanding from a latent zero-point slumber and clothing itself in the universal fluid of our atmosphere? But what does that even mean? Another observation from that particular experiment was as the substance emanated from my left eye the skin on my face felt exceptionally taught. This is something I have experienced before. In my opinion, it relates to the uncommon high density of that unusual psycho-spiritual medium.

But what's really at play? What is that bizarre emanation? Why does it sometimes project as a crystal-clear bubble or fluid-like medium of such rarefied clarity as to shame the transparency of air; and why does it sometimes project as a rapidly spiralling unstoppable torrent of truly bountiful proportion? How far can it stretch? Where is it anchored? What is its source and what is its composition? Could that substance be argued as evidence of an immortal principle within? Are my eyes and my ego marvelling at something much greater than they? Questions in respect of the mysterious mechanics are at play in these experiences cannot remain whispered or unspoken. What actually occurs within my brain after the

DMT molecules arouse that organ? How does DMT so powerfully arouse my psycho-spiritual self? That is to ask: How does DMT arouse the occult me through the vehicle of the physical me? If a neuroscientist is able to authoritatively answer half of that question then who is best qualified to answer the second part of the question?

In experiment #59, I had an experience that brought previously forgotten boyhood memories flooding into my mind; memories of awakening in the morning as a small boy and finding my clenched teeth momentarily stuck together with a thin and tactilely gummy film. Why did I re-experience that very same occurrence after inhaling 27mg of dimethyltryptamine? I can assume the strange short-lived gummy substance upon my teeth was somehow related to the psycho-spiritual substance which had emanated from me and rendered my surroundings with remarkable visual clarity? That same dose was sufficient to attract an entity from hidden nature. And although it remained unseen, its presence to my amplified psycho-spiritual self was without any doubt whatsoever. To my mind, that is a really fascinating observation. Principally because it forces me to suspect that whatever emanated outwardly from me, it had power of perception at distance from my physical self. I could certainly perceive the entity mentally or emotionally, but I could also perceive it palpably too. I could somehow feel the power of its discarnate presence without me. But I could also sense it within me too! In some strange way, I could also vaguely see the entity too, despite the overall invisibility of its presence within my own exceptionally transparent psycho-spiritual medium. Its rapid departure was visible and palpable somewhere between hasteful and immediate.

A frequent occurrence when powerfully amplifying my psycho-spiritual substance with dimethyltryptamine outdoors was the appearance of snowflake-like geometric patterning, appearing to adorn the clouds. I have ventured to assume the naturally occurring mineral accretions within my pineal body are involved. These mineral accretions are also known as brain sand:

https://en.wikipedia.org/wiki/Corpora_arenacea

Corpora arenacea (or brain sand) are calcified structures in the pineal gland and other areas of the brain such as the choroid plexus. Older organisms have numerous corpora arenacea, whose function, if any, is unknown. Concentrations of "brain sand" increase with age, so the pineal gland becomes increasingly visible on X-rays over time, usually by the third or fourth decade. They are sometimes used as anatomical landmarks in radiological examinations. Chemical analysis shows that they are composed of calcium phosphate, calcium carbonate, magnesium phosphate, and ammonium phosphate. Recently, calcite deposits have been described as well.

[From: Wikipedia, the free enyclopedia]

Could the energetic oscillatory arousal of the pineal gland, caused by a sudden surge of DMT molecules, act upon the minerals therein in a fashion best explained by cymatics?

https://en.wikipedia.org/wiki/Cymatics

Cymatics...is a subset of modal vibrational phenomena. [...] Typically the surface of a plate, diaphragm or membrane is vibrated, and regions of maximum and minimum displacement are made visible in a thin coating of particles, paste or liquid. Different patterns emerge in the excitatory medium depending on the geometry of the plate and the driving frequency.

[From: Wikipedia, the free enyclopedia]

The following from *Correlation of Sound and Colour* by Paul Foster Case sheds some light on the matter, suggestively at least:

The higher brain, or cerebrum, is the organ for expressing this Mercury vibration. Of the brain centres through which it functions, the most important is the pineal gland, or conarium. This is a reddish-white, cone shaped organ, almost at the centre of the brain. It contains a yellow granular substance known as brain sand. Adepts complete the function of this centre by making the particles of brain sand cohere, so as to form a crystalline body. This crystalline body is the true stone of the Wise, or Philosophers' Stone. When the Life-power is specialized through this centre, one experiences superconsciousness. Anatomists know nothing of the crystalline formation of the pineal gland, simply because they never have an opportunity to dissect the brain of an adept.

[From: Correlation of Sound and Colour, (1931) by Paul Foster Case, Page 10]

Assuming the DMT-induced oscillatory activity upon the pineal body really does impose a crystalline-like structure throughout the brain sand therein, does that crystalline structure then impose geometric patterning upon my psycho-spiritual output during DMT inebriation? Or could it simply be that my eyes, in working through an uncommonly dense medium emanating from me, results in the appearance of such geometric patterning? In Michael Cremo's *Human Devolution: A Vedic Alternative to Darwin's Theory,* we read:

A popular, but incorrect view is that Descartes thought that the pineal gland in the brain mediated an interaction between mind (consciousness) and matter. This organ was, according to this account, sensitive to both mind and matter and could link them. Modern philosophers now believe that Descartes simply suggested that the pineal gland was the place where an interaction between mind and matter took place. As to how the interaction actually took place, Descartes could not say.

[Human Devolution: A Vedic Alternative to Darwin's Theory (2003) by Michael Cremo. This quote references Parapsychology, Philosophy, and Spirituality: a postmodern exploration (1997) by David Ray Griffin]

Where exactly and how exactly is that mysterious mind-matter interaction anchored? What are the occult mechanics at play as DMT powerfully projects an otherwise hidden aspect of one's being into one's immediate surroundings? Exactly which part of my occult self is it that temporarily, fluidically and elastically projects? If I say it is my psycho-spiritual substance, what exactly does that encompass? If I then begin musing that my psycho-spiritual substance has a latent zero-point existence anchored to my physical, cellular, molecular, atomic and sub-atomic matrix, what do I believe I am actually saying? Am I saying my psycho-spiritual substance exists within every fibre of my being, but also outside of three-dimensional space and time? But isn't that really the same as saying my psycho-spiritual substance remains invisible to me because of my incarnate existence and the limitations of my ordinary incarnate perceptions? If my range of perception was truly broad band along all frequencies and throughout all dimensions then that which is now occult within and without would be all too evident – and quite likely alarmingly and overwhelmingly so! But such a level of perception simply cannot be achieved with the ordinary organs of human perception, and in my opinion, cannot be achieved by human consciousness in its present qualitative state of evolution.

Perhaps the pineal gland works in something of a polar opposite fashion to our lateral eyes. Light streams into our lateral eyes and informs our mind of the configuration of the environment through conditioned learning from birth. But if the pineal body really is an interface between our hidden self and our physical self, we find that when it is prised open (in my case through the inhalation of freebase DMT) psycho-spiritual substance expansively projects – amplifies or streams out in a very definite and very observable fashion. But if one's occult constitution from a previously invisible state can stream out from within, what else that is otherwise invisible can stream in from without?

What more may be said about the audible human psychic signal? That unmissable cranially-housed sound that manifests or responds so strikingly to a boost of dimethyltryptamine? What might we suppose that sound actually is, beyond the moniker of tinnitus? Could that sound be considered as a mysterious but natural characteristic of the numinous element within humankind? Can we reasonably consider that sound as evidence of one's soul or spirit interfacing with one's physical body? Is there a place where one's spiritual constitution becomes anchored to one's physical constitution? Given its central focus within occult lore, the pineal gland has to be the most obvious anchor point. And that certainly seems to be the general location that sound within my head increases terrifically in audibility. If that suspicion is correct, how and why does spirit produce audibility of its presence within the flesh? Does that sound arise from perpetual high frequency oscillation of the pineal gland resulting from anchoring of the spirit? Perhaps that interface really is something like a singularity, where factors relating to density, space and time cannot be apprehended without recourse to abstract speculation? The questions quickly become weighty, taxing and profound. My research has shown me that inhaling DMT in the vaporous form has a tremendously energising effect upon the acoustic qualities of that sound. Are we then to suppose the pineal body serves as some kind of valve or regulator to a bountiful reservoir of our psycho-spiritual self?

With a sufficient dose of DMT inhaled, the occult signalling properties of that mysterious transmission rapidly attracts something from without. Something immensely powerful from hidden nature. Something with the capacity to effectuate a bizarre and life-changing experience upon the DMT percipient. There was one particular class of entity that seemed to respond most frequently to my dimethyltryptamine-amplified psycho-acoustic signal. I chose to refer to that class of entity as, Occult Masters. There was an overwhelming sense of stupendous high-mindedness, incredible intellect, deep wisdom and great power in abundance. But more so, those entities seemed to have a practical working knowledge of my psyche and my physiology. But what is the proper classification of such entities? At least as far as cataloguing occult lifeforms is concerned? It is at least interesting to speculate as to who or what they could be:

https://en.wikipedia.org/wiki/Ascended_master

> ...Ascended Masters are believed to be spiritually enlightened beings who in past were ordinary humans, but who have undergone a series of spiritual transformations originally called *initiations*. [...] Ascended Masters are believed to be individuals who have lived in physical bodies, acquired the Wisdom and Mastery needed to become Immortal and Free of the cycles of "re-embodiment" and karma, and have attained their "Ascension"... [...] This knowledge is believed to have previously been taught for millions of years only within "Ascended Master Retreats" and "Mystery Schools". [...] It is further claimed by various groups and teachers that the Ascended Masters serve as the teachers of mankind from the realms of Spirit, and that all people will eventually attain their Ascension and move forward in spiritual evolution beyond this planet. According to these teachings, they remain attentive to the spiritual needs of humanity, and act to inspire and motivate its spiritual growth.

> [From: Wikipedia, the free encyclopedia]

The interpretative possibilities from such speculations are intriguing. They prise the imagination wide open; which is something occult literature tends to achieve and oftentimes strikingly and sometimes discomfortingly so. One could argue that Rick Strassman's research with the Spirit Molecule has unwittingly opened a door that will ultimately lead to much wider practical occult research with dimethyltryptamine – at least by those whose heart and mind is wont to explore such realities. There can be no doubt that the experiences reported in such mind manifesting explorations will ultimately furnish science with new dimensions of inquiry. But such a mindset was already under development before Strassman's research, and such a mindset is still under development:

https://en.wikipedia.org/wiki/New_Age

> The New Age is a term applied to a range of spiritual or religious beliefs and practices that developed in Western nations during the 1970s. [...] As a form of Western esotericism, the New Age movement drew heavily upon a number of older esoteric traditions, in particular those that emerged from the occultist current that developed in the eighteenth century. Such prominent occult influences include the work of Emanuel Swedenborg and Franz Mesmer, as well as the ideas of Spiritualism, New Thought, and the Theosophical Society. A number of mid-twentieth century influences, such as the UFO cults of the 1950s, the Counterculture of the 1960s, and the Human Potential Movement, also exerted a strong influence on the early development of the New Age movement. [...] Despite its highly eclectic nature, a number of beliefs commonly found within the New Age movement have been identified. Theologically, the movement typically adopts a belief in a holistic form of divinity which imbues all of the universe, including human beings themselves. There is thus a strong emphasis on the spiritual authority of the self. This is accompanied by a common belief in a wide variety of semi-divine non-human entities, such as angels and masters, with whom humans can communicate...

> [From: Wikipedia, the free encyclopedia]

In Steven Turner's *Panegyric to Spirit: The Final DMT Diaries,* Turner quotes from Luke A. Myers', *Gnostic Visions*:

> As you have already seen, the Gnostics claimed that the whole spiritual and material universe was peopled with countless numbers of entities and spirits that were known to

make up the many varied levels of existence. [...] They gave the name Aeon to the high classes of inhabitants, those which beckon humanity upwards. The inhabitants of the lower classes, those below the level of the human kingdom, they call Archons. These entities are depicted as jealous of the higher state that mankind has reached. They constantly try to pull him back into a lower, more material realm.

[Ref: Panegyric to Spirit – The Final DMT Diaries (2015) by Steven Turner, page 112; Quoting from: Gnostic Visions by Luke A. Myers]

Turner's commentary is equally informative and fascinating:

The Gnostics would attempt to map out and chronicle this spiritual Multiverse, as a guide to other explorers within this complex cosmogony. And they would also try to describe the activities and natures of the diverse beings which they encountered there. Most of the beings within the higher realms were more spiritually progressed than mankind, and usually benevolent. The beings of the lower levels of this dimensional strata, were more base and mischievous, and often resented mankind – and often sought to drag it down to their level. One must always be cautious of one's dealings with such creatures, as they might not have your best interests at heart. Within the Gnostic doctrine the world of matter constituted one of the lower levels of existence, a baser ontological realm, and was usually seen as the physical prison which entrapped the most divine aspect of mankind: which was *soul* or *spirit*.

[Ref: Panegyric to Spirit – The Final DMT Diaries (2015) by Steven Turner, pages 111 - 112]

Gnostic philosophy is unambiguous and stark. It addresses profound and mysterious matters authoritatively and knowledgeably. Turner's panegyric ultimately brings those metaphysically-gnostical matters of the past into the present:

Such metaphysical models of the world are again arousing interest, and in many ways, it is within the field of psychedelic research which is opening this debate. The questions raised by psychedelic states, as giving access to different planes of reality which are normally imperceptible to us, is at present attracting more and more academic interest. Particularly with the scientific research which is currently underway through the western-world's discovery of *Ayahuasca,* as a legitimate scientific subject of study (the indigenous South American entheogenic brew has made many inroads recently within western culture, and is now a source of attraction to many spiritual seekers). As well as the pioneering work of *Rick Strassman* whose years of study and medical trials with DMT may profoundly shake our concepts and models of the universe.

[Ref: Panegyric to Spirit – The Final DMT Diaries (2015) by Steven Turner, page 122]

Is there anything of value to be gained from scrutinising the metaphysical mysteries of the DMT phenomena against the UFO phenomenon? Perhaps more appropriately considered as Unidentified Aerial Phenomena (UAP) because under a very strict interpretation of the UFO acronym a great many things would qualify as UFO. Unsurprisingly my view of the UAP mystery is coloured by the lens of my occult-influenced mind. The Ultraterrestrial Hypothesis is not too dissimilar in outlook. The following quote is taken from John Michael Greer's, *The UFO Phenomenon: Fact Fantasy and Disinformation*:

The starting point of the ultraterrestrial theory is the argument that UFO's and their occupants do not behave like physical nuts-and-bolts spacecraft at all. They appear and disappear like ghosts, and sometimes can be seen by some witnesses and not by others in a situation in which a physical object would be visible to all. They show close similarities to themes from contemporary popular culture, but they also closely resemble legendary beings recorded in the folklore of cultures around the world. Thus, according to this way of thinking, the answer to the UFO phenomena is to be found somewhere in the complex realm of human experience that reaches from the mind through the debatable ground of psychic phenomena into the world of myth, magic, and spirituality.

[Ref: The UFO Phenomenon (2009) by John Michael Greer;
Pages 144 – 145; Llewellyn Publications]

However, it was Jacques Vallée that gave the UFO phenomena the original and insightful popular analytical scrutiny that freed it from the illogical and wholly improbable nuts-and-bolts spacecraft theory; aka, the Extra-terrestrial Hypotheses. Vallée's arguments took the matter into occult territory. He arguably remains one of the pre-eminent authorities in UFOlogy. It is Vallée who shaped the argument and directed it towards the highly emotive occult dimension.

https://en.wikipedia.org/wiki/Jacques_Vall%C3%A9e

Vallée proposes that there is a genuine UFO phenomenon, partly associated with a form of non-human consciousness that manipulates space and time. The phenomenon has been active throughout human history, and seems to masquerade in various forms to different cultures. In his opinion, the intelligence behind the phenomenon attempts social manipulation by using deception on the humans with whom they interact.

Vallée also proposes that a secondary aspect of the UFO phenomenon involves human manipulation by humans. Witnesses of UFO phenomena undergo a manipulative and staged spectacle, meant to alter their belief system, and eventually, influence human society by suggesting alien intervention from outer space. The ultimate motivation for this deception is probably a projected major change of human society, the breaking down of old belief systems and the implementation of new ones. Vallée states that the evidence, if carefully analyzed, suggests an underlying plan for the deception of mankind by means of unknown, highly advanced methods. Vallée states that it is highly unlikely that governments actually conceal alien evidence, as the popular myth suggests. Rather, it is much more likely that that is exactly what the manipulators want us to believe. Vallée feels the entire subject of UFOs is mystified by charlatans and science fiction. He advocates a stronger and more serious involvement of science in the UFO research and debate. Only this can reveal the true nature of the UFO phenomenon.

[From: Wikipedia, the free encyclopedia]

Ungrounded and feverish speculation upon the UFO-cum-UAP subject may lead one into powerful conspiratorial paranoias. And whilst some of those mistrusting speculations may have some validity, the antidote to such paranoia has to be calm-headedness and careful, insightful, analytical thinking. Vallée's suggestion that the UFO phenomena operates as a spiritual control system is, in my opinion, metaphysically ground-breaking. The following is taken from his *Dimensions: A Casebook of Alien Contact*, originally published in 1988:

> After forty years of puzzlement, we have plenty of data to document the impact of the UFO phenomena on our society. We have only to look around us and examine the shift that takes place right now in human mythologies. We need only observe to what extent the subject of contact with extra-terrestrial life has become fashionable.
>
> As a society, we are developing a great thirst for contact with superior minds that will provide guidance for our poor, harassed, hectic planet. I think we may be ready to fall into a trap, perhaps a kind, benevolent pitfall. I believe that when we speak of UFO sightings as instances of space visitations, we are looking at the phenomena on the wrong level. We are not dealing with successive waves of visitations from space. We are dealing with a control system. [...] I propose there is a spiritual control system for human consciousness and that paranormal phenomena like UFO's are one of its manifestations.

[Ref: Dimensions: A Casebook of Alien Contact (1988) by Jacques Vallée]

What are the grander occult influences upon the earth's manifold and interconnected systems of nature? Can and do occult influences impose upon the technological, political, social and economic dimensions of empires and civilisations? Could there really be far greater powers at play than science has hitherto been bold enough to imagine; discarnate powers of mind and emotion that no telescope and no microscope can ever hope to magnify and amplify? Were the Gnostics of yore far ahead of our modern minds insofar as they actually recognised not only the unseen realms, but the actual nature and characteristics of the inhabitants therein, and the influences therefrom? What are we to make of the Gnostic division between higher classes of discarnate inhabitants (Aeons) and lower classes of discarnate inhabitants (Archons)? Could the most relevant qualification for scientists who shape the future of that inquiring and scrutinising discipline be one of both literal and practical open-mindedness?

Experiment #7, reports how I was psychically outmuscled by a very powerful entity of a qualitatively very different character to those I have termed Occult Masters. The entity manifesting in that experience was of markedly different order to anything I had ever experienced before. The density of its mind was easily palpable within me and without me, by virtue of the perceptive capacity inherent in my own dimethyltryptamine-amplified psycho-spiritual bubble – a forced expansion of my own superdense psycho-spiritual constitution. Visually, emotionally and psychically, its appearance and its energy were overwhelmingly – even pseudo-tangibly – apparent to my heightened psychic perception. The unmistakable sight of a spiralling projection slowly descending from within that energetic mass was as fascinating as it was frightening. But why did that psycho-spiritual protrusion of the entity spiral down towards me? Why not simply put forth that portion of superdense mind as an appendage? One has to suppose there are genuine occult mechanics involved in these interdimensional encounters. But really and truly: What was that thing that had emerged into my bedroom? Had my amplified psychic signal attracted something benevolent or something malevolent? Was it imposing heavily upon me as something of an initiation; possibly in order to see whether I would return to further my research after such a frightening experience? I don't think it was that. There was something about that manifested entity that was humungously weighty and very far removed from my incarnate human consciousness. Even speculating upon the evolutionary path of such an entity feels like a terribly presumptuous enquiry.

At the time of the experience it was beyond frightening. And I did not doubt for one moment the entity could snuff me out with as much ease as I may blow out a candleflame. But I cannot help myself from wondering exactly what class of entity that would be classified as in the occult cataloguing of discarnate intelligences. And to commit myself to further opinion, it be no lie to say that particular entity seemed like the polar opposite of those I have come to term, Occult Masters. It was no less lacking in potency and strength, but it somehow seemed differently configured, at a very fundamental level – it was full of willful drive and resolute purpose, with little by way of care or compassion.

To once again reiterate my fundamental finding: Inhaling dimethyltryptamine in the vaporous state powerfully amplifies an aspect of one's occult constitution to such extent that a discarnate intelligence from hidden nature will likely manifest and interact with the research percipient in such an overwhelming manner as to cause profound astonishment. I readily concede that I have very likely experienced nowhere near to a fraction of the experiential possibilities. And I am happy to acknowledge the limitations of my doses and route of administration. But even without the manifesting discarnate occult intelligence, the emanation of one's own otherwise hidden psycho-spiritual self is a hugely mysterious and immensely rewarding sight. In the appropriately titled experiment #61, what the pigeon saw really was sufficient for it to make a sudden about-turn in mid-flight, rather than fly through the superdense psycho-spiritual mass ranged above the garden. I must assume the strange optical effects of that superdense medium were sufficient to convey to the pigeon that all was not quite as it should be with the local airscape. There have been many other occasions where a bird has flown through or glided through that medium without making any apparent fuss. Oftentimes their passage produces incredible tracer trails in the wake of their flight. In addition, those powerful discarnate entities seem intelligently capable of creating bizarre magnifying effects, simply by configuring their psycho-spiritual constitution in order to create bizarre illusion-inducing optics, as one looks through their superdense and highly transparent body-of-mind.

In experiment #54, the form of the manifested entity was simply spectacular to behold in that it resembled a huge psycho-spiritual multi-faceted diamond. The sighting of such an epic visual revelation felt entirely purposeful and planned. Could it be at all possible the entity knew full well that I was faithfully recording my experiences with an ambition to publish? I don't see why that could not be so. If only the great naturalist Sir David Attenborough could have shared that sight with me. I wonder what he would've made of it? And what would modern day king of physics, the late Stephen Hawking have made of such a sight? Such learned and highly knowledgeable men. But what in the name of all that is holy would they have made of that gloriously configured occult form that emerged out of the thin air above a non-descript suburban back garden?

The terrific increase in energy these entities expend as they emerge – apparently from out of thin air – and impose themselves within one's immediate setting is unmissable and unmistakably perceptible; audibly and pseudo-tactilely, within and without. Occasionally that power has commenced after the entity imposed forcibly upon the ground, or upon indoor floor and wall surfaces with sufficient energy to create audible sounds and perceptible vibrations. In experiment #48, the discarnate entity thumped heavily into the garden, causing the ground around my head to momentarily shake under the incredible otherworldly impact. It's absolutely astonishing that something intangible can impose so obviously physically. To qualify the term 'pseudo-tactilely', I am stating that one's amplified psycho-spiritual constitution has a capacity of perceiving other psycho-spiritual presences in a manner that is most similar to the sense of touch.

As well as a capacity to impact upon solid matter, those entities have also displayed a capacity to easily penetrate my living tissue, in a manner that has enabled me to have an incredible appreciation of my skeletal self and my cranial anatomy. I have also found those powerful entities can impose themselves in such a manner as to make a portion of their psycho-spiritual constitution seem physically perceptible. They seem to have the ability to configure or transform a portion of their body-of-mind into something of a quasi-physical appendage or impossibly taught membranous field. As outlined above, it is actually the aroused and expansive emanation of my own psycho-spiritual substance that enables me to perceive such apparent solidity as well as the unimaginably prodigious force behind it.

In commenting upon the apparent intelligence of those powerful entities, I am conscious I can really rely upon my own incarnate consciousness as a yardstick. And as much as I may place a premium on verbal and written communication as a sure sign of high intelligence within the wider mammalian ménage, I am instinctively drawn to conclude that many if not all of the higher energy interactions I have experienced have been with entities to whom oral speech and the written word are either wholly redundant or directly impractical forms of communication. However, I am conscious that my dose choice and chosen route of administration are possibly limiting factors in wider experiential possibilities with these entities. In experiment #41, I experienced a debilitating lightning-like jolt into the crown of my head that rendered me completely insensible. I suspect that had I not been seated so nonchalantly upon a garden chair the experience would have been very different. I could take an interpretive view that I was taught a salutary lesson against seating myself so leisurely when researching with such an uber-potent, occult-entity inducing, mind-manifesting substance. Looking back at experiment #11, I must assume the entity that was both within me and without me was absolutely cognisant of my emotional state. Indeed, not only was it cognisant of my emotional state but it actually acted in a way that shaped them. It bunched a small portion of its own psycho-spiritual substance either around my trachea or within my trachea and then gradually constricted my breathing, until, filled with genuine fear for my life, I sat bolt upright on the verge of succumbing to a very ugly panic. It was only after the experience had concluded and I'd had a few minutes to reflect that I realised who had the controlling hand all along.

The sealing up of my lips from within was a reasonably frequent occurrence. But it wasn't until experiment #16 that I was courageous enough to test the integrity of that seal, and thereby find it was far stronger than my mouth was able to overcome. The slow and purposeful movement of the psycho-spiritual substance moving upwards through my oral physiology, towards the opening of my mouth, indicated knowledge and intention. The improbably thin psycho-spiritual film coating my cheeks ultimately proved absolutely impossible to overcome as it secured its resolute seal over my lips from within. The firmness of the otherworldly grip upon my mouth opening and the general area around my jaw was truly prodigious.

It seems rather silly to talk about unexpected occurrences when I am already dealing with such bizarre goings on. Yet clearly there are some constants at play when powerfully amplifying one's psychic signal with DMT, and thereby attracting and securing overwhelming interaction with one of the classes of discarnate entities from hidden nature. The latter end of the experience reported in experiment #36 was especially bizarre in that the discarnate intelligence was clearly undertaking some kind of activity upon my teeth. Whatever was underway in my oral environment it felt purposeful, methodical and even beneficial. Arguments arising from such an occurrence in support of health benefits from such interactions are intriguing, surprising and profound.

It is interesting to speculate on the esoteric mechanics behind these incredible interdimensional interactions with powerful beings of hidden nature. These interactions can diminish significantly because of an unexpected disturbance, or by willfully diverting one's attention. I have found shifting my eyesight or my focus has greatly diminished the strength of some interactions. There must be a reason why that is so and I suspect it has something to do with breaking those temporarily melded psychic energies that are so central in these mind-to-mind interactions. It is only by asking relevant questions and then being as open-minded and as receptive as possible to the possibilities, no matter how unrealistic they may sound, that sense can made of the apparently unreal and improbable. Some relatively low dose experiments have been incredibly rewarding in terms of providing insights into the occult mechanics at play. They have proved incredibly informative in providing strong visible evidence of the fluidic effects of my psycho-spiritual emanation. Other low dose outdoor experiments have given short-lived visual sighting of what appear to be millions of infinitesimally small vibrating particles appearing within my visual field, just a few arms lengths distance from me, immediately preceding the obvious fluidic psycho-spiritual emanation. Those two apparently different states clearly appear fundamentally related. I might assume the appearance of those apparent particles represent visual evidence of the initial wavefront of psycho-spiritual substance emanating from me. What aspect of my being could give rise to such an unusual particulate appearance of my psych-spiritual self under the influence of dimethyltryptamine? In *Panegyric to Spirit*, Steven Turner begins Chapter 1 by referring to the 'Orch OR' model of consciousness. In outline:

https://en.wikipedia.org/wiki/Orchestrated_objective_reduction

> Orchestrated objective reduction (Orch-OR) is a hypothesis that consciousness in the brain originates from processes *inside* neurons, rather than from connections *between* neurons as in the conventional view. The mechanism is held to be a quantum physics process called *objective reduction* which is *orchestrated* by molecular structures called microtubules. The hypothesis, which was put forward in the early 1990s by theoretical physicist Roger Penrose and anaesthesiologist and psychologist Stuart Hameroff, has so far been rejected by the majority of cognitive scientists.
>
> [From: Wikipedia, the free encyclopedia]

I am not going to pretend I am qualified to understand the full complexities of a controversial new model of brain processing and consciousness. But in reading Chapter 1 of Turner's book, it becomes evident that microtubules are a key aspect of that model:

Many scientists cite the astonishing number of connections produced through the synaptic firings of the roughly one hundred billion neurons within the brain, as the explanation of complexity of human consciousness. The number of microtubules in the human brain (which form the outer casing of the neuron), however, dwarfs this number by a staggering amount, as they create the fine lattice structure of the neurons shell. And it is at this molecular scale that Hameroff suggested that quantum processes could in fact interface with the brain at the biological level.

[Ref: Panegyric to Spirit – The Final DMT Diaries (2015) by Steven Turner, page 12]

I cannot help but wonder whether it is the structure of those microtubules that influences the apparent appearance of countless infinitesimally small psycho-spiritual particles immediately preceding the wavefront. Turner takes an encouraging stance on the ongoing Orch OR debate:

Such a model of consciousness has complex and deep implications within the philosophical questions of free-will and conscious self-determination. [...] The questions which it poses are still open to many different interpretations, such as the very source and location of individual consciousness. And these theories are likely to be challenged and disputed within many scientific and intellectual fields – from material-reductionists, humanists, religious philosophers, or simply other neuroscientists. In fact, it should be a challenge to thought for all thinking human beings.
[Ref: Panegyric to Spirit – The Final DMT Diaries (2015) by Steven Turner, pages 25 – 26]

The location of individual consciousness is still a great puzzler for the very best of human minds. Can traditional science ever furnish mankind with a comprehensive answer that will completely satisfy every valid and highbrow occult enquiry made of that same mystery? And equally, can existent or developing occult doctrines ever provide a full and satisfactory account of the same enigma that will meet the exacting demands of science? Or will science and the occult have to go to bed together and see what comes of that relationship, in the fullness of time, after a period of troublesome gestation? Perhaps if the science that has become mainstream was far more ready to admit that it does not have all the answers, and it remained open-minded rather than choosing to scoff at that which it cannot explain, the discipline would be far less dogmatic than what it has become. And if the occult wasn't so addled with the cloak of secrecy, and especially with the negativity borne from its perceived lowlier and seedier practices, then we may be able to adopt a change to our thinking in a way that promotes evolutionary betterment?

Experiments #47 and #56, both convey relatively rare experiences wherein a mental state of introspection became terribly overbearing. The title of each report suggestibly conveys the extent to which my amplified inward-looking negativity afflicted me. From here we can reasonably venture to ask: What kind of mindset best suits commitment to research of this nature? The capacity for asserting self-control over one's mood and one's stream of thought should never be undervalued. I found, very much to my own surprise as my research progressed, that I almost always maintained an improbably calm sombreness. An emotional neutrality before, during and sometimes even after some really truly astounding experiences. Whilst maintaining that sombre mindset was not always possible, I certainly found it beneficial when approaching the DMT experience from an investigative and analytical perspective. I have in fact wondered whether some of the entities that have interacted with me may've slightly tweaked an aspect of my psyche in order to lessen what was clearly an otherwise innate propensity towards excitability. I believe I can say with some degree of confidence that my commitment to smoking the molecule, and submitting myself to those profoundest of experiences, has significantly strengthened my emotional intelligence.

I still find one of the most fascinating sights in this research being that initial period of emergence, where one's psycho-spiritual constitution responds to the effect of the dimethyltryptamine, and visibly begins to faintly emerge ahead of oneself, as though manifesting from out of thin air, and quickly becomes increasingly evident to such extent that geometrically cellular characteristics become all too evident as that increases in visibility prior to or during expansion. I have recorded experiments wherein the initial appearance of that psycho-spiritual substance has emerged so smoothly and so subtly as to make it appear that it was in fact present exteriorly and invisibly all along. Perhaps our otherwise occult psycho-spiritual constitution does naturally exist interiorly and exteriorly. Perhaps the mechanics that play out from boosting my brain with additional DMT molecules is something like the opening of a sluice gate to that psycho-spiritual substance; such that within mere seconds, something previously unseen becomes increasingly evident and then, within a few more seconds, has expanded to a size that makes my bodily anchor appear comparatively small.

Turning my analytical attention to those phenomenally highly defined and wholly immersive hallucinatory vistas and visions that characterise a great many of the interdimensionally interactive DMT experiences, I contend that they are constructs formed within the mind of the entity in whose psycho-spiritual mind-substance one is engulfed in a temporary state of mesmeric rapport. I came to wonder why there was a relative absence of such hallucinatory experiences when researching outdoors in the rear garden, when clearly some of the doses were sufficient to attract immensely powerful entities. I don't doubt those entities could easily impose their wonderful hallucinatory constructs upon my amplified mind. Could it then, have anything to do with the proximity of the neighbouring properties? Is there any possibility that someone looking upon our small rear garden would not see me (because of the height of the fence and my recumbent position) but may catch sight of some bizarre visual refractory effect when unknowingly looking through the transparent body of the entity ranged above the garden? I don't really suspect it is quite that, or quite that simple, but I retain the argument in print as indicative of my thinking in that regards. I could also entertain the notion that those entities are able to intuit that I have garnered some basic understanding of their capacity to function in that regard – as grand and as outlandish as that may sound – and have therefore decided not indulge me with highly defined colourful visual vistas. It's really very difficult to know exactly what the reason is when the styles of communication are so at odds between the incarnate and discarnate mode of existence. Once again, I recognise the limitations of my own research and my chosen route of administration in that particular regard.

In preparing to draw this work to a close, I have perhaps overlooked the Don (Vito) Corleone of the psychedelic movement, certainly as far as DMT is concerned:

https://en.wikipedia.org/wiki/Terence_McKenna

Terence McKenna advocated the exploration of altered

states of mind via the ingestion of naturally occurring psychedelic substances. For example, and in particular, as facilitated by the ingestion of high doses of psychedelic mushrooms, ayahuasca and DMT, which he believed was the apotheosis of the psychedelic experience.

His notion was that Western society has become "sick" and is undergoing a "healing process", in the same way that the human body begins to produce antibodies when it feels itself to be sick, humanity as a collective whole (in the Jungian, sense) was creating "strategies for overcoming the condition of dis-ease" and trying to cure itself, by what he termed as "a reversion to archaic values."

[From: Wikipedia, the free encyclopedia]

Terence has been called one of the leading authorities on the ontological foundations of shamanism and the intellectual voice of rave culture. He conducted lecture tours and promoted natural psychedelics as a way to explore universal mysteries and stimulate the imagination. Terence shared his ideas about DMT in a 1993 lecture entitled: Rap Dancing into the Third Millennium. This was originally issued on cassette. It has since been re-issued on CD and is available on YouTube. In that lecture Terence speaks about the DMT experience and wonders why it is not considered headline news:

...this experience is of a fundamentally different order than any other experience this side of the yawning grave. And why religions have not been built around it? Why empires have not risen and fallen around the control of its sources? Why theology has not enshrined it as its central exhibit for the presence of the other in the human world? I don't know. I can tell the secret. As you notice, nothing shuts me up. But why this is not four-inch headlines on every newspaper on the planet I cannot understand because I don't know what news you were waiting for, but this is the news that I was waiting for.

[Ref: https://www.youtube.com/watch?v=EZAMKn2xr9E]

I wholeheartedly agree, the experience is of a fundamentally different order to anything else within one's lifetime, save for birth and death, and arguably the classic OBE, the genuine NDE, and astral travel in its truest sense. But his question about why theology has not enshrined the DMT experience as an exhibit proving "the presence of the other," and asking, "why this is not four-inch high headlines on every newspaper on the planet," are totally valid and provide tantalising opportunity for further literary work and debate outside the limited scope of this work. However, not wanting to not have a stab at that, one only has to recognise the dogmatically authoritarian controls at play within institutionalised religions, and to contrast those with the powerful and individualistically enlightening experiences provided by powerful psychedelic entheogenic substances, to give some hint of an answer. Can you imagine the social uproar that would follow were the news headlines to suddenly run a report about a psychedelic compound common throughout the living kingdoms of nature that facilitates subjective experiential proof of occult realities? There is no doubt the DMT experience can, and will, and already is altering the western mindset. The speed of that sea change will depend upon many factors and when historians look back on this period of cultural change, perhaps they will recognise that unseen powers were very much at play – just as they always have been.

In his original ground-breaking publication, Dr Rick Strassman spent some time justifying and arguing about the importance of nomenclature for DMT. I found the arguments fascinating:

> First, what do we call it? Even among researchers there is little agreement over this crucial point. Some don't even use the word *drug*, preferring instead *molecule, compound, agent, substance, medicine* or *sacrament*.

> Even if we agree to call it a drug, look how many different names it has: *hallucinogen* (producing hallucinations), *entheogen* (generating the divine), *mysticomimetic* (mimicking mystical states), *oneirogen* (producing dreams), *phanerothyme* (producing visible feelings), *phantasticant* (stimulating fantasy), *psychodysleptic* (mind-disturbing), *psychotomimetic* and *psychotogen* (mimicking or producing psychosis, respectively), and *psychotoxin* and *schizotoxin* (a poison causing psychosis or schizophrenia, respectively).

> This focus on name is not trivial. If everyone agreed about what a psychedelic is or does, there certainly would not be so

many words for the same drug.

[Ref: DMT The Spirit Molecule (2001) by Rick Strassman, MD; Park Street Press; page 30]

At the time I did not consider the matter of nomenclature to be such a big deal. But now that I have committed so much time and energy to this research under an unashamedly occult interpretation – and furthermore sought to publish that work with a view to securing myself a position of authorship within that genre – suddenly the matter of nomenclature seems more important than it previously did; certainly to the extent that I wish to give my two-penneth's worth of opinion and input. To my subjective perception, the DMT experience has given me ample evidence of occult reality within and without. If I commit to asserting that what I have actually seen is evidence of my psycho-spiritual self (something relating to my mind, my soul, my spirit) and evidence of powerful psycho-spiritually-composed beings of hidden nature, then I could propose a conjunction of 'pneuma' and 'delic', and suggest 'pneumadelic' as both an alternative name and an apt descriptive of the profound effects induced through DMT inebriation. Psychedelic is derived from the Greek words *psyche* (soul, mind) and *delein*, (to manifest), hence "soul-manifesting" or "soul revealing." *Pneuma* is an ancient Greek word for 'breath' and in a religious context refers to spirit or soul. But no matter whether referred to as Psychedelic or Pneumadelic, DMT is going to change this world!

Reference Bibliography and Source Material

BOOKS:

The Coming of the Guardians
Compiled by Meade Layne
The Book Tree, 2009

Correlation of Sound and Colour
Paul Foster Case
The Hestia Publishing Company, 1931

The Cosmic Pulse of Life
Trevor James Constable
The Book Tree, 2008

Cyber-biological Studies of the Imaginal Component in the UFO Contact
Experience Edited by Dennis Stillings Archaeus, Volume 5, 1989

The Dark Gods
Anthony Roberts and Geoff Gilbertson
Panther Books, 1985

Dimensions: A Casebook of Alien Contact
Jacques Vallée
Contemporary Books, 1988

DMT The Spirit Molecule
Rick Strassman, MD
Park Street Press, 2001

Gnostic Visions
Luke A. Myers
iUniverse, 2011

The Great Secret
Maurice Maeterlinck
The Century Co., 1922

The Greenhaven Enyclopedia of World Religions
Jeff Hay
Greenhaven Press, 2007

Human Devolution: A Vedic Alternative to Darwin's Theory   Michael
Cremo
Bhaktivedanta Book Trust, 2003

Isis Unveiled
H. P. Blavatsky
Theosophical University Press, 1998

The Key to Theosophy
H. P. Blavatsky, 1889
https://www.theosociety.org/pasadena/key/key-hp.htm

A Manual of Occultism
Sepharial
William Rider & Son Ltd, 1914

Panegyric to Spirit: The Final DMT Diaries
Steven Turner
CreateSpace Independent Publishing Platform, 2015

The Philosophers Stone
Israel Regardie
Llewelyn Publications, 2013

The Spirits' Book
Allan Kardec
Brotherhood of Life, Inc., USA 1989

The Secret Doctrine
H. P. Blavatsky
Theosophical University Press, 1999

Studies in Occultism – Collection of Articles from Lucifer, H. P.
Blavatsky's magazine, between 1887 – 1891
https://www.theosociety.org/pasadena/hpb-sio/sio-hp.htm

The Theosophical Glossary
H. P. Blavatsky,1892
http://theosophy.org/Blavatsky/Theosophical%20Glossary/Thegloss.htm

The UFO Phenomenon: Fact Fantasy and Disinformation
John Michael Greer
Llewellyn Worldwide, 2009

INTERNET LINKS:

Wikipedia – Animal magnetism

    https://en.wikipedia.org/wiki/Animal_magnetism

Wikipedia – Ascended master

https://en.wikipedia.org/wiki/Ascended_master

Wikipedia – Corpora arenacea

https://en.wikipedia.org/wiki/Corpora_arenacea

Wikipedia – Cymatics

https://en.wikipedia.org/wiki/Cymatics

Earth Lights

http://www.pauldevereux.co.uk

Wikipedia – Jacques Vallee

https://en.wikipedia.org/wiki/Jacques_Vall%C3%A9e

Wikipedia – Michael Taylor (Ossett)

http://en.wikipedia.org/wiki/Michael_Taylor_(Ossett)

Wikipedia – New Age

https://en.wikipedia.org/wiki/New_Age

Wikipedia – Orchestrated objective reduction

https://en.wikipedia.org/wiki/Orchestrated_objective_reduction

Wikipedia – Pelican

https://en.wikipedia.org/wiki/Pelican

Wikipedia – Roc (mythology)

https://en.wikipedia.org/wiki/Roc_(mythology)

Wikipedia – Terence McKenna

https://en.wikipedia.org/wiki/Terence_McKenna

Terence Mckenna – Everything you need to know about DMT [rapdancing into the 3rd millennium]

https://www.youtube.com/watch?v=EZAMKn2xr9E

Wikipedia – Thunderbird (cryptozoology)

https://en.wikipedia.org/wiki/Thunderbird_(cryptozoology)

Wikipedia – Thunderbird (mythology)

https://en.wikipedia.org/wiki/Thunderbird_(mythology)

Wikipedia – Will (philosophy)

https://en.wikipedia.org/wiki/Will_(philosophy)

Wikipedia – Wren

https://en.wikipedia.org/wiki/Wren

Earth Lights: Spooklights and Ghost Lights -

http://inamidst.com/lights/earth

Printed in Great
Britain
by Amazon

Sari Reams
Sadaf Saaz

 The University Press Limited

The University Press Limited
Red Crescent House, Level 6
61 Motijheel C/A, G.P.O. Box 2611
Dhaka 1000, Bangladesh
Phones: (8802) 9565441, 9565443, 9565444
e-mail: info@uplbooks.com.bd
website: www.uplbooks.com.bd

First published, November 2013

Cover design by Journeyman
Cover photography by Shahriar Rahman
Author photograph by Safia Azim

ISBN 978 984 506 137 7

Published by The University Press Limited, Red Crescent House, 61 Motijheel Commercial Area, Dhaka-1000. Book designed and produced by Journeyman and printed at the One Stop Printshop, 60/A Purana Paltan, Dhaka-1000, Bangladesh.

To Nick,

Hope you have enjoyed your time in Bangladesh, and ~~my~~ collection will hopefully help you remember us!

With warm wishes,

Sadaf

Sari Reams

CONTENTS

To the memory of my father
Jamal Nazrul Islam
(1939-2013)

ACKNOWLEDGEMENTS

There are many people who have been with me on my journey as a poet, without whom this collection would not have been possible.

I am grateful for the generosity and enthusiasm of my motley crew at Writers Block; Saad Z Hossain, Masud Khan Shujon, Srabonti Narmeen Ali, Samir Asran Rahman, Awrup Sanyal, Iffat Nawaz, Tisa Muhaddes, Sabrina Ahmed and Sal Imam, with a special thanks to Shazia Omar, Munize Manzur, M K Aaref, Lori Simpson and Farah Ghuznavi, for encouraging me to share my work with the outside world. My thanks also to Farhan Quddus, Moshiur Khandaker, Naila Azad, Sharbari Ahmed, Mukul Agarwal and Safia Azim, for their support.

I would like to express my gratitude to my friends Tahmima Anam, Ahsan Akbar and K Anis Ahmed for their constant support and advice.

I would like to thank Shireen Huq, Lubna Marium and Naila Z Khan for blazing the way, and to my Naripokkho sisters who help me believe that we can make a difference.

I would like to thank Kaiser Haq and Arundhathi Subramanium for their helpful and sensitive feedback. I am indebted to Syed Shamsul Haq, Fakrul Alam and Gillian Clarke for their valuable inputs and encouragement, and to Mahrukh Mohiuddin for being the best publisher I could hope for.

I am grateful to my sister and best friend, Nargis, and brother-in-law Alex, for their unwavering love and support, and to Amma, for her love and guidance.

I would not be the person I am today without the unconditional love, support and encouragement of my beloved father and mother, Jamal and Suraiya Islam, who taught me about the wonder of life, the power of love, the richness of books, the thirst for knowledge, the need to stand up against injustice, and the value of commitment and *shadhona*. Most of all I would like to thank my dear husband Kamel, the love of my life, for painstakingly typing up my poems so they wouldn't get lost (in the days before computers!), for supporting me in all my endeavours, and for being the person he is.

Dhaka, November 2013   Sadaf Saaz

FOREWORD

What struck me most as I read *Sari Reams* is the passion with which Sadaf Saaz has woven the poems she has collected in her book. Her debut collection of verse will attract other readers too because they have been created by a poet who is intensely involved in everyday life in Bangladesh and in relationships that stir her poetic spirit strongly. Sadaf's poems, in other words, come straight from the heart. However, they also reveal her strength of mind and her ability to craft poems in a style that is quite expressive as well as distinctive.

Sari Reams reflects throughout the poet's ardour and commitment to her country. In a number of poems Sadaf writes endearingly about her determination to immerse herself in the sight, sounds and smells of Bangladesh. "Among this all" is thus a poem that has her declare delightfully that she is "High on the idea/That this place is mine/It's part of me/That this is the way it was meant to be". Her taste bud is aroused by the land's produce, her eyes feast on its colours, and her imagination is kindled by "the beauty and imagination it fires". In "*Tikli* and glass bangles" she is fully fascinated by the clothes women wear in the land that is her destiny: "Red *paar*, *zari* edge/Black shades and all". Is it any surprise, then, that she chose to title her first book of poems, *Sari Reams*?

Sadaf's passionate side comes out of course in her poems about loving. The first poem of her collection, for instance, shows her engrossed in a tender moment as she comes closer and closer to her beloved. Another tender poem about loving that I found refreshingly original and captivating is "I love our low bed". In fact, Sadaf has it in her to pleasantly surprise the reader again and again with the kind of sensibility that can never become jaded because it is based on what John Keats had characterized in a famous letter as "the holiness of the heart's affections and the truth of imagination". This is the type of sensibility that I found in another poem about loving included in the collection titled "As the Angels bite the dust" which concludes feelingly with the following appeal to the beloved: "As your doing and undoing/Is sensitive as the leaf rustles/At the hint of a new day/As dawn for you it must/So don't give up on me/Or in my trust".

What makes Sadaf's collection of poems distinctive too is her passionate commitment to all sorts of causes and to her fellow activists. She is certainly not the kind of person who would end up being "Silenced/Guilty by acquiescence/of the status quo". She is thus quite contemptuous of the "Mixing mingling crowd/of the powerful/who convinced themselves/and those with a say/that this is normalcy/This is the way" ("Mixing and mingling"). Her commitment to Bangladesh and its future make her wonder : "Will this land see sparks of sunrise/To nurture a future just born?/Shall we merge at last with our conscience?" ("Nation"). She confronts in a number of poems injustices inflicted on women and then cloaked with "the sound of silence" ("The sound of silence", "Birangona", "Women of the night"). Her elegiac poem "An artist and an activist", indicates not only her devotion to the memory of her friends but also underscores her determination to campaign against breast cancer and for all sorts of "freedoms" for women.

Passionate in love, devoted to her country, determined campaigner for the rights of women though she is, *Sari Reams* displays for me the lighter, wittier side of Sadaf as well. Taking off from E. E. Cumming's immensely funny poem, "May I feel said he", she creates almost as ingeniously a Bangladeshi version of the lighter side of mating rituals between men and women in "Underneath the jackfruit tree". However, she ends the poem with an epilogue that provides a feminist twist to amatory encounters that go all the way. "Horn, horn" is another comic poem (reminiscent of Sukumar Ray's *"Chole hon hon/Chhote pon pon ..."*) that makes light of the maddening midday commotion heard in her beloved but crazy city: "Horny horns/Honking horns/Loud horn/LOUDEST horns/Too many horns" is what overwhelms her (and every Dhakaite) through its "midday jam/Jamma jam/Jamming horns ... ."

In fact, I have been fascinated by the variety of topics, the range of emotions, and the array of voices Sadaf has assembled in *Sari Reams*. Sometimes her poems tantalize by offering glimpses of a sensitive woman's private world of feeling ("The memory"). She writes poems too of pain, frustration or convoluted emotions ("Across the table", "My castle in the air"). But in at least a few poems she tries to convey either in a dramatic monologue or through narrative poems the fate of women trapped by scheming men or pitiless people ("Saving him", "Women of the night") or the drama of the life of an unsung hero of the Rana Plaza disaster ("After Rana Plaza fell"). In contrast are poems that delight in sensuous apprehension ("Mango love", "Dhaka beat").

Although Sadaf's poems demonstrate a wide variety as far as their subject matter is concerned, she has been able to create a unique style to deal with her disparate subjects. She prefers to use free-flowing lines and flexible rhyming patterns and juxtapose Bengali words with English ones to forge her signature style and to convey the pulse of life in contemporary Dhaka. It is obvious too that she likes to play with words and experiment with structure. All these traits are evident in a poem such as "Dhaka Beat" which weaves Rabindranath Tagore's beautiful poems *"Aaji Jhoro Jhoro Mukhoro Badoro Dine"* into a tapestry displaying the impact on the poet's senses of a Dhaka thunderstorm.

There is then much to recommend then in Sadaf Saaz's *Sari Reams*. Her debut work will appeal to readers because of the lively sensibility and talent everywhere evident in the poems she has assembled. *Sari Reams* reveals a confident and exuberant poet and suggests that there is much more that we can expect from Sadaf in the future. The signs are finally propitious for Bangladeshi writing in English and with this collection Sadaf appears set to contribute significantly to its inevitable flowering.

University of Dhaka   Fakrul Alam

HOLD ME CLOSE...

Hold me close
Shield me
from susceptibilities
and pulling tides
Draw me tight
As I fit your form
And we move together
The hypnotic rhythm
That still drugs me
Into your trance
And hours pass
As the moment lasts.

THE MEMORY

The memory
The lightening
Goes back further
To the dawn of life
To strive
Thus rooted it grew
Into me and you
Whatever the beginning
The sure sure end
So this was fate
This urge after all
Our existence call
Fooling us all
For it was always within
Evolving over centuries
A mere fraction of time
Slowly to climb
While building our technology
Intellect and power
Yet the urge to tower
Our nuclear might
To press the button
And give up the fight
So in my flash
Time did stand still
Yes
We did exist
For a mere fraction of time
Believe it or not.

AMONG THIS ALL ...

Strange sensations
The foreign and familiar
Entice me to take a dip
In this sensuous abode
As I journey this road.

High on the idea,
That this place is mine
It's part of me
That this is the way it was meant to be
As I begin to see
The world as it is.

Among this all ...

Green mango with red hot chilli and salt
Crushed, not shaken.

The all too known, and unknown
Imbibing through me
Till intoxicated by the notion
That out of this
Pain, despair and high speed stress
We'll bear testament to the test
Of how to live and strive
And feel really alive.

Among this all ...

Against the canvas backdrop
Of a mixed potion of all the frustration and hope it inspires
With the beauty and imagination it fires

Drenched in the hypnotising tropic heat
To rise and meet
That ultimate challenge
Of survival and revival.

Among this all ...

The land of sunsets, and sunrises
Red, yellow and *shonar* orange
Light up the sky glow
And I throw
Fragments of judgment
Wild peaks of *dhan khet* green
And specks of *godhuli* light
Flicker as an old 35mm
Camera projects
The good old days.

The parade of possibilities excites
And ignites
The longing and determination
To overcome
As if just begun.

Among this all ...

The stench of long days of toil with little to show
The vibrant rainbow rickshaws flashing as they go
The high-rise contradictions, and sensory overload
The strength and quiet dignity of those on silent mode
The indomitable spirit of *biplobi* past
The colour array of women breaking tradition at last
The dynamic exports of international fame

The migrant masses from whose savings we gain
The corruption of politics by those with no shame
The constant madness of this insane game
The mind-pounding struggle of countless miles
The enduring bonds of family ties
The shining resilience of warm smiles
The haunting Sufi song on wooden boat
The fascinating mega-city about to choke
Nazrul, Tagore; the epics they wrote.

Among this all
You can dance.

You can dance
In the pouring moonlight.
Jotsna raate ...

As night shapes
Take the stage
And escort your spirit
To its own destiny.

TIKLI AND GLASS BANGLES

With *tikli* and glass bangles
A swish of *aanchol* with sandal toe
Secured in this jigsaw web
As pieces come and go
Am I in too deep?
Sometimes not at all
Red *paar, zari* edge
Black shades and all.

Untamed as sweat glistens
A shake of tangle with jet mane
I've awoken again
To the destiny I foresaw
The dream that I bore
To many who had glimpsed
The black and white prints
Bear a chronicle of sorts.

Yes I've emerged
With uncorked gushing froth
Cutting energy raw
Stamping my horizons
And others I saw
With askance purdah eyes
And dormant riches within
I enveloped floating worlds
Till chains became rings.

And freedom another space
As the wilderness grew
I with it too
Yes I've ridden cotton clouds from strength
Driven by the call
Black denim, bootlace
Raw silk and all.

ACROSS THE TABLE

Sitting opposite
Across the table
My beat pounding in my head.
Still nothing said.

As I don't look up
And sip my coffee
In silent air
Like you don't care.
The fear kicks in
Tension waves spin
My heart.

Disconnected.
As your eyes don't smile
At me.

Palpable air
Every sense of me aware
I'm cold and alone
Frozen out on my own.

Emotions run high
Slow hand ticks by.
Contained in this web
Reasons swarm my head.

So convoluted can't think
A severed broken link
Bursting through every pore
Pain cuts me raw.

Frustration and desperation deflect
My reasoning to reflect
And respond rationally.

Instead erupt in anger.
Words to retract
Can never take back.
Or remain reigned in.

A Brownian craziness in my mind
No thought helps me find
A way to make things right
To get out of the fight.

Unable to pass your moat
To ease, laughter and happy times
From this desolate place we find
Ourselves in.

Thousands of things pending
Stood still in this quiet battle
Of wills, needs and senses.
And history.

Want to communicate
And reach for your soul
To feel, cherish and hold.

But can't get through
To you...

MIXING AND MINGLING

Diamonds and ruby bling
Saris, a month's housekeeping
Mixing and mingling
with those who I would
rather not give the time of day
Don't deserve their say
Plump cats
On the backs
of the system they abused
when it could be said
they had the privilege
of not needing to.

Or some
get their pay
milking their way
with muscle and force
on their course
to owning multi-storey gold
which we all sold
our souls to accept.

Those have 'made it'
oiling the machinery
No sugar coating
They actually were
stealing from our land
Yet among us they stand
Without shame
Or blame
No hard work deserved
No old fashioned ethic preserved
Money under table exchange hands
Wired to some other land

Normal days work
Yet we all shirk
Mouths sealed
Nothing revealed
Iron clad shield
Of all in the know
And on show.

Disconnect.
Alienated in this fallacy
Living in surreal reality.
Silenced.
Guilty by acquiescence
of the status quo.

When I speak up
Gazes avert
as I try and assert
the truth out loud
Mixing mingling crowd
of the powerful
who convinced themselves
and those with a say
that this is normalcy
This is the way.

Conscience.
Doesn't seem to exist
When we persist
To embrace them in the fold
as if it is the done thing to do
Which makes us all
part of it too...

MY CASTLE IN THE AIR

Clouded by shrubbery of solitude
Prevailed by a sense of hope to seed
Yet trapped by the chagrin which follows
The realization of a futile need.

My estranged castle in frozen air
Strangled by its choking cry from my throat to call
My proud silence preventing its fall
As a succinct symbol of all my dreams
Which before long dissolves and seems
As if it never existed at all.

MANGO LOVE ...

That sweet distinctive
Mango *shango*
Imbibe, inhale
A fragrant tango
In quarts, peeled, slurped, sucked whole
Nectar of gods
Indulge my soul
While I savour
your familiar flavour
Chosha, Fojlee, Lengra gold
Irresistible and bold
Mouths mingle
with tasty tingle
As delicate, delicious converge
textures, touches merge
a lustful surge
seducing this urge.

Delightful morsels,
yellow, orange tease
temptations with ease
Tongues, lips
gorge the golden
shonali sight
unsung delight
of succulent *aam.*
unique *ghraan*
on gooey palm.

The perfume
of breezy orchards
infiltrates our heat
as our breaths meet

You penetrate me
with that heady aroma
Of familiar childhoods
Grown-up escapes
Midday breaks
Soaking *jhorna* rains
Hot siesta days.

Dripping, oozing, arms and face
Licked with your expert grace.

Our desires erect
gorging the juicy wet
as I forget
myself
in the tropical riches
of our bounty.

NATION

In a crowd with a blur of faces
A heightened purpose in time suspends
A mingling of emotions
To question the beginning and end.

Each with different theories
Shall we emulse, shall we be torn?
Will this land see sparks of sunrise
To nurture a future just born?
Shall we merge at last with our conscience?
Shall we shadow as the masks we wear?
Shall we fight as prodigal heroes
To follow convictions we swear?
Or let them scatter ashes to ashes
Crushed down dust to dust
To flow with flirting breezes
Or burn deep with no dignity or trust.

Shall rigid principle paralyse
And compromise betray?
Till wrong is right
And is believed.
And given words
Are imbibed and received.

Shall freedom be worn like a noose around my neck?
Eroded driftwood
From a dying shipwreck.

SARI REAMS

She will wrap around encircle gold
Embedded with tresses of time
Weighed down by river folds
Embodied and Enshrined.

Mothball stale in silent air
Unravelled as time stood still
As I bring water-filled hands to cover my face
I see my mother's reflection
And within her, her mother's too
And in the void wonder
Visage of my daughter's queue.

With heavy dampness as monsoon
Waters cast the dice
This entwined piece of cloth
With centuries embroider worn
Intricate a form
Engraved to bodies desire
Clings to droplet perspire
To carry on with defiance
Or shield space within
Each thread with the past cushions
Our place in the future we are in.

She will carry it on her
Proud and hair piled high
Or cascading free and wild
Whatsoever her choice.

I remember the faded picture
My mother's wedding one
With a gold circle nose ring.

And now I see it in my own.

NOTHING I COULD DO

Grains of sand on a beach
Lifted high on breeze
A guilty guilty piercing whirl
That hid the girl.

Within easy reach she was
The last I saw
And yet I missed
The danger raw.

And for a moment
The sand blinded my sight
As it rose to its height
And I only knew that she had drowned
When the wind died down.

THE SOUND OF SILENCE

The sound of silence
Excruciatingly loud
Deafening those
Who still remember
that lilting walk
Carefree talk
Charming twinkle
of sidelong glance
Poignant dignity of stance
Carrying her subtle style
An infectious smile
Generous
with her laughter
As it now echoes
In the sound of silence.

So beautiful, so young
Long thick shiny hair
Oiled with care
To waist
Can still taste
Blood in air
Gushing from her throat slashed rare
Punctuating flashes
Pierced those nearby
As visiting nightmares
were hid under a silent shroud.
Never uttered aloud.

She fought valiantly as he grabbed
her waist down as she
tried to break free
Found she could not
while he violated her every orifice
Triumphantly.
She was now his.

She ran as
torn bloodied
scraps fell.

As she tripped
that sharp sharp glint
was held against her neck
Used with a deliberate intent.
She never stopped her screams
until they finally died
with her.

His father, her father's brother
Her *chacha-to-bhai*
Own family and kin
Why reveal the shame and sin?
Family ranks closed in.

Her mother
wept till her heart bled
and begged
when the police came
to break it down.
The wall of silence.
In the bedroom her mother's plea
to her husband
That her daughter would not
sacrifice her right
to find justice in death.

It was not to be.
Preserving 'face'.
Allowing vicious violation, murder and rape
to escape
Into the sound of silence...

THE ONLY ANSWER

Silence
Yes I give silence
To fortify my shrinking reason
And indulge your fantasies
To leave
A histrionic trail
A tale.

Does it show me
For what I am
Debauched and ignominious
Imbibing idle gossip.

Till I'm caught in the vortex
And nonchalant I lie
So nothing can touch me.

As the subjugation
Becomes impalpable
To my languid form.

SAVING HIM

Looking down on uneven grey
forging the cement array
to hold me steady.
As his hand hit my cheek
it was more the shock
than the smarting red
and the words he said
which cut me inside
Those piercing eyes cold, hard, distant, snide
Brown green glints boring into me
as he tells me that he will continue to see
those others
whether I like it or not.

We met among better times and friends
when in an HSC college in Jessore
He just had that air with self-assure
that I wanted to know more.
That's what got me.
His fiery eloquence in spite of odds
This sense of righteousness to stand up
for those who were not able.
He, from a minority Bihari community
They had been failed by our society
Holes in the Bangla status quo
An intensity simmering just below
Got me hooked to want to know
what was underneath
that exterior of defiance.

His tall stance with the intent look
made me melt when he took
my hand one day and said I was his.
And I could think of nothing else but him.
He was doing his B.Com pass
trying to get away from past

I was studying too to stand on my own
Had the confidence as I had grown
with faith in my ability
and intellectual capacity
determined to get that job
in Dhaka city
The place of opportunity.
My mother, a teacher
gave me the dream and strength
that helped take me to the lengths.
She was tough, and forthright and expected it of me
As I did too.

He called me beautiful though I was not
the forgiving fair *phorsha*
but *shyamla* – that medium colour, average face.
But with good taste
And sparkling eyes and wide white smile
that kept his attention for a while.

He followed me to Dhaka
We had good times
In Sadharghat, the Balda gardens,
Ashulia
and *addas* at the c*ha er tong*
Our feelings were too strong
Bibi he would say, my wife
what is wrong in being with me
You are mine, everyone can see
As he loved I gave in
to his touch
After all, a (marriage) certificate seemed a technicality.

He wanted to know more and more
where I go, where I've been
who I've seen
Wanted to be in charge of everything.
At first I knew it was cause he cared

and what we shared.
Yet could not ask the same of him.

It became suffocating.
After intense interrogating
with me apologizing, weeping
He would cry and I would melt at seeing
the tenderness he had for me
under it all.
With a pride that that this gorgeous creature
was mine, and I his.
Me, of medium colour, and average face.

He became more possessive
and more nonchalant
Sometimes
Full turned on electric charm
Other times
Reticent and dark
The hugely stark
gulf between his two selves.

Yet I had already given myself
as his wife
and could only think
would never find someone such as he
Clinging to the memory
of his loving gaze.
Nothing will faze
me from saving him.

Cannot tell my mother
Or any other.

No one will understand.

SOMETHING WITHIN

It stirs up sometimes from within
Nurtured by an alien force
A piece of imagination
A cry from the heart
Who knows?
Waves take over
From head to toe.

A feeling of surprise, disbelief and fear
Mixed blessings
Joy, hurt
Happiness and pain
Then it is gone again.

UNDERNEATH THE JACKFRUIT TREE...

You can touch, said she
This much? said he
Not that way, said she
Whatever you say, said he

That's enough, said she
It's tough, said he
I can't, said she
Ok, shan't, said he

(just a bit then, said she
As you wish, said he)
Feels too good, said she
Don't think we should, said he

A bit more, said she
Are you sure? said he
Not sure, said she
I want more, said he

Never felt this before, said she
I'm turned on, said he
Like a tap, said she
You flow, said he

Don't stop yet, said she
What? said he
Nice and slow, said she
You glow, said he

Not there, said she
Where? said he
Where you be, said she
Too late, said he

Feel amazing, said she
You are, said he
What have we done? said she
We are one, said he

... ...

It's been three months, said she
How are you? said he
It's yours, said she
Maybe not, said he

What do you mean? said she
Please no scene, said he
What to do? said she
Go figure, said he

One afternoon? said he
All it takes, said she
Life's ahead, said he
Living it now, said she

Kill it, said he
But it's mine, said she
Not my problem, said he
But it's mine, said she.

I LOVE OUR LOW BED

I love our low bed
Raw silk head.

White crisp sheets with satin stripe sheen
Freshly laundered nice and clean
Compliments the dark wood teak
Underneath
A sanctuary of calm
The cooling balm
Of the gentle outside breeze
My core at ease
It flows through wide open door
Overlooking glistening water, wooden boats and more
Removed from madness of regular day
In this frenzied city we stay
The touch I crave
Your body and mine
Flesh on flesh comfort divine
Basking in that special time
The essence of our being
Wrapped up
With cosy contentment
Just the warmth of snuggling up
You with your book, listening to iPod stuff
And I insist to read
Then promptly fall asleep.

I love our low bed
Raw silk head.

BIRANGONA*

Heroic one.
The name bequeathed you
But you would have to
Be much more than that
In the years to come.

The wrong we did by you
We all knew
What you went through
Never black and white
Fighting through the greys
The multiple ways
You had to.

That official line
Our mothers and sisters
Lost their honour
Rather than the other way around
Those who found
They got away
With crimes against humanity
While all that remains
Is the shame
Stuck on you
Whatever you do
Can't shrug off
The stain we create.

You survived your fate
To find family won't take you in
Woman of sin
Difficult to find work
Not paid if you do
After all

Why pay
When one can say
She is loose
To discard and use
And abuse.
When the police and military
Came next time round
It was you they offered
What did it matter
If they soiled you some more?

You are no longer
The mother of your son
Who found out
What you had done
Didn't want to hear what
Had been forced on you
Terrified and disgusted
He, and you, back then
To bear wounds never to heal.
Which changed your life
And death
As no one gave you
A piece of cotton
To wrap your lifeless body
Though your soul left
40 long years ago
When you were cornered as you ran
Then it began
Men like giants on you

Till you got used to it
And when you found 'freedom'
In joy and longing

You were reviled
And defiled
By your own.

You are the one
Who dressed up and wore gold
And you sold
Your dreams
To the enemy
But your menfolk and homes
Were left alone
For the sacrifice of this
Unsung dilemma.

You are the one
Who was caught
When ten of them
Found you in the *dhan khet*
Left you half dead
As you jumped in flowing waters
But found yourself still alive
On the other side
As you were pulled out like a
Fish in a net.
Afterwards not able to say
That your faeces dripped constantly
Till the day when you could
Take your own life.

You are the one
Who was stripped bare
When you dared
To tie the sari-length around your neck
And when you tried again
Using your thick long braids

Your head was shaved
And like a captive animal
You were starved
To get you to obey
To what they say
Till you had no other way
Out.

You are the one
Whose husband shunned you
When you could no longer satisfy him
Of course never yourself
Too scarred inside
And out
Even though your mother-in-law
Said it was not your fault
And ensured you a home.

You are the one
Whose husband cradled you
After their semen dripped
Down your swollen insides and legs
And loved you till
He was killed by local thugs
Greedy over land
And you were turned out
By his family and left to beg.

You are the one
Whose beautiful brown-eyed girl
Has blossomed in a far-away place
In a different time and space
The chosen land
She will never understand

And will never know how
You could bring all to tears
With your sweet lilting voice
Milking ballads of your soul
Or the endless years of anguish and pain
You felt at giving up
A very part of you.

You are one of countless
Whose story was never told
And never will
As all records were burnt.
And you will never come forward
As your people brutalized you over again.
As your government
Washed its hands
Of you and your sacrifice
And doesn't want to know
What you went through then.
And still are now
If you managed to survive.

---

* In 1971, during the Liberation War of Bangladesh, Pakistani soldiers carried out
a brutal rape campaign against Bangladeshi women as a strategy of war. Exact
figures are not known, but unofficial estimates put the number of rape victims at
over 200,000.

The term given to the rape survivors of 1971 was "*Birangona*". Initially intended
to signify a brave woman, this title has effectively become a pejorative label
within the context of a conservative society because it is associated with the
shame of rape.

After 1971, many rape survivors were not accepted back into their communities;
they were ostracized by their families, often refused employment, and did not
receive any form of compensation from the newly-independent government.

The Pakistani Government has still not officially apologized.

THE DANCER'S CALL

She dazzled, with her beat
A dancer's adorned riches
Heavy anklets gripping feet
And body swaying hypnotise
Her movements discovering surprise
Coy dark rimmed eyes bewitching all
Her hands align a dancer's call.

Yes drowning all in sight
By animating night.

So rich in gold and jewels and red
As the many men, whose hearts she's led.

Yet when the performance is finally done
No more the dancing one
The end to wonder, frenzy, hope
So swiftly swept off with the cloak
Of charm so long attired.

Who is she underneath the case?
Stripped of glory
A faceless face.

AS THEIR PATHS CROSSED

They were living each their lives.
It was
Not going so far as to say fate
When their eyes met.

And
Somewhere a gain
Somewhere a loss
As their paths crossed.

AS THE ANGELS BITE THE DUST

As the Angels
Bite the dust
As you have shone
And shown
I have grown
The sky you unknowingly held
And let go
As we sip foreign fragrances
Of ripe mango
We're mixed
In a sweet strange potion
That drugs our bond
Which is what it was.

As the sand dunes
Of a desert stand
Proud, daunting in wonder
Must change as the wind
As you fed me from the solitary drop
Let not go of it
For what the rains give later.

As the rays converge
To tears I shed
Watching you turn from the unrecognized
Truth you have found
Inside you.

As I attempt to understand
As rage melts to despondency
Pity to despair
A crushed fruit seeps no juice
It dries before ripe.

As your doing and undoing
Is sensitive as the leaf rustles
At the hint of a new day
As dawn for you it must.

So don't give up on me
Or in my trust.

DHAKA BEAT

The thunder clouds loom afar.
Ominous yet welcome.
Reminders of her abeyant mood.

As the oppressive midday heat
Doesn't miss a Dhaka beat.

Stifled in traffic jamming jam
Nerves taut with overflow like inbox spam
Hot wet heavy droplet galore
Sticky sauna sweat from every pore
Anticipating the coming *jhor* ...

The cosy comfort of moist warmth
Hit by mock cool a/c air
Immediate relief from the cutting glare
Tempering feelings of despair
Savouring the seasons that we share.

Reminiscent of Tagore songs
heralding the arrival of *borsha* ...

Soothing around her.
Waiting for the refreshing sheet
A shock of quenching surround sound
Liberating the space
With that different pace
Of the coming of the rains ...

For when they came
They took her breath away

Washed away that feeling
Put in its place
The connection
With all that is
Here and around.

The pouring sound
Made her catch her breath
As she cast her eyes
She soared and dived
Though her senses connived
To take it all away.
Before she was ready
To savour the moment.

On this thundery stormy rainy day...

Showered by the sudden rain
Childhood exhilaration reincarnated again.
To the amazement
Of discovering
What it is all about.

Yes
The rains and storm came
Bringing breath and life
Lush lush *kola pata* green
That fresh wet sheen
Washing out the dusty haze of months before
Cleansing her senses
And much much more.
Challenging the dense dark damp hot heat.
Finally rejuvenated to seek
That Dhaka Beat...

REGRET

Now despondent.
As rage and deep sorrow
with grief
wrap me.
Scems to mean nothing.
What I have had.

So this
Is how it feels
To not have the option
No world as my oyster
No endless paths to take
Or dreams to make and break
To not have
The promise of the future
Meandering before me.
A vast labyrinth of openings and pathways
To savour and step into.

Is this real and is this me?
Can this be the way
it was supposed to be?

Crushing fear
Suffocates hope.
Desperately desperately
trying to cope.
As the glimmer fades
into darker days.

How will I
Get over the piercing cry
Of those wasted years?

Regret.
Something had not met.
Yet.
Gnaws at my soul
Spinning me down a hole.
To black nothingness and blame
And shame
At myself for not being here before
And thus ignore
The situation for what it was.

SHE

She exhibits her convex grace
As arching her delicate branch
Her virginal white head
Flutters indifferent to the caressing breeze.

A rancorous lump deep in my throat
As I see her lovely blooming flower
Her innocence astutely piquant
Engendering my malignant jealousy
Of her peremptory aura.

Oh her cryptic beauty
Immures me with all its impetus
My whimsical prison
Drives me into this anomaly
As her aroma envelops
A wave of calm
To enhance her charm.

AFTER RANA PLAZA FELL[*]

Today Rana Plaza fell.

He stares, in fearful air,
as white ghosts emerge,
like walking dead of a 9/11 scene.
Desperate
for familiar eyes to lock in recognition.

Her last words; that rushed morning
on a mobile, now ringing hollow on their bed.
Left in haste,
not to miss a day,
for a cut of pay.

He enters
a hole from next-door RS tower,
to the sandwiched third, fourth and fifth.
Blunt metal hammering by unlikely heroes,
to a claustrophobic nightmare.

A sticky, redness drips.
From a stuck head between pillars,
fixed eyes stare,
as he prepares
to find her.

Two days since Rana plaza fell.

Perspiration with pungent decay.
Hideous swollen arms blocking way
in mine-like shafts,
serendipitous paths of 15-inch beams,

on elbows,
past cloth stacks, cartons spilling jeans, MANGO label reams,
to persistent, weakening cries,
of a group huddled alive.

His new sister stifles her pain,
while freedom finally gained, from pinning concrete.
As he saws off her arm
his crude instrument and virgin hands shake,
a two-minute lesson by doctors who could not take
the risk.
He, who used to faint at a vaccine jab.

No joyful reunion.
A grateful stranger grasps
till he let go, that afternoon, or was it night?
Difficult to tell,
when time stood still, as it was running out.

Exhausted hours of searing will,
for the lucky to have another chance.
He must have brought out over 200 alive.

A wet patch of brown-red.
A baby born a few hours ahead,
shocked into silence,
till a heartening scream in the blinding sun,
swathed to her mother's belly,
pulled out on fabric rolls strewn
in tunnels on the brink of collapse.
Held by flimsy car jacks.

Seconds and minutes creep by.
Spotlights catch terrified eyes
with sudden hope, after unbearable heat
made them strip bare.
Holding onto life; taking in urine, licking up sweat.

A handyman, foreman,
gardener, student, and cook.
A motley team, with no names,
On whom his life depends.

Take a break, they say, but how, when this
unexpected calling
blots out reason.
Snatches of sleep on a neighbour floor.
Adrenalin propels him back for more.

Several days since Rana Plaza fell.

He tastes that smell
despatching dignity to the dead.
Later, unable to eat for days.
Gasping oxygen
under shifting plates.

Skulls seem to look up.
Hands, with no body parts.
Heart still leaps, with a reminiscent ring on bare bones.
Just so he could bury her.
Even if never to feel her warmth again.

He heard
of someone like him,
left with a battle of his own,
without use of arms and legs.

Five months since Rana Plaza fell.

Still no job, after that fateful month.
Saving souls and reuniting the dead
was not enough to keep it.

His grip tightens on his daughter's hand.
Her mother's teasing tones echo.
Visit his dreams.

As do the screams
of those he left behind.
Begging him not to.

---

* On 24th April 2013, an eight-storied building housing half a dozen garments factories, collapsed at Savar, Bangladesh, after developing cracks in its pillars the previous day. Ad-hoc rescue workers, mostly untrained, worked day and night for 19 days, managing to rescue 2,438 people alive. According to official records, 1,127 persons lost their lives, including two rescue workers. Many more were injured, suffering from physical injuries as well as psychological trauma.

DELTA BLUES

River rhymes.
Your moods like mine
turn at the behest of whims.

Tempestuous or still.
From shimmering dancing,
to murky choppy flows.

Sea-wave waters run deep.
I'm frivolous like jumping dolphins,
amidst working dredges, overladen with dangers,
between scattered rust orange sails.
As quaint postcards of old
dotted with engines and steel.

And suddenly a happy day of blue
turns to a shock sheet of grey,
coloured by dark demons.

THE ADDICTS

They mask it well
Like a painted shell
Only you cannot tell
It is.

Conversation and charm
No sign of harm
Behind the calm
We see.

Come across okay
The things they say
Can't catch the fray
That is.

But signs are there
Shared gossip aware
Friends who care
Do know.

Articulate, well versed
They hide the worst
Spell of the curse
From all.

For creative juice
There is no ruse
The need to use
To fly.

The natural game
To actually claim
The kick is the same
With it.

Have they fooled us so
We really don't know
Or is it not a show
At all.

Are they not addicted
As predicted
Signed, sealed and convicted
By us.

That's the illusion
To create the confusion
Part of the collusion
By them.

THE GLASS BLOWER

Reflections are shaping
Curves begin to mould
Softly slowly forming
Delicate and bold
With his expertise and technique
Creating a vase unique.

Emerging it silently forms
Masterful, he performs
The glass sparkles like crystal
So proud it stands alone
So beautiful its every contour
Shaped by his hands alone.

Yes she was his creation
She loved every second he took
She loved him with all her naivety
His every expression and look
Yet he left the vase to stand there
Her perfect sculptured form
His creation finished and done
To create another one.

THE FINAL GARDEN OF EDEN

Drop by drop
Falling slowly by
Joining thread for thread
A knotted tie
Gathering a tangled form
An involute storm
To envelope all with darkness, as it pours.

Yes, a reckonable force
Washing with thorough solicitude
And only by chance and serendipity
The thespian of reality
Will finally tumble and converge
The wrath once and for all to merge
Till annihilating the fraud
Gives birth to the eager, cognizant sword
Of a fruit not yet plucked
For the new born babe with no name
Its innocent juice to finally claim.

WOMEN OF THE NIGHT

They laugh a cacophony of camaraderie
And you could mistake them
For savvy 30 somethings
Getting together
Having a drink at day end
From signals they send
As they relax and chat
Yet they are not in a bar
Somewhere far
They huddle together in flickering light
Ill-fitting heels, blouses bursting tight
Light powder, musty rose, *attar* and lipstick red
Time for them to finally shed
Their attired façade.

Some complain, others refrain
End of hard working day
Having a *biri*, and a laugh
Gossiping about their 'other halves'
The one who brings her flowers so sweet
He who insists on his special treat
Another who beats her out of her wits
Or confides to her his family twists
Without the baggage of domesticity
Playing the role of mother, lover
And whore-in-one.

Some have regulars,
Lungis, safaris, frayed suits or vests
BO stained shirting, baring belly chests
Rick pullers, bankers, pen pushers or the like
Stingy *baksheesh* givers, those rich *Gulshanites*
College goers cheating on paying their nights.

Glitter, gaudy, bright colours entice
Women hair grooming, picking their lice

They vent, chatter and share mundane news
Routine sex, police hassles and landlord blues
Local *gundas* threaten with constant demands
Under iron veil of the madam's high command.

Noshto women 'spoilt' by reality
Pierced by a sharp ferocity
To the very edge of desperation.
Surviving by sheer fortitude
Against all odds.

Scratch beneath the surface.
You'll find deep loneliness
Hidden amidst buried horrors.

Their trajectory.
Sealed by a tragic misstep of fate.
Maternal death, second wife
Vicious gang rape
Lost in the city, seeking streets of gold
Tied up, kidnapped, sodomised and sold.
Outcast by those who needed to care
Rejected by those who should have been there.

With no safety net to catch as they fell
Innate power from earth on hell
Keeping them afloat while vilified
Their basic rights repeatedly denied.

These are survivors,
With no choice.
We denigrate as 'beneath us',
Without a voice.

Not taking time to see
How it would be
If circumstance and destiny
Had been doled out differently.

HORN, HORN

Bus horn
Cow horn
Car horn
Truck horn
Train horn
Scoot' horn
Mo' horn
Bike bell
Is a bella horn
Morning horns
Horny horns
Honking horns
Wonky horns
Loud horn
LOUDEST horn
Too many horns
Orchestra horn
Midday heat
Horns to the beat
Midday jam
Jamma jam
Jamming horns...

AN ARTIST AND AN ACTIVIST

Part I
Eyes sparkling, energy high
The cliché; everything to give
Infectious love of life
That's what they had
These two amazing women.

Together.
The comfort of girl power
We were all there
Dipa said
Sing that *Rabindra Shangeet*
Though not trained.
I did.

And tears came in my eyes
She valiantly fought every cell
To stay
But lost her long battle
When it took over
Till her soul could no more have a home.

We continued
To campaign for Breast cancer
Following heart and conscience
Giving and receiving
All life had.

Nasreen.
Laughter and warmth
Caring and courageous
Fearing nothing for the right way
Till this day
Inspired by how she lived

No one was too less
Nothing was too more
For her to be.

The day she left
This precious place
There was no warning.

An accident?
She bled to death
And took with her
That zest.

Standing for the unjust
Did she pay the price
With her life?
When laid in earth's bounty
Her sister, my dear mentor, said
Sing that *Rabindrasangeet*
Though not trained.
I did.

Part II

And tears fell
As I picked up red earth
Scattering it on her as we said farewell.

The following month
I was in Shelaidah.
Gentle breezes in golden afternoon
Passed the stretch of Padma
Through simple villages
Scattering happy children
Vast skies of fresh air
When I got there.

On the *ghat* of the pond
Relieved by temporary escape
From urban madness.

As I sit
On the *ghat* at Shelaidah
Where Tagore wrote his song
The casual soul strumming
Of an ektaara reach me
Familiarity pervades
The old man's hand with a young boy's tone
Though not trained.
He sang.

Part III
Tears flow out of me
His sweet folk style
Milking me
Remembering my own mortality
The presence of something greater
In the place
Tagore watched moonlights
Where I am told
He wrote this very song.
And I thought of
The transience of it all.

Memories flood in
They had fought for freedoms
And asked me to sing
That Tagore song...

Jokhon porbe na mor payer chinho aye bate...

When my footsteps will not fall anymore
On the path of life...
That's when
You may not remember me

Sitting on Shelaidah's *ghat*
Their spirits resonate.
And I still do...

SHADHONA

Twilight night
Fades as the *roshni* light
Infuses a pastel hue
Stirring
The silent earth.

Sheer pure sound
Breaks dawn with *komol Ré*
The bending *meer*, that soul-hitting note
Invites *bhairab's* early morning.

A life-changing union.
Technical brilliance with mindfulness
Nurtures spirit and craft.

That perfectly aligned split second.
Achingly beautiful.

PLOUGH ON

Plough on
Plough on
As sodden wheel must tread
As toiling toiling days
Drip from your head
As your forefather's omen
Of the bullocks you led
And though fed water
They did not drink
They turned their heads
They did not think.

And while turning the dirt
Bared of shirt
Passing fancies did flirt
But, I kept on looking at the churning dirt
To plough
Plough on
So it could not hurt.

GLOSSARY OF LOCAL TERMS

Aam	mango
Aanchol	end of Sari which falls past the left shoulder when worn
Adda	casual conversation while hanging out
Attar	perfumed oil
Baksheesh	tips
Bhairab	early morning raga
Borsha	rains, monsoon
Bibi	wife
Biplobi	revolutionary
Biri	local hand-made cigarette
Chacha-to bhai	paternal cousin brother
Cha er tong	road-side tea stall
Chosha	a type of mango
Dhan khet	rice field
Fojlee	a type of mango
Gulshanites	residents of Gulshan; a posh residential area in Dhaka
Godhuli	the light at the time of sunset, when the herd of cows return home blowing dust in the air
Ghat	jetty
Ghraan	aroma
Gundas	goons, hoodlums
Jhor	storm
Jhorna	waterfall, fountain
Jotsna raate	moonlit night
Kola pata	banana leaf
Komol Ré	flattened 2nd note of a raga
Lengra	a type of mango
Meer	gradual joining of two notes with a bend, in Indian Classical Music
Noshto	spoilt, damaged
Paar	border, edge
Phorsha	fair complexioned
Rabindra Shangeet	Tagore songs
Roshni	early morning light rays
Shyamla	medium complexioned
Shadhona	arduous endeavour or practice
Shonali/shonar	golden
Tikli	pendant worn on the forehead, traditionally for weddings
Zari	gold thread